PROJECTIONS OF PASSING

PROJECTIONS OF
PASSING

Postwar Anxieties and Hollywood Films,
1947–1960

N. MEGAN KELLEY

University Press of Mississippi / Jackson

www.upress.state.ms.us

Designed by Peter D. Halverson

The University Press of Mississippi is a member of the Association of
American University Presses.

First printing 2016

∞

Library of Congress Cataloging-in-Publication Data

Names: Kelley, N. Megan, author.
Title: Projections of passing : postwar anxieties and Hollywood films,
    1947–1960 / N. Megan Kelley.
Description: Jackson : University Press of Mississippi, 2016. | Includes
    bibliographical references and index.
Identifiers: LCCN 2015045695 (print) | LCCN 2015048294 (ebook) | ISBN
    9781496806277 (hardback) | ISBN 9781496806284 (epub single) | ISBN
    9781496806291 (epub institutional) | ISBN 9781496806307 (pdf single) |
    ISBN 9781496806314 (pdf institutional)
Subjects: LCSH: Identity (Psychology) in motion pictures. | Passing
    (Identity) in motion pictures | Motion pictures—United
    States—History—20th century. | Motion pictures—Social aspects—United
    States. | BISAC: PERFORMING ARTS / Film & Video / History & Criticism. |
    HISTORY / United States / 20th Century. | SOCIAL SCIENCE / Discrimination
    & Race Relations.
Classification: LCC PN1995.9.I34 K35 2016 (print) | LCC PN1995.9.I34 (ebook)
    | DDC 791.43/653—dc23
LC record available at http://lccn.loc.gov/2015045695

British Library Cataloging-in-Publication Data available

Dedicated to the memory of my brother Michael and my sister Ana

CONTENTS

PROJECTIONS OF PASSING

INTRODUCTION

Iago: *I am not what I am[1]*

In 1952, Langston Hughes published the short story "Who's Passing for Who?," which playfully exposed postwar ambiguity about race, authenticity, and identity in America.[2] In the story, an unnamed black writer chats with members of "Harlem's literary bohemia," who "considered [themselves] too broadminded to be bothered with questions of color." The narrator recounts their introduction by another black acquaintance, Caleb, to two men and a woman from Iowa, and how they dined together at a Harlem restaurant. In the recounting of the story, the "red-headed" man disrupted the evening with a chivalrous attempt to stop a black man from hitting a blonde woman he assumed was white. The interruption stopped the assault, but the black man informed the red-headed man, with a vaudevillian deadpan, "She's not a white woman. She's my wife." Shocked, the man from Iowa apologized. This offended the "colored painter," who told them, "I don't like it, the way you stopped defending her when you found out she wasn't white." Caleb tried to defend the man from Iowa by pointing out that he could not be expected to know better, but was interrupted by the suggestion that the woman might have been "just passing for colored." This triggered a lengthy discussion about race, color, and passing in American society. The narrator and his "Harlem bohemians" thought it fun to chide the white folks from Iowa, but it was they who got a surprise, he explained:

> [We] all settled down comfortably to shocking our white friends about how many Negroes there were passing for white all over America. We were determined to *pater le bourgeois* real good via this white couple we had cornered, when the woman leaned over the table in the midst of our dissertations and said, "Listen, gentlemen, you needn't spread the word, but me and my husband aren't white either. We've just been *passing* for white for the last fifteen years." ... Well, that took the wind out of us ... Then everybody laughed. And laughed! ... All at once we dropped our professionally self-conscious "Negro" manners, became

natural . . . talked and kidded freely like colored folks do when there
are no white folks around.[3]

Hughes's punchline occurs at the end of the story when the "light-colored"
woman from Iowa leaned out the window of a taxi and shouted, "Listen, boys!
I hate to confuse you again. But to tell the truth, my husband and I aren't
really colored at all. We're white. We just thought we'd kid you by passing for
colored for a little while—just as you said Negroes sometimes pass for white."
The story concluded, "We didn't say a thing. We just stood there on the corner
in Harlem dumbfounded—not knowing now which way we'd been fooled.
Were they really white—passing for colored? Or colored—passing for white?"

Unlike most stories about passing, Hughes refused to reveal the identities of his characters. Their ancestry and racial status remained ambiguous
throughout the story. Hughes played with reader's assumptions about identity.
His refusal to assign race made categories that appeared stable suddenly
more fluid: the color line revealed as imaginary. He used passing to mock the
ideologies and cultural assumptions about race in postwar America, albeit
leaving more rigid gender politics intact. (Hughes himself pushed assumptions about gender and sexuality, but these reflections would be left to other
stories). At the same time, Hughes's story suggested it was more fun to be
in on the secret, an interesting twist on postwar perceptions about passing.
Hughes was in tune with the times. A key question of the period really was
who was passing for whom.

This short story is an example of the anxiety and issues raised by passing
in postwar America. The contradictions and anxieties exposed by individuals who passed were reflected in literature, art, and film. Representations
of passing framed postwar anxieties about identity. Despite shifts in how
identity was understood, lingering beliefs in essential categories remained,
especially with regard to race and gender. Passing was not simply a social
phenomenon, but an epistemological dilemma.

As an epistemological conundrum, passing threatened to destabilize all
forms of identity, not just the longstanding American color-line separating
white and black. There is a rich literature on racial passing, which this book
not only builds on but expands in a new direction by examining how the
question of "Who's passing for who?" extended to many fields.[4] In the imagi-
native fears of postwar America, identity was under siege on all fronts: not
only were there blacks passing as whites, but women passing as men, gays
passing as straight, Communists passing as good Americans, Jews passing
as Gentiles, and even aliens passing as humans (and vice versa). By showing

how pervasive the anxiety about passing was and how it extended to virtually every facet of identity, this study broadens the literature on passing in a
fundamental way.

Projections of Passing begins in 1947, a watershed year, with the House
Un-American Activities Committee (HUAC) attack on Hollywood. The year
1947 also marked the release of *Gentlemen's Agreement*, Hollywood's first
postwar "social problem" film that addressed passing. It is important to map
out how passing was first represented and then chart how that changed. In
early representations of passing, it was portrayed sympathetically as a social
strategy in an unjust world. Narratives dealt with questions of behavior: the
passer was condemned for violating social norms or admired as a trickster for
challenging social barriers. However, throughout the 1950s, representations of
passing changed. Passing became associated with deeper internal psychosis
and betrayals of inner self. The traumatic events of World War II combined
with new theories of psychology to create anxiety in America about the
nature of identity and authenticity. Passing became an indicator of inward
pathologies rather than external social behavior, reflecting the influence of
popular psychology. Under the glare of therapeutic culture, passing became
a crisis about identity.

This study ends in 1960, amid the beginnings of another major shift in
cultural trends and ideologies in both Hollywood and American politics. In
Hollywood, the studio system and the blacklist began to disintegrate while
the election of John F. Kennedy signaled political and social change. More
important here, by the early 1960s, cultural discourses about identity, passing,
and authenticity changed. How Hollywood represented and replicated passing anxieties was a defining phenomenon of the long 1950s, but not beyond.[5]
Hollywood's obsession with themes of passing and questions of authenticity
came to an end. Passing was no longer a useful metaphor for understanding
cultural anxieties.

The potency of the imagined fear of passing linked the language and anxieties of passing to other postwar concerns. American culture was obsessed
with threats from within. While the practice of passing was rooted in social
inequality, anxieties about passing were obsessed with modern issues of identity and authenticity. As Henry Louis Gates Jr. notes, "to pass is a sin against
authenticity, and 'authenticity' is among the founding lies of the modern
age."[6] Reflecting this, the "specter of passing" rather than its actual incidence
fueled anxiety about the nature of identity.[7] The distinction is important. This
specter related to a person's questioning of his or her own authentic internal
identity and his or her fears of truly seeing other people's identities correctly.

The specter of passing became more threatening in the postwar era because it fed anxiety about subversively hidden blacks, Communists, homosexuals, or "others" who could threaten the stability and security of the white status quo. Discursive passing fears were used to express anxiety about the nature of Selfhood and identity but never reflected real-world numbers.

Passing was connected to postwar anxieties because it illustrated the boundaries of the self. Social categories deemed rigid were permeable. Although passing was a narrative device in literature before World War II, films after the war used it as a metaphor for cultural anxieties about identity. Filmmakers across genres used tropes of passing to reflect fears that social categories were blurring. Films were obsessed with people who were not what they seemed to be: husbands could be former Communists (*Woman on Pier 13*); husbands could be aliens from outer space (*I Married a Monster from Outer Space*); girls could be men (*Some Like It Hot*); the Jewish man next door could be Christian (*Gentleman's Agreement*); and the white folks you lived and worked with could be black ("Daytime Whites," *Pinky, Lost Boundaries, Imitation of Life*). At the same time, films like *Peyton Place* and *The Man in the Gray Flannel Suit* suggested that conformity was itself a performance: everyone was passing for "normal."

While Hollywood films were obsessed with passing as a subject, passing as an act resonated in Hollywood because the industry was built and staffed by those who made a living performing, by people who invented and reinvented themselves both on-screen and off-screen. Passing imagined a malleability of identity, based on performance, which challenged binary concepts. While film has always been about acting and performance, in the 1950s Hollywood underscored the performative nature of identity while raising questions about the relationship between authenticity and identity. Passing became more problematic in the postwar era because of its troubling resemblance to public performance. One of the central dichotomies of postwar American culture was that on-screen public performances of acting were celebrated, while off-screen passing performances were feared. The dichotomy between praiseworthy cinematic performances and blameworthy passing helps explain this period.

Passing plays with identity and how we determine who is who. The postwar pressures for Americans to conform became cultural clichés that survive to the present day. In the culture of postwar America, how one dressed and how one looked dictated who one was and how one socialized. The omnipresent "men in gray flannel suits" and cookie-cutter suburban housewives epitomized a drive towards homogeneity over individuality. However, while the dictates of American culture emphasized conformity, the idea of who one was and how one looked became an increasingly unreliable way to define each other. The fact that the signifiers for conformity were so easy to aspire to resulted in insecurities about the meaning of these visible signifiers. It was possible they meant nothing at all.

While passing is an Americanism that involves "crossing any line that divides social groups," in American history, passing has most often referred to blacks passing for whites.[8] Passing was particularly considered a black/white phenomenon in the nineteenth and early twentieth centuries because of the "one drop rule" where one drop of black blood made a person legally black.[9] This illogical racial identification and the discrimination of Jim Crow laws provided opportunity and motivation for crossing the color line. The focus on an imagined color line also had the perverse effect of making white identity suspect.[10]

Ideologies of identity and passing changed as new psychological discourses about identity gained currency after World War II. Moreover, the emerging civil rights movement of the 1940s and 1950s shifted the nature of the debate. New civil rights ideologies posited that political battles about race should focus on a culture where the practice of passing would be unnecessary. Discourses about racial passing were caught between older essentialist categories of racial identity (defined by blood) and rising liberal ideologies of race shaped by civil rights discourses (defined by color). This greatly influenced how racial passing was understood.

Langston Hughes's story reveled in the playful side of passing and mocked American obsessions with an imagined stability of the color line, marking a shift in the representation of racial passing. Prior to the 1950s, attitudes toward racial passing vacillated between a sympathetic, sometimes joyful treatment of racial passing and the more serious, unsympathetic narrative of the "tragic mulatto."[11] However, essentialist aspects of this nineteenth-century trope (blood equals race) did not resonate comfortably in a postwar American culture infused with liberal ideologies about race and shifting psychological discourses about identity.

After World War II, racial passing moved from being a popular fictive device to an open debate. Magazines increasingly published real-life stories about blacks who stopped passing. These have been termed post-passing narratives. Examples include Reba Lee's 1955 memoir *I Passed for White* (made into a film in 1960) as well as magazine articles like Janice Kingslow's "I Refuse to Pass" and *Ebony*'s "Why I Never Want to Pass."[12] By the mid-1950s, post-passing narratives were a dominant literary trend in fact and fiction. The decline of narrative fictions about racial passing in the 1950s marked an end to a century of the trope as a narrative device in African American literature, including celebrated works like James Weldon Johnson's *The Autobiography of an Ex-Colored Man* (1912), Nella Larsen's *Passing* (1929), and Fannie Hurst's *Imitation of Life* (1933).[13] Authors like Hughes became a transition between older nineteenth-century tropes of passing and postwar tropes that rejected passing as a social strategy.[14]

Ironically, broad representations of passing became popular precisely at the historical moment that racial passing was less likely to be employed as a social strategy. Statistical estimates for the number of people who passed as white in the interwar period vary enormously from a few million to ten million. In 1948, William M. Kephart suggested that "the wide disparity in figures suggests the real answer, namely, nobody knows."[15] However, the well-documented rise of post-passing literature in the 1950s, together with frequent pronouncements by 1960 of the end of passing, all suggest that passing was understood as a strategy of the past, not the future.

By the time journalist John Howard Griffin's *Black Like Me* was published in 1961, "passing was already beginning to 'pass out' of style for African Americans, going the way of Jim Crow buses and segregated lunch counters."[16] And by the 1970s, after the civil rights movement and identity politics had changed the discourse, the subject of racial passing was no longer assumed to be dramatically relevant. In 1979, when young comic Steve Martin played the son of a Southern black family in Carl Reiner's hit film *The Jerk*, this Hollywood reference to passing was framed as unimaginable except as over-the-top comedy. The time when white actors could play black characters in seriousness was gone. Passing no longer resonated in American culture.

The goal of this study is to explore why anxieties about passing did resonate on so many levels in the long 1950s, and analyzing films of the era is key to understanding this. Films are intertwined with fantasies and fears, representations and realities. Accordingly, representations in film are potent reflections and creations of postwar ideas about identity. While films are never simple mirror-images of broader sociological trends, Hollywood both reflected and exerted influence upon cultural discourse. In an era defined by anxiety and psychology, the best reflections came out of Hollywood, America's "Dream Factory." Hollywood films that exposed anxiety about authenticity, identity, and passing transcended genre. People and things were not what they appeared to be. Fears about passing as dangerous to the self and subversive to the nation assumed unprecedented importance in postwar American culture. The films discussed in this book all received substantial critical or box-office attention upon their release and have been studied by both film historians and cultural theorists. This study, however, is unique in addressing the films as a thematic group, revealing the broader but interconnected concerns and anxieties about passing.

Chapter 1 considers influential cultural contexts that affected how films were produced and consumed looking in particular at the rise of psychology, cultural anthropology, and the culture of the Cold War to understand how concepts about identity changed after World War II. These cultural shifts focused on questions of authenticity and identity. Understanding changes in cultural ideas about identity informs how representations of passing were used as a metaphor for fear and anxiety.

Chapter 2 looks at representations of racial and ethnic passing in Hollywood films produced in the late 1940s. Race is a logical, theoretical entry because of the literary tradition of equating passing with blacks passing for white. Beginning in 1947, films about race and racial identity were part of the postwar "social problem" or "message" films. Films like *Crossfire* and *Home of the Brave* addressed race issues in ways that also illustrated the psychoanalytic turn in American culture. Racial passing was directly addressed as a theme in *Gentleman's Agreement, Lost Boundaries*, and *Pinky*; in these films, passing was sympathetically represented as a response to external social injustices. This model did not survive long, but it was an important milestone in cinematic constructions of racial identity, one that reflected specific postwar ideologies about passing.

Chapter 3 focuses on the dramatic shift in later representations of racial passing in Hollywood films. While earlier films were sympathetic to those who passed, films from this period portrayed passing unsympathetically. Films like *Island in the Sun* and *Imitation of Life* no longer represented passing as an accepted response to external social pressures, but rather as a failure to accept an imagined authentic identity. This shift reflected a change in attitudes toward passing because of the civil rights movement, the rise of black stars and post-passing narratives, and equally important, the psychoanalytic turn in Hollywood.

Chapters 4 and 5 extend the examination of passing representations beyond biology. The fourth chapter looks at political passing, in which the specter of passing was utilized in films produced in the context of the Cold War. Anti-Communist films like *My Son John* and *Woman on Pier 13* focused on the "enemy within" and featured Communists infiltrating America as patriotic citizens passing undetected in society. Science fiction and horror films have often been similarly interpreted as allegories for Cold War politics, but here it is more crucial to examine the way these films exploited anxieties connected to postwar ideas about identity. The fifth chapter considers science fiction, arguably the most successful film genre to tap into the fears and anxieties about politics and issues of identity. Films like *Invaders from Mars*, *Invasion of the Body-Snatchers*, *I Married a Monster from Outer Space*, and *The Day the Earth Stood Still* featured aliens who passed as humans, raising important questions about the nature of identity.

The last two chapters study gender representations and passing anxieties, including how Hollywood negotiated imagined ideas of normalcy and authenticity and the fear that gender categories were collapsing. Chapter 6 considers the crisis of masculinity as represented in Hollywood and on film. Postwar films charted a perceived breakdown of secure gender categories and by implication, a breakdown of sexuality. "Crisis of masculinity" films gave rise to ambiguous masculine ideals, personified by the postwar "sigh guys." Films like *The Man in the Gray Flannel Suit*, *Rebel without a Cause*, *Rope*, *Tea and Sympathy*, *Vertigo*, and *Some Like It Hot* explore the passing guises of masculinity. The final chapter analyzes representations of women and issues of femininity and feminine performance with respect to anxieties about authenticity and passing. Images of masculine women in *Calamity Jane* and *Johnny Guitar* coexisted alongside the hyperfeminine and manufactured women in films like *Gentlemen Prefer Blondes*. Other films, such as *All about Eve* and *Peyton Place*, suggested that femininity itself was a performance, raising the issue of "passing for normal." Whether framed in masculine attire or glamorized as the ideal blonde, femininity on the screen revealed gender to be a manufactured construct, performed by actresses both on and off the screen.

By asserting the connections between all these different films, this work reveals how representations of passing allowed Americans to express anxieties about who they were and who they imagined their neighbors to be. This study is not about lived experience or delineating the differing consequences for passing and exposure, important as those things are. This is about exploring the world of representations and discourse to capture and illuminate the threads of a pervasive, if tangled, cultural trend. To analyze postwar culture without considering the importance of imagined passing specters is to misunderstand the historical context of the long 1950s.

CHAPTER ONE

HOLLYWOOD'S PASSING CONTEXTS

The Rise of Psychoanalytic Discourse, Identity Studies, and Cold War Culture

Man had been tossed into the vestibule of another millennium. It was wonderful to think of what the Atomic Age might be, if man was strong and honest. But at first it was a strange place, full of weird symbols and the smell of death.[1]
—*Time* (1945)

The successful splitting of the atom at the end of World War II signaled the beginning of the atomic age. In 1945, *Time* suggested: "With the controlled splitting of the atom, humanity, already profoundly perplexed and disunified, was brought inescapably into a new age in which all thoughts and things were split—and far from controlled."[2] Fear of this new technology, the ability to split the atom with an unknown destructive intensity, became a key cultural anxiety. The nature of identity, how individuals defined themselves and their communities also became split in this period. Postwar American culture was obsessed with identity. A new vocabulary emerged featuring ideas of authenticity, alienation, "the enemy within" and "identity crisis" that focused on fear and anxiety.

Postwar concepts about identity reacted to shifting ideologies about race, gender, and sexuality. Postwar therapeutic culture developed through the marriage of cultural anthropology and psychology in the interwar period, but only became popularized after the Second World War. At the same time, the social sciences fostered new ideas about individual and cultural identities. For the first time culture and identity were understood as malleable social constructs that could evolve and change, a proposition that was in conflict with cultural desires for stable, unchanging identities. These competing discourses and disciplines intersected in Hollywood films where the Dream Factory met dream analysis and where popular psychology framed representations of identity, aided by a desire for social engineering and a shift to Method acting.

America came home from the battlefields of Europe searching for a better world. The experiences of the war demanded new approaches to identity, Selfhood and culture. In the postwar period the threat to America changed from the physical battlefields of the Second World War to the psychological terrain of the Cold War. The physical defense of the nation was couched in psychological terms. The Cold War was fundamentally "a psychological phenomenon," and the combination of such Cold War factors and events as the National Security Act of 1947 and the Korean War "added up to a 'dream come true' for psychological experts."[3] Psychology became the ideological key to power on the war front while ensuring loyalty and good citizenship on the home front.

In postwar America, FBI leader J. Edgar Hoover used "the enemy within" to justify sweeping investigations of government workers and Hollywood filmmakers.[4] In this culture of fear, Communist threats were described as "contagions" and "viruses." America became the body politic and medical metaphors imagined that Communism could spread through America like a disease. Metaphors like this made Communism an invisible threat that could appear anywhere in America.

In popular memory and historical accounts, the 1950s is remembered through a prism of competing narratives. It is seen as an age of conservative conformity and political repression: the McCarthyite witch hunts, the Cold War dogmas of Truman and Eisenhower, the rigid cultural norms of appropriate gender behavior, the legal racial segregation of Jim Crow laws, and the repression of homosexuality. According to this narrative, the fifties were a time of fixed and rigid identities when people were classified by gender, national, racial or sexual orientations.[5] It was the "age of conformity."[6]

In contrast, a competing narrative posits the 1950s as an "age of anxiety."[7] It was a time of atomic fears and existential angst in the aftermath of World War II and the Holocaust.[8] Rather than being a time of certainty, historians suggest that it was an era under siege.[9] This interpretation has its own potent set of cultural icons: Elvis Presley's transgressive dancing, Marlon Brando's angst-ridden portrait of masculinity, Rosa Parks's fighting for civil rights and beatnik poet Allen Ginsberg's celebration of same-sex desire. While both these views are important, they are not mutually exclusive. Conformity and anxiety were sides of the same coin. Imagined conformity masked a wide range of insecurities. Anxieties about identity were intertwined with ideological and political values in postwar literary and cultural discourse.

Cold War political culture was shaped by a cultural emphasis on popular psychology and identity. The work of cultural anthropologists like Margaret Mead and Ruth Benedict became well known to the American reading public.[10] Pre–World War II attempts to delineate personality types characterizing particular societies, such as Ruth Benedict's *Patterns of Culture*, became national character studies that grew out of the experiences of World War II.[11] The American military sought the aid of cultural anthropologists to understand these "alien" and "exotic" cultures.

Ruth Benedict's 1946 study *The Chrysanthemum and the Sword* exemplifies many national character studies of the 1940s and 1950s.[12] The government's faith in the new tenets and approaches of cultural anthropology was made explicit in 1940 when Ruth Benedict and Erik Erikson, among others, were employed by the government. These "behavioral experts" acted as consultants for committees (including the Committee for National Morale) to aid in the war-time analysis of "national characters." Japan, Germany, and Russia figured prominently in national character studies as America sought to find its place in the world politically and militarily.

Cultural anthropologists became famous and produced best-selling books that were widely read. The popularity of books by anthropologists reiterated the desire to understand identity, both on an individual and a national level. At the heart of these studies rested "the conviction that microscopic questions about individual personality and behavior and macroscopic questions about societal patterns and problems were nothing but two sides of the same coin."[13] From such studies came notions that socialization molded the personality of individuals, and that identity was a part of the personality that was created. Margaret Mead's view that people were "made" not "born" and Benedict's famous dictum that culture was "personality writ large" became part of American cultural literacy in the 1930s.[14]

During this period the language of psychoanalysis became part of the lexicon of identity. While these ideas percolated during the 1930s, it was not until after World War II that mainstream culture adopted the shift from biological to psychoanalytic understandings of self and society. Identity and Selfhood became a journey, a rigorous process of soul searching. Jung's questing hero was popularized in the 1950s in the works of Joseph Campbell and Northrop Frye.[15] At the same time, Erik Erikson's studies of cross-cultural personality patterns influenced how Americans thought of identity. His work influenced by the experience of the war was also indebted to the ideas fostered by cultural anthropology. In this "age of Erik Erikson" the language of authenticity became pervasive, changing how the Self was understood and represented.[16]

After the war, a cultural ideology of authenticity ruled.[17] The ideal of authenticity, as a distinct postwar discourse about identity, drew upon the philosophical language of existentialism and the therapeutic language of psychoanalysis. Prior to this, the normative notion of proper behavior was sincerity, which meant being true to the conventions of society. Selfhood was understood as a product of sincerity, as an external signifier. Authenticity, by contrast, was an internal ideal, involving fidelity to an inner, irreducible core. Because identity could not be taken for granted and required a quest or journey, the search for authentic identity became a source of cultural anxiety. Psychiatrists framed the "quest for identity" as a universal problem.[18] Not coincidentally, "identity crisis" entered the culture "as a common term for the first time" in the 1950s.[19]

While the Great Depression encouraged a reevaluation of the impact of social conditions on individual behavior, an emphasis on environment over biology, the truly radical shift in racial ideology occurred after World War II: "Hitler gave racism a bad name."[20] Gunnar Myrdal, in his influential 1944 book *An American Dilemma: The Negro Problem and Modern Democracy*, argued that World War II made racism "inherently un-American."[21] It was not lost on African American soldiers that while fighting abroad for the "four freedoms," discrimination and segregation reigned at home. The "Double Victory" campaign demanded that any victory abroad defeating fascism must be matched by a victory at home, ending discrimination.[22] Veterans of World War II called for the desegregation of the armed forces and demanded their civil rights—demands that informed the nascent civil rights movement, ushering in an ideology of racial liberalism. The ideology of race shifted from biological determinism, discredited by Nazi ideologies and crimes, to a more psychological understanding of difference and Self.[23] This meant that race relations in postwar America became viewed as a struggle within individuals as much as it was between them.[24]

After the war, as biology became suspect, psychology and the social sciences offered new ideologies for solving old social problems. In addition to the work by Myrdal, important studies by Abram Kardiner, Lionel Oversey, and Gordon W. Allport all defined identity and race relations as psychological problems.[25] The government influenced by these experts used these ideas to address problems of race, defined best by Truman's report entitled "To Secure These Rights."[26] Postwar civil rights victories, including *Brown v. Board of*

Education, reflected an acceptance of these psychological arguments. The language of the couch informed government decisions as a burgeoning number of psychiatrists and psychoanalysts were employed. The psychoanalytic turn in American culture had a direct impact on everything from Supreme Court decisions to representations in film.

At the same time, psychology informed ideas of gender. Seemingly contradictory ideologies about gender coexisted in postwar American culture. Conservative and immutably binary gender ideals were heavily promoted. Such representations also epitomized Cold War "containment culture."[27] A stereotypical image remains the mythical white nuclear family with a male breadwinner as head of the household and wife as nurturing center. This new postwar stereotype, rooted in the suburban domesticity of the baby boom, was evoked by June Cleaver and Donna Reed. Underneath these superficial images, the culture was rife with anxieties and beliefs that categories of gender and sex were breaking down.

Lines were drawn between categories of "normal" and abnormal. New restrictive ideals about femininity developed in conjunction with a "crisis" in masculinity.[28] The surge in the popularity of psychotherapy was part of a broader trend to de-institutionalize mental illness, showing that "normal" people had psychological problems.[29] Popular magazines promoted not only the terminology but the ideas: "The women's magazines also provided women with an entirely new language for expressing their feelings of dissatisfaction, terms such as *unconscious, ego, inferiority complex, psychoanalysis, defensive reaction*, and *self-esteem*."[30] There were also new drugs to help with the new anxieties. Advertisements for psychiatric drugs skyrocketed in the 1950s, marketing these drugs as a solution for "normal" if gendered problems. Miltown, the first widely distributed tranquilizer, was prescribed for unhappy women. Similarly, businessmen could "fix" the stress of their job by taking Seconal.[31]

While gender roles changed so too did concepts of sexuality. Debates about authenticity, Self, id, ego, and identity formation entered the nation's bedrooms. Psychoanalysis claimed that sexual identity was a cornerstone of Selfhood. Sensational headlines about Christine Jorgensen, the first male-to-female transsexual, contributed to a growing sense that gender and sexual identities were permeable and unstable.[32] The public identities of transsexuals destabilized core binary categories of male and female. It was difficult for Americans to separate ideas of gender from ideas of sexuality. World War II marked the beginning of sexuality as a category of identity.[33] Just as the war tarnished ideas of biological determinism about race, postwar ideologies about sexuality shifted toward psychological and social conditioning.

In the 1940s and 1950s, the psychoanalytic ideas of Jung, Freud, Erick Fromm, and Erik Erikson intersected with the cultural anthropology of Edward Sapir, Ruth Benedict, Margaret Mead, and Franz Boas. Both professions addressed problems of alienation, personality, and identity, and used "national character" studies as the foundation of popular books and debates. "Character studies" informed other influential works, including David Riesman's *The Lonely Crowd*.[34] Together these social theorists, psychologists, and psychoanalysts shaped the psychoanalytic turn in postwar American culture.

The idea that identity and personality traits could be shaped was developed and publicized by anthropologists and social scientists alike. Major studies showed the correlation between aspects of culture and personality.[35] Postwar theorists argued that the early childhood years featured in the development of healthy identities, and that healthy identities could eliminate social problems, like racism or sexual deviancy.[36] In keeping with the therapeutic turn, postwar literature framed prejudice and discrimination as "human deficiencies," which could be "cured" or "reformed" through "social engineering." In the politically conservative postwar years, education became a tool of social engineering. Preventing prejudice was accomplished best in childhood. William Menninger's 1948 study *Psychiatry in a Troubled World: Yesterday's War and Today's Challenge* argued that a happy, "healthy" home was necessary to breed happy, "healthy" citizens. Mothers, as the caretakers of the home and the young, became the key for eliminating prejudice. Mothers became "cultural architects because families were personality factories."[37] Liberal ideologies equated racism with ignorance and asserted that "tolerance propaganda" was best begun at an early age in the home.

While social scientists could disagree about how these structures worked, all prioritized nurture over nature. The home was the best place to begin engineering the new Self. Of course, if mothers were the key to this new Self they could also be blamed for current social problems. Philip Wylie, in his 1942 book *Generation of Vipers*, coined the term "Momism" to explain this problem.[38] Edward Strecker expanded this theme in *Their Mothers' Sons* (1946), as did psychiatrist Marynia Farnham and sociologist Ferdinand Lundberg in their bestselling book *Modern Woman: The Lost Sex* (1947).[39] At the core of these reactionary books was the belief that psychiatry could be an "antidote" to societal problems, a belief held by many postwar social theorists.[40]

Not surprisingly, pop culture aimed at children, like comic books, was not immune from the psychoanalytic shift that placed it under the scrutiny of experts. Psychiatry, sexuality, and youth culture intersected in the ideas and

BUY THIS BOOK TODAY!

University Press of Mississippi

Popular Culture Association / American Culture Association
2017 Annual Conference
San Diego, CA

Title: *Projections of Passing*

$65.00
List Price

$32.50
50% Off

- ✂ -

Title: <u>Projections of Passing</u>

List Price: $65.00   50% Off: $32.50

University Press of Mississippi
Popular Culture Association / American
Culture Association
2017 Annual Conference | San Diego, CA

Sold to:

MISSISSIPPI

University Press of Mississippi
3825 Ridgewood Rd., Jackson, MS 39211
1-800-737-7788 | 601-432-6205
press@mississippi.edu
www.upress.state.ms.us

- ✂ -

_____
Name

_____
Address 1

_____
Address 2

_____
City, State, Zip

Paid with:
☐Cash ☐Check ☐MC ☐Visa ☐AmEx ☐ Discover

Account No. _____

Exp. date _____ E-mail _____

Signature _____

Phone (_____) _____

advocacy of psychiatrist Fredric Wertham, popularized in his 1954 bestseller *Seduction of the Innocent*. Like other social scientists, Wertham's expertise was called upon by the government. In televised hearings before Congress, the psychiatrist argued that comic books led to juvenile delinquency and sexual deviancy, singling out Batman and Wonder Woman for special condemnation. In most respects, Wertham embodied a postwar liberal progressive ideology—he supported the Rosenbergs, opposed HUAC, and most importantly, believed in the power of psychiatry and social science to eliminate racism and sexism in society. But those same beliefs made him fear the corruptive influence of comic books on confused and developing adolescent personalities, a framing used by conservatives with their own agendas, including the creation of the Comics Code, which he himself opposed.[41] However, what is important here is that his cultural and political authority derived from his expertise in psychiatry, reflecting a specific postwar context. Wertham's attacks on comics emerged from his own studies on the psychological development of youth, and while his data was flawed (or, as some suggest, manipulated), his concerns and theorizing about social development and identity were in keeping with the times.

Popularly disseminated psychiatric studies, whether concerned with race or gender, shared the basic goals and characteristics of identity and personality studies under the rubric of social sciences. In a more limited academic circle, this search for understanding values and identity was reflected in projects like the Ramah Values Study.[42] Under the direction of Clyde Kluckhohn at Harvard, this multidiscipline group of anthropologists, philosophers, psychoanalysts, and sociologists worked together, studying five societies living in the vicinity of Ramah, New Mexico. The Zuni and Navajo were native groups that had been in the area for centuries; the Spanish Americans were descendants of Spanish/Mexican immigrants over several hundred years. The Mormons and a group of Texans who had immigrated from the dust bowl of West Texas were more recent arrivals. Seeking to express the values of each of the five groups, Kluckhohn's team developed a tripartite scheme that analyzed the relationship of each culture to the supernatural world, to other humans, and to the natural world. The hope was that a profile of each culture's values would create a profiling technique to be used on other cultures. This study, as well as the B. F. Skinner psychology experiments in socialization and the Whiting studies, all occurred at Harvard in the same period.[43]

At the same time, deprivation studies, psychology experiments, and socialization studies sought to discover correlations between practices and outcomes that would be cross-cultural and universal. Deprivation studies looked at individuals under conditions of stress to identify the essence of a person when all the "superficial" layers of identity were stripped away. These studies were done on institutional prisoners, on concentration camp survivors, and retrospectively on slaves.[44] These particular attempts to extract the essence of personality and cultures are illustrative of a wide range of approaches to this general topic that indicate how important such quests were during the 1950s. It was thought that the self reflected the culture in which it lived; in essence, the goal was to understand the formation of identity. Understanding identity became the key to understanding culture.

Sexologists contributed to the study of identity, especially Alfred Kinsey with his bestselling studies on male and female sexuality (published in 1948 and 1953 respectively).[45] Kinsey's six-point sliding scale of sexual identification suggested a fluidity of sexual categories in marked opposition to existing heterosexual-homosexual binaries.[46] Moreover, the study suggested that cultural signifiers of masculinity or femininity were not indicators of sexuality, disconnecting external signifiers and behavior from internal conceptions of sexual identity. Kinsey's work "changed the way homosexuality was conceptualized in mainstream society as well as among scientists. Just as the research obliterated the idea of a clear-cut homosexual type, it effectively erased the possibility of such a thing as a distinctly homosexual body."[47] Postwar sexologists broke down not only the sexual binary but the idea that gender predetermined sexuality. For the first time, concepts of gender and sexuality were decoupled.

Social scientists in this period argued that normalcy was socially constructed, and conversely, that no action or identity that was culturally possible could be labeled abnormal.[48] These cultural ideas became heavily intertwined with new theories of psychoanalysis. An ironic consequence of identity studies was that normalcy was challenged.[49] The American public became increasingly pathologized and medicated. Individually Americans began searching for their "true Selves," while national character studies encouraged the nation to find itself. Culture and personality studies reflected cultural quests for identity, while normalizing a crisis about the nature of identity.

The wide acceptance of psychological interpretations across so many disciplines gave Americans a language and ideology for understanding culture and identity. Social scientists, anthropologists, and philosophers all used and adapted psychological theories to answer questions about the meanings and development of culture, personalities, and identities. Identities were malleable and no longer fixed. Anxieties arose about individual and national identities. If previously stable categories of race and gender were not determined by biology, was it possible for anyone to know who they truly were?

It is telling that Erik Erikson understood the relationship between anxiety and identity: "However much the psychotherapist may wish to seek prestige, solidarity, and comfort in biological and physical analogies, he deals, above all, with *human anxiety*."[50] Erikson distinguished between fears and anxieties: "Fears are states of apprehension which focus on isolated and recognizable dangers so that they may be judiciously appraised and realistically countered. Anxieties are diffuse states of tension . . . which magnify and even cause the illusion of an outer danger, without pointing to appropriate avenues of defense or mastery."[51] Paraphrasing FDR, he concluded: "We have nothing to fear but anxiety."[52] Both fear and anxiety, as Erickson defined them, were widespread during the postwar era.

Fears sprang from the dangers of the atom bomb and military invasions, while cultural anxieties were rooted in issues about personal identity and the inability of people to occupy appropriate stable categories. The government reacted to and fostered this climate. In 1947, President Truman initiated a loyalty oath program within the American government, and the Attorney General and the FBI developed lists of subversive organizations. At the same time, J. Edgar Hoover publicly stated: "Communism is really not just a political party, it is a way of life, an evil and malignant way of life, it reveals a condition akin to disease that spreads like an epidemic, and like an epidemic, quarantine is necessary to keep it from infecting the nation."[53] The use of medical language mirrored terminology used in popular culture to describe "dangers" to American ideals, like the "virus" of prejudice that was "infecting" America. Contagion became a metaphor for the body politic. Similar language was used to describe the danger of other perceived subversive groups like homosexuals.[54]

In 1949 and 1950, political events reinforced fears about Communism; the State Department "lost" China, the Soviets detonated an atomic bomb, and Alger Hiss was "unmasked" and convicted in January 1950. These political events laid the groundwork for Senator Joseph McCarthy's famous speech at the Republican Women's Club in Wheeling, West Virginia, where he held up a "list of 205 Communists" (a number that later dropped to 57).[55] William Chafe argues "in such a context, fantasies of subversion multiplied with geometric progression."[56] The "enemy within" was used by ideological true believers and partisan political opportunists alike as the catch-all indictment of anyone suspected of Communist "tendencies" or "affiliations." It was hard to distinguish where the reactionary position against Communism ended and the search for a recognizable American identity began.

Individuals targeted by FBI investigations were described as having suspect political tendencies. Many of those targeted by HUAC had been involved in leftist politics during the 1930s. Writers like Dorothy Parker, Lillian Hellman, and Dashiell Hammett organized the "Motion Picture Artists Committee to Aid Republican Spain," a group that included Hollywood directors and actors like John Ford, John Garfield, Paul Muni, and Fredric March. HUAC's list of "suspicious" organizations, which they imagined were Communist "fronts," included Hollywood's Anti-Nazi League, whose members included Humphrey Bogart and James Cagney.

Civil rights activists, "premature anti-fascists," and New Dealers alike were subject to investigations, but most of the targeted individuals fit political *and* sexual profiles.[57] In public rhetoric, the pink and red menace overlapped; "increasingly, accusations of homosexual and Communist tendencies became interchangeable."[58] Homosexuals in the government were imagined to be "security risks" and "Communist sympathizers" if not outright Communists.[59] The purging of suspected homosexuals illustrated what happened to those perceived to be deviant.[60] Inflammatory speeches by religious and political leaders, parroting sensationalist exposés in tabloids, linked the "sins" of godlessness, homosexuality, and Communism.[61] Tabloid magazines like *Confidential* and *Whisper* published allegations of same-sex scandals, usually about film stars, but when they exposed people in government agencies, the link between Red and pink was made clear. Consistently, these political tracks implied that both Washington and Hollywood were dens of deviant subversion.[62] The State Department directly linked these threats in a 1950 report entitled "The Employment of Homosexuals and Other Sex Perverts in Government": "Like Communists who would presumably infiltrate and destroy the society, sexual 'perverts' could spread their poison simply by association.'One homosexual can pollute a Government office.'"[63] It is difficult to ascertain whether sexual or political deviancy was perceived as the greater threat to the status quo at the height of McCarthyism.

Hollywood proved to be a microcosm of the contradictions and anxieties of Cold War culture. In both 1947 and 1951, the "enemy within" became a fact of life in Hollywood as the FBI and Congress, under the auspices of the House Un-American Activities Committee, investigated the film industry for Communist influences and political subversion in two rounds of hearings.[64] In 1947, film critic Bosley Crowther condemned the persecutions, stating:

A dangerous perversion of privilege has been happening in Washington . . . Dissident witnesses and their counsel have been bullied and muzzled flagrantly, witnesses "friendly" to the committee had been treated by it with kid gloves—all of which obscured the main question of whether there has been "un-American" propaganda in American films and fattened instead the innuendo that Hollywood is shot through with "Reds," and so far, the House committee has failed completely to specify what it considers "un-American" or "subversive" in the content of recent films.[65]

HUAC's attack on the film community echoed fears that movies could shape attitudes and affect politics both at home and abroad. Investigators focused especially on the screenwriter's guild. Anti-Communist crusaders believed that the organization hid Communist members who were trying to insert propaganda to subvert the American way.[66] The committee used the investigations to promote partisan politics, suggesting that the wartime government "under F. D. Roosevelt" encouraged Hollywood to make "pro-Soviet" films. More specifically, HUAC focused particularly on those involved in the making of three wartime films: *Song of Russia* (MGM, 1943), *The North Star* (RKO, 1943), and *Mission to Moscow* (WB, 1943). Breaking with a tradition of autonomous self-regulation, studios collaborated with the political witchhunts of HUAC, accepting the rationale for persecutions and blacklists.

The "Hollywood Ten" were the most famous of those called before HUAC in the first round of hearings in 1947.[67] The Hollywood Ten included Alvah Bessie, Lester Cole, Edward Dmytryk, Ring Lardner Jr., John Howard Lawson, Albert Maltz, Sam Ornitz, Robert Adrian Scott, Dalton Trumbo, and Herbert Biberman. The national publicity accompanying the Ten's prosecution demonstrated that those called before the committee had no way to effectively defend themselves or invoke their rights. Each of the Ten invoked the First Amendment and refused to answer the committee's key question: "Are you now or have you ever been a member of the Communist Party?" All were cited for contempt of Congress and sentenced to prison in the summer of 1950. Just before the Hollywood Ten were imprisoned, they made a short documentary film entitled *The Hollywood Ten*.[68] Produced by Paul Jarrico, the film explained who they were and what position they had taken in testifying before HUAC. They attacked the hypocrisy of the hearings: "These investigations are actually traps—you're damned if you do and damned if you don't."[69] The documentary's director, John Berry, was later named to HUAC by director Edward Dmytryk.

In reaction to the initial hearings, the studios released the "Waldorf State-ment" on December 3, 1947, in which they agreed to suspend the Hollywood Ten and bar the employment of Communists, thus creating the blacklist. Like the Production Code this "self-regulation" instituted by the studios sought to avoid outside control and regulation of the industry. Over 200 people were blacklisted and barred from working in the film industry, while others were listed on a more ambiguous graylist. Those that were called before the com-mittee divided into two camps: "friendly" versus "unfriendly" witnesses (based on whether or not they voluntarily agreed to appear and give evidence). A second round of investigations occurred in 1951, and from these proceedings there developed a blacklist that lasted until 1960.[70] Although conservatives like Ronald Reagan later dismissed the existence of the blacklist, publications of blacklists attest to their existence during the 1950s.[71]

From the outset, writers and artists responded to the political trials, the blacklists, and the charged political atmosphere. Howard Fast published *Spartacus* in 1952, Arthur Miller wrote *The Crucible*, and Lillian Hellman wrote *Scoundrel Time*, all allegories about McCarthyism and the blacklist. Blacklisted filmmakers also responded. Paul Jarrico, who produced the *The Hollywood Ten*, also produced *Salt of the Earth*, arguably the single most important political film of the period. Directed by Herbert Biberman and written by Michael Wilson, *Salt of the Earth* was made outside of Hollywood with the cooperation of the International Union of Mill, Mine, and Smelt-ers Workers. The film focused on strike organizer Ramon Quintero (Juan Chacon) and his wife Esperanza (Rosaura Revueltas), who gradually asserts herself and joins the other women as they take over the picket line to win the strike. Based on an actual mining strike in New Mexico, the film depicted racism experienced by miners and the misogyny they created in their homes. Many of the real-life strikers played themselves. The film's transcendence of racism and misogyny made it a "suitable crime" to warrant the punishment of the blacklist. Both the film and the filmmakers continued to act as a flash-point in American politics; the American Legion called for a boycott of the film and members of Congress denounced it as a "new weapon for Russia."[72]

Being blacklisted left few options. Some returned to the more liberal world of the theatre while others moved to Mexico or Europe to keep working. Ironically, writers, who were disproportionately targeted by HUAC, found it the easiest to assume new identities and continue working. Those in front of the camera could not hide who they were, but those behind the camera often could, especially writers. Blacklisted writers continued to work using a series of assumed names and fronts.[73] They became what HUAC feared: subversive authors.

Politics, ideology, and fear polarized Hollywood. The newly created "Motion Picture Alliance for the Preservation of American Ideals," which included Clark Gable, Walt Disney, John Wayne, Barbara Stanwyck, Ronald Reagan, and Ayn Rand supported the government and HUAC, while the "Committee for the First Amendment," which included Gregory Peck, John Garfield, Jane Wyatt, Danny Kaye, Sterling Hayden, Gene Kelly, Lauren Bacall, John Huston, Myrna Loy, Edward G. Robinson, and Humphrey Bogart, declared their support for the Hollywood Ten. The Committee flew to Washington with the Ten for the hearings.[74] This trip by the stars to the capital was noted in the press, but their initial belief in the power of the committee proved optimistic: "They came back wilted by the overwhelming power of the Committee and of the vitriolic tabloid press."[75] The Committee was called into question during the late 1940s and the 1950s, even by newspapers like the *New York Times*, which described them as Communist "dupes." Some, including Bogart, had to make public statements explaining or recanting their earlier public defense of the Ten.[76]

Hollywood remained fractured by fundamental political divisions throughout the 1950s. The paranoia about Communism and investigations into the political beliefs of filmmakers blurred the line between Hollywood and politics. Political scientist Michael Rogin suggests that "the atomic spy trials of the late 1940s merged with the House Un-American Activities Committee investigation of Communist influence in Hollywood. Since HUAC exposed both Alger Hiss and the Hollywood Ten and since the accused spies, writers, and directors all went to jail, the distinction collapsed between microfilm and film. The celluloid medium of secret influence became the message."[77]

By the early 1960s, tensions eased with the effective repeal of the blacklist. In 1960 two films vied for the honor of publicly breaking with the blacklist: *Exodus* and *Spartacus*. Otto Preminger announced that he would defy the blacklist by hiring blacklisted screenwriter Dalton Trumbo for *Exodus*, while actor/producer Kirk Douglas claimed his production of *Spartacus* was the first to do so.[78] Not wanting to play favorites, right-wing gossip columnist Hedda Hopper called for a boycott of both films, but attacks no longer had the same power to hurt box office or critical reception.

Even during the "blacklist era," when Hollywood was polarized along seemingly clear political lines, contradictions abounded. Progressive filmmaking and conservative ideologies vied for dominance. During the second HUAC focus on Hollywood (1951–54), the Supreme Court ruled in the 1952 *Miracle* decision (*Burstyn v. Wilson*) that motion pictures were entitled to the same First Amendment protection of free speech as written works.[79] These progressive decisions acted in contrast to other legal rulings that worked to limit cultural freedoms, like *Eugene Dennis v. United States* or the Subversives Activities Control Act enacted in 1950. Such contradictions are perhaps best explained by the concept of "cold war liberalism" that Steven Whitfield suggests is the "soundest guide to historical consideration of the period."[80] In many respects, Cold War liberalism is a useful construct to understand individual leftists—including filmmakers, who struggled with the often conflicting twin beliefs of social justice and anti-Communism—and to understand what film topics could be pursued without drawing the attention of HUAC or censorship. However, Cold War liberalism is a less useful construct for interpreting the wider cultural context. Discourse about the "enemy within" was just one dimension of larger cultural anxieties about authenticity and identity, which ultimately interested Hollywood most. One thing all sides of the political spectrum agreed upon, including social scientists, was that film was a powerful medium for social change.

In 1950, cultural anthropologist Hortense Powdermaker published her bestselling study, *Hollywood: The Dream Factory.*[81] She believed dissecting America's most powerful and popular cultural generator was the key to understanding American personality and identity. Hollywood, she argued, was overwhelmed by anxieties rooted in the horrors of the two world wars, by the possibility of a third world war that would be more destructive because of the atomic bomb, and by the "frightening global struggle" between democracy and totalitarianism: "Anxieties are further deepened by difficulties in understanding national rivalries, the conflicts in ideology, the complex theories of psychoanalysis and of relativity and so on, which whirl about the average man's head."[82] Like cultural anthropologists who came before her, Powdermaker treated her tinsel-town subjects in the same way she had interacted with aborigines living in the South Seas, the subjects of her previous research. She noted that in Hollywood, "There is far more confusion and anxiety than in the society which surrounds it . . . Now, fear rises to panic. Anxiety grips everyone from executive to third assistant director."[83] *Time* magazine tellingly reviewed this book in the cinema section. "After a year's safari into darkest Hollywood," the review noted, "Dr. Powdermaker concluded that the denizens of Hollywood are even more primitive, more superstitious, more beset by anxieties than Stone Age tribesmen."[84]

Powdermaker's observations led her to a paradox in the Hollywood system: "stars" were obsessively admired in the "real" world, but within the film world they were treated with virtual contempt, almost as "subhuman." Actors "are often described as children who do not know what is good for them, immature, irresponsible, completely self-centered, egotistical, exhibitionist, nitwits, and utterly stupid. Part of this description is reminiscent of white attitudes in the Deep South toward Negroes. Hollywood attitudes towards actors range from pitying condescension to contempt, hostility, and hatred."[85] For good reasons, Powdermaker believed postwar cultural anxieties about identity were magnified in Hollywood, but like most postwar cultural theorists she also believed that movies could be used by regular Americans safely outside the Hollywood world to explore or escape such anxieties.

Another study that brought together psychology, anthropology, and film was Martha Wolfenstein's and Nathan Leites's *Movies: A Psychological Study* (1950), which explicitly acknowledged a psychoanalytic framework and an intellectual debt to Margaret Mead.[86] They addressed the implications of actors "play[ing] themselves" in films: "The temptation to break through the aesthetic illusion is generally countered by a tendency to build it up again. Where stars play themselves they are apt to produce an unsettling double image, an uncertainty about what is real, rather than a simple voyeuristic gratification." They concluded that the "same applies to the revelations of fan magazines . . . The process is a kind of striptease in which as much is put on as is taken off."[87] This duality, while inherent to film acting, opened up other unsettling ideas about what was real and what was not. Hollywood films, fan magazines, and social scientists were all embedded in the quest to understand identity and in the language of the couch.

In American culture, the Dream Factory met dream analysis and formed a merger that defined postwar America. Hollywood films featured representations of psychologists, used psychologically motivated story lines, played with the language of psychology, and depicted a range of abnormal personalities. Equally influential was the well-publicized off-screen trend of movie stars and filmmakers actively participating in psychoanalysis. While psychology, psychoanalysis, and psychiatry are distinct disciplines, the lines between them blurred in popular culture. Hollywood films inserted their own undisciplined and generic understanding of popular psychology and Freud into the broader culture. The late 1940s and 1950s were the heyday of psychoanalytic moviemaking. There were Freudian-influenced horror and science fiction films, social problem films that addressed mental health issues and American institutions, and comedies that employed an almost tongue-in-cheek approach to the language of the couch.

Most films in the long 1950s featured psychoanalytic language, regardless of genre. Writing in 1959, Norman Holland lamented the inevitable psychiatric turn in Hollywood and its films, marking 1941 as Year One:

> First there was sound, then the wide, wide screen—someday, psychoanalysis had to come to the movies, too. In the good old silent days, characters did not even have motives, let alone complexes and fixations … This reprieve ended in 1941 with Alfred Hitchcock's *Spellbound*, a film apparently designed to prove that psychoanalysts on their own time are entitled to be as crazy as anyone else … Oddly enough, this amiable balderdash marked a milestone.[88]

Comedies like *Pillow Talk* (1959), which featured Tony Randall's character referring repeatedly to his therapist, were standard fare. The science fiction hit *Forbidden Planet* (1956) had psychoanalytic "subtext" so omnipresent in the narrative that it could substitute for a Freudian reader (in the film there was even a literal interpretation of the menacing "id" of the scientist). There was also the emergence of the "psychological western," a new genre of sorts, including *The Gunfighter* (1950) starring Gregory Peck as the antihero Jimmy Ringo, *Johnny Guitar* (1954), and *The Searchers* (1956). Other "psychiatric-centered" films that featured psychiatric professionals as core characters included *The Snake Pit* (1948), *Home of the Brave* (1949), *Whirlpool* (1950), *Harvey* (1950), *Miss Sadie Thompson* (1953), *The Caine Mutiny* (1954), *The Seven Year Itch* (1955), *The Opposite Sex* (1956, an MGM musical remake of *The Women*), *Invasion of the Body-Snatchers* (1956), *I Was a Teenage Werewolf* (1957), *The Three Faces of Eve* (1957), *Oh, Men! Oh, Women* (1957), *I Want to Live* (1958), *Vertigo* (1958), *Anatomy of a Murder* (1959), and *Suddenly, Last Summer* (1959).

The depth of the psychoanalytic turn in Hollywood reflected not only the stories on-screen but also how actors lived their lives off-screen. In particular, Hollywood's postwar infatuation with Method acting reflected and promoted concerns about authenticity, inner truth and popular psychology. The Method was a philosophy of performance that altered postwar Hollywood. Developed by Konstantin Stanislavski at the Moscow Art Theatre, it took what was essentially an older philosophy about acting and formalized it with specific exercises and techniques. Stanislavski created the Method because he became "dissatisfied and disenchanted" with the "conventions and artificiality" of the theatre. He wanted "to bring naturalism and truth back into the theatre, to force the actor to play from the inside rather than the outside."[89] Method acting was part of a widespread "naturalistic revolution" within the art world, the theatrical counterpart to then-modern playwrights like Ibsen and Chekhov. This system was first brought to America in the 1920s by two of Stanislavski's students (Boleslavsky and Ouspenskaya), but the powerful influence the system eventually had in American theatre and film rests more surely on two of the early devotees of the "Method," Harold Clurman and Lee Strasberg.[90] Throughout the 1920s and 1930s devotees like Strasberg championed the Method and successfully revolutionized acting in theater.

However, the theatrical revolution of the Method did not hit American culture with full force until after the Second World War, when Hollywood discovered it, along with psychoanalysis and therapeutic culture. The Actors Studio, founded in 1947, immediately became the center for promoting Method acting as the new system of training for actors and performing.[91] The Method was first popularized by the Actors Studio on Broadway, but it traveled to Hollywood with the many New York actors who went west to work in films: "The Studio's most significant contribution [was] the creation of a committed state of mind about acting—committed about its relevance to contemporary life and its seriousness as a craft."[92] Out of this school came stars like Marilyn Monroe, John Garfield, Dorothy McGuire, Shelley Winters, Tom Ewell, Kim Stanley, James Dean, Paul Newman, Ben Gazzara, Anthony Perkins, Julie Harris, Eva Marie Saint, Rod Steiger, and Marlon Brando, the actor most associated with the Method technique.

The Method was immensely popular in postwar Hollywood, especially among young stars, who saw acting as an extension of the desire to find an inner truth. To achieve this truth, an actor had to channel their emotions and connect to the characters, using techniques like "emotional recall." Method actors did not just play a part; they sought to become the character. As in psychoanalysis, actors explored their own subconscious and past experiences to trigger emotions as the role demanded. Method actors were therefore concerned about the motivations of their character and the inner workings of their minds. In Method acting, "the text is just the 10 percent of the iceberg that shows. The rest is subtext . . . The subtext involves what's beneath the language of the script: not what people say, but what they really want but are afraid to ask for. Spoken dialogue is always secondary to Method actors. Their concern is with an inner dialogue."[93] In its original definition, "subtext" consists of the hidden meanings "beneath the text," specifically in reference to acting in film or theatre. Interestingly, "subtext" only entered common usage following the Second World War and was first cited in 1950 by the OED dictionary in relation to Stanislavski and the Method.[94]

Postwar American culture was "a new age in which all thoughts and things were split."[95] In the words of Erik Erikson: "Man remains ready to expect from some enemy, force, or event in the outer world that which, in fact, endangers him from within: from his own angry drives, from his own sense of smallness, and from his own split inner world."[96] The idea that identities were malleable coexisted with discourses about authenticity and "identity crisis." Atomic angst, Cold War fears, identity anxiety, and the rise of psychoanalytic discourse were both reflected and promoted by Hollywood. All the divergent ideological strands and cultural beliefs that defined the postwar period—from Cold War fears of an "enemy within," to the rise of psychoanalytic culture and the proliferation of identity studies, to the Method shift in acting—impacted how Hollywood represented racial, gender, sexual, and political identities on-screen and how audiences interpreted those representations.

CHAPTER TWO

PASSING AS SOCIAL STRATEGY

The Early Postwar "Message" Pics

Because our American whites are so stupid in so many ways, racially speaking . . . I have great tolerance for persons of color who deliberately set out to fool our white folks . . . passing for white is, of course, the most common means of escaping color handicaps.[1]
—Langston Hughes, "Fooling Our White Folks" (1950)

After the war, Hollywood addressed passing as a subject. Characters that passed appeared in films in the 1930s, most notably in early screen adaptations of *Show Boat* and *Imitation of Life*, but passing was neither the focus of the plot nor the subject of these films. The first film to address passing as its central theme was *Gentleman's Agreement* in 1947. The public and critical success of a film addressing anti-Semitism encouraged filmmakers to then tackle racism in "race prejudice" films like *Lost Boundaries* and *Pinky*, both released in 1949. Not so coincidentally, the House Un-American Activities Committee began investigations into Hollywood at the same time, affecting representations of race and the politics of racism, both on and off the screen.

A key lesson learned from World War II was that film was a powerful tool of propaganda. During the war, Hollywood studios answered to the Office of War Information (OWI) and the PCA. The OWI was concerned with promoting "propaganda nonce words [like] 'unity,' 'tolerance,' and 'brotherhood'" as part of the war effort.[2] The OWI used cultural anthropologists and Hollywood filmmakers to make films supporting the war effort. Anthropologist Philleo Nash and movie reviewer Dorothy B. Jones worked with Walter White, head of the NAACP, "to pledge to award 'citizenship' to African Americans in their movie roles, meaning the roles would no longer be limited to menial stereotypes but rather would include bourgeois extras."[3] The "Double Victory" extended to the integration of actors in the film industry. Race became a conscious part of the war effort in Hollywood.

The war fostered a "liberalism of the heart," a philosophy that came to define leftists in postwar Hollywood.[4] Filmmakers viewed film as a tool that could promote social development in society. There was "an emerging consensus about the potential efficacy of cinematic representation to shape political discourse about race and national identity."[5] After World War II, filmmakers "earnestly insisted on making serious, mature, and trenchant films, considering their responsibilities to be related to the problems of the world in which they live. Some of these men [were] war veterans—Hollywood artisans who returned to their jobs inspired with a new comprehension of the significance of the medium in which they work."[6] Progressive-minded liberals emerged from the war convinced that films with the right message could affect real social change.

Postwar filmmakers used films to address serious issues, elevating the "social problem" or "message" pictures to new levels of prestige and popularity and redefining the genre.[7] These films dealt with a range of topics, including alcoholism in men in *The Lost Weekend* (Paramount, 1945); as well as alcoholism in women in *Smash-up: The Story of a Woman* (Universal, 1947) and *I'll Cry Tomorrow* (MGM, 1955); female insanity in *The Snake Pit* (20th Century-Fox, 1949) and *The Three Faces of Eve* (20th Century-Fox, 1957); crippled veterans in *The Best Years of Our Lives* (RKO, 1946) and *The Men* (UA, 1950); racial prejudice in *Home of the Brave* (UA, 1949), *Go for Broke!* (MGM, 1951), *Japanese War Bride* (20th Century-Fox, 1952), and *Three Stripes in the Sun* (Columbia, 1955); prison reform in *Brute Force* (Universal, 1947) and *Caged* (Warner Bros., 1950); and the death penalty in *I Want to Live* (UA, 1958), an anti-death penalty film. Previously taboo and controversial subjects were accepted and encouraged. Problems of racism, anti-Semitism, and prejudice were ripe for commentary amidst the disillusionment of postwar culture. With pleas for tolerance tied to a denial of difference, these films established a framework for Hollywood representations of race. Underlying the production of these films was the idea of representing and fighting prejudice.

In 1947, Hollywood released two message films about anti-Semitism, *Crossfire* and *Gentlemen's Agreement*. The success of these films allowed Hollywood in 1949 to address racism in films that *Variety* dubbed the first cycle of "Negro prejudice films."[8] These included *Pinky, Lost Boundaries, Home of the Brave*, and *Intruder in the Dust*. All of these films featured characters that passed, except for *Crossfire* and *Home of the Brave*. In these two films, racism was a product of a twisted psychosis. It is important to consider how race and racial identities were constructed in these two films, not only as a counterpoint to discussions of racial passing in films, but as a way of showing the trajectory of pathological figures in Hollywood films, from twisted psychosis wrought by racial prejudice (late 1940s) to the twisted psychosis wrought by racial passing (late 1950s). Usually, the message films are linked thematically and chronologically with the cycle of anti-Semitism films of 1947, followed by a consideration of the "Negro prejudice" film cycle of 1949. It is more useful, however, to link the "psychoanalytic" prejudice films like *Crossfire* and *Home of the Brave*, in which passing was not present, and contrast these with films in which passing was the central motif, including *Gentlemen's Agreement*, *Lost Boundaries*, and *Pinky*.

Social issue films sought to expose and cure the "virus of prejudice." Medical metaphors abounded in reviews and commentaries. Frank Sinatra used typical language for the times in an interview with *Ebony*, stating, "Bigotry is a disease—worse than any medical disease."[9] Film reviewers talked of the "virus of prejudice" and suggested that films could act as a "specific cure of certain forms of race prejudice" in the fight against discrimination which afflicted the nation.[10] Dore Schary, the producer of *Crossfire*, used medical metaphors when discussing the film, suggesting that it could act as a "vaccination" against prejudice in "mild" cases.[11] Rose Pelwick suggested *Crossfire* was "not merely a step forward. It's a step into another world of thinking and doing ... there will always be people who object that public treatment is not the best method for such diseases of society as race prejudice. But others have a strong argument in the fact that most diseases of the mind and of the body thrive in the darkness and silence of those who try vainly to ignore an enemy out of existence."[12] Prejudice was framed as an unwanted and contagious disease, and Hollywood films offered the cure.

The broad scope of these goals made contradictory representations inevitable. Contradictions between the aims of directors and the images that played out on the screen illustrate competing forces that drove the social issue films. There was a tendency to present stable divisions of race or ethnicity, such as black, white, Jewish, or Christian, when the goal was harmony between all groups. At odds with these representations were filmic assertions of the essential sameness of all people under the skin, regardless of race, religion, or gender, where the goal was assimilation. Too often, there was a simplistic conflation of "race relation" issues and prejudices. The problems of minorities were framed as interchangeable. This was reinforced in how the Hollywood machine changed the nature of "otherness" in characters within Hollywood scripts. Scripts about anti-Semitism in the army became stories of racism, and novels that explored homophobia became films that explored anti-Semitism.

RKO's *Crossfire* (1947) offers a case in point. In Richard Brooks's novel *The Brick Foxhole*, on which the film was based, the original motive for murder was homophobia. In the film, however, homophobia became anti-Semitism. The erasure of the homosexual in *Crossfire* was typical of the whole genre of "social problem" films at that time, in part because of the limitations imposed on the subject matter by the Production Code. But the logic behind the thematic switch to anti-Semitism was more complex. The chief advocate for making the victim Jewish was producer Adrian Scott, a noted leftist activist in Hollywood, aided by screenwriter John Paxton.[13] So what began as a "novel treating various veterans' frustrations including homophobia became a project about the suddenly salable issue of anti-Semitism."[14] The film's director, Edward Dmytryk, later dismissed this change as inconsequential: "As you know . . . the original thing in that, the man who was killed was a homosexual, and he was killed on that basis. We figured that wasn't anything worth talking about then, and that we could make it a Jew."[15] In the eyes of radical Hollywood filmmakers like Dmytryk and Scott, the "otherness" of gay men and Jews was interchangeable if it suited their larger goals. The film was well received by critics and became one of the definitive Hollywood films on the subject of anti-Semitism. Film critic James Agee applauded the goals of the film but called it "safe fearlessness . . . It is as embarrassing to see a movie Come Right Out Against Anti-Semitism as it would be to see a movie Come Right Out Against torturing children."[16]

More important for this discussion is how *Crossfire* framed the bad guy, Montgomery (Robert Ryan), as an irrational, bigoted killer. Shot in black and white in the style of postwar investigative thrillers, the detective—played by Robert Young— slowly identifies the sole motive for the murder as "extreme prejudice."[17] Montgomery's anti-Semitism is pathological. His victim, on the other hand, is represented as such an outstanding person that the sole homicidal motive had to be Montgomery's deep-seated pathological prejudice. This mode of representation made anti-Semitism an individual's pathological problem, not a product of systemic societal prejudice. The death of Montgomery implied a triumph over anti-Semitism. The film's narrative acted against the goals set forth in the film's marketing, reflecting contradictory ideas that society was at once violent and corrupt, but the right films and therapeutic theories could change society for the better. Reviews recognized the conflict of intent. *Life* magazine called *Crossfire* a "grade A thriller," but noted that in making the killer sergeant "a villain of the deepest dye," it discouraged "the audience from disliking him solely for being a Jew-hater." Even worse, it made the story less relevant, because "a man whose feeling against Jews is so intense that it drives him to murder seems far removed from the problems of a nation whose anti-Semitism is expressed largely in the insidious but less spectacular methods of social discrimination."[18]

Despite its faults, *Crossfire* was central to debates about the place and effectiveness of films addressing social issues. There was a heated debate between Dore Schary, executive of RKO, and Elliot E. Cohen, the editor of *Commentary: A Jewish Review*, about the role of art in social change.[19] Schary defended the picture, saying that it "was never intended to convert the violent anti-Semite. It was intended to insulate people against violent and virulent anti-Semitism . . . It might move slightly anti-Semitic people into the liberal camp." He admitted that it "is not a definitive picture aimed at readjusting the *real* anti-Semite. No one picture, nor one book, nor one group of professionals, has succeeded or can succeed in achieving that Nirvana."[20] Cohen replied, arguing that the "point at issue is whether *Crossfire* is effective in fighting anti-Semitism." Ultimately, Cohen concluded it wasn't because those who saw the film not only thought the killer Montgomery was crazy but also were self-righteous in thinking that the film had nothing to do with "them." For the average American, he said, "The film can hardly be insight-giving; it presents anti-Semitism as an irrational trait of an irrational man—the product of a mysterious virus that breeds hate indiscriminately against Catholics, Jews, Tennesseans, men with striped ties—a pasted-in, slick formula, transparently false. There is no effort to illuminate the psychological, economic, or political factors that make anti-Semites."

Cohen pleaded with studio executives for three things: "(1) study by the movie-makers of available knowledge on the causes and mechanisms of anti-Semitism; (2) scientific testing of the effect of film dramas on the social attitudes of film audiences; and (3) the development of a more sensitive, mature film art to deal more adequately with such complex human issues as race hatred."[21] While lamenting the muted message of *Crossfire*, Cohen's promotion of studies to probe the relationship between film and human behavior was an interest shared by many in Hollywood.

In response, Schary approved an unscientific but well-intentioned study of the social impact of *Crossfire*.[22] Researchers devised a questionnaire for audiences in Boston and Denver. As part of the study, the film was shown in schools in Ohio, where students were "tested" on their levels of intolerance before and after viewing the film. The social scientists concluded that there was an increase in tolerance after the film had been seen and that "obviously *Crossfire* made the students stop and think."[23] The filmmakers admitted this was the best they could hope for. Virginia Wright put it best: "While agreeing that a single picture would not produce a great basic change in attitude the educators felt that *Crossfire* would stimulate audiences to rethink many ideas of their own relating to prejudices of one kind or another."[24]

The film received, among other awards, "Best Social Film" at the Cannes Film Festival and *Ebony* magazine's award for "improving interracial understanding." The film was later nominated for Best Picture at the Academy Awards, and Dmytryk was nominated for Best Director. Eric Johnson, head of the Motion Picture Producers Association, was "presented with an 'Americanism' award for 'Crossfire.'"[25] But while Schary was busy accepting awards for *Crossfire* across the country, he was purging his studio of "premature anti-fascists," including both the producer and the director of *Crossfire*, Adrian Scott and Edward Dmytryk, who were members of the Hollywood Ten.[26] Ironically, the anti-prejudice message occurred just as Hollywood began persecuting filmmakers. *Crossfire* was a flashpoint between personal political convictions and studio politics in the wake of the first round of HUAC investigations. According to the press, *Crossfire* was also "the first film to break with Hollywood's policy of shutting its camera eye on controversial subjects," and this "paved the way" for the "race-prejudice" films that followed.[27]

If anti-Semitism was the hot topic of 1947, then racial prejudice was the hot topic of 1949. The cultural distance between these issues was small, because in practice Hollywood saw all minority and "racial" issues as interchangeable. The *Los Angeles Times* noted, "Racial Intolerance Feature in Full Swing."[28] Film critic Jesse Zunser suggested that *Crossfire* marked a leap forward in Hollywood's willingness to be daring: "Racial antagonism, along with bigotries, has lately had a considerable airing in the newspapers, on the stage, and in best-selling novels. But until now it has been included in Hollywood's list of taboos because, like other controversial subjects, it might spell bad box office."[29] Hollywood finally addressed racism and prejudice in a thematic trend that dominated the end of the 1940s. And the doomsayers were wrong: these racially themed message films turned out to be great box office.

Among the "Negro prejudice films" released in 1949, *Home of the Brave* not only beat its competitors to the box office but was thematically very different. It was the only film to focus on the psychological damage inflicted by racism. Directed by Mark Robson and produced by Stanley Kramer with a screenplay by Carl Foreman, *Home of the Brave* told the story of a black GI's experiences with racism from his fellow soldiers while serving in the Pacific Theatre during WWII.[30] The film was shot in secrecy under the working title of "High Noon."[31]

As with *Crossfire*, Hollywood changed the subject of the source material. The original 1945 Arthur Laurents play *Home of the Brave* focused on anti-Semitism rather than racism. *Variety* magazine suggested that "One of the difficulties of recognizing the script was that in Laurents's Broadway version the principal character, suffering a nervous disorder as a result of bigotry in the Army, was a Jew. It was felt that theme was worn thin. Decision was made to rewrite it with a Negro substitute."[32] Michael Rogin argues that changing the story from anti-Semitism to racism made the film more radical: "However vicious, American anti-Semitism was not the racism that organized the society. While the United States was defeating Nazism with a Jim Crow army, there was a growing recognition that American Negrophobia was the counterpart of European anti-Semitism."[33] The potential for radical social commentary (and for profit) appealed to the filmmakers. In interviews, producer Stanley Kramer explained he choose to switch the identity of the lead character to make the film more timely and forceful: "If the story of a Jew forced to feel different was gripping on stage then in motion pictures, the story of a Negro would be much more so, because an audience could see the difference in terms of color rather than seeing one white man saying he was Jewish and another saying he was Christian."[34] Kramer's statement reflected the contradictions of a culture that promoted racial and ethnic tolerance while suggesting that prejudice was more understandable when visible markers of identity were apparent.

Newcomer James Edwards was cast as the now black World War II soldier Peter Moss, aka "Pete Mossy," who becomes paralyzed from the waist down after a traumatic incident during a top secret mission. Bosley Crowther acclaimed the film's "fascinating plot which combines a battle melodrama within a psychological mystery," stating that "Mr. Kramer's picture comes directly and honestly to grips with the evil of racial defamation, which is one of the cruelest disturbers in the land."[35] Posters for the film highlighted the fact that Edwards was both a veteran and an accomplished actor, coming "straight from his sensational success in the smash stage hit 'Deep Are the Roots.'"[36] A publicity photo for *Home of the Brave* featured five GIs in a row, guns pointing forward, with Edwards in the center of the group. The image encapsulated racial integration Hollywood style: a visualization of the "melting pot" platoon.[37] Truman desegregated the armed forces in 1948, and Hollywood filmmakers promoted this idea in subsequent WWII films. Film historian Thomas Cripps notes how films like *Home of the Brave* embraced the "metaphor of lone black warrior thrust among a white platoon, which had been put forth as an icon of a multiethnic war effort."[38] *Ebony* described

Moss's predicament: "Attempting to accomplish his surveying mission as just 'one of the guys,' he is excluded and friendless. Edwards breaks under the strain of being forced 'outside the human race' although feeling 'inside' like everyone else."[39]

The film opens with a montage of Navy-focused world-at-war shots with a brief narration: "Not so very long ago a great many Americans were asked by their government to take over a vast number of islands in the Pacific Ocean. This is the story behind one incident in that war, one island, one American." The scene cuts to an army office where Major Robinson (Douglas Dick) asks the army psychiatrist (Jeff Corey) if Private Moss will be okay, to which he responds: "I'm a psychiatrist, not a clairvoyant! The boy suffered a severe traumatic shock. He's paralyzed, lost his memories. Cases like his are curable sometimes, but I need help." He has the facts but he needs more. He asks the major and Corporal TJ Everett (Steve Brodie) to tell him as much as possible about what happened, and they start talking about the mission they were all on together, allowing the story to unfold in flashbacks.

In the first flashback, the scene fades to a shot of the 293rd Reconnaissance and Intelligence Detachment on an unnamed naval base in the Pacific. The major recounts how it all began with an order from HQ to survey and map a nearby island held by the Japanese. Robinson picked three men from his outfit: TJ Everett, Finch (Lloyd Bridges) and Sergeant Mingo (Frank Lovejoy). He emphasizes to the men it is strictly a volunteer mission and then gives them ten minutes to think about it. The major makes sure to inform them that survey specialist Private Peter Moss from one of the engineering battalions has already volunteered. On cue, Moss walks in, reporting for special assignment as they are weighing their decision. The entrance of the black serviceman causes a stir, but Finch is the first to recover and walks right over, making it apparent they are old friends. Finch explains they went to high school together and were on the same basketball team.

While they reminisce, the unexpected appearance of Moss causes the major to retreat into his office and call his commanding officer, Colonel Baker (Cliff Clark): "Sir, that engineer you've given me to do the surveying. He's—he's colored, Sir." The Colonel replies: "Is that so? What color is he?" The major begs pardon, but the Colonel takes him to task: "Look, Major, you do know the time element here, don't you? Well, for your information in this particular MOS I have 3 men in the hospital, 2 in a rest camp, and another in a top priority job. And furthermore, let me remind you that he is the only available surveyor specialist who's volunteered. So I wouldn't care if he was purple all over and had green stripes down his back! Is that clear? And if I may ask, what do you think this is? A war or a country club tea dance?" The Colonel stakes out the liberal claim for color-blindness by arguing that racial intolerance was more than unjust; it was a hindrance to the war effort. When the major returns the men all volunteer, though TJ complains that the army "does not have the right" to make them serve with a black man on a dangerous mission.

The mission is simple: survey the island and get the maps back to base. The men are dropped off on the far side of the island, and they hide their raft before heading into the jungle. Moss does the surveying, Finch draws the maps, and the others help out. Early scenes on the island establish racial tension. On the first night, the men pull out their dinner rations, except for Moss, who unpacks fried chicken that he made himself, neatly setting up TJ to make a racist remark about what "wonderful cooks the coloreds are, great entertainers too." In another scene the major confides in Mingo: "You know it's funny; ever since we got to the island I never think of [Moss] being black." Mingo chides him: "It is funny; I never think of you being white." However, real discord affects the group when the tension between Finch and TJ flares up into a physical brawl after TJ taunts Finch and calls him a "nigger-lover." Mingo tries to de-escalate the conflict, telling Moss that TJ's attitude is not personal, and TJ is just a thirty-five-year-old resentful civilian in army clothing, but the incident triggers anger in Moss about all white people, including Mingo: "You make us different. What do you want us to do? What do you want us to be? Tell your wife to write a poem about it Mingo!" When Mingo tries to tell him, "But at least you know Finch doesn't feel that way," Moss just replies, "I don't know anything."

On the final day of their mission, the stress of war gets to them all. Moss's insecurities and heightened sensitivity lead him to fight with Finch over whether they should risk their lives to retrieve the map case that Finch dropped or just evacuate. They make up and recover the case, but when Finch is shot, Moss is faced with the dilemma of staying with his buddy or completing his duty as a soldier. He does his duty. Finch is captured and tortured by the Japanese. Moss wants to go back for Finch, but the major says no; their priority must be to get the survey maps back to HQ. Finch escapes, making it to the rendezvous clearing, but lives just long enough to die in Moss's arms. A firefight erupts, forcing the team to evacuate. When Moss realizes he cannot even bury his friend, that he has to abandon Finch, he suddenly loses the use of his legs and collapses. Mingo's arm is wounded in the shooting, so he cannot help get Moss out. It is ironically the virulent racist, TJ, who picks up Moss and carries him out of the jungle to the waiting boat, AVR 114, and to safety.

When the group without Finch returns to the base, Moss's paralysis is diagnosed as psychological and not physical. The army psychiatrist first tries to cure him through "narcosynthesis," injecting drugs to unlock memories. Other psychological treatments are tried, including talk therapy. The immediate paralysis was induced by a "guilt complex" because he, as a black soldier, survived when his white buddy did not. On top of the guilt, Moss also felt betrayed because Finch, one of the few white people he had ever completely trusted, had almost called him a racial slur in a heated moment during the mission before catching himself and saying "nitwit" instead. After many sessions, the psychiatrist concludes that a lifetime of discrimination is the root of Moss's trauma, and he suffers from the "disease of too much sensitivity." As treatment, the psychiatrist spews racist comments. But Moss is only fully cured when he realizes his guilt is not unique to him because of his race; his feelings are normal. All soldiers are glad when a bullet misses them, even if it hits a buddy. Mingo helps Moss with these issues at the hospital, as he adjusts to his own new disability with the loss of his arm.

The heart of the film is the friendship of Finch and Moss and its representation of liberal ideals of racial harmony. In later flashbacks from Moss's point of view, in high school together they are as close as two friends could be, inseparable at work and play, even studying together. They have a running gag where they greet each other with affectations of "delighted" and "charming," and they use minor insults like "nitwit" and "dolt" as terms of endearment. Their friendship is reignited on their mission together, and they discuss how they will open a restaurant or bar together back home when the war is over.[40]

When Finch dies, Mingo steps in. In an earlier scene during combat, Sergeant Mingo quotes a poem by his wife to calm down the hysterical Moss: "We are only we two, and yet our howling can encircle the world's end. Frightened, you are my only friend. And frightened, we are everyone. Someone must take a stand. Coward, take my coward's hand."[41] In the final scene, a new interracial friendship is presented as Moss quotes these lines back to Mingo, offering his hand to help him with his gear as both are being sent home, and Mingo tells him that perhaps they should go into business together and open a restaurant, just as he and Finch had planned.[42]

This kind of "buddy" dynamic was at the core of many war genre films in the 1940s. Soldiers fighting wars together in the male world of the military allowed for the intensity and love between men to be represented by

Hollywood, even if the overtones of homosexuality were never explicit.[43] Whether or not the love and friendship between Moss and Finch (or Moss and Mingo) crossed sexual boundaries, it crossed the wartime racial boundaries of a segregated army and promoted the postwar ideal of racial integration. If bravery and soldiers coming together in missions like the one depicted in *Home of the Brave* helped win the war, the film also suggests that psychiatry and racial integration would help win the peace.

Home of the Brave begins and ends in the office of the army psychiatrist at the military hospital. The psychiatrist is the primary if unacknowledged filter through which the story is told. At its core, the film exposes the "psychic toll that prejudice extracted" and suggests that therapy and psychoanalytic theories are the solution to the social problems of discrimination and prejudice.[44] While this framing led some reviewers to complain that "the arguments against discrimination get badly mixed up with the abracadabra of psychiatry," it situates the film perfectly in postwar discourse about race and identity.[45] This representation gave narrative life to popular psychoanalytic ideas; racism and discrimination not only damaged self-esteem but could literally cripple their victims. But the film more uncomfortably suggests it is victims like Moss who must learn not to be "sensitive" to racism, absolving racists like TJ from bearing the burden of change towards progress. Moreover, while the flashbacks of Finch and Moss together in high school were heart-warming, the film fails to address the implications of Moss being the only visible black student in these scenes. Ultimately, by relying on the trope of the "lone black warrior" to make its plea for racial tolerance, the film sent mixed messages, inviting critiques.[46]

There was an uneasy tension between these texts of progress and racial tolerance and the subtexts that contradicted those messages. Sympathetic media and reviews usually focused on the positive spin. Under the headline "Film Has Telling Lines on Bigotry," *Ebony*'s review of *Home of the Brave* fully recounts the scene where the major reacts to the "alarming" news that a "Negro" has been assigned to his mission, and the Colonel memorably exclaims: "I wouldn't care if he was purple all over and had green stripes down his back!"[47] This exchange captured the popular postwar idea that universal color blindness was in the best interest of the military effort (and society). An underlying tenet of films like *Crossfire* and *Home of the Brave* was the humanist, liberal ideal that humanity trumped difference. Jews were just Christians who attended synagogues instead of churches, and blacks were really just folks with darker skin. Ethnic, religious, or racial traits were negligible when compared to the common bond of "Americanness."

There was an idealistic and integrationist agenda to many of the "social problem" films that never fulfilled itself off screen. James Edwards never became a major star, despite his highly acclaimed performance in *Home of the Brave*, because America was not ready for African American stars. As Donald Bogle puts it, "Racial tolerance as a theme was fashionable but Negro actors were not."[48] The actor Edwards may have been a few years ahead of his time, but the character, Private Peter Moss, was close to a perfect embodiment of the postwar cultural dynamics of racial liberalism and psychoanalytic discourses that garnered Hollywood's attention in the late 1940s.

Both *Home of the Brave* and *Crossfire* featured the psychological damage of racial discrimination: to a perpetrator in *Crossfire* and to a victim in *Home of the Brave*. The films critiqued unchecked prejudice and discrimination while offering films as therapy to solve American racism. Their psychoanalytic bent was the perfect mirror for postwar reflections about social issues, racial identity, and an integrated society. Despite their faults, *Crossfire* was viewed as a strong postwar indictment of anti-Semitism by Hollywood standards, just as *Home of the Brave* was seen as a strong indictment of racism.

Like *Crossfire*, *Gentleman's Agreement* also dealt with anti-Semitism and was released that same year in 1947. The timing of two major films addressing the same issue did not go unnoticed. Zanuck was miffed that Schary made the "first" film addressing anti-Semitism. In his autobiography, Schary explained, "We exchanged a few notes . . . then a phone call during which I was compelled to tell him he had not discovered anti-Semitism, and that it would take far more than two pictures to eradicate it. The conversation ended with both of us not having budged one inch."[49] Thomas Brady of the *New York Times* noted that Darryl F. Zanuck's *Gentleman's Agreement*, in contrast to *Crossfire*, was "dealing with the small social and economic discriminations by which most American anti-Semitism finds expression."[50] Zanuck's film offered a glimpse of the problem of polite bigotry in America. More importantly, while not the first to tackle anti-Semitism, *Gentlemen's Agreement* was the first Hollywood film to centralize passing as the key theme of its narrative.[51]

Gentleman's Agreement (20th Century-Fox, 1947), based on a screenplay by Moss Hart, was produced by Darryl F. Zanuck and directed by Elia Kazan. It starred Gregory Peck as Philip "Schuyler" Green, Dorothy McGuire as Kathy Lacy, and John Garfield as Green's best friend, Dave Goldman. Supporting actors included Anne Revere as Green's mother, Dean Stockwell as Green's son Tommy, Celeste Holm as Anne Dettrey, and June Havoc as Elaine Wales, with a cameo by Sam Jaffe as Professor Fred Lieberman. The film was nominated for eight Academy Awards in 1948, winning three in the categories of Best Picture, Best Director, and Best Supporting Actress (for Holm, who beat out Revere for the award). In addition, it received the New York Film Critics' vote for best picture, and was one of the big box office successes of the year. Prestige and profit packaged together became the most socially relevant film of that year.

Ebony situated the film as part of a socially progressive agenda in Hollywood under the headline, "*Gentlemen's Agreement:* New daring movie exposes 'nice people' who spread racial hatred":

> Most of the 98,000,000 Americans who attend the movies every week, settling down comfortably in soft cushioned seats with nickel candy bars, will be shocked by a new 20th Century-Fox film which is not about love, prisons or psychopaths, but about ordinary, everyday Americans who hate other Americans because of their race. Undoubtedly the most daring picture ever made in Hollywood, *Gentlemen's Agreement* is about Americans who hate Jews—but easily substituted for Jews could be Catholics, Italians, Negroes or any other minority in the U.S. [The movie] is, in fact, a more aggressive exposure of "nice," "good" people in America who spread racial and religious hate than the original novel. Without compromise the film rips the veil of hush-hush from the subject of anti-Semitism and blasts the blindness of "Typhoid Mary's" who unknowingly carry the germs of intolerance and bigotry.[52]

While reviewers described the film using the language of the couch, the film was surprisingly free of psychoanalytic language. This was in marked contrast to *Crossfire* and to every other "message" picture in production.

The source for the film was Laura Z. Hobson's best-selling novel, which she had written after witnessing anti-Semitism in Congress.[53] On the floor of Congress, Representative John Rankin of Mississippi "referred to Walter Winchel as 'a slime-mongering kike.' *Time* reported that, despite his inflammatory rhetoric, no one rose to protest."[54] Hobson was upset that such Southern-styled racism was accepted in the House of Representatives. The book illustrated how silence in the face of racism allowed bigotry to exist and spread. Originally serialized in *Cosmopolitan*, where "its 20,000,000 readers were startled at its daring," it later became a novel.[55] Both the book and the film focused on those who remained silent in the face of prejudice. The protagonist, a white Protestant male played by Peck, was a sympathetic guide to help American audiences understand anti-Semitism. Hobson's Phil

Green was the perfect gentleman, ensuring that prejudice could only occur because of anti-Semitism. In conjunction with the release of Zanuck's film adaptation of *Gentlemen's Agreement, Movietone News* noted, the book "led all bestseller lists . . . no story of the last decade has hit the literary world with such terrific impact."[56] The film exposed the "quiet anti-Semite" to show how prejudice and discrimination worked through silence.

The "gentlemen's agreement" of the title is the silence of polite society. Ironically, neither the Second World War nor the Holocaust is referenced in the film; instead, the picture calls for tolerance to stem prejudice. The film-makers were cautious about discussing anti-Semitism both on and off the screen, fearing anti-Semitic violence. As a consequence, compromises were made. Before filming began, Zanuck acknowledged that the film "had been greeted by some protests, the majority coming from admittedly anti-Semitic letter writers. A few objections have come from Jews, who feel that the picture *may increase rather than diminish intolerance*, but a far larger proportion of Jewish opinion approves the venture."[57] Rabbi Magnin, the "spiritual leader of the Hollywood Jews," was one of the people who feared that mention of the war and the Holocaust might increase anti-Semitism: "All they talk about is the Holocaust and all the sufferings. The goddamn fools don't realize that the more you tell gentiles that nobody likes us, the more they say there must be a reason for it. They don't understand a simple piece of psychology . . . They've got paranoia, these Jews."[58] Zanuck noted the "nervousness" of Jewish studio heads, who had all turned down the project as too controversial.

The movie opens as Phil Green and his son, Tommy, arrive in New York City after moving east from California. Phil, a widower, has moved east for a new life. He begins a job at *Smith's Weekly* magazine, where his new boss, John Minify (Albert Dekker), asks him to write a series addressing anti-Semitism. As Minify explains, "it's the wider spread of it that I want to get at. The people that would never go near an anti-Semitic meeting or send a dime to Gerald L. K. Smith." The romantic interest, Minify's niece, Kathy, reflected Zanuck's belief that "message" pictures were not profitable unless tied to a traditional love story. Kathy was also a divorced woman, a new character in postwar films. Kathy explains to Phil that she had married and gotten her dream home in Connecticut, but that her marriage fell apart before she had a chance to live in the house.

Not only did the film challenge anti-Semitism, it also tackled the Produc-tion Code's ideas about representations of marriage. The film makes it clear that Kathy left her husband not because he was abusive or an adulterer, but simply because she stopped loving him. Phil and Kathy meet at a cocktail party attended by her ex-husband, evidence of their "friendly and civilized" divorce. Representing a divorced woman as a heroine provoked battles with the censors and the Legion of Decency, but Zanuck and Kazan refused to bow to such pressure. Phil and Kathy's romance is tempered with tension brought on by Phil's journalistic obsessions, but the film ends happily, with them engaged.

The debates about anti-Semitism that occurred behind the scenes were replicated in the film's narrative. These discussions blurred the lines between the film's narrative and the cultural narrative of the film's production. A Jewish co-worker at *Smith's Weekly* argued that a series on anti-Semitism was a bad idea because it would stir up trouble: "you can't write it out of existence."[59] The WASP editors of the magazine dismissed such criticism with the rebuttal that not running the series would pretend that anti-Semitism was nonexistent and would "add to the conspiracy of silence."

Phil is initially disappointed with the assignment, questioning whether anything new can be said, but his mother chastises him: "You mean there is enough anti-Semitism in real life without people reading about it?" Deciding to tackle the subject, Phil wonders how to frame the story to make the series stand out. At first he is stumped, but again his mother clarifies things, reminding him how he solved previous journalistic problems by becoming what he was writing: "When I wanted to find out about a scared guy in a jalopy, I didn't stand out on Route 66 and stop him so I could ask a lot of questions. I bought some old clothes and a broken-down car and took Route 66 myself. I lived in their camps. Ate what they ate. I found the answers in my gut, not somebody else's. I didn't say what did it feel like to be an Okie. I was an Okie." On another assignment, Phil says: "I didn't try to dig into a coal miner's heart. I was a miner." Journalism allowed him to make a professional career of passing. Phil decided the only way for him to investigate prejudice and to expose anti-Semitism was to become Jewish, to pass as a Jew. He had his angle and his title: "I Was Jewish for Six Months."

Looking in the mirror, Phil concludes that there is little difference between him and an old army buddy, Dave Goldman: "He's the kind of fellow I'd be if I were a Jew." He further notes that Dave's hairstyle, facial features, and mannerisms are similar. Nothing in their physical appearances was different; neither Phil's nor Dave's physical bodies marked their ethnicity. "All I gotta do is say it," he declares, and "see what happens." While denying the "racialization" of Jewishness in the film, the filmmakers hired Jewish actor John Garfield to play Dave Goldman, in contrast with the Protestant Gregory Peck to play Phil. The actors could have replicated the dialogue in the film word for word.[60] Hollywood's representations of passing always invoked the dilemma of casting, authenticity, and performance.

Equally important is Phil's ability to cross boundaries without being discovered because he had moved from the west coast to the east coast. Phil recognizes that his ability to pass is easier because he is new to New York City. This means that no one except for his family, his editor, and Kathy know he is a Gentile. Ultimately, to pass successfully, there has to be a "conspiracy of silence" by those close to him. His mother, his son, and his fiancé Kathy all have to pretend he was Jewish. Unlike racial passing, this does not involve their invisibility or separation from him, but it does mean they are implicated in his masquerade. In the end his performance, what Michael Rogin calls "Jewface," involves simply changing his name from Green to Greenberg.[61]

This framing exposes a key contradiction of the film's message: for Phil to be seen as Jewish (and thus experience anti-Semitism) he must actually tell people his name is "Greenberg." Jewish identity here is culturally invisible, save for the name. In contrast, Dave Goldman is always seen as Jewish, as in one scene at a restaurant where Dave, in his military uniform no less, is confronted by a man who picks a fight and calls him a "Yid." Phil, who is at the same table, draws no notice from the bigot.

Nonetheless, Phil's passing is effective. While trying to register at an upscale hotel where he had stayed before as Phil Green, he is refused as Phil Greenberg, and he is also turned down for a job. The experience shows how anti-Semitism operates for Phil, but it also impacts Tommy, who is beaten up at school and called a "kike" by fellow students. At the same time, Kathy exhibits polite anti-Semitism. She argues there are risks to passing: "It will mix everybody up; people won't know what you are ... it will keep cropping up." Kathy worries what others (specifically her Connecticut relatives) will think about her relationship with Phil Greenberg. Even if he stops passing, there would be issues. Once that door is opened, it cannot be closed again, and his authentic identity would always remain unstable. She feels it only reasonable for her family and good friends to be in on the secret that he is not Jewish. Disappointed by her attitude, Phil sees her polite prejudice as part of the problem.

While the "quiet prejudice" of American society is the core of the film, other issues are raised. Supporting characters voice alternate philosophies. As the fashion editor, Anne Dettrey is the only woman on the editorial board at *Smith's Weekly*, but she holds her own with the boys and expresses an authentically liberal even feminist attitude. The smart and fun fast-talking career gal, a staple in 1940s films, is used here to great effect. Anne's quick wit challenges any intolerant behavior, whether at the office or a fancy restaurant, even berating an erstwhile acquaintance for bigotry after he tried to claim he was not prejudiced because he had Jewish friends, pointing out that though "some of his best friends are Methodists, he never brings that up." Suitably, it is at a cocktail party given by Anne that the nature of Jewish identity itself is contemplated. With drinks in hand, Professor Lieberman, described as a world-renowned physicist, articulates a complicated understanding of identity and passing. Lieberman explains: "I've no religion so I'm not Jewish by religion. Further, I'm a scientist, so I must rely on science, which tells me I'm not really Jewish by race since there is no such thing as a distinct Jewish race. There isn't even such a thing as a Jewish type. Well, my crusade will have a certain charm. I'll simply go forth and state flatly I'm not a Jew. With my face that is not an evasion but a new principle." Lieberman continues:

> There must be millions of people nowadays who are religious only in the vaguest sense. I've often wondered why the Jewish ones among them still go on calling themselves Jews. Can you guess why, Mr. Phil? Because the world still makes it an advantage not to be one; thus for many of us it becomes a matter of pride to go on calling ourselves Jews. So you see I will have to abandon my crusade before it begins; only if there were no anti-Semites could I go on with it.

Interestingly, Laura Z. Hobson in a 1947 interview gave the same response. She was raised politically aware, but without religion: "I grew up in an agnostic and broad-minded family. I think of myself as a plain human being who happens to be an American. But so long as there is anti-Semitism in this country, so long as it remains an advantage not to be Jewish, I can never simply say, 'I am agnostic,' but must say, 'I am Jewish.'"[62]

Professor Lieberman and Hobson's views about identity revealed the contradictions between assimilation (the denial of difference) and passing (the racialization of identity). The issue is addressed again when Phil asks his secretary to send out two sets of applications to a long list of hotels, country clubs, and medical schools, one marked "Phil Schuyler," the other "Philip Greenberg." His secretary takes the opportunity to reveal to him that she changed her name from Estelle Walowski to Elaine Wales to get the job where they work. She explains how she sent two applications to "the great liberal magazine that fights injustices," and how the one marked Walowski was rejected, while the one marked Wales got her the job.

Elaine explains that she experienced prejudice until she learned how to act like a middle-class WASP. She also admits she does not support the hiring of "openly Jewish" workers, because any problems would "come out of us," and she had learned the "hard way" that "it's no fun being the fall guy for the 'kikey' ones." At this point, Phil critiques her language and accuses her of promoting anti-Semitism. However, her speech reveals as much about class as it does about ethnicity, rooted in a desire to pass as middle class. Phil's condemnation of her attitude is condescending, especially since he comes from that unspoken world of privilege. It is telling that Elaine Wales (nee Walowski), the one person who genuinely passes in the film, accepts Phil's "Jewface" without question. She never questions his Jewish identity, only how he deals with anti-Semitism.

Ironically enough, a film that sought to expose the "quiet" anti-Semitism is championed by a character who only pretends to be Jewish, but is framed as more righteous and willing to fight against racial injustice than those who are Jewish. What's more, after the masquerade is revealed, Phil is portrayed as heroic for subjecting himself to such discrimination. The explanation for this can be found with the book's author. Hobson asked: "Would anybody say he was Jewish if he wasn't Jewish?"[63] She felt the answer must be no. This premise underlies the whole film. Phil's Jewishness is never challenged or put to a test.

Hollywood was left asking what constituted Jewish identity. In Hollywood the political stakes of this question were often personal.[64] Complicating the issue, in the movie business changing a person's name was a rite of passage and was common. While some name changes sought to disguise ethnicity, others simply strove for star-sounding names. Lou Hollis commented, "if this name game has any rules at all, one is that the star should have an Anglo-Saxon name," but he does allow exceptions to this "for the very few who either became famous with their old monikers prior to hitting Hollywood or who pick a foreign sounding name because it types them well."[65] In the language of Hollywood, Margarita Cansino "repositioned" herself and became Rita Hayworth, while Natalia Nikolaevna Gurdin, the daughter of Russian émigré parents, became the more audience-friendly starlet Natalie Wood, just as New York Jewish girl Betty Joan Perske became Hollywood's Lauren Bacall. Tabloids and newspapers frequently asked: "Would you like Martin and Lewis just as well if they were billed as Crocetti and Levitch? And who are those famous Academy Award winners William Beedle and Sarah Fulks?" William Beedle became William Holden, Sarah Fulks became Jane Wyman, Dodo Kappelhoff became Doris Day, Lucille LeSeur became Joan

Crawford, Shelley Schrift became Shelley Winters, Bernie Schwartz became Tony Curtis, while Issur Danielovich became Kirk Douglas.[66] The enormous public interest in the Hollywood "name game" meant that passing was part of the language both on and off the screen in Hollywood.

The relationship between passing and Hollywood's name game became clear when name changes involved disguising Jewish or "foreign sounding" names for something more marketable and Anglo. Name changes were made, sometimes under orders from the studios, to protect stars against the prejudicial nature of American audiences, but it was often an open secret. Audiences knew that John Garfield was Julius Garfinkle and that he had been forced to change his name to secure leading-man roles. Likewise, they knew that Judith Tuvim, the daughter of Russian Jewish immigrants, had changed her name to Judy Holliday at the behest of her studio (20th Century-Fox). It was also no secret that Laura Z. Hobson, the author of *Gentlemen's Agreement*, was born Laura Zametkin, and that she kept the "Z" from her maiden name to remind her of her Jewish identity. Edward "G." Robinson added a middle initial to his Hollywood name for exactly the same reason, an unobtrusive but public display of his Jewish identity.[67] The discourse about the name game made it hard to distinguish between the rituals of Hollywood stardom, American assimilation, and issues of discrimination.

"What's in a name?" became a highly politicized question in the era of HUAC investigations. While movie tabloids treated the "name game" lightly, those outside the industry imagined a more sinister agenda. In 1947, Congressman John Rankin, the inspiration for Hobson's novel, unleashed barely concealed racism as he read a list of names on a petition that Congress had received in support of the Hollywood Ten:

> One of the names is June Havoc. We found out from the Motion Picture Almanac that her real name is June Hovick. Another name was Danny Kaye, and we found out that his real name was David Daniel Kaminsky . . . Another one is Eddie Cantor, whose real name is Edward Isskowitz. There is one who calls himself Edward G. Robinson. His real name is Emanuel Goldenberg. There is another one who calls himself Melvyn Douglas, whose real name is Melvyn Hesselberg. There are others too numerous to mention. They are attacking this Committee for doing its duty in trying to protect this country and save the American people from the horrible fate the Communists have meted out to the unfortunate Christian people of Europe.[68]

Rankin, the former chair of HUAC and a driving force behind the postwar resurrection of the Committee, judged who was subversive and who was patriotic.[69] In HUAC investigations, Rankin focused on stars who had had Jewish or "foreign sounding" names. The Committee imagined that changing names meant subversive agendas. John Garfield was targeted with accusations of "leftist sympathies." Garfield died of a heart attack in 1952 just before he was supposed to testify again before HUAC. June Havoc, who played Phil's secretary Elaine in *Gentleman's Agreement*, was also investigated because her last name was suspicious. Being part of films with socially conscious themes was also grounds for investigation. Character-actress Anne Revere (who played Phil's mother) and Albert Dekker (who played Minify), were both investigated, and Revere was blacklisted.

A cultural schizophrenia existed between Hollywood's message of tolerance and Washington's attacks on the civil liberties of Hollywood's liberals. The idealistic goals of filmmakers were jeopardized by the compromises deemed necessary to make films addressing social problems. The most quoted comment about the impact of *Gentlemen's Agreement* is a story often repeated:

Moss Hart (who scripted *Gentlemen's Agreement*) is said to have had an encounter which is at least significant. A minor technician working on the picture told him afterwards that being associated with such a film had made a deep impression on him; when the gratified writer asked for details he said, "I'll be more careful in future; I won't ever ill-treat a Jew in case it turns out he's really a Christian."[70]

The "soon to be blacklisted" Ring Lardner Jr. similarly observed that "the movie's moral is that you should never be mean to a Jew, because he might turn out to be a gentile."[71] Variations of this story abounded; missing the message of the film, audiences walked away thinking prejudice was bad because the victim could be a Gentile—a tragedy because of mistaken identity, not systemic prejudice.

Gentlemen's Agreement and *Crossfire* marked Hollywood's first round of "message" films about prejudice. On-screen, these films examined aspects of American anti-Semitism, while off-screen, the drama between Hollywood and HUAC conflated Judaism and Communism as justification for persecution. This Cold War context made the issue of anti-Semitism in America more salient, but the possibility of Jews passing as gentiles did not invoke deep-seated fears in postwar American culture, especially when Jewish passers looked and acted like Gregory Peck. Stories like *Gentleman's Agreement* arguably contributed to the specter of passing, but in America race trumped ethnicity. However, the success of films that addressed anti-Semitism allowed Hollywood to finally tackle the issue of race.

In 1948 *The Boy with Green Hair* was released, described as an antiwar message picture that "blasted color discrimination."[72] Directed by "accused Communist radical" Joseph Losey, this film told the story of "The Boy," Peter Frye (Dean Stockwell again), who comes to learn how small differences can lead to great prejudices. The film begins in a police station where a young runaway with a shaved head will not tell anyone his name. A child psychologist, Dr. Evans (Robert Ryan), is called in to talk to him, and the story unfolds in flashbacks. The boy is an orphan, his parents "war casualties," but the child still believes his parents are alive and will come back home to him. He gets passed from relative to relative until his singing Irish "Gramp" (Pat O'Brien) takes him in. After kids at school call him a war orphan, he can no longer avoid the truth that his parents were killed; he is traumatized. The next morning after a bath, the boy looks in the mirror while drying his hair and is shocked to see it has turned green. The change to his appearance causes the people around him to react in fear and suspicion. This young white boy with his Irish grandfather became a victim of prejudice. Because of its "race" theme, *Ebony* reviewed this film and noted: "Unlike *Gentlemen's Agreement* or *Crossfire* which blasted religious prejudice, this new $1,000,000 Technicolor production fearlessly blasts color discrimination—and strangely enough through the effective medium of an all-white cast."[73]

However, it was in 1949, with the release of *Home of the Brave*, *Intruder in the Dust*, *Pinky*, and *Lost Boundaries*, that Hollywood initiated its first serious foray into "Negro prejudice films." These films reflect an agenda of racial tolerance that promoted civil rights. Long before their release, there was speculation about the casting and subject matter of these much-hyped racial prejudice films. The only exception was *Home of the Brave*, whose storyline was a well-kept secret.[74] Two of these films, *Lost Boundaries* and *Pinky*, prominently featured racial passing, an issue that was presented as a fundamental part of the battle against racial prejudice.[75]

The media discussion surrounding the production and release of *Pinky* and *Lost Boundaries* gave the idea of racial passing unprecedented visibility in American culture. Popular magazines like *Reader's Digest* and *Collier's* featured stories showcasing the issue. The most dramatic was the 1948 *Ebony* cover story estimating that "five million" blacks were passing within American society, noting that it "cannot but startle the unknowing white people to whom it is news that between 40,000 and 50,000 Negroes 'pass' into the white community yearly."[76] Magazines like *Ebony* forced an acknowledgement that passing was a widely used pragmatic strategy available to mixed race individuals.[77] Similarly, a popular docudrama TV show, *Confidential File*, featured an episode on racial passing called "Daytime Whites" that represented the issue both sympathetically and matter-of-factly, noting it was a reality that millions of blacks in big cities like Chicago or New York had to pass for white in order to work.[78] The focus on passing "forcefully brought the question before the white community and many whites are looking around for the elusive 'mulatto in the woodpile,' so to speak."[79] However, seeing the "mulatto in the woodpile" was not an easy task. These stories playing on journalistic sensationalism were designed to prove that it was difficult to differentiate blacks from whites when provided with rows of pictures.[80]

Other articles made passing sound like an adventure that was an acceptable social strategy to mock Jim Crow attitudes and legislation. Those who passed acted as Trojan horses inside white America. One such article described a "social experiment" designed to see if whites could identify Negroes who were "passing" by having a "light-skinned girl" go to schools, restaurants, and beauty shops that barred Negroes.[81] The goal was to "violate the sanctity of their Jim Crow institutions." The article contained photos showing a young lady successfully passing at a dance club, at a college, and at a "swank" hotel. She even managed to get a massage and go bowling, a feat that the article implied was the toughest assignment, because most bowling alleys in Chicago observed "rigid Jim Crow" rules. The article noted: "With an estimated 12,000 light-skinned Negroes annually joining the army of colored Americans who pass, Jim Crow zealots are having an increasingly difficult time in maintaining race lines in their institutions . . . The dilemma of Jim Crow advocates is the source of thrills for many Negroes who get a kick out of fooling whites."[82]

The popularity of stories about passing led to blind items in tabloids about passing in Hollywood. There were rumors about the blackness of celebrities like Dinah Shore: "Ava Gardner revealed in her autobiography that producer Dore Schary wanted Dinah Shore—'of all people,' Gardner wrote—to play the role of Julia in the 1951 version of *Show Boat*. Perhaps Schary's desire to cast the Jewish Nashville native had been rooted in a misbegotten sense of realism: Shore, after all, had been rumored for years to be a 'Secret Negro.'"[83] In Hollywood's pantheon of otherness, ethnicity and race were interchangeable, creating a "spiritual miscegenation" between the two in American culture.[84] Despite rumors, the articles stopped short of naming names, preferring to allude to the sheer "number of prominent people high in American life today who are 'passing,'" including "a Midwest U.S. Senator, a famous girl band leader, a top movie glamour boy, and a well-known girl radio singer."[85] Passing was no longer tragic but subversive. Writers like *Ebony's* Roi Ottley emphasized how blacks knew about racial passing but whites did not, and this is important to claim because it directly challenges the core premise of segregation that whites can tell, determine, and enforce racial boundaries.

Pinky and *Lost Boundaries* represent the first cycle of racial passing films in 1949. In these films, passing was sympathetically portrayed, with a suggestion that the ability to pass enhanced the chance for achievement of professional status and middle-class respectability. The lack of any psychological dimension to Hollywood's early vision of racial passing is all the more striking when contrasted with the prevalence of psychoanalytic theories in non-passing racial message films like *Crossfire* and *Home of the Brave*.

Lost Boundaries (1949) was produced by Louis De Rochemont and directed by Alfred Werker originally at MGM, but the studio dropped the project, forcing De Rochemont to make it outside of Hollywood. The film was based on the real-life story of Dr. Albert Johnston, who passed for twelve years in Keene, New Hampshire. After enlisting in the Navy in 1941, Johnston's commission was revoked when Navy Intelligence discovered he had belonged to a black fraternity at Chase College Medical School. Recalling the incident, Johnston admitted most people's reactions to him and his family were unchanged; "I would say 80 percent of the people didn't care, didn't make any difference. Why would it?"[86] The film, however, enhanced the drama by having the townspeople reject the family after disclosure, then eventually having a change of heart.

Aside from minor dramatic license, the film reflected Johnston's story as it was told in William L. White's "Document of a New England Family" in *Reader's Digest*. The verisimilitude was enhanced by the documentary style of filmmaking for which De Rochemont was known for.[87] In the film Mel Ferrer plays Scott Mason Carter (the changed name of the protagonist), who moves to New England and passes to secure a job as a doctor. The film begins in 1921 with Carter's graduation from medical school, his marriage to his light-skinned girlfriend Marcia (Beatrice Pearson), and the offer of a medical internship in the South. After his arrival in Georgia he is told by the clinic that they must hire a Southerner, implying that his skin was "too light" to work in a Southern black hospital. Carter's first experience with discrimination is from other blacks.[88] He then moves to Boston with his pregnant wife and tries unsuccessfully to get a job. Rejected, he is told that there just "aren't any openings for Negro doctors." He considers working as a red-cap in the train service but is reluctantly persuaded to take an internship at Portsmouth Hospital, where "for one year of his life he's going to be a white man." While there, he saves the life of a Dr. Walter Brackett who offers him his late father's practice in New Hampshire. Carter refuses, confessing to Brackett that he is black, but Brackett's reply is that "no one has to know."

Carter accepts the job and he moves with his wife into the elder Brackett's house. This is followed by a montage of his rescuing children from drowning and fighting forest fires. For twenty years, the Carter family lives in this community without incident. By 1941, their son Howard (Richard Hylton) attends the university and their daughter Shelly (Susan Douglas) enjoys town dances and boyfriends. But their lives are turned upside down when their racial identities are exposed as a consequence of Carter's application to serve in the Navy.

The pros and cons of racial passing are vividly debated in the film's narrative, with both black and white characters favoring Scott's decision to pass. His reluctance to pass is framed as a virtue, and his view of passing as a necessary social strategy is contrasted with other passing characters who are portrayed less sympathetically. The negative side of passing is indicated by example rather than by argument. Marcia's parents are represented as lacking in racial pride. They pass but are so fearful of exposure that they shun contact with visible blacks, even family members. Her father refuses to attend Marcia's wedding to Carter because there would be blacks there. In a later scene, Marcia's father advises his daughter against giving birth in a hospital just in case the child was noticeably "colored." The film represents such actions as cowardly.

The film emphasizes the contrast between Carter's healthy attitudes about race and the unhealthy, self-hating attitudes of Marcia's parents, especially her father. While out of work and looking for a job, Scott and Marcia lived with her parents. Marcia's father makes it clear that he does not want to limit his daughter's opportunities: "Marcia's never been identified as colored. Luckily, there's no reason for you to be either . . . I won't have my daughter seen in the company of Negroes." Carter's reaction is to tell him that "when Marcia married me she decided for herself to be a Negro." The mother defends this: "We did agree to let Marcia make up her own mind about this, Mort." But the father dismisses this: "You agreed. Scott, we've built a new life up here. When we left the South, Marcia was a little girl. Down there as Negroes we had nothing. Absolutely nothing. Now I've got a good job—a white man's job. I live in a white neighborhood. Our friends are white. We don't know any Negroes. Even my own sister has never set foot in this house. Are you going to risk all we've gained by being seen with blacks?" His discomfort with his black identity, which is not portrayed sympathetically, foreshadows passing subjects in films of the late 1950s. The focus of the film is the sympathetic portrayal of Carter and his wife Marcia.

The subject of passing is raised repeatedly in the film by different characters. Scott and Marcia attend a party at the house of his mentor and friend, Dr. Howard (Emory Richardson), who is not only a well-respected physician, but also a leader in the black community. At this get-together of professional black men and women, alternative views on passing are discussed. Surprisingly, the men and women separate to discuss issues of segregation and race, but the gender segregation of these discussions is not addressed.

The men in the dining room, professionals all, get deep in conversation about the pros and cons of passing. One of them says: "I'd like to ask Scott why he objects to passing." Carter responds: "If a Negro wants to help his race he should have the courage to stand up and say 'I'm a Negro!'" Dr. Howard interjects: "Don't look at me, Scott; I've never had to worry about passing." Another man is heard: "You know what they say down South? If you white, you alright. If you brown, you can hang around. If you black, stand back." A different man (who is equally light-skinned as Carter) says: "Carter, until you establish a practice you should at least consider passing." Carter tells him: "I have. I've also considered what happens when the truth comes out." The other man replies: "It needn't. If you watch your step." The last word on the subject belongs to Dr. Howard, who says: "After all, this has been a big problem with our people for generations. Each man has to work it out his own way." In this simple statement, Dr. Howard invokes the long history of racial passing without judgment.

While living in Keenham (the name to which Keene is changed in the film), the Carter children are unaware of their own status. A key dramatic element is that the children do not know they are passing; they never question who they are. The children echo the racial prejudice of the culture around them. Shelly betrays her own racism when she reacts to the news that her brother is bringing home a black friend, Arthur Cooper (William Greaves), from college, "He's colored! What will the gang say? With all the boys at college my brother's got to bring home a coon." Shelly's response reflects the deep-seated cultural racism that existed in communities like Keenham, New Hampshire.

The children's ignorance about their background is surprising because their father maintains ties to the black community, albeit secretly. The narrator intones: "No one suspected that Carter's weekly trips to Boston were to work with his old classmate Dr. Jesse Pridham. Together they had helped build the Charles Howard Clinic. In Boston, one day a week, Scott Carter practiced medicine as a Negro among Negroes." In doing this, the film implies that Scott remained true to himself, but at the cost of having to juggle his life strategically to accommodate both his passing and non-passing worlds. Scott never forgets where he came from or rejects his past associations, a crucial framing that ensures audience sympathy for his actions. But strangely, his own children never question his weekly departures, and he never takes the opportunity to show them that part of his life. For twenty years, the children accept their status as a white American family, and no one in the town questions the identity of the Carter family.

Only after Scott loses his Navy commission do Scott and Marcia tell Howard about his heritage, waiting to tell Shelly at a later date. Howard is confused: "But I'm white! That's true, isn't it? I am white?" His mother simply replies, "No, it isn't true. We're all Negroes." In reaction, Howard tellingly looks down at his hands as if seeing them for the first time, an image used in several of the film's posters. Howard's loss of self is further dramatized when, after learning about his racial identity, he runs away to experience his "negro heritage" in Harlem. *Variety* captured the intention of the scene: "With cold focus, the camera picks up the squalor and rancor within the colored ghetto, pointing to the fate the boy missed through an accident of his skin's shade."[89] Howard's experiences in Harlem include a striking dream where he tosses and turns as he sees all his family and his girlfriend shift from white to black, causing him to wake, as if from a nightmare. Howard is frightened by the nightmare and his own insecure racial identity.[90]

Howard becomes progressively more despondent and engages in reckless behavior, ending in a fight where he is arrested. He refuses to give his name to the arresting officer, but tells the police that he just found out he was "colored" and that was why he ran away from home. The police captain nods with authority and explains that in situations like this, where someone finds out their racial background is not what they thought, "they really do go screwy." A black police lieutenant named Thompson (Canada Lee in a notable cameo) is chosen to talk to Howard because the other cops believe he can best empathize with Howard's crisis. In the ensuing conversation, Thompson articulates postwar liberalism, telling the boy: "Whether they're white or whether they're black, people are pretty much the same." Howard reacts in frustration, saying: "Except me. I'm neither white, nor black. I'm both." "You're a Negro," Thompson responds, "And there are plenty of other Negroes whose skins are light enough to be mistaken for white. Eight million or more." To this news, Howard replies: "And my father was one of them." The lieutenant cuts him short: "Wait a minute. Before you start passing judgment, remember what you've seen in Harlem since you've been here. It's not much like New Hampshire, is it?" Having absorbed a lesson about the privilege he has experienced, Howard returns home to his family in New Hampshire.

In a later scene, Carter consoles his son Howard by telling him that he was raised white and there is no reason why he should not continue to live as white and think of himself that way. This quiet moment radically suggests that their passing is not a racial trespass at all. In this line of thought, their choice was not about hiding an authentic identity and "passing" for white; rather, the choice was between being white or making the equally valid choice to maintain a black identity. The film ends as the town gathers for Sunday church, the Reverend preaches against discrimination, and the Carter family humbly receives forgiveness for their trespass of racial boundaries.[91] But the happy ending is made more ambiguous by the final shot of the daughter alone outside the church.

Posters for the movie openly revealed the passing narrative. An advertisement in *Ebony* featured a large image of the son staring down at his hands in anguish and a smaller superimposed image of the mother and father leaning down over their son with the quote, "I should have told you this years ago, son . . . we are Negroes!" At the top of the poster was the tag line "The true story of a New England family who lived a lie for twenty years!"[92] This framing in the promotional material of passing as a shameful secret was in opposition to most of the film's narrative, where passing did not invoke the tragic mulatto. Such seeming contradictions reflected how complicated the issue was, made more so by casting choices.

When the film was released, it created a minor stir because of the use of white actors to play the black to white racial passers.[93] *Ebony* reviewed that "casting white actors in the roles of 'passing' Negroes, the producers of *Lost Boundaries* were under fire of the Negro press during the filming of the story."[94] However, the article noted the ethnic background of the actors, which belied their racially "fixed" white status:

Dr. Scott Carter is played by Mel Ferrer . . . of Spanish descent by way of South America . . . His wife is played by Texas-born Beatrice Pearson, last seen with John Garfield in the film *Force of Evil*. Oklahoma-born Richard Hylton has the role of the son. He is part-Indian and his father, who divorced his mother, re-married to a Negro woman. Negro actors in the film include William Greaves, Bai Saunders, and Emery Richardson.[95]

The ethnicity and background of the actors was important for *Ebony* readers, who wanted to celebrate the achievements of black and ethnic actors in a major film. The magazine coded these mestizo and mulatto actors as both white and nonwhite while collapsing ethnicity and blackness. Nonwhiteness was transferrable. Those of Spanish, Jewish, or Native descent were more authentically black than purely WASP actors.

While *Lost Boundaries* featured nonblack actors in lead roles, the film represented a spectrum of racial types and exposed key contradictions about race and identity in American culture. Just as Gregory Peck helped American audiences to understand anti-Semitism, so did white actors expose racism. The recital of the ethnic and racial makeup of the actors magnified the cultural disjuncture between the stated goals of the project, the elimination of prejudice, and the unspoken assurances of racial boundaries. Despite the desire to underscore the essential "sameness" of all people and the importance of ending racism, it was still important to assure readers and film audiences about the racial categories of actors and characters. By fixing the racial identities off screen, racial binaries were reinforced rather than challenged.

While *Ebony* focused on how the film was cast, other reviews focused on the message of tolerance. One review summed up the conclusion of the film, "In the moving finale, the New England folk are also led to understanding of human brotherhood through a church sermon and demonstrate their continued warm affection for the doctor and his family."[96] The film's uniqueness was addressed in *Variety*:

> The story of a Negro medico is traced from his early failure to surmount barriers of discrimination to his emergence as a respected member of a community deceived by the whiteness of his skin. Initial half of the film sharply poses the moral problem involved in this deception, which is finally solved by necessity and the advice of the doctor's colored friends. Later, the problem shifts upon the doctor's two children who have been raised as whites and who have absorbed some of the anti-Negro prejudices of their friends. The future dilemma of the parents is painfully foreshadowed during a sequence in which the daughter shouts at her parents "I don't want any coons visiting my house." Later, the deception falls apart when both father and son are rejected for Navy commissions during Second World War on racial grounds.[97]

While critics were impressed, reactions in the South were hostile. The film was banned by Southern censors, which provoked lawsuits from the studio.

To circumvent censorship, De Rochemont even tried to show the movie on television in Memphis and Atlanta, but stations refused "on the assumption that they would only be 'used' to help De Rochemont in his fight against the censors."[98] Despite such battles, the film received wide distribution and was popular at the box office. The difficulties in showing the film gave its social message more cultural resonance.

The topic of racial passing was also addressed by the high profile 1949 studio production of *Pinky*, directed by Elia Kazan and produced by Darryl F. Zanuck, with Philip Dunne and coauthor Dudley Nichols as screenwriters.[99] Based on the 1946 novel *Quality* by Cid Ricketts Sumner, it was produced as an A-list film. The term "Pinky" was "the tag hung by Negroes on a member of their own race who [was] light-skinned enough to pass for white."[100] The same film reviewer noted that while there was "no actual passing shown ... it is made clear that Miss Crain had passed herself off as ofay for a number of years while studying in Boston to become a nurse. However, when she returns to the home of her grandmother (Ethel Waters) in the South, the scripters always have her quickly reveal herself as a Negro."[101] *Pinky* is built on three important points: Patricia "Pinky" Johnson is black, she can and does pass for white, and because of this she must continually assert her racial identity to stabilize her blackness.

Pinky's narrative is straightforward. Patricia/Pinky Johnson returns home to her grandmother, who is known as Aunt Dicey and who had sent her North to study nursing. Back home in Georgia, Patricia becomes Pinky once more as she takes over the care for Miss Em because the work is too much for her granny. After dying, Miss Em leaves her plantation home to Pinky. Jealous relatives fight the bequest, but in a dramatic courtroom scene Pinky is awarded the estate. An interracial love story adds to the drama as Pinky is engaged to a white doctor from the North, Dr. Thomas Adams (William Lundigan), who had not known Pinky was black until he sees her in the South with her grandmother. He still wants to marry her, "despite the color line." Pinky must ultimately choose between her fiancé and her home. The film ends with a shot of Miss Em's plantation transformed into a school and nursery designed to help improve the situation of black children in the South.

The simple narrative belies the complicated issues about race and gender addressed by the film. Jeanne Crain, a white actress, plays the title character of Pinky, a young Southern black woman who passed for white while studying and working in the North. Two other prominent actresses compliment Crain's performance: Ethel Barrymore as the wealthy and "sharp-tongued" white matriarch Miss Em, and Ethel Waters as Pinky's black granny, called Aunt

Dicey. All three actresses were nominated for Academy Awards. The fluidity of Pinky's ability to pass is juxtaposed against the fixed racial constructs of the two Ethels. Together these three actresses compose a trinity that is used to interrogate concepts of race. Pinky is the "in-between" but no longer tragic mulatto.

Dicey's blackness is represented as a fixed construct, using racist stereotypes. From her first appearance on the screen, carrying laundry out to the yard to hang the clothes to dry, she is shown doing domestic labor.[102] Dicey works for others until she herself gets sick. Miss Em's whiteness is an equally fixed construct in the film, with Barrymore's legacy as a film legend adding to the stability of her race off-screen. By juxtaposing these characters, the film depicts an inconsistent approach to racial identity. The fixed racialized identities of the older women exist in deliberate contrast to the unsecure and unfixed racial identity of Pinky. In the scene that introduces Miss Em's greedy and bigoted relative, Mrs. Melba Wooley (Evelyn Varden), Pinky answers the door and Melba exclaims, "Oh, so you're the one. I'd heard you were light but I'd no idea you were (pauses) . . . well, you're practically white." Then upstairs when she is alone with Miss Em, Melba says, "My goodness, she's whiter than I am," to which Miss Em just responds, "Prettier too."

The film begins with Pinky's return home, the prodigal daughter. It opens with her walking down the dirt road of a small town until she walks up to the porch of a poor house in the black part of town. An old black woman hanging out laundry spies her, greeting her with "Ma'am", until Dicey recognizes her as her own granddaughter Pinky. From Pinky's response, "Yes, Granny, it's me," the audience understands that they must see Pinky as black. Whiteness in *Pinky* depends on the "double-take."[103]

In the film, Pinky's racial identity must be repeatedly assigned through these kinds of double-takes. That is, because Pinky's skin "is, in and of itself, unreliable as a signifier of her identity, Pinky must always be 'seen' twice, this second sighting functioning as a moment in which she is re-sited within racial hierarchy."[104] This double-take occurs not only within the film narrative but also for the audience watching the film. By showing the same woman as first white and then black, the film exposes and contrasts the treatment accorded white and black women in the South. A sheriff comes to Pinky's defense when he perceives her as a white woman being harassed by a black couple, but he becomes abusive when informed she is black. The most shocking incident occurs between Pinky and two white men. They spot her in the black section of town and insist on escorting her out of the area. When Pinky informs them she lives there, the offer of a ride becomes instead a threatening chase. What was first chivalry towards a white woman becomes a sexual assault for a black woman.[105] A less violent example of the double-take occurs when Pinky tries to buy a veil for Miss Em's funeral. The shop lady is helpful, until a white customer complains she is being ignored in favor of Pinky. Melba forcefully demands the attention of the shopkeeper: "Since when has it been your policy to wait on Negroes before white folks?" The shop owner reassures Melba: "I'm sure that Miss Viola just didn't see you." However, the implication is clear; the shop lady failed to see Pinky as black. After Pinky's race is revealed, the price of the veil doubles, a reminder of the economic and social penalties exacted in the South on second-class citizens.

These scenes show how Pinky learns to accept and reclaim both her black and Southern identity, and in the process they allow the audience to understand why someone would want to pass. Dicey is aware from the beginning of the film that Pinky passed in the North: "Yes, Pinky, I do see . . . I do know and I know what you done—and you know I never told you pretend you is what you ain't!" Pinky responds, "I didn't mean to, Granny; it just happened." Dicey responds: "But that's a sin before God and you know it . . . Oh shame, shame on you, Pinky! Denying yourself like Peter denied the good Lord Jesus!" Dicey then tells Pinky she should kneel down and pray to God for forgiveness for her sins and transgressions.

Dicey encourages Pinky to stay and work for old Miss Em as a duty to her profession and her grandmother. Predictably, as patient and nurse, Miss Em and Pinky come to love and respect each other, but tension remains about issues of race and Southern heritage. In an early confrontational scene, Miss Em argues that it is Pinky's duty to stay in the South and live like her granny. Pinky asks her: "What do you want me to do? Stay here, live this sort of life when I don't have to?" Miss Em responds, "Just prove you're addicted to the truth like you pretend. Wherever you are, be yourself." For Miss Em, Pinky must assert her blackness, something that passing makes problematic. The difficulty in following this simple dictum represents Pinky's dilemma, and she replies:

> What am I then? You tell me. You're the ones that set the standards. You whites. You're the ones that judge people by the color of their skins. Well, by your own standards, by the only ones that matter to you, I'm as white as you are. That's why you all hate me. What should I do? Dye my face, grovel and shuffle, say yes'sem and no'sem, marry some man like Jake Walters, carry a razor in my stockings so I won't upset you?

Despite the reassurance of Em's response, "Nobody hates you, Pinky," the uneasiness with Pinky's racial fluidity remains.

Both Dicey and Em disapprove of passing. Dicey tells Pinky it is wrong to pretend that "you is what you ain't" and Em tells her she must "be herself" in the name of authenticity and truth. When Pinky begins nursing Em they articulate ideas of identity and place. Pinky asserts: "Nursing is my profession" and "In some places a nurse is treated with respect." Em responds: "Nobody deserves to be treated with respect as long as she pretends to be something she isn't." Racial passers are not respected because they are not true to themselves.

In the end, Em provides the means for Pinky to remain in the South by willing her estate to Pinky, so she could open a clinic and nursery run for "her people." Pinky could then reject passing in the North. At first Pinky wants to return to her life in the North to rejoin her fiancé Tom, but that gradually changes. Those from the black community suggest that Pinky should let Em's cousins get the estate to avoid a dangerous conflict. Dicey's friend, Jake Walters (Frederick O'Neal), expresses a fear for his own security because he has a nice house and "no fire insurance." Against the wishes of those around her, Pinky decides to stay and fight. But her fight is further complicated for Pinky by the illness of Dicey, forcing Pinky to become the town washerwoman to pay court costs. In doing so she literally takes on the visible signifiers of her grandmother's Southern and racial identity. Just as Pinky assumes her role and her rights vis-à-vis the fight to keep Em's estate, her fiancé Tom enters the picture to make the cost of her decisions clear.

The nature of the court case is publicized even as far north as Boston, alerting Tom, Pinky's Northern fiancé, of her predicament. Tom journeys south to ask her to quit the trial and go away with him as he has "plenty [of money] for them both." He dismisses the value of Em's estate and asks Pinky to explain what it is she's fighting for. For the first time in the film Pinky talks about "her people," Southern blacks. Tom responds, "They're not your people, Pat. Not really. There will be no Pinky Johnson after we're married. You'll be Mrs. Thomas Adams for the rest of your life." But Pinky replies, "You can change your name. I wonder if you can change what you really are, inside."

Pinky challenges her continued passing by invoking the ideals of Dicey and Em. In contrast, Tom advocates escape and continued passing so they can be together. In the South her connections to her community prevent her from hiding her racial identity and Tom is unwilling to live in an openly interracial relationship. All the publicity of the court case meant that resuming her passing life in Boston would similarly be impossible because too many people there knew or could find out. Tom suggests instead another option, a move to Denver where no one would know who they were so they could be together and keep their secret.

In court, Miss Em's relatives fight her will on the grounds of "undue influence" by Pinky, but ultimately the judge decides in Pinky's favor because it was clearly Miss Em's "wishes" to pay back Pinky "a debt owed." However, in the original script a blood connection between Em and Pinky was understood. Deleted courtroom scenes included Judge Walker (Basil Ruysdael) questioning Dicey as to who Pinky's father was, who reluctantly answered, "Mr. Sam," Em's brother. Another scene, championed by Francis Harman, had Doctor Joe corroborating the testimony that Sam was Pinky's father:

Dr. Joe: "Miss Em suspected the truth. She made me tell what I knew. She told me she was going to leave her property to Pinky. I remember her exact words: 'Joe,' she said, 'Some of us Southern white people talk high and mighty just to keep up appearances. We act as if we were Lords of creation when deep down inside we know very well that girls like Pinky are the tragic victims of a caste system which tolerates racial equality on the level of vice while opposing it on the level of virtue. Pinky has the blood of my family in her veins. She is going to get the family place. I'll see to that in my will.'"[106]

However, these scenes would have meant the filmmakers would have to acknowledge the issue of miscegenation, which they did not want to do. Zanuck responded to Francis Harman's arguments, suggesting it would be better to erase the "illicit miscegenation angle."[107] His letter is a reminder of the cultural unease with miscegenation, both on- and off-screen. *Pinky* allowed the representation of a passing subject but not an explicit recognition of how those who could pass were born to interracial unions. The way the court case plays out in the film deftly evades the issue of miscegenation, but the estate remains a concrete symbol for what could not be talked about.

Despite Zanuck and Kazan's sleight of hand, Em's estate allowed Pinky a real choice: to be an independent Southern black woman or to pass with her white fiancé Tom somewhere else. The courtroom scene has the predictable if unrealistic ending of Pinky's victory against the Southern justice system. This reveals the optimistic faith of the filmmakers in an objective legal system that remained above racist attitudes. Some reviewers called this the triumph of justice, but others argued it was a vindication of the fairness of the Southern courts and paternalism, and therefore an injustice to the realities of civil rights in the Southern states.[108]

Following Pinky's courtroom victory, Tom assumes she will sell the house and leave with him for Denver. Instead, she ends her love affair with him. She cannot marry and hide, because she would "lose her identity as a Negro," she tells him: "I'm a Negro. I can't forget it and I can't deny it. I can't pretend to be anything else. I don't want to be anything else. I can see it now clearly for the first time. You can't live without pride." It is not possible for her to claim all of her identities on her own terms. She must choose. And her "choice" to break it off with her fiancé allows the film to sidestep the politics of Pinky's interracial engagement. The film ends with a shot of Em's home transformed into "Miss Em's Clinic and Nursery School," filled with black women in crisp white nurse's uniforms and their charges.

Pinky was the second highest grossing film of 1949, suggesting that the American public was ready for such stories. Northerners could get smug satisfaction from seeing racism as a Southern problem, and Southerners enjoyed a vindication of the Southern justice system. Culture in postwar America was fractured as much by region as by race. After release, *Pinky* received mixed reviews. Positive reviews focused on the potential to fight racial discrimination. Mainstream magazines like *Time* commented that *Pinky* was one of many films dealing with "the sorry plight of the U.S. Negro," but argued it was exceptional:

> By daring to suggest that some Negroes may be villains—and some white Southerners decent men—*Pinky* will annoy those who insist on their propaganda with only good and evil labels. Anyone who is deter-mined to look for clichés of the anti-discrimination propaganda might charge that the sour-sweet old plantation owner (Ethel Barrymore) is a "symbol" of white paternalism and the Ethel Waters role a "symbol" of Aunt Jemimaism. But *Pinky* is the most skillful type of propaganda: in avoiding crude and conventional labeling, it leaves a strong impression that racial discrimination is not only unreasonable but evil.[109]

In contrast, there was marked opposition to the film by proponents of segre-gation in the South who feared the film might cause social unrest. Ironically, this muted protests on the left about compromises made in the film. Thus, when Texas counties banned *Pinky*, civil rights leaders supported the film, focusing on the courage of the film rather than its limitations.[110] Representa-tions of racial passing always meant walking a tightrope between sympathy for the characters while not alienating white Southern audiences. In the end, Pinky was given the green light by censor boards in the South.[111]

Negative reviews were direct about the film's shortcomings. *Ebony* sharply pointed out how the "casting of Ethel Waters as an out-and-out Dixie mammy and Nina Mae McKinney as a razor-toting hussy is certain to offend Negroes."[112] The review also noted: "NAACP secretary Walter White, a close friend of Zanuck's, read the story and told Zanuck it would be resented by Negroes. White also submitted it to a panel of five Negroes who were even more critical of it than he."[113] These critics attacked what they perceived as racial stereotypes and hints of Southern paternalism in the film.

Acknowledging some of the negative press, Kazan "admitted limitations in the film after its completion but insisted: '*We do show a real Negro as our central character*, not a fawning person but the average Negro who, I think, is bitter, goes around thinking white people don't like him and who is a fighter.'"[114] This seems ironic, given that Jeanne Crain was that "real Negro" character. In a later interview, Kazan admitted, "There was some essential cop-out in casting a white girl in the lead."[115] Kazan was not the first and would not be the last director to cast a white actor to play someone who passed.

The symbolic use of white actors to play black characters who then passed for white was common, if controversial. It allowed the studios to make socially relevant pictures to fight prejudice while using stars to sell pictures. Audiences knew that miscegenation on-screen was being performed by white actors, muting the radicalism of the on-screen relationship. Hollywood's representations of racial issues were complicated by the film industry's contradictory desire to champion social justice on-screen while implicitly refusing to confront its own racist ideologies off-screen. Studio memos encouraged ambitious actors who could pass for white to do so if they wanted to get long-term contracts in Hollywood.[116] The film industry's failure to integrate and hire blacks or visible minorities and the Production Code's continued prohibition against "miscegenation" mirrored the "unjust world" that liberal filmmakers like Zanuck and Dunne claimed they were fighting to change with these message movies, but the irony did not go unnoticed.

The NAACP protested the casting of Jeanne Crain for the starring role. Even *Variety* commented on the casting choice: "While generally commended, many Negro newspapers criticized 20th Century-Fox for casting a white girl, Jeanne Crain, in the central role." Film critic Richard Winnington praised the film when it came out, but in 1950, he wrote a stronger critique arguing that *Pinky* had sold out:

Pinky (well, but not brilliantly played by Jeanne Crain) is a Negro girl of unblemished white pigmentation whose old darkie grandmother (beautifully played by Ethel Waters) has pinched and saved to send her to college. There she had fallen into the easy temptation of passing for white . . . Returning as a graduate nurse to the Cabin in the South, the sensitive and civilized Pinky is subjected to a full litany of racial prejudice . . . Pinky's ordeal is brought home . . . But Pinky's dilemma—shall she forsake her race and become "white" or proclaim it and lose her lover?—is side-tracked into never-never-land . . . The cardinal crippling evasion of *Pinky* lies in the selection of an established white film actress to play the heroine. Thus, the audience is insulated against the shock of seeing white and Negro embrace, against any effect of realism.[117]

Crain was herself aware of issues, but focused on the acting challenge rather than the principles at work:

"I asked myself," she notes, "how a young Negro girl would feel almost every day. And I remembered times in school when I was humiliated horribly. I used those times as a base for understanding my part. I think everyone has experienced what colored people face daily and I hope this movie does some good. So many people have told me not to stir up anything that I feel we've really got to move them into feeling for Pinky and her problems."[118]

Crain echoed postwar liberal beliefs about race, but also suggested good actors could understand and convey the perspectives of others. The influential *Pittsburgh Courier*, however, declared that "Hollywood made a right decision in giving the part to Miss Crain since white audiences would tend to more easily identify with her predicament."[119]

The use of a white actress not only served as a guide for white audiences but also helped the filmmakers dodge the issue of miscegenation.[120] The Production Code banned the depiction of interracial relationships, but it was not clear about characters that passed.[121] No matter what, the issue of miscegenation, both in the PCA code and the minds of the audience, was part of the film's history. The ability to pass implied past miscegenation. No denial in the script or censor by the PCA could erase the meanings of bodies that could pass. This unspoken history of miscegenation complicated Hollywood's attempts to represent race both on and off the screen. In his review of *Pinky*, Ralph Ellison criticized the film's narrative evasion of miscegenation, noting how Pinky's "racial integrity, whatever that is, was violated before she was born."[122] The filmmakers were naïve to think that erasing the discussion in the narrative actually meant erasing the issue. Script changes easily eliminated scenes that clarified Pinky's heritage, but they could not eliminate the meaning of Pinky's racial ambiguity.

As the film's reception attests, the racially passing subject reinforced and denied stable racial boundaries, a contradictory framework that invited confusion and compromises by all those involved in telling their stories, including genuinely conscientious filmmakers and activists. Because film is a visual medium, filmmakers faced a dilemma writers did not: how to put a face—literally—to racial passing. Philip Dunne, one of *Pinky's* screenwriters, wrote to Zanuck about the difficulty of representing passing without addressing miscegenation and racism:

> The legal position taken by many Southern states and seemingly upheld in the film—that even one drop of Negro blood made a person a Negro—is "far from a universal definition . . . If you or I . . . were to discover suddenly that we had a near Negro progenitor, would we feel 'different' inside?" He felt certain that whatever position he took, they might raise trouble by criticizing the current American take on race, but that "the key point is that she doesn't say she *is* a Negro, but that she *chooses* to be one."[123]

Dunne thought about the implications of passing and racial identity, but failed to acknowledge the contradictions in the plot and the casting of the film. "A trace of Negro blood" did make people different, at least in Hollywood's hiring practices. The producers did not want to offend Southern audiences and were careful to avoid showing physical contact between blacks and whites. Thus, Pinky had to sacrifice the love of her white doctor but also any other possibility of love because that would involve another example of miscegenation: a white actress with a black actor.

To avoid such issues, Dunne and Zanuck made Pinky choose. In a letter to the Fox lawyers in February 1949, Zanuck explains Pinky's choice not to pass:

> I do not believe that in this kind of picture you can afford to compromise . . . you cannot in the last reel give Joan of Arc novocaine to ease her pain. She has to burn at the stake. It is a sacrifice that Pinky makes in which she loses her love but in which she finds herself . . . Pinky

chooses to be a Negro. It is her choice and it is made voluntarily, and in doing so I think she rises in the estimation of the audience.[124]

In the letter Zanuck frames Pinky's identity as conscious choice. However, if it is true that Pinky could choose to be black, then equally she could choose to be white. If the two options are equivalent, passing is no longer relevant. Passing implied injustice. In the end, the film allowed a discussion about racial identity in America while acknowledging both the existence of passing and the contradictions that passing implied.

Postwar message films like *Pinky* also illustrated how seriously filmmakers took themselves and the subject matter of race after WWII. Screenwriter Philip Dunne captured the scope of their agenda:

We have throughout remained conscious of our obligation to society in projecting such a film. The experience of war has taught us that the motion picture is a powerful and persuasive vehicle of propaganda. What we say and do on the screen in productions of this sort can affect the happiness, the living conditions, even the physical safety of millions of our fellow-citizens.[125]

Dunne's attitude about his responsibility as a filmmaker reflected dramatic postwar shifts about culture and identity. However, it is unsurprising that the first major studio film to promote racial tolerance featured a passing character. Passing was proof of the fallacy of biologically determined racial identities, which appealed to liberals like Dunne but also unintentionally exposed broader contradictions about how identity was understood. Passing exposed the fictions of race while demonstrating that stabilized racial categories still had the power to define social and cultural ideologies.

Situated as black but visibly white, Pinky remained a potential racial passer throughout the film, a notion that complicates the film's place in postwar discourse about racial identity. Even the film's key compromise, casting a white actress in the lead role, offers destabilizing possibilities if one accepts that audiences were expected to read her as black. In other words, the "triple cross-dressing" phenomenon of "white as black as white" complicates rather than denies the instability of racial identity.[126] Because of this, even these compromised representations were able to foster anxiety about identity and authenticity within American culture and contribute to the specter of passing.

Earnest Hollywood "message" pictures defined American culture in the late 1940s. Hollywood mapped out the boundaries of postwar ideas about

race, ethnicity, and identity in the films *Crossfire* (1947), *Gentleman's Agreement* (1947), *Lost Boundaries* (1949), *Home of the Brave* (1949), and *Pinky*
(1949). Darryl Zanuck and Elia Kazan notably produced and directed two of
these films, *Gentleman's Agreement* and *Pinky*. All these films had an impact
on public discussions of racial identity. They featured liberal ideas about
racial and ethnic passing that reflected postwar beliefs in the power of film
to effect social change and the desire to champion civil rights. The naïve
campaign to eradicate social injustice was embraced by Hollywood and by
social theorists who studied the impact of films on American attitudes. The
stated purpose of such message films was no less than to end racism. There
was an irony in Hollywood's wish to tackle race and ethnicity on-screen while
refusing to address such issues effectively off-screen. James Edwards could
star in a film about racial tolerance, but he could not yet become a star.

The postwar trend of earnest message pictures and Hollywood's sympathy
for racial passing was equally short lived. *Gentleman's Agreement, Pinky,* and
Lost Boundaries were pioneering films in their representations of the ethnic
and racially passing subject, but they were the last sympathetic representations of racial passing. These films framed passing as a viable social strategy,
not a sign of an internalized confusion about identity. Pinky knows she is a
Southern black woman. It is the prejudiced attitudes and behaviors of others
that cause anxiety, not her sense of self. The film asks instead whether she
will accept that reality or pretend to be something else. In the 1950s, Hollywood's understanding of racial prejudice and representations of racial passing shifted dramatically. Representations of passing that showed the fluidity
of racial identity became problematic. The psychoanalytic demons that had
earlier plagued both victims and perpetrators of prejudice in *Home of the
Brave* and *Crossfire* finally caught up with racial identity. By the mid-1950s,
filmmakers presented racial passing as an internal sign of mental instability.
Passing characters were no longer understood sympathetically but were
instead framed as psychologically unstable.

CHAPTER THREE

PASSING AS IDENTITY CRISIS

The Psychoanalytic Turn in Hollywood

There is nothing wrong in passing.
The wrong is in the world that makes it necessary.
—Fannie Hurst, *Imitation of Life* (1933)

Films that framed passing as a sympathetic and rational strategy in an unjust world were short lived. By the late 1950s, passing became a pathological psychological failure to accept an imagined authentic identity. Questions about passing became linked to ideas about identity. Psychoanalysis and the language of the couch became part of American culture and Hollywood films. At the same time, "post-passing narratives," the rise of black stars like Dorothy Dandridge and Harry Belafonte, and the civil rights movement redefined how Americans understood race. *Imitation of Life* (1959) and *Island in the Sun* (1957) show this new view of passing. Racial passing, which was previously represented as an accepted external social strategy, became an indication of a psychologically motivated internal crisis about identity.

While Freudian terminology was familiar to the American public in the 1930s, it took another generation for it to become part of American culture. Psychoanalytic and therapeutic discourse moved from the rarefied air of psychologists, cultural anthropologists, and government strategists to the general public through Hollywood movies. Wartime psychological thrillers like *Cat People* (1942) and Hitchcock's *Spellbound* (1945) paved the way for a multitude of postwar films about psychiatric subjects, including *The Snake Pit* (1948), *Home of the Brave* (1949), and *The Three Faces of Eve* (1957). The language of the couch informed film narratives and Supreme Court decisions. High profile cases like *Brown v. Board of Education* used psychological terminology and argued that discrimination and segregation harmed the "self-esteem" of black children, creating an "inferiority complex" and leading to a "defeatist" attitude in blacks. Terms like "guilt complex," "temporary insanity," "submerged second self," and "psychopathic behavior" became part of the cultural lexicon and crept into films of the day.[1] Shifting postwar concepts about self and identity reconfigured how Hollywood represented passing subjects.

Not surprisingly, psychoanalytic discourse became commonplace in films as major Hollywood personalities also sought therapy. Postwar stars were diagnosed and pathologized in therapy and popular culture. Media stories revealed who was in therapy and discussed who should be. A tabloid headline capitalized on the trend: "Hollywood Headshrinkers Squeal on the Stars! *Hush-Hush* Magazine reveals where some of the gossip about film folk starts: on the analyst's couch."[2] Blaming the stars themselves for the gossip leaks, the article describes how "Many of the stars pride themselves on their own instability . . . and take refuge in the overabundance of sex, liquor, and money in Hollywood. 'When these fail' an analyst [commented], 'some of them get desperate and turn to us.'" The story claimed that Shelley Winters, Doris Day, Gene Tierney, Rita Hayworth, June Allyson, Robert Mitchum, Frank Sinatra, Ava Gardner, Harry Belafonte, and Gregory Peck all visited the "analytic couch." Hedy Lamarr, it claimed, "used to lug her analyst along wherever she went, like a lapdog, even on her European jaunts," and "Marlon Brando felt such an urge to consult his analyst while he was making movies in Hollywood that from time to time he would vanish from the set and turn up on the couch of a Manhattan soul-searcher."[3]

The reporter had gone to an analyst to get the dirt on the "Freud-happy stars." He suggested that analysts were the "best informed people in Hollywood. In front of them the stars wash their soiled linen without an iota of shame or inhibition, in the hope that the analysts, knowing all, will pull them out of their psychological predicaments."[4] Another exposé, "The Truth about Psychiatry and Hollywood Love," declared: "Some of the stars who seek the aid of head-shrinkers are really sick, sick, sick. But to others, it's just a meeting of the minds!!"[5] These articles suggested that therapy was as common as signing a contract with a studio and was a sign of success: "The great majority [of stars] . . . wear the badge of their illness brazenly, talk openly about the results of their latest trip to the analyst. This school might best be summed up by hip-swinging Sheree North when the Broadway baby moved to Hollywood: 'I've finally made the grade,' she cracked, 'I now have my own psychiatrist.'"[6]

Articles pathologizing Hollywood stars increased throughout the 1950s. A front-page tabloid headline in *Confidential* magazine screamed: "Are Most Movie Stars Mentally Ill? Yes! says a psychiatrist, and the facts are even worse than people think!"[7] Writer Victoria Thorn declared, "Three quarters of the Hollywood acting population is either insane, just getting over being insane or about to go insane," adding that within Hollywood, "suicide attempts are so common they cease to be news."[8] The tabloid revelations of neuroses focused on behavior that a decade earlier might have been labeled immoral but not "psychotic." In the prewar period, therapy itself had been considered abnormal.

The psychoanalytic discovery of a "crisis in identity" both on and off the screen contributed to anxieties about the nature of identity and the instability of boundaries. Films like *Pinky* and *Lost Boundaries*, with white actors playing black characters, reflected concepts of identity that were in flux and where binary categories were questioned. Racial identity was supposed to be inscribed on the body. As passing makes clear, the body can lie. It is an unstable signifier. Over time, such racial indeterminacy became loaded with psychoanalytic meaning. By the 1950s, those who could racially pass created confusion and anxiety because categories broke down in the face of psychiatric interpretations of behavior and identity.

The only exception was the usually positive reception given to on-screen or onstage passing performances by actors. For instance, black actress Juanita Hall managed to cross racial boundaries with impunity. She played the Tonkinese woman Bloody Mary and the Chinese woman Madam Liang in both the film and Broadway versions of the musicals *South Pacific* and *Flower Drum Song*, respectively. In reviews, Chinese friends of the actress were humorously quoted: "You see, Juanita Hall is Chinese after all. She's been passing for colored all the time!"[9] Casting choices that crossed racial or ethnic lines were often critiqued, but the performances were praised and seen as business as usual in Hollywood. Off-screen there was no such understanding.

It is not surprising that discourses about racial passing became increasingly dismissive, even hostile, in the popular press and literature. There was a sharp a rise during this period in "post-passing" narratives that focused on authenticity and identity. Typical was a confession in *Ebony* of a young woman who decided to "drop the mask and return to her people," stating that "after 12 years of having been 'white' I can truthfully say that I'll never make that choice again. I'm through with passing, through with all the hiding, all the dodging, all the miserable lies that turned my life into a confused, frustrated existence."[10] While earlier discourses normalized the practice of passing, post-passing narratives in the face of the civil rights movement framed the practice as outdated. It was now a psychologically problematic response to societal discrimination.

At the same time, the currency of the 1940s "message pix" fell out of favor with Hollywood filmmakers and audiences in the 1950s. Earnest social issue films like *Pinky* became passé. Although Hollywood still promoted films about racial tolerance in the 1950s and continued to put social issues on the screen, representations of race and related narratives changed. Films like *No Way Out, Island in the Sun, Sayonara, Imitation of Life*, and *The Defiant Ones* marketed racial issues in a more "courageous" and direct fashion. Hollywood became more outspoken in the fight against racial bigotry. In 1958, *Ebony* interviewed Frank Sinatra:

In my own profession, show business, we have always felt proud of our tradition that performers should be rated and accepted on merit and nothing else. Entertainment on the whole has generally been ahead of the rest of the country in the matter of equal treatment and real democracy . . . Hollywood has matured remarkably, especially in the last ten years in its treatment of racial themes in movies and its use and acceptance of Negro actors and performers. Stereotypes have just about disappeared. *Kings Go Forth* is the latest of a series of films dealing intelligently with interracial relations in the last ten years, and I think it should do an enormous amount of good. I am a strong believer in the subtle treatment of controversial issues like the racial problem as opposed to straight preaching which is seldom effective . . . *Sayonara*, starring Marlon Brando, is another example of sensitive and honest treatment of interracial love. In this picture the love of a Japanese girl and a white American ends in marriage.[11]

Representations of passing subjects changed as ideas about identity changed. The change in attitudes about race allowed the rise of black stars like Harry Belafonte, Dorothy Dandridge, and Sidney Poitier to become box office draws.[12] Dandridge, an actress who could have passed, has a special place in American film history because she starred in three important and controversial films in the mid-1950s: *Carmen Jones* (1954), *Tamango* (1957), and *Island in the Sun* (1957). She was also the first black actress to be nominated for Best Actress at the Academy Awards in 1955 for her role in *Carmen Jones*.[13] Her films pushed social boundaries. In *Tamango* and *Island in the Sun*, Dandridge's characters engaged in interracial relationships that challenged the Code's strictures against miscegenation. In *Jet* magazine promoting *Island in the Sun*, Dandridge argued she played a West Indies girl who, unlike an "American Negro girl," was not "self-conscious about or sensitive to an interracial love affair" because "it happens all the time in the West Indies."[14] Marguerite Rippy notes that "Both Dandridge and *Jet* avoided discussing interracial relationships as a facet of 'reality' that had long gone underrepresented in American society."[15]

What was occurring on-screen was replicated in lives lived off-screen and the public's desire to know who was sleeping with whom. Dandridge married Jack Denison and had an affair with director Otto Preminger. The tabloid press fixated on Dandridge's love life and on interracial love affairs of black stars in general. Sammy Davis Jr. made headlines for his romance with Kim Novak, sold alongside stories like "How Pearl Bailey Hooked a White Husband!"[16] Sex sells, and tabloid articles focused not only on interracial sex scandals, but on any affairs that suggested "miscegenation" amongst stars. Rita Hayworth was attacked and became tabloid fodder for her marriage to Prince Aly Khan.[17] The tabloids even analyzed their own marketing of interracial relationships in such articles as "Racy or Racist?: What Is It the 'Expose' Magazines Think They're Exposing in All Those Articles?"[18] This article notes: "On the cover of the largest selling 'expose' magazine, on every street corner, in every drug store, magazine browsers are treated to the sight of Negroes paired sexually with whites—three times as often as they see Negroes alone," and just "what is being 'exposed' in these stories is seldom very clear, but such terms as 'tan lover,' 'chocolate bon bon,' 'tan Tootsie,' 'bronze boxer,' and other 'cute-talk' for the simple word Negro abound."[19] Such self-reflection did nothing to stop the trend. Interracial relationships and identities drew attention both on and off the screen.

Together, the popularity of the language of the couch, post-passing narratives, the rise of new black stars, the cycle of film genres, and the burgeoning civil rights movement all changed how passing was represented and understood in the 1950s. Hollywood films with racial passing figures included *Show Boat* (MGM, 1951), *Love Is a Many Splendored Thing* (20th Century-Fox, 1955), *Island in the Sun* (20th Century-Fox, 1957), *Band of Angels* (Warner Bros., 1957), *Kings Go Forth* (UA, 1958), and *Imitation of Life* (Universal, 1959). In all these films, the passing subjects were women, connecting race to gender.

Saffire (1959) was the lone British film dealing with the issue of racial passing, but it also connected race and gender. Directed by Basil Dearden, the film begins with the murder of a girl who is initially assumed to be white until her visibly black brother (Doctor Robbins) comes forward and overturns this assumption. The revelation of her racial identity immediately changes the attitudes of those investigating the case. As in other 1950s films, the black identity of the girl becomes sexualized. Sexy outfits found in her apartment are evidence of the "black under the white," as is the dead girl's taste in jazz music and its implied association with promiscuity and night life. The investigation reveals that the girl had "passed for white" and led a "double life." A review summed it up: "A light-skinned girl of mixed parentage has been killed, and it is discovered that she was pregnant by a white man. The fear that the child might have been black provides a possible motive; and another is the jealousy of the colored friends whom she had cast aside. Thus, racial prejudice, in one form or another, is encountered throughout the investigation (the mystery of who-done-it becoming the mystery of human responses)."[20] This film replicated many of the same tropes about racial identity and passing as Hollywood films, but its small budget and British setting meant it garnered neither the media attention nor the controversy of its American produced counterparts.

Island in the Sun (1957) was based on Alec Waugh's *The Sugar Barons*, a best-selling novel controversial for featuring interracial relationships. The film overtly dealt with themes of miscegenation and racial passing, but also implicated white identity as imitative, adaptive passing. Waugh "intended it as a Caribbean metaphor for American racial relations, and 20th Century-Fox had purchased it for the same spirit—as much a crusade as a moneymaker."[21] Waugh's book was adapted by Alfred Hayes, and directed by Robert Rossen, who previously made the social issue films *Body and Soul* (1947) and *All the King's Men* (1949). The producer was Darryl F. Zanuck, a decade after he put together *Gentlemen's Agreement* (1947) and *Pinky* (1949). This was Zanuck's first independent production after leaving Fox Studios in 1956, and he had high expectations for the thinly veiled critique of race relations in the American South.[22]

While the filmmakers choose to address social issues, how race and identity was represented was different from earlier films. Geoffrey Shurlock, head of the PCA, worried about "the much more subtle and difficult question of whether or not this story constitutes an unfair portrayal of the Negro race, and whether or not the story is told in such a way that it could reasonably inflame Negro people."[23] The controversial nature of the film ensured heightened communication between the Production Code office, the studio, and concerned interest groups.

Truman K. Gibson, who previously had worked for the Pentagon, worked for the PCA and was consulted to give a "black" perspective. "20th Century-Fox," Gibson believed, "is due tremendous credit for courage in tackling the ticklish issues in the screenplay and for demonstrating an increasingly evident maturity in the selecting and treatment of screen material."[24] When released, critics chided the filmmakers for failing to make a daring film about race relations. They acknowledged the potential "courage" of the film, but dismissed the final product:

> The script by Alfred Hayes is jumbled, the acting leaves a lot to wish for ... Result is a picture that is flat and even tedious, that hints at raw sex but stops short of even a kiss for fear it might offend ... Because it attempts to deal with white-black relations on an island in the West Indies under British rule, and because the race angle has been injected so prominently (to the exclusion of other values in the book), "Island" will be thought of [as] a courageous picture by some. Actually, it barely comes to grips with the problem. It is just candid enough to offend the South and disappoint those in the North who are expecting to see the Alec Waugh novel come to life ... Probably aware that there is a price on "courage," Zanuck has pulled quite a few punches in this one. The picture somehow doesn't hang together, and some of it is so theatrical that the audience—at the opening at least—broke out with guffaws at a dramatically critical moment.[25]

Despite being critically panned, the film did well at the box office.[26] One key reason was that Harry Belafonte received star billing, alongside James Mason, Dorothy Dandridge, and Joan Fontaine.[27] The heavily promoted love affair between Belafonte's character, union leader David Boyeur, and Fontaine's Mavis Norman, added to the controversial nature of the film. Cut from the screenplay was the most politically charged character, the lawyer activist Grainger Morris who had been the man that Mavis had loved and admired in the novel. Truman K. Gibson, wrote: "I did have a feeling of disappointment in the character development of Boyeur. Since the lawyer was omitted from the screenplay, the development of Boyeur as a cynical exploiter of his people diverts attention from some of the basic reasons why people in that area now are actively and rapidly pushing towards dominion status; and also why the Caribbean World has so radically changed in the last few years."[28] This character's voice and love interest was collapsed into the Boyeur character. However, members of the Fleury family remained central to the story.

It is a complicated plot. Mavis is the sister-in-law of Maxwell Fleury (James Mason), a man who is Boyeur's political rival. An impressive supporting cast included newcomer Joan Collins (as Maxwell's much younger sister Jocelyn Fleury), and Stephen Boyd (as the Governor's son Euan Templeton). Dorothy

Dandridge played Margot Seaton, and John Justin played her love interest (the Governor's aide Denis Archer). The film also starred Michael Rennie (as Hilary Carson) and Diana Wynyard (as Mrs. Fleury).

This film weaves together four separate love stories, a high-profile murder, and a political contest, all set on the fictional Caribbean island of Santa Marta during the sunset of British colonial rule. All of the love stories are interracial. *Life* magazine described the film as "a lush Technicolor romance with so many interracial subplots that telling white from black becomes a guessing game."[29] Mavis Norman and David Boyeur form one couple, and Margot Seaton and the Governor's Aide Denis Archer form another, while Jocelyn Fleury and the Governor's son Euan Templeton make up a third relationship. The relationship of Maxwell Fleury and his wife Sylvia, not a traditional love story, merited a lot of screen time. The film's willingness to deal with the issue of miscegenation indicated a change from earlier depictions of passing subjects. In the films of the 1940s and the 1950s, black women were routinely desexualized on the screen to sidestep the problem of on-screen miscegenation. The Production Code specifically prohibited "miscegenation," defined solely in terms of black/white relationships: "Sex relationships between the white and black races are forbidden."[30] In the mid-1950s, the code was altered, leaving the handling of the issue to the "discretion" of filmmakers.[31] This more lax interpretation did not prevent Geoffrey Shurlock from sending a memo stipulating that "the affair between Mavis and Archer will not be portrayed as a sex affair."[32] The filmmakers tried to negotiate between pressures from the PCA, the predicted outrage of Southern censors, and progressive ideals. Ultimately, the "passion" between the interracial leads was minimized but not eliminated in compromises that inevitably pleased no one.[33]

Despite demands for the "sex affair" between Denis Archer and Margot Seaton to be played down, it is implied when Denis marries Margot. While working with him at the Governor's House as a secretary, they secretly become engaged. When the Governor reads the story about the Fleury family, he asks his aide: "What is your opinion, Denis? Having the wrong sort of grandmother?" He replies: "Well, it's difficult to pick one's ancestors, sir." With this statement, Denis sums up a liberal understanding of the social construction of race that would not have been so casually represented on the screen a decade earlier. Not a single kiss is shared between Denis and Margot on the screen, but they fly off to England together at the end, boarding the same plane as the white married couple, Euan and Jocelyn.

Another much-publicized love affair develops between white liberal Mavis Norman and black activist David Boyeur. Mavis has a habit of always falling for the wrong man. Despite promotions highlighting Belafonte and Fontaine together, it is telling that this romance is the most restrained on the screen. The relationship between a black man and a white woman was still the most politically charged and controversial relationship in the film. As Margot leaves with Denis, Boyeur comments, "Maybe the men looking at Margot at some party in Bloomsbury, or some literary tea, well, they'd envy Denis Archer. Their own wives look sort of dull when she walks into a room." Boyeur pointedly explains to Mavis the cultural difference in terms of the acceptability of a white man having a black wife, which was tolerated and envied by others as "exotic," and a black man having a white wife, which was threatening. Boyeur admitted an additional problem for them; if he became publicly involved with Mavis, blacks on the island would see it as a betrayal, and the relationship would thus be detrimental to his political career. In the end, although Mavis was willing to damn social conventions to be with him, he gives her up for his career. While there is sympathy for their predicament, they do not even actually share an embrace on-screen.

A deeper issue was the instability of white identity. In the film, the Fleury family is revealed to have black ancestors. This is especially visible in the evolution of Jocelyn Fleury's love affair with Euan Templeton, the Governor's son and heir. A newspaper article by a reporter named Bradshaw (Hartley Power) exposes the Fleury "family tree," featuring the headline "The Color Problem." Bradshaw's story reveals that Julian Fleury's biological mother was a Jamaican who died in childbirth. Julian had always known, but he kept it a secret from his family. The article begins, "The Fleury family is the perfect example of the problems faced by many of the old families on this island." The scene cuts to the patio at the Fleury's plantation family house as Julian reads the front page story aloud: "For 300 years there has been marriage and intermarriage with nobody sure of their precise ancestry. But a veil of secrecy, whispers, innuendos has been drawn across the problem . . ." This recital is interrupted by Jocelyn, who has been visibly disturbed by the revelation: "To believe that you belong to one kind of world and then suddenly . . . When I asked you if there was any reason why I shouldn't marry Euan, you said no!" Her father replies: "I said there was no GOOD reason." Jocelyn then asks: "How can you say that? Euan's heir to a title! Can you picture a black man sitting in the House of Lords if we had a son?" Her father merely responds, "There is no need to exaggerate. My mother was ¾ white. I've only ¹⁄₁₆ colored blood. The chances are your children will be completely white." This reassurance falls on deaf ears. Jocelyn only hears that she is no longer white. Her racial identity becomes unfixed. Julian dismisses the significance of the revelation advising them to hold their heads high and behave normally after the family secrets are published.

Jocelyn experiences a crisis not only about her racial identity but also her gender and sexual identity. She breaks off her engagement to Euan because she feels she is no longer pure enough to marry a British Peer. The movie suggests a direct connection between her unstable racial identity and the sudden relaxation of her sexual morals. This is confirmed when she reveals she is pregnant. Jocelyn states she became pregnant after deciding she could not marry Euan because of her "ancestry," deciding instead to become his mistress. The PCA's chief Geoffrey Shurlock insisted that "Jocelyn's affair with Euan will be treated with proper compensating moral values. Some reason had to be given for her sin, and the most probable reason was the shock of discovery that she has black blood. In the scene with her mother there needed to be a proper voice for morality."[34] It is interesting that the shock of black ancestry justified bending the Code's rules about sexuality on the screen. Jocelyn's mixed race identity allows her to have sex and love, but not married respectability. However, she still places enough value in family pride to consider running away to Canada to preserve appearances.

Euan still wants to marry Jocelyn, despite knowing about her past. While miscegenation is discussed and Euan accepts that Jocelyn has mixed heritage, there is no discussion of what that means in terms of her racial identity. While Jocelyn believes that Euan does not care about her ancestry, she is unsure about his father's feelings. She tells Euan that his father's agreeing to the engagement does not mean he supports their getting married: "It wouldn't be very diplomatic, would it, for the Governor to offend the whole colored population of Santa Marta? Engaged. And now no one can say that GH draws a color line. Do you think he'd run the risk of having a grandson, an eventual heir, who's part Negro? He'll see to it that you go back to England. It doesn't matter. The marriage is not that important anyways." She understands the unwritten codes of race relations and identity that have dictated her life on the island. This would have resonated with American audiences, as these codes echoed the strictures of race relations and identities in America.

The film then sidesteps the issues of miscegenation and racial ideology by restoring Jocelyn's racial heritage. Jocelyn's mother Sylvia informs her that she had an affair with an indisputably white British Lord, telling her, "You need have no qualms about marrying Euan. There isn't a drop of African blood in your veins. My husband isn't your father." Jocelyn is shocked and relieved: "I never conceived the possibility of you with another man in your life." Sylvia replies: "Children don't. They think mistakes are their privilege." With this secret and the corresponding assurance of her whiteness, Jocelyn decides to marry Euan. Jocelyn's racial identity is disassembled and then restored without ever addressing the contradictions exposed by this plot device.

Such contradictions were highlighted by the casting decisions. In contrast to the fixed racial identities in the film, actress Joan Collins must embody a racial identity that is contrasted both with Dandridge's blackness and Joan Fontaine's whiteness. Collins's black hair and tanned complexion, visibly darker than Fontaine's, signify a position of racial ambiguity that can be read as both black and white. These physical markers of racial instability do not fully lose their meaning even after her character is securely realigned with whiteness. It was strangely plausible that as Jocelyn, Joan could go from white to black and back again, regardless of outward appearances.

Unlike Pinky, Jocelyn never endures the "double-take." Nobody treats her differently. Those around her see her behavior simply as the common mistakes young women make. She struggles with her own prejudice about racial identity, not with the external world around her. She experiences a psychological rather than social dislocation about her racial identity.[35] Jocelyn's racial body is not marked by definite visual signifiers, but is suggestively marked in a gendered and sexualized manner.

Unlike Jocelyn, however, Maxwell is his father's child. The revelation of his ancestry affects more than Maxwell's identity. According to the rules of the island his marriage to Sylvia is also de facto miscegenation, an issue the film sidesteps. Significantly, Maxwell's psychological issues are not as easily resolved as Jocelyn's. Following his father's advice to "behave normally," Maxwell goes to the Club, making a show of thanking the reporter: "You said things that needed saying." Maxwell then explains how the information that has been made public will help in his bid to run for the legislature:

> I've not been trusted. They thought of me as a feudal planter. But now, I combine black and white. The new and the old. I've got a foot in both camps. Your article gave me the courage that I needed. I didn't see this before, but now I can look into those faces and say to them my grandmother was of African ancestry. She came over on the slave-trader just as yours did. I'm one of you now.

Shortly after this speech, Maxwell encounters Hilary Carson, a man he suspected of having an affair with his wife. Carson denies the affair, adding insult to the denial by saying he would never take something from a man "with the tar-brush rubbed across his face!" Maxwell explodes and chokes Hilary to death, all the while repeating "Tar-brush! Tar-brush!" Film critics interpreted Carson's murder as revenge for being the cuckolded husband, but Maxwell's repeated recital of "Tar-brush" suggests his injured pride about racial identity.

The Fleury family tree and the murder of Carson become the talk of the island. The detective assigned knows that Maxwell has killed Carson, but admits he has no proof. The two men meet and the detective gives Maxwell a copy of *Crime and Punishment*, explaining how some men are unable to live with their actions. Maxwell desperately tries to put a positive spin on his family heritage, but falls into a psychological spiral.

Maxwell briefly tries to publicly reconcile his racial and political identity, claiming affiliation with both the black and the white sides of Santa Marta. In their competing bid for the same seat in the legislature, both Maxwell Fleury and David Boyeur give major political speeches to a predominantly black audience assembled on the docks of the island. Maxwell begins:

> I've passed you in the fields or in the cocoa sheds and you've been just a name or a face or a number in a book. And I've lived in a world through which you moved only in shadows to be feared or ignored. I've now lived in the two worlds of Santa Marta. I know how they both think. How they both feel. I also know that they cannot exist if they're cut off from each other by suspicion and fear, each in its loneliness. This bridge I can help you to build. I ask for your faith, your trust.

Maxwell's suggestion that he is "one of them" is ridiculed and denied by Boyeur, who does not accept that Maxwell can ever speak for the "black" world of the island. In effect, Boyeur denies the validity of privileged racial passers to claim blackness. The notion of whiteness may be fragile, destabilized through a simple newspaper article, but black identity is not. Boyeur asks whether Maxwell is saying that "the only issue here is one of color? Is he saying that that is the reason we should vote for him? Is he saying vote for me because I am one of you?" Then Boyeur directly challenges Maxwell: "You said you came here tonight to only speak the truth. Wouldn't it also be true to say that the only reason you seek the election is to revenge yourself upon the whites whom you now think despise you. That the only reason you want to be black is because the white world will not let you be white anymore?" Boyeur frames whiteness as a psychological problem, stating it was not part of the social realities of the island's black world. Beaten, Maxwell admits, "He's right. I don't want to be one of you. I never did." Maxwell's claims to blackness are ludicrous when juxtaposed against Boyeur's blackness.

Maxwell's failed political bid and the recognition that his wife's infidelities were imagined cause him to spiral into depression. He considers suicide, but instead dramatically smashes the mirror (more psychology), telling his wife Sylvia to call the inspector. He confesses to the murder of Carson and is arrested, but the charge is reduced to manslaughter. He is given three years in prison. In the original novel, Maxwell commits suicide, but Geoffrey Shurlock wrote to Harry Cohn, objecting to this ending: "We have read the synopsis of the novel *The Sugar Barons*, and wish to report that, in its present form, it is in violation of that provision of the Production Code which states that 'suicide should never be used to defeat the due processes of the law.'"[36] Whether his story ends in suicide or in jail, Maxwell is the most psychologically damaged character in the film.

In *Island in the Sun*, white masculinity is portrayed as unstable and in decline. James Mason's Maxwell Fleury is portrayed as weak and riddled with doubts about his masculinity and his place on the island. He knows that he does not belong anywhere else and that he exists in limbo. It is clear that Maxwell represents an outdated and repressive past that has become corrupt and useless. He does not represent the future. The future of masculinity belongs to Boyeur, who attains political leadership even though he doesn't end up with the girl.

If masculinity is fractured, race is strangely less so. Although the film toyed with ideas of blood-equals-blackness, the middle ground of the mixed race individual was erased as a viable category. Race is defined as the binary of black and white, the "two worlds" of Santa Marta. At best, the film suggests that Julian passed for most of his life, but this reading is undermined by Julian's complete comfort in his role as the white patriarch of a wealthy plantation family, which to him is not in conflict with the knowledge that his mother was black. It is Maxwell's and Jocelyn's crises about their racial identities that are showcased, not his. The psychological trauma of Maxwell and the sudden sexual immorality of Jocelyn are products of their trauma about racial identity, and yet the people around them are never concerned. Maxwell's problems are framed unsympathetically as his own psychological failure. By the film's end, he fails to become a great and respected man like his father, becoming instead a figure of crippled masculinity.

The complicated ending of *Island in the Sun*, with its mixed messages of race, gender, and politics, reflected the aspirations and ultimately the compromises of those involved in the film. The filmmakers wanted to address the issue of interracial relationships in a controversial and open fashion, but had to hedge their bets cautiously. Geoffrey Shurlock, who demanded that the affairs of Denis and Mavis be kept chaste, made no reference to the delicateness of Jocelyn's affair with Euan. The romance of Joan Collins, the white actress, gets more screen time than the romance of Dandridge, the black actress. However, both women were allowed more romantic screen time than Harry Belafonte and Joan Fontaine. As noted earlier, not even a touch between them made it through the final editing.[37] Moreover, both Jocelyn Fleury and Margot Seaton marry by the film's end, while Mavis and David separate. Despite compromises in the film, it was part of a trend that signaled a shift in how Hollywood addressed issues of civil rights. Just as Boyeur embodies the future of the island politics, it is clear that the future of black images in Hollywood belonged to stars like Harry Belafonte and Dorothy Dandridge, who gave depth to their roles as David Boyeur and Margot Seaton. Black actors were finally allowed to replace white actors playing black.

Ironically, the portrayal of miscegenation in films like this was strikingly old-fashioned compared to the attitudes found off-screen in Hollywood, which was more supportive and accepting of interracial relationships and marriages. The reality of Harry Belafonte's marriage to Julie Robinson at the time of the premiere of *Island in the Sun* was in sharp contrast to the film-maker's cautious refusal to allow him an on-screen relationship with Joan Fontaine, an irony not lost on the movie-going public.[38]

In 1959, two years after the release of *Island in the Sun*, the last important 1950s Hollywood film featuring a passing character was released: Douglas Sirk's remake of *Imitation of Life* (Universal-International), based on a popular novel by Fannie Hurst.[39] It has been described as one of the last true melodramas, and it reflects a sea change in attitudes towards race, gender, and identity. The cast included Lana Turner as Lora Meredith; Sandra Dee as her teenage daughter, Susie (the epitome of a privileged white girl); and Juanita Moore as Lora's longtime companion, Annie Johnson. Annie's passing daughter, Sarah Jane, was played by the Jewish actress Susan Kohner. Like *Island in the Sun*, this film was critically panned but did well at the box office. Critic Bosley Crowther quipped, "Everybody hates it but the public."[40]

Arriving in theatres a decade after *Pinky* and two decades after the original 1934 screen adaptation of Hurst's novel, the film shows how attitudes towards race had changed. Hal Erikson at the *New York Times* stated that "this glamorized remake . . . bears only passing resemblance to its source."[41] Changes were made to the names and occupations of the characters. In the novel, Lora is a "businessman," not an actress. Her business cards read "B. Pullman," allowing people to assume she is a man. Playing with the Aunt Jemima myth,

Lora makes her fortune using Annie's pancake recipes and her image to sell them. The novel also has Sarah Jane marry a white engineer. Together they moved to Bolivia, where she is sterilized to avoid the problematic issue of miscegenation. Thus, passing as a white woman was predicated on giving up motherhood.[42] In both films, the daughter decides to stop passing and returns to her mother, but the films also differ in important ways. The *Hollywood Reporter* argued that the original film's plot "would not have stood up in today's era of integration," so a new rationale had to be provided for the interdependent relationship of the two main characters.[43] When asked about the changes made to the 1934 script, Sirk admitted that the character of Annie was somewhat less empowered than in the original, but he explained:

> In Stahl's treatment of the story the white and the Negro women are co-owners of a thriving pancake business—which took all the social significance out of the Negro mother's situation. Maybe it would have been alright in Stahl's time, but nowadays a Negro woman who got rich could buy a house, and wouldn't be dependent to such a degree on the white woman, a fact which makes the Negro woman's daughter less understandable. So I had to change the axis of the film and make the Negro woman just a typical Negro, a servant, without much she could call her own but the friendship, love, charity of a white mistress. This whole uncertain and kind of oppressive situation accounts much more for the daughter's attitude.[44]

Lana Turner's performance was praised as "outstanding in the pivotal role."[45] At the time of the film, Turner was still coping with the legal drama following the murder of her lover Johnny Stompanato, publicity that did not hurt the movie's box office returns. The "slippage between the character Lora Meredith and the person Lana Turner made this self-reflexive tale about imitation and white motherhood meaningful."[46] The overlap between Turner playing a successful actress who is neglectful of her daughter and her life off-screen was perceived by the studio and the public.[47] The conflation of a theatrical role with life lived off-screen raised questions about the blurred lines between fiction and reality. Lora's change from a businesswoman to a successful and glamorous actress was inescapably linked to Turner's own star image.

While Turner was the star, reviewers also praised Susan Kohner's performance, noting that "Miss Kohner, as the light-skinned daughter who frantically tries to 'pass' for white, gives a fascinating performance."[48] *Variety* went further, asserting that "The secondary plot of a fair-skinned Negress passing as white becomes the film's primary force."[49] Even critics who disliked the film praised Kohner's acting. One reviewer commented that the film was a "tear-jerker, but it didn't jerk my tears. I was too aware of it as manufactured, or remanufactured, melodramatics;" however, the reviewer adds, "Miss Kohner's role proves a showcase for her rather considerable ability as an actress; it is unusual today—and never easy—to attempt to play one of another race."[50] Sarah Jane was a marginal character, yet she was also the heart of the film. Susan Kohner gave a "great performance" playing an unsympathetic character. Despite the praise, some critics suggested that Hollywood had taken a step backwards because the role of the passing daughter in the original 1934 adaptation was played by black actress Fredi Washington.

Casting Susan Kohner in the role of Sarah Jane highlighted Hollywood's continued discomfort with showcasing a black actress who could pass for white and its continued use of white actors to play blacks passing for white. In *Pinky*, the casting of Jeanne Crain was rationalized to sell the message to movie-goers by attaching a "star." In contrast, far from being a box office draw, Kohner was an unknown and was not the star of the film. Her casting was not that controversial because of the supporting nature of her character. Also, by casting a Jewish actress with Latina roots, Hollywood again conflated ethnicity with race.[51] Kohner's mother was famous Mexican-born actress Lupita Tovar (who was Catholic), and her father was Czech-born Hollywood producer and agent Paul Kohner (who was Jewish and who counted Lana Turner among his clients). Somehow her Jewishness and ethnic background gave Kohner access to racial difference and made her performance of blackness more authentic. This contradictory discourse about racial identity and passing informed both the production of the film and its reception by critics and audiences.

By the time *Imitation of Life* was made, the media was more interested in documenting civil rights: the "tragic mulatto" of the past was no longer relevant. Reflecting this, the studio marketed the film as a "women's picture" and not a "race problem" film.[52] In this vein was Bosley Crowther's review: "It is the kind [of film] that used to be called a 'woman's picture' until the feminists let out a howl. It still may be called a 'tearjerker' without pointed offense to any group." The film's publicity emphasized the universal aspects of this melodrama for women and mothers. The filmmakers underscored how they understood the "problems" encountered by the female characters in the synopsis, summed up as follows.[53] Single mothers Lora and Annie meet accidentally at the beach on Coney Island in 1947 and strike up a friendship. Lora is white and Annie is black. However, their daughters, Susie and Sarah Jane, both look white. Annie explains that the girl's father looked "almost white," but he left shortly after she was born. Desperate for work and a home for her and her daughter, Annie asks Lora if they can live with them in exchange for doing the necessary work around the home; "You wouldn't have to pay me no wages, just let me come and do for you." The two single mothers live together and their lives become intertwined as they form a household, with the girls raised as sisters.[54]

In the 1959 film version, Lora desires to be a great actress and Annie becomes her domestic caretaker. Their economic fortunes increase dramatically, but neither mother is very successful with her daughter. Lora succeeds as an actress while her daughter grows to resent her. She also sacrifices love in order to achieve her ambitions. Annie's relationship with Sarah Jane is also strained; "Sarah Jane is resentful of the segregation and restrictions on her future imposed by her race. She even disclaims her mother to camouflage her ancestry and eventually she runs away to become a showgirl. Broken-hearted, Annie grows ill."[55] The movie ends with an elaborate funeral marking Annie's death as Sarah Jane returns, mournful and repentant, begging forgiveness over her mother's coffin. Lora welcomes her back with open arms, and the three remaining women ride off together in a limousine.

In 1971, director Rainer Werner Fassbinder paid homage to Douglas Sirk and *Imitation of Life*, interpreting the film as a representation of contradictions in American culture:

> *Imitation of Life* (1959) is Douglas Sirk's last film. A great, crazy movie about life and about death. And about America. The first great moment: Annie tells Lana Turner that Sarah Jane is her daughter. Annie is black and Sarah Jane is almost white. Lana Turner hesitates, then understands, hesitates again and then quickly pretends that it is the most natural thing in the world that a black woman should have a white daughter. But nothing is natural. Ever. Not in the whole film . . . It's not because white is a prettier colour than black that Sarah Jane wants to pass for white, but because life is better when you're white. Lana Turner doesn't want to be an actress because she enjoys it, but because if you're successful you get a better deal in this world . . .[56]

Fassbinder reflected Sirk's idea that "nothing is natural," and there were only imitations of imitations everywhere. Fassbinder and Sirk were both sympathetic to Sarah Jane's confusion and understood that systemic racism was the underlying cause of her disturbance.[57] Yet the film focuses on Sarah

Jane's psychology rather than sociology. Sarah Jane is disturbed because she passes and is obsessed with white identity. The "tragic mulatto" becomes psychologically unstable.

When Susie first meets Sarah Jane, she offers her a black doll as a present, upsetting Sarah Jane, who wants a white doll instead.[58] Later, the two girls perform a "blood experiment," precipitated by talk at their school: "after class one of the kids said that Negro blood was different, so . . . Sarah Jane wanted to compare her blood with Susie's." Shortly after, Susie asks Annie what color Jesus was, and before she can answer, Sarah Jane states, "He was like me, white."

These early scenes establish Sarah Jane's obsession with whiteness. Later, she is caught passing with devastating consequences. Annie takes some things to Sarah Jane's school, only to be told by the teacher, "I'm afraid you've made a mistake; I don't have any little colored girls in my class." Annie sees Sarah Jane and goes to her, but Sarah Jane runs out of the school. Realizing that her daughter was passing, Annie confronts her, but Sarah Jane responds, "They didn't ask me; why should I tell them?" Annie answers, "Because that's what you are, and it's nothing to be ashamed of." Back at home, both Annie and Sarah Jane are upset, and Annie confesses to Lora, "Sarah Jane's been passing at school, pretending she's white." Hearing this, young Sarah Jane shouts, "But I am white. I'm as white as Susie." Lora dismissed it, telling Annie, "Don't be upset, children are always pretending." But Annie is not convinced: "No, it's a sin to be ashamed of what you are, and it's even worse to pretend, to lie. Sarah Jane has to learn that the Lord must have had his reasons for making some of us white and some of us black." Here it is clear that the burden is on the ambiguously racialized body to commit to the right racial identity, which Sarah Jane refuses to submit to, no matter the punishment.

The most disturbing scene shows Sarah Jane being beaten by her white boyfriend after he discovers the "truth" about her race. He yells at her, "Is your mother a nigger? Are you black?" She tells him, "No, I'm as white as you are!" But in response, he just screams, "You're lying" over and over again as he slaps her face. Sirk explained that he deliberately used clean-cut teen heartthrob Troy Donohue to make the audience uncomfortable, underscoring how the scene could not be "violent enough" because Donohue was "impersonating Whitey."[59] Yet the extreme violence of his reaction makes audience identification difficult. He is framed as a bad romantic choice because he is a delinquent bad boy. Sympathy for Sarah Jane is undermined by her transgressions, the secrecy of their romance, the lies she tells Annie, and the implication that he is a pickup she met at an ice cream shop.

Sarah Jane's determination to pass for white and her gendered transgressions escalate. When she is supposed to be in the city working at a library, Annie discovers a pamphlet for "Harry's Bar" in her daughter's coat. Taking a taxi to confront Sarah Jane, Annie discovers that she is again passing, singing in suggestive skimpy clothing in "a low down dive." Annie is upset by the immorality of the place, and Sarah Jane is fearful of her mother's visit. When the boss finds out that Annie is her mother, Sarah Jane is fired. Because Annie's blackness endangered her masquerades of whiteness, Sarah Jane rejects and denies her mother.[60] Passing is equated with a rejection of motherhood and racial heritage and with the acceptance of a sexualized, degraded lifestyle. Yet Sarah Jane had to pass to get those jobs; even if they were bad, the discrimination was not all in her head.

Nonetheless, Sarah Jane's decision to cut ties with her mother makes her an unsympathetic character, *Ebony* declared:

The present-day version does not shirk from the dramatic implications of a light-skinned daughter of a humble black woman disowning her mother and seeking identity in the white world. While her mother toils faithfully as companion, maid, and confidante to the actress, Sarah Jane Johnson reaches out for the larger world of white people. Annie Johnson's ordeal reaches its climax when her daughter contemptuously denies their relationship.[61]

Sarah Jane's passing is intertwined with sexual immorality and gender transgression. Her desire to pass becomes a symptom of an unstable and confused psychological problem. After leaving home, she works in the chorus of a Hollywood nightclub called "The Moulin Rouge" under the assumed name Linda Carroll. Sarah Jane as Linda is shown performing in suggestive musical sequences, including the "Rockin' Blues Chair" number. The gaudiness and colors of this scene represent urban decay and vice. It is as colorful as it is sinful. The nightclub echoes Howard's visit to Harlem in *Lost Boundaries*, conveying a similar atmosphere of moral outsiders. The scenes further connote an exploitation that Lora manages to avoid in her rise to stardom, yet the lines of racial respectability are not so clear. It is Sarah Jane's racial ambiguity that allows her to perform at segregated nightclubs in the first place; the white showgirl lifestyle would have been forbidden to her as a black woman. To add to the representational fog, the nightclub used for these scenes was an actual Hollywood club of the same name, one of Sirk's deliberate attempts to blur the lines between filmic imitations and the off-screen world.[62]

The message was indicative of both gender and racial transgression. These representations highlighted a cultural shift, as anxiety about passing moved from race to gender. Sarah Jane flees her WASP fantasy world so that she could "pass for white," but the chorus-girl lifestyle that she embraces evoked Hollywood's coded representations of moral otherness and therefore blackness. Thus, in this representation, passing was an externalized threat safely located on the fringes of society, associated with drugs and prostitution. One reviewer noted, "Tragically resentful of her Negro blood and *callously spiteful* in her efforts to abandon her mother, this character . . . evokes both pity and hatred. The heights (or depths) of irony are reached when she blindly prefers the life of a white stripper and call girl to that of Negro respectability."[63] The reviewer does not acknowledge that the choice was less strange, given that the film equates respectability with servitude.

All these issues come to the fore in the final scenes, as Annie tracks Sarah Jane to Los Angeles and flies out to see her. Sarah Jane is cruel, refusing even to let her ailing mother sit down. Recognizing Sarah Jane's need to pass, Annie calls her "Miss Linda" and lets the other showgirls think she was Sarah Jane's "Mammy." Sarah Jane is tearful when Annie departs but she cannot give up her masquerade as a passing white woman. More tragically, Sarah Jane's rejection literally kills Annie as the mother returns home "brokenhearted."

While Sarah Jane's passing is represented as a psychological problem, everyone else in the film passes in one way or another. All the characters perform imitations of real lives. The film reflects cultural discourses about the nature of identity and issues of passing in the 1950s.[64] Douglas Sirk said he would have "made *Imitation of Life*, in any case, just for the title," and went on to explain how the main theme of the movie was simply "you cannot escape what you are."[65] He believed that an "authentic" self existed, and that this self would always assert itself. Throughout the film the use of mirrors illustrated these "reflected existences." Sirk repeatedly uses shots where the reflections of the characters take center stage while the physical character is ignored. All the characters are symbolic reflections of whole people, further made ethereal being reflections on a movie screen, reflections played by actors who were themselves imitating a part.

Sirk argued that the film featured multiple forms of passing, with all the characters except Annie passing in one manner or another, a theme that he felt informed the whole film:

The only interesting thing is the Negro angle: the Negro girl trying to escape her condition, sacrificing to her status in society her bonds

of friendship, family, etc., and rather trying to vanish into the imitation world of vaudeville. The imitation of life is not the real life. Lana
Turner's life is a very cheap imitation. The girl (Susan Kohner) is choos-
ing the imitation of life instead of being a Negro. The picture is a piece
of social criticism—of both white and black. You can't escape what you
are . . . I tried to make it into a picture of social consciousness—not only
of a white social consciousness, but of a Negro one, too. Both white
and black are leading imitated lives . . . There is a wonderful expression: seeing through a glass darkly. Everything, even life, is inevitably
removed from you. You can't reach, or touch, the real. You just see
reflections. If you try to grasp happiness itself your fingers only meet
glass. It's hopeless.[66]

While Sarah Jane is the only character who racially passes, the theme of
reflected, imitative lives is central to the film.

No character raised questions about identity more than Lana Turner's
Lora Meredith. Her character was the center of the film because of Turner's
star status. As an actress, Lora wears masks for a living. She lives her life by
putting on other people's identities the way other people put on clothes. In
the film, Lora only plays with identity. At the beginning of her career she
lies to get into a meeting with an agent, telling the secretary that she is a
Hollywood film star sent by her studio to get some Broadway experience.
When the agent, Mr. Loomis catches on, however, he is not angry: "You lied.
All actresses lie. I know that. But I believed you . . . you took me for all of
twenty seconds, but I don't mind. It was a good acting job." The agent suggests
that to succeed as an actress Lora needs to prostitute herself on the casting
couch. She refuses, but her compromise is ambiguous. In the end Mr. Loomis
becomes her agent, admitting, "I'm a man of few principles and they're all
open to revision." Lora, however, realizes her goal and becomes a celebrated
theater actress. After establishing her career, Lora reveals that she only feels
complete onstage. Other characters repeatedly tell her to "stop acting." She
does not know where her stage identity ends and where her offstage life
begins.

Lora is not the only character unsure about her identity. The film's other
main characters also were represented as passing in different ways. Susie,
the most self-absorbed and least developed character, chats to Annie about
her love life as Annie is dying in her bed. She is a pale imitation of her
mother Lora, even having a crush on her mother's boyfriend: "Sirk reinforces
the screen persona of Sandra Dee . . . and makes of the character a vacant

personification of the dominant culture's bankruptcy. In perfectly coiffed hair and costumes that seem to echo her mother's, Susie appears rather like a Lora Meredith Doll."[67]

Even token male roles in the film were not represented as leading genuine lives. The romantic lead Steve Archer (John Gavin) cannot make a living as an artist-photographer and compromises himself by working in advertising to make money. Likewise, the agent Allen Loomis (Robert Alda) and the playwright David Edwards (Dan O'Herlihy) perform their identities more than they live their lives. The common theme was lies. Actors were professional liars. Advertisers were liars. The film suggested that all the characters were liars who performed identity, just like Sarah Jane.

The only stable character not represented as inauthentic and false is Annie, Sarah Jane's black mother. Annie is idealized as the good mother to both girls and as Lora's solid friend. Against this image of maternal compassion, Sarah Jane is represented as a disturbed and ungrateful daughter and Lora as a bad mother. If viewers were encouraged to reject the value of Sarah Jane's passing and rejoice when she symbolically reclaimed her blackness at her mother's funeral, they were also encouraged to view Lora's acting ambitions as fraught with problems. Ironically, Sarah Jane and Lora are represented as true soul mates because they both want what they are not supposed to desire. They both cross racial and gender boundaries by refusing to accept the roles of black daughter and good mother, preferring instead the "imitative" lives of passing showgirl and working actress.[68] Both Sarah Jane and Lora claim they will reform themselves and live more authentic lives, but the film's ambiguous ending leaves open the question of whether Sarah Jane has accepted her blackness and given up passing and whether Lora has likewise given up the false identity of nonstop performance as an actress.

Imitation of Life featured two sets of mothers and daughters that paralleled and contrasted each other in interesting ways. A promotional poster for the film captured the female world and dramatic maternal issues at the heart of this film with three overlapping images.[69] Dominating the poster is a large picture of Lana Turner and Juanita Moore as the mothers Lora and Annie, featuring the caption, "As women there was no barrier between them! ... As MOTHERS they must face two different worlds!" Another image of Annie and Sarah Jane suggests a mother's worry and a daughter's anguish: "The color line won't stop me, Ma! I look, feel, think white! And I'm going to marry white!" The third image of Lora and Susie suggests maternal failure and a daughter's unhappiness: "You've given me everything a mother could, but the thing I wanted most ... your love!" The poster and the film reflected broader cultural anxieties about the precarious boundaries between authentic and imitative identities and the psychological traps that framed racial and gender identity in this era. The film itself represented authentic racial and gender ideals only to dismantle them and raise the specter of passing. Is Lora a bad mother or an admirably ambitious woman? Is Annie a maternal ideal or a racial stereotype? Is everyone really passing for something else?

By the film's ending, even Annie's projection of an authentic identity can be questioned. The dramatic funeral that accompanies her death subverts the humble and submissive figure of maternal ideals that she epitomizes throughout the film. Lora's love interest, Steve, aptly notes that until her death, Annie is "everybody's Rock of Gibraltar." The Mammylike, sacrificing stereotype needed to be acknowledged in death with a dramatic scene. Referring to the funeral scene, Sirk felt that "the only escape for the blacks then was death" and that Annie's saving for her big funeral was a kind of "victory over the white race, equality at last."

Whatever Sirk's intent, the scene upends Annie's representation until that point. This was one of the most elaborate funeral sequences ever filmed. Annie's character is finally and publicly honored as an important leader in the black community, complete with four white horses pulling the coffin and a black marching band leading the way. To top it off, Mahalia Jackson sings "Trouble of the World," further emphasizing Annie's "after-death achievement." Sirk noted that "there is an outburst of Black Power, which is unprecedented. First of all, this is a terrifically gifted singer, and to have [her] singing down over the mute crowd below her is a triumph."[70] The result was moving enough to cause Jack Moffitt to note that the scene provides "the comforting thought that this great and good woman had the sympathy and admiration of members of her own race. Furthermore, they say to us that in accepting the Negro as an equal, we accept him as a Negro and not as an imitation white person."[71]

Ironically, the Annie who suffers as a mother and friend has carefully planned a funeral that was far from humble. The funeral finally acknowledges Annie's status outside of the orbit of Lora's circle, subverting earlier representations that defined Annie solely in terms of her relation to Lora, Susie, and Sarah Jane. It also suggests that Annie's submissive performance as a black woman is just as much a passing performance as Lora's acting or Sarah Jane's desire to pass. Moreover, the disjuncture between Annie's submissive life and her "after-death achievement" also complicates negative readings of Sarah Jane's passing to get jobs—like being a showgirl—that otherwise would be denied to her when the "respectable" alternative open to her is the equally dishonest life of servitude and passing pretenses performed by her mother.

Annie passed too. And despite Sirk's politicized good intentions and the significance of her "after-death achievement," the role of Annie was fraught with problems, leaving critics unsure how to evaluate the character and the performance by Juanita Moore. One article gave a glowing review of Moore's performance as a positive representation of a black mother, but disingenuously denied this related to a Mammy stereotype, stating that while Moore was "Mature, beautiful, and intelligent, she is not the 'mammy' type that in the past has been associated with the role ... she is a figure not of the Negro as a figure in political controversy but as a Woman, the homemaker and guardian of the young—the universal mother." The biases become transparent as the reviewer concludes: "It is my belief that she will be especially appreciated in the South where so many whites have known and loved and felt friendship for colored people such as she is in their households."[72] In contrast, other articles focused on the controversy such stereotypical representations stirred up: "Since its press-preview of its remake of 'Imitation of Life' last week, U-I has been caught in the middle of a battle over merits of the film."[73] Battle lines were drawn between those who protested the stereotypes of the black roles, especially the character of Annie Johnson, and those who celebrated Moore's performance in the role. Almena Lomac, an editor of the *Los Angeles Tribune*, publicly condemned the film as "a libel on the Negro race. It libels our children and the Negro mother and should be banned in the interest of national unity, harmony, peace, decency, and interracial respect."

However, the article went on to argue that the film as a whole dealt with racial passing in a realistic way: "it is a fact as everyone knows that 'passing' exists in this country. A reliable source estimates that as many as 10,000,000 Americans 'pass.' 'Imitation of Life' then relates to a factual situation."[74] This estimate doubled *Ebony's* 1948 number of five million Americans who were passing, but greater numbers did not correlate to greater fears.[75] The specter of racial passing in America was metaphorically contained in films that pathologized racial passers.

When Annie tells her daughter, "It's a sin to be ashamed of what you are, and it's even worse to pretend, to lie," she echoes the admonitions of Miss Em telling Pinky that "pretending you is what you ain't" was wrong. Original sin equals racial shame. Both films expressed disapproval for racial passing, but between the making of *Pinky* and *Imitation of Life*, the rationale for disapproval changed. In both *Pinky* and *Lost Boundaries*, characters pass to achieve respectable middle-class employment and stop passing when they are able to work in their chosen fields. Passing in these films is understandable, although dishonest. In contrast to these sympathetic representations, racial passing in *Imitation of Life* is portrayed as a sign of a psychological problem.

By the late 1950s, passing was no longer simply dishonest; it was a sign of a deeper internal psychological disability. Passing became marginalized and relegated to unsympathetic and/or supporting characters. Anxiety about racial ambiguity became framed as a crisis about sexual deviance and mas- culinity. Sarah Jane in *Imitation of Life* was a counterpart to Maxwell's tragic character in *Island in the Sun*; both characters existed in psychological traps made by their own aberrant internal psychologies. They represented a racial- ized and gendered crisis of identity. Their irrational behavior was contrasted with the rationality of the film's stable black characters. The trope of the "tragic mulatto" resurfaced, but the central motif was an internal crisis of identity.

As racial passing disappeared from the screen, unstable identity moved to the forefront. Films like *Island in the Sun* (1957) and *Imitation of Life* (1959) illustrate how discourses about race, passing, and identity changed. The specter of passing shifted from a fear that others might not be who they seemed to be to a fear that one's own identity might be inauthentic. Passing was no longer a black/white issue; it became a metaphor to explain a crisis about identity.

CHAPTER FOUR

"HIDING IN PLAIN SIGHT"

Political Passing, Communist Fears, and Hollywood

Higgledy-Piggledy, my Red Biddy.
She lays eggs for the Un-American Committee.[1]
—Gracie Allen, "Hollywood Nursery Rhymes" (1949)

In the late 1940s and early 1950s, all of the major studios produced anti-Communist films. These films were made to show Hollywood was not subversive to avoid political regulation and control of Hollywood by Washington. Anti-Communist films normalized representations about hidden identities and passing Communists. Postwar discourse about Communist fronts, fellow travelers, and infiltration fostered a political climate defined by fear, suspicion, paranoia, and hysteria. Hollywood reflected this. Films about political passing called into question not only who was who, but also the nature of identity. The idea that people could pass politically mirrored fears about racial passing, complicated by postwar obsessions with Communism. Americans saw Communists everywhere. Communists could be passing as regular Americans, hiding their true nature and the dangerous threat they posed. The implication was that Communists owed their allegiance to the Soviet Union and were a threat to a vaguely defined "all-American" way of life. What was less clear was what "all-American" meant. The unofficial slogan of the politicized 1950s was "trust no one!"

In anti-Communist films, Communists became the villains. Characterizations of Communists were always overblown and negative. They were deceitful, subversive, traitorous, treasonous, and perhaps even evil incarnate. Unlike earlier representations where passing was represented as a sympathetic social strategy, political passing was always represented as having a sinister agenda. Anti-Communist crusaders believed Communists who passed were intent on destroying democracy itself. No one was safe. Families could be deceived, the FBI could be infiltrated, and the military could be breached. Film representations of Communism were complicated by HUAC investigations, the blacklist (and graylist), and the desire of studio heads to make propaganda pictures showing the evils of Communism and defending a vaguely defined "all-American" way of life.

From 1947 to 1960, linkages between the politics of Washington and Hollywood were created by the HUAC hearings and the resulting Hollywood blacklist. Senator Joseph McCarthy's hearings about Communism made political identities a volatile issue both on and off the screen. As a result, the treatment of Communists in film shifted dramatically after the war. Before 1947, Communists were represented as visibly foreign-born, while Communism itself was represented as a minimal external threat. Communists and Communism could even be treated lightly in comedies like *Ninotchka* (MGM, 1939) and *He Stayed for Breakfast* (Columbia, 1940), where love triumphed over opposing political beliefs. When WWII ended, so too did this playful openness about Communism. In postwar films Communists became sinister, lurking anywhere undetected. In 1950, columnist Penelope Houston noted: "Since the war, Communism has become an enemy within the state, and no subject for humour; the propaganda of *The Iron Curtain* (dealing with Canadian spy trials) was solemn portentous, unrelieved; the Russians were brutal and ruthless."[2]

After the war, Communism became an internal rather than an external threat. Ironically, after WWII, "the Communist Party itself had fallen on hard times," but numbers did not matter to anxieties based on fear.[3] Nor did it matter that strident anti-Communists like Senator Joseph McCarthy never gave consistent numbers in the search for "Communist spies."[4] At best, they gave vague lists of subversives that they claimed were hidden in powerful places throughout American society. Communists were no longer a comic threat to the American "way of life," but became J. Edgar Hoover's "enemy within." In 1947 Hoover called members of the American Communist party "masters of deceit." The specter of passing was invoked for political ends.

The "enemy within" loomed large in the administrations of both Truman and Eisenhower. Anti-Communist crusaders fueled fears that Communists could be hiding anywhere, but were especially dangerous in places of power like the military and the government. Truman's Attorney General J. Howard McGrath added to fears by declaring that Communists "are everywhere—in factories, offices, butcher stores, on street corners, and private business. And each carries in himself the death of our society."[5] In 1952, Billy Graham opened a session of the Senate with a prayer alluding to "barbarians beating at our gates from without and moral termites from within."[6] Vague fears about passing Communists as a domestic threat gained such a strong hold in American culture precisely because Communism was imagined to be an invisible menace, a germ that could infect the whole country.

The language of contagion and of the "enemy within" shaped Cold War investigations and legal decisions of the courts. A culture of fear took hold. Justice William O. Douglas, dissenting in *Eugene Dennis v. United States* (1951), suggested that the court's decision amounted to a "twisted interpretation" of the "clear and present danger" test established in *Schenck v. United States* (1919).[7] The court denied the right of Communist Party members to protection under the Fifth Amendment, and argued that subversion was determined by an individual's *intent* rather than *words or actions*. Moreover, *Dennis* argued that courts could interpret the hidden meaning of any language used by subversives to spell anti-government intent.[8] Thus, if an alleged Communist argued in writing for nonviolent advocacy of their goals, courts could interpret their hidden message as the violent overthrow of the government and prosecute accordingly. The person was judged, rather than the ideas.

In practice, this meant that even teaching Marxist theory implicated those teaching it as subversive. If one was accused of subversion, *Dennis v. United States* allowed the accused only to challenge their membership in organizations, not the overzealous ideology of crusading anti-Communists. Accused subversives could not question the validity of investigations or the politics behind them. They could not even challenge whether the organization was itself subversive, just whether or not they belonged. The use of this ruling by the courts and by the government meant that some beliefs were inherently subversive, which made defense against them impossible and suspect. The Subversives Activities Control Act enacted in 1950, over a veto by President Truman, strengthened the principles of this ideology.

Hoover and anti-Communist zealots were aided in the prosecution of suspected Communists by the Smith Act and the McCarran Act. Passed in 1940, the Smith Act stated that Communism advocated the overthrow of the American government. In 1950, the Internal Security Act, also known as the McCarran Act, required Communists to "register" with the federal government.[10] It also stated that individuals who belonged to the Communist party automatically "repudiated" their American allegiance in favor of a foreign government. Together, these acts created a catch-22; if Communists complied and registered under the McCarran Act, they could then be convicted under the Smith Act.[11]

Public trials of suspected Communists put faces to the "enemy within" in ways that challenged old stereotypes, fueled partisan politics, and created new stereotypes about American Communists. The primary targets of the FBI's sweeping anti-Communist investigations were government employees. These investigations polarized the nation, especially the charges brought against Alger Hiss and Julius and Ethel Rosenberg, who were unmasked as spies in high-profile political trials.[12] Of these two cases, the Hiss case is the more important here because of its passing implications.

Alger Hiss was convicted in January 1950 on charges of perjury; "its importance derived not from the weightiness of the indictment or the length of the sentence but from the stature of the defendant."[13] As a Roosevelt New Deal official, Hiss's conviction gave the Republicans the chance to paint the federal government of the Democratic Party in the 1930s as sympathetic to Russia and infiltrated by Communists. Whitaker Chambers was a key witness for the government, and his testimony used phrases like "close friendship," "deep friendship," and "very intimate" to describe his association with Hiss. Chambers admitted that until 1938 he was a Communist and a homosexual, at which point he found "God and the FBI," in that order, but this information was kept secret.[14] Jurors admitted in interviews after the trial that they could not understand the association between Hiss and Chambers without some sort of "Communist conspiracy."[15] During the trial the FBI refused to release information about the possible sexual relationship between Hiss and Chambers. Either way, the trial forced Americans to rethink what Communists "looked" like: "Hiss wore no beard, spoke with no accent, moved casually in the best circles ... The stereotype of the Communist agent was irremediably shattered. Hiss looked like the man down the block in Scarsdale or Evanston, the man in the office across the hall on Wall Street or State Street. If this man could be a spy, anybody could."[16]

In this climate of fear, the only option was self-censorship: to pass and avoid being investigated.[17] In practice, this meant monitoring one's behavior. Fandom became evidence of ideology. Anything peculiar, like admiring jazz or being a fan of accused Communists like Paul Robeson, was grounds for investigation.[18] In the wake of the emergence of the national security state, Americans scrutinized themselves "for any indications of sexual and/or political deviance that might call into question their loyalty to the nation."[19] Self-censorship and passing as a good American was better than the alternative. To be called a Communist meant losing all one's civil rights, one's job, and often one's family and friends.

Once a person had been investigated, his or her options were limited. The political and legal atmosphere allowed little room for self-defense. Many HUAC witnesses took the Fifth Amendment, which the committee cited as proof of something to hide and which proved equally inadequate as a defense. Fighting charges of subversion was difficult under legal rulings that allowed courts and government committees to use Constitutional defenses as proof of guilt because innocent people would not resort to those tactics. For unfriendly witnesses, there was no safe defense.

In 1954, journalist James Wechsler admitted to the House Committee on Un-American Activities that he had been a member of the Communist party while an adolescent in the 1930s, adding that he had become an ardent anti-Communist and that this shift earned him abuse from former comrades.[20] This narrative of youthful folly did not satisfy McCarthy. "How do we know," the Senator asked, "that you didn't quit them on Moscow's order?"[21] Those suspected of Communist ties were damned: if they stayed within the party, they were Communist; if they left the party they could still be viewed as dangerous subversives, who were only passing as loyal Americans. There was simply no way for Wechsler to prove to McCarthy he was a patriotic citizen.

The attitude of anti-Communist crusaders was summed up by Lela Rogers, mother of dancer Ginger Rogers. She wanted legislation to "preserve the Bill of Rights to the people for whom it was designed—that precious Bill was never intended to protect enemy agents, saboteurs, and spies whether they're American or alien born."[22] Following a similar logic, in the pro-HUAC film *Big Jim McClain* (1952), the hero explains how "only subversives hostile to legitimate authority would hide behind Constitutional niceties," adding that "a democratic society should not misinterpret the Bill of Rights as a suicide pact."[23]

While anti-Communists fought against liberty in the name of national security, important figures like Albert Einstein attacked the right of HUAC to conduct their investigations. In 1953 he released a statement, entreating: "every intellectual who is called before one of the committees ought to refuse to testify . . . [because] it is shameful for a blameless citizen to submit to such an inquisition and that this kind of inquisition violates the spirit of the Constitution."[24] But arguments challenging the committee's right to prosecute proved inadequate in stopping the investigations.

In this climate, anti-Communist books written by "informers" and "professional ex-Communists" became best-sellers. Focused on the domestic Communist threat, they capitalized on passing fears, including Matthew Cvetic's

I Was a Communist for the FBI, Herbert Philbrick's *I Led Three Lives*, Angela Calomaris's *Red Masquerade*, and Hede Massing's *This Deception*.[25] These "professional anti-Communists" became major sources for television and movies. Herbert Philbrick's book became a top-rated television show which ran from 1953 to 1956,[26] and Matt Cvetic's book was turned into a film with the tag line: "I had to sell out my own girl—so would you! I was under the toughest orders a guy could get! I stood by and watched my brother slugged … I started a riot that ran red with terror … I learned every dirty rule in their book—and had to use them—because I was a Communist—but I was a Communist for the FBI!"[27] These books suggested that Communists were a grave threat because they could not be spotted by the average American. These themes even popped up in a series of comic books about ex-Communists and undercover agents published between 1951 and 1955, with titles like "I Was a Spy!" and "Communist Kisses!"[28]

Undercover agents and informers who worked for the American government confused the boundaries between Communists and those pretending to be Communists. Calomaris saw passing agents and passing subversives as the same: "The blunt facts are that there will be undercover agents as long as there are conspirators who can be detected in no other way."[29] Undercover agents obscured the lines between agents pretending to be subversives and Communists pretending to be Americans. Nobody was what they seemed.

Herbert Philbrick's memoir articulated the paranoia brought about by the specter of passing Communists: "Where Communism is concerned, there is no one who can be trusted. Anyone can be a Communist. Anyone can suddenly appear in a meeting as a Communist party member—close friend, brother, employee or even employer, leading citizen, trusted public servant."[30] But Philbrick was more nuanced than many, making distinctions between Communists and liberals, even including an appendix in his memoir on how to distinguish the two: "If the inexperienced Red hunter cannot distinguish between a Communist and an innocent liberal, then he is also unable to distinguish a bona-fide Communist from a government counterspy."[31] More worrisome for Philbrick was the fear that if he played a Communist long enough he would actually become one. Sounding more like a Method Actor than a professional anti-Communist, Philbrick explained:

> I was sinking so deep that it was no longer possible for me to "play" the role of a spy. I could no longer simply make believe that I was a Marxist. Like an experienced actor, who must sublimate himself to his part and immerse himself in the playwright's creation, whenever I walked into

the stage setting of a cell meeting, I had to be a young Communist. The costume was not enough. No disguise would have been adequate.[32]

The "psychic compartmentalization" used by political agents was vividly described by one of their own, atomic spy Klaus Fuchs, as "controlled schizophrenia."[33]

These political narratives in print and film were informed by the psycho-analytic turn of postwar culture. In *The Enemy Within* (Republic Pictures, 1949), also released under the title of *The Red Menace*, a disillusioned ex-Communist agent named Henry Solomon moans: "I thought I could be an American liberal and a Communist," but he found out the Communist committee was "composed of psychopathic misfits, seeking an outlet for their frustrations."[34] Shortly after this scene, the young agent gets expelled from the Communist Party and is persecuted until he is finally murdered and his death is portrayed as a suicide. Solomon is described as an "intense young Jewish communist poet." *The Enemy Within* ends as another Communist character is taken into an Immigration Office and loses control, screaming, "The revolution has come! They'll be here!" The officer in charge diagnoses her as "psychopathic."

Although these kinds of psychologically damaged characters were a postwar specialty, they were anything but invisible. Psychopathic agents of Communism might be dangerous, but not hidden. This was a representational problem. Hollywood seemed confused as to how to represent the threat of Communism on the domestic front. Publicity for a variety of anti-Communist films tried to play upon cultural fears that devious Communist agents could pass for Americans and maybe even be the boy or girl next door. Worse yet, they suggested that passing political deviants might be hiding within American families undetected. Daughters, sons, husbands, or wives could be dangerous subversives. People were unsure about who was who and about the motives of everyone around them. The fear that nobody was whoever they seemed to be fed fears that passing was endemic. That was the hype.

Yet anxieties about hidden subversives did not always fit their filmic representations. Framing Communists as visible psychopaths was just one common contradiction in these narratives. Formulaic movies that caricatured Communists made them hard to tell apart from any other B-movie bad guys, adding to the confusion. Moreover, while filmic Communists would stand out in most American towns, ironically they could often pass as their film counterparts in the FBI. It did not help that both FBI agent "good guys" and Communist subversive "bad guys" were played by the same roster of B-movie actors who typically "lack distinguishing features: they simply look alike."[35]

Despite the contradictions of the film genre, the culture of Cold War politics gave the premise of anti-Communist films their edge, especially when they conflated fact and fiction to exploit the fears heightened by the "based on a true story" subgenre of anti-Communist films. How the films were shot and cast further blurred the line between what was perceived as real and what was not. For instance, while *I Was a Communist for the FBI* (1951) was dramatic fiction, it was shot as a political documentary. It so successfully mirrored this style that it was nominated for "Best Documentary" at the 1951 Academy Awards. This deliberate blurring of fact and fiction by mimicking documentary was a broad practice in the 1940s, referred to by the industry as "newsdrama cinematography." Other "confessional" exposés of Communism, like the popular TV series *I Led Three Lives: Citizen, "Communist," and Counterspy*, used the same techniques. Whether Americans looked to films and books or to the news of the day as their guide, it was hard to differentiate between real and imagined subversives and between undercover agents and Communist spies.

One thing was crystal clear, however; the climate of political paranoia and blacklists meant that participating in anti-Communist films became a litmus test in Hollywood: "Willingness to make these lurid and simplistic movies was not only a loyalty test for Hollywood, participation in these projects also became such a test *in* Hollywood."[36] A surprising number of stars found themselves in these essentially B-productions. For instance, Elizabeth Taylor and Robert Taylor starred in *Conspirator* (1949), a forgettable political propaganda picture made in Britain, which, as *Variety* noted, was not in tune with the British political situation, but the review predicted that the film "will probably have a better success in the U.S. than in Britain."[37] Whether motivated by fear or ideology, Hollywood produced many anti-Communist films. Ironically, the prerequisite for playing a Communist in Hollywood was not being one.

Hollywood's overtly political films reflected the external fears of the Soviet Union and the internal anxieties about passing American spies. Films like *The Iron Curtain* (20th Century-Fox, 1948) framed Communism as an external threat, representing Russians as Communists. Foreigners were easy to spot. *Red Danube* (1949) starred Janet Leigh as a deported ballerina, and was directed by George Sidney. *Invasion U.S.A.* (Columbia, 1952) was a low-budget, predictable take on Soviet Communists as the ultimate enemy (with the title giving away the plot), but it had enough conservative cachet to get a tag line quote by Hedda Hopper: "It will scare the pants off you!" Other anti-Communist films that received a lot of press coverage and hype because of their overt politics included Samuel Fuller's *Pickup on South Street* (20th Century-Fox, 1953), and John Wayne's *Big Jim McClain* (Warner Bros., 1952). Set in Hawaii, *Big Jim McClain* starred Wayne as a heroic HUAC investigator who called into question the patriotism of those who used the Fifth Amendment or "hid under" the Constitution. The unusual cross-genre film *The 27th Day* (Columbia, 1957) featured a science fiction twist that saw Communists across the planet wiped out by a suicide pill provided by aliens.

What is surprising is that while anti-Communist books and exposés were voraciously consumed, the American public did not flock to theatres to see overtly political films, even when they were packaged with spaceships. Anti-Communist themes were popular with Hollywood studios, but not with audiences. *Variety* declared that the "anti-Commie cycle" of films was a "lightweight b.o. contender," especially when compared to the extreme popularity of socially significant "message pics," possibly because of "the public's alleged distaste for political polemics on celluloid."[38] Almost all of Hollywood's anti-Communist films had "disappointing" box office returns, including RKO's *I Married a Communist* (1949, then in the process of being renamed), 20th Century-Fox's *The Iron Curtain* (1948), and Metro's *Red Danube* (1949), Republic's *The Red Menace* (1949), which was distributed abroad with the ironic title *The Enemy Within*. Even in the United States, such poorly executed political propaganda films did not bring in the audiences in any great numbers.

However, like other B movies, some anti-Communist films gained wider appeal by being billed with more bankable features. And what they lacked in audiences, some of them made up for in critical acclaim and cultural influence.[39] Importantly, the most prestigious, *My Son John* (1952) and *I Was a Communist for the FBI* (1951), showed Communism as an internal domestic threat, tapping into wider cultural anxieties about passing. Of the fifty or so anti-Communist films Hollywood made in this period, *My Son John* (1952) and *The Woman on Pier 13* (originally titled *I Married a Communist*, 1949), best illustrate both the potential message and the failure of its execution. In these films the threat of subversion is located within the family unit, a framework that personalized ideological fears about Communism and heightened the dramatic stakes about political passing. The iconic image of the postwar nuclear family, previously imagined to be a safe place, is shown to be untrustworthy.

My Son John (Paramount, 1952), directed, produced and co-authored by Leo McCarey, was not a B-grade film. McCarey had previously helmed the Marx Brothers classic *Duck Soup* (1933), Mae West's *Belle of the Nineties* (1934), and Cary Grant and Irene Dunne in *The Awful Truth* (1937), for which he won his first Best Director Oscar, and the comedies *Going My Way* (1944), for which he won his second Best Director Oscar, and *The Bells of St. Mary's* (1945). He is also remembered as the man that created the comedy duo of Stan Laurel and Oliver Hardy. In addition, McCarey later directed such acclaimed films as *An Affair to Remember* (1957).

My Son John was a departure from McCarey's comedies, but it reflected his staunch anti-Communist views and active membership in the "Motion Picture Alliance for the Preservation of American Ideals" at the time the film was made in the early 1950s. McCarey's casting, however, was typically impressive. Broadway actress Helen Hayes played the mother, Lucille Jefferson; Van Heflin played the FBI agent, Stedman; Dean Jagger played the father, Dan Jefferson; and Robert Walker played the titular son, John Jefferson. One review noted that the film was "a staggering piece of propaganda, emotional in its treatment and irrational in its approach."[40]

My Son John focuses on "all-American" parents who discover that their grown son is a Communist and a traitorous spy. Even though the only two books she reads are the Bible and her cookbook, Lucille proudly describes her son as "having more degrees than a thermometer." Gradually the mother grows suspicious of her son, seeing danger in his intellect. Secretive phone calls and odd behavior make it clear that John is involved with something bad. He avoids the family farewell dinner for his brothers who have enlisted to go fight in Korea, and when he does visit home, he immediately goes to see an old professor, who is framed as a suspicious person, probably the one who led John into political subversion. Making things worse, an agent of the FBI named Stedman creates a pretext to get closer to the family, eventually admitting to Lucille that John is under suspicion. Lucille follows John back to Washington, where she comes to believe that her son is a spy and tries to convince him to give himself up.

John's exact profession in Washington, as well as any specific crimes he may have committed, are absent from the narrative. The closest the film comes to invoking a real-world threat is a shot of a newspaper with a headline about the arrest of a female spy, but the charges are vague. The film implies a connection between the female spy and John in the form of a key to her apartment hidden in clothes John left at home, which is framed as hard evidence of nefarious activity. It is literally the key on which John's guilt or innocence rests. When Lucille finds the key she takes it to Washington, goes to the woman's apartment, and tests the lock. It opens the door. This is what finally convinces her that John is a traitor. The whole scene is shot through the watchful eyes of the FBI; Lucille is under continual surveillance. She confronts her son, and John unconvincingly explains he had the key because they were having an affair; it is personal, not political. In the end, what exactly John did for Communism is not represented or even relevant. John is guilty of Communist thoughts, and in keeping with other anti-Communist films, he pays for his association with Communist ideology with his life.

The film is an extreme expression of postwar hysteria and an attack on liberal intellectualism. John is typed as an intellectual government worker in Washington, a reference to Hoover's attacks on the State Department as a breeding ground for the "enemy within." The Communist protagonist in this film is "an intellectual, seduced into the CP by 'superior minds' and 'daring thoughts.' These characterizations, like Joe McCarthy's attack on 'twisted thinking intellectuals,' introduced an element of anti-intellectualism into the stew, as if intelligence were somehow subversive in itself."[41] Robert Warshow described the bad son in 1952:

[John's] a brilliant and rising young government official (already one's suspicions are aroused) . . . he is a figure to fill any ordinary human being, let alone any red-blooded American, with loathing: pompous, supercilious, as sleek and unfeeling as a cat, coldly contemptuous of his father, patronizing to his mother; also, though nothing is said of this, one feels that he might be a homosexual. In fact, as will eventually be revealed, he is a Communist and a traitor . . . Robert Walker's characterization is essentially the same as in *Strangers on a Train*, where he played the role of a pathological murderer.[42]

For Warshow, the anti-intellectualism was the most dangerous aspect of the film, as it implied that anyone who read or had any intellectual curiosity was somehow un-American. For this, Warshow condemned the director's lack of vision: "The fact is that Leo McCarey is not enough of an artist to imagine why anyone might become a Communist . . . The hidden logic seems to be: since we cannot understand Communism, it is likely that anything we cannot understand is Communism . . . For in the end we are left in no doubt: what is being upheld is, precisely, stupidity."[43] This theme was shared by many anti-Communist films, as Karel Reisz noted: "There is in these films a general distrust of people who read books, know anything about wicked science, people, in other words, who think and argue."[44]

The film attacks more than intellectualism. In the psychoanalytic atmosphere of the 1950s, it also attacks mothers. Lucille is presented as potentially unstable. Shortly after her younger sons, Ben and Chuck leave home to go serve in the military, the family doctor makes an uninvited house call to Lucille because a woman "her age" needs help to stop her from "busting a bustle" and going crazy. The concerned doctor hands her a bottle of pills and tells her to take three a day to calm her nerves. He explains it is normal for women like her to use medication to the handle stress of advancing years and an empty nest. At first she jokes about this and hides the pills, but she becomes increasingly hysterical as she begins to suspect John might be a traitor. Lucille is framed as responsible for failing to recognize her son's betrayal. John and his mother are portrayed as too close for a mother and son. There is an Oedipal undertone in John's antagonism to his father and his closeness with his mother. John tells his mom: "We talk the same language, we think the same way . . . But I warn you, this is liberal thinking. To Dad, we're leftists, Communists, subversives!" Lucille is reluctant to accept John's political beliefs and tries to reconcile father and son. Out of the dozen or more films in this political genre, this movie "comes closest to blaming mom for Communism."[45] Lucille is guilty of fostering liberalism, but in the end she is credited for convincing her son to repent and to double-cross his co-conspirators.

While Lucille is most to blame for John's attraction to Communism, her husband Dan is faulted for failing to exert his patriarchal authority. Dan's masculinity is contrasted with John's. Dan likes sports, is unquestioning in his patriotism, and is hostile to intellectuals. The father talks a lot about the "red, white, and blue" and is a proud member of the American Legion. John is openly disrespectful and ridicules his father, saying no one can say they were not brought up on "jingoistic bromides." To drive the point home about how far apart they are, Dan hits his son over the head with the family Bible. Only at the end is Dan redeemed, when Lucille says he has more wisdom than all of them, because he trusted his "gut" over heart and mind and recognized John as traitor. The family's "good" sons Chuck and Ben (Richard Jaeckel and James Young) mirror Dan's masculine patriotism. The two boys are athletic football heroes with no interests in intellectual pursuits, who dutifully go to church on Sundays and patriotically sign up to serve in the military together. Ben, Chuck, and their father are represented as less intellectually engaged than Lucille and John, safely insulating them from dangerous ideologies. Yet, in the end, these bulwarks of American masculinity are unable to counteract John's interest in Communist ideology. To do this, the family calls in the FBI.

It is FBI agent Stedman, not her husband, who convinces Lucille that John is guilty and that she must help John to recognize the error of his beliefs and repent his Communist sins. In separate scenes, both Lucille and Stedman urge John to return to his American roots in defiance of his Communist orders. Lucille invokes God and football in her plea, apologizing for supporting his desire to learn instead of pushing him to play football like his brothers, saying that now John must "take the ball from her" and repent. John ignores this plea and escapes, but then has a change of heart and phones Stedman from the airport. The FBI agent tells him that "everybody's life has purpose, even Judas" and pleads with him to "use whatever free will you have left and make your own decision and get over here!" John makes the decision not to use his ticket to freedom in Lisbon because he wants to do one decent thing. In retribution, the Communists target him. A car chase and some gunfire end symbolically on the steps of the Lincoln Memorial. Stedman and the forces of the law are present as John dies. John tells Stedman, "They got me," and Stedman says, "I know who," but the film does not name names or even use the word "Communist." John's dying request is for Stedman to play the speech he recorded for the graduates, which he tells him is back at his apartment.

The film ends with John's taped speech, which acts as both confession and propaganda. John's death prevents him from being there in person to give the commencement address at his alma mater, but Stedman follows through on his promise, allowing John to be there in spirit. Stedman plays John's recorded speech verbatim as a light shines on the empty podium in front of the assembled graduates. In the speech, John not only condemns Communism, but attacks intellectual curiosity as inherently dangerous. John explains how his experience as a student made him an "intellectual" and encouraged him "to defy the only authorities" he had ever known: "Church and his parents." He admits the intellectual environment of college was stimulating, but "stimulants lead to narcotics as the seller of habit-forming dope gives innocents their first inoculations with the cunning of the serpent." He warns them how Soviet agents were lurking to take advantage of bright young minds. The scene cuts back and forth between shots of the lighted podium and the faces of the graduates listening. John continues, "I am living a lie. I am a traitor. I am a native American Communist spy, and God have mercy on my soul." Religion and political symbolism play heavily throughout the film. The final scene has John's mother and father leaving the commencement to go to the chapel to "pray for John" and to pray "they forget what he did and remember what he said this day," as a chorus sings in the background.

God and football triumph over Communism and intellectual curiosity, but beyond this simple framework, the film stumbles. The role of the FBI in this film is ambiguous. The FBI represents the force of peace and order. Stedman, the FBI agent, has John under surveillance and believes he is a traitor because of his association with a woman charged as a spy. While seemingly a force for good, in the film the FBI employ the same subversive tactics used by Communists. They lie, manipulate and intimidate to achieve their ends. At the beginning of the film Stedman instigates a minor accident with the Jefferson's car as an excuse to enter their lives. Stedman hides his identity from the family and befriends the mother in order to manipulate her and confirm his suspicions about John. Stedman admits, "I know our methods are very often criticized, but nobody objects to a firm that protects its business by investigating your credit." The FBI is the catalyst that brings about the destruction of the family, ending with the death of John and almost causing the total breakdown of Lucille. While America is protected by the FBI, the postwar nuclear American family is destroyed in the process.

My Son John was a defining production in the anti-Communist genre, yet the film's representation of the threats of Communism or Communist ideology is strangely ambiguous. At no time does the film show behavior that could be considered treasonous or even subversive; nor are any of the Communist threats ever seen in the flesh. John's former professor, an assumed Communist, is not given any screen time; neither is the female spy, the requisite femme fatale with whom John claims to have an affair. In fact, all John's alleged Communist co-conspirators are more implied than shown (except in the car chase), and while many scenes feature phone calls, the audience only hears John's side of the dialogue. The only Communist represented is John.

Moreover, the audience is supposed to believe that John is an "invisible" menace. The narrative relies on the belief that he passes, keeping his identity hidden from his family. In a key scene, John swears to his mother on her Bible that he is not nor has he ever been a Communist, and this convinces her, if not the audience. Visually John does conform. He is camouflaged in that he wears clothing appropriate for his job in Washington, including the ubiquitous gray flannel suit. Ironically, the suits John favored were almost indistinguishable from the clothing that FBI agents like Stedman wore in the film. The fashion made all men, good or bad, invisible as individuals. Despite this, the audience cannot fail to see John as a Hollywood "bad guy." Like other film noir or gangster Hollywood "bad guy," John looks more sinister in his suit and trench coat with a hat pulled down to cover his eyes than his good guy counterparts. He is also frequently shot lurking in shadows to meet other nefarious characters, and he receives mysterious phone calls. His attitudes are equally suspicious: he is openly disrespectful of religion, insulting a priest; he is also rude to his father and mother, while giving lectures that are Communist in tone. John was marked from the opening scenes as a Hollywood Communist with his espousal of ideology and guilt by association. He was a visible bad guy.

The metatext surrounding the actor Robert Walker playing John also contributed to the visibility of the threat he posed. The audience knew Walker as the "pathological murderer" Anthony Bruno in Hitchcock's 1951 film *Strangers on a Train*.[46] Vito Russo argues that Walker played Bruno as queer, allowing audiences to collapse deviance and Communism.[47] If that link was not strong enough, the audience also knew that leftover footage of Walker from Hitchcock's film was used to fill in scenes for *My Son John* because Walker died before completion of filming, so Bruno and John are literally parts of the same performance.[48] Walker as John was simply not convincing as a hidden political threat.

Ultimately, even without the layers of Walker's persona, the way that *My Son John* represented Communists was shallow and one-dimensional. Critics like Warshow argued that such simplistic depictions of Communists were dangerous because they misled the public about how passing operated. He believed this film was an example of the irresponsible and wrong kind of anti-Communism (the sort that threatens American freedom as much as the Communists do) and argued that it therefore "might legitimately alarm any thoughtful American, whether liberal or conservative."[49] The "bad guy" gangsters of the 1930s became the Communists of the 1950s.[50] For Warshow, this was a mistake: "Communists are not like gangsters; they are usually more complex and their lives much duller. In their own way they are often the epitome of stodgy respectability (think of Alger Hiss, for instance)."[51] But then Warshow himself becomes guilty of collapsing liberalism and Communism, arguing that Communist threats were much more likely to be eastern Ivy League liberals than gangsters.

Because filmmakers made Communists unsympathetic characters based on earlier representations of criminals, the message of Communism was depoliticized. The title character in *My Son John* may have been guilty of being a Communist, but the film was circumspect as to why that was a political threat, and the story did not depict any specific crimes he had committed in the name of Communism, let alone any that would warrant his investigation by the FBI and his ultimate death. McCarey wanted to show Communists as the ultimate "bad guys," but in so doing he undermined what made them so frightening. He created a film where realism and complexity were dismissed in favor of simplistic propaganda and a Hollywood ending.

McCarey was not alone in failing to make filmic Communists believable as internal threats who could hide and subvert America from within. The anti-Communist film *The Woman on Pier 13* (RKO, 1949), directed by Robert Stevenson, revealed similar anxieties about the invisibility of people's political identities.[52] Stevenson was chosen after Joseph Losey declined to direct this film, leading to Losey's later blacklisting and exile to England.[53] The film starred Robert Ryan as Bradley Collins, an average American man who had been a Communist, with actress Laraine Day as his new wife, Nan. The film was again located in the family, but this time in the marriage bed. It is worth noting that the original title of the film, *I Married a Communist*, was changed because the Studio believed it gave away too much of the story.[54]

Like *My Son John*, the Communist characters were updated versions of 1930s gangsters or WWII Nazis, simplistic and two-dimensional. The *New York Times* noted the studio substituted "Communists for gangsters" in a formula flick. Acknowledging the mandatory melodrama and fast-paced action, the review suggests that the movie nonetheless "paints a fairly ugly picture of Communist machinations in stirring up labor strife along the San Francisco waterfront and demonstrates that the party is quite ruthless when it comes to disciplining its erring or backsliding members. But all this is dramatized in such emotional fashion that the picture speaks without authority."[55] Communists are depicted as irredeemable. Gene Arneel's 1949 review summed up the film's flaws:

> The film appears to be highly flavored fiction all the way, reminiscent of the more flamboyant anti-Nazism films of the war circa, but audience appeal is what counts and "I Married a Communist" seems to have it in sufficient quantity ... Thomas Gomez is the Red agent whose nefarious activities are more suggestive of an underworld czar than of a political revolutionist. Janis Carter, also a Communist in the film, is by far more good-looking than the general conception of active Party workers.[56]

Other reviews of *The Woman on Pier 13* gave it a mediocre rating and commented on its exploitative and melodramatic nature. Despite these stylistic drawbacks, the film is an important study in identity.

The filming and production of *The Woman on Pier 13* was an example of the politics of the time, reflecting Hollywood's negotiations with HUAC. Howard Hughes, the owner of RKO, wanted to make an anti-Communist film while countering accusations that left-leaning politics ruled Hollywood. Daniel Mainwaring was Hughes's first choice for writing the screenplay, but when he refused to work on the script, Hughes had him fired. Mainwaring recalled that Hughes "used that project to get rid of a lot of writers, directors, and actors. If you turned it down, out you went."[57] Other writers proved more cooperative, and the screenplay was given the green light by the studio's executives and the industry's PCA censors. Once released, the only real issue for the PCA censor was a suggested tag line for a poster campaign in Los Angeles that used the phrase "Trained in an Art as Old as Time." It was supposed to refer to femme fatales' penchant for criminality, but the censors did not like the implication of prostitution. The tag line was thus changed to the extended line: "Trained in an art as old as time—She follows a vicious pattern, first an innocent flirtation, then pretended love, then disgrace, finally murder!"[58]

The movie opens with a couple on their honeymoon at a nice hotel. It is made clear that they were married after a brief courtship, which allows secrets from their previous lives to intrude. Echoing film noir conventions, the husband's past includes a femme fatale named Christine Norman (Janis Carter), who led him to the Communist party. By sheer coincidence, Christine is staying at the same hotel as the newlyweds. As Brad orders two champagne cocktails, Christine, a sophisticated looking blonde woman, approaches. Brad buys her a "Ward 8." Christine explains to Nan that she used to know her new husband, revealing that Ward 8's (also known as boilermakers) were their favorite drink in New Jersey: "In the good old days I used to think your husband invented it." The drink is a symbol of the earlier relationship between Brad and Christine and their working-class origins.

The scene shifts to San Francisco, where Brad becomes executive vice-president of his company. Christine enters the picture and reveals to him that "they" (meaning Communists) have opened a "branch" in San Francisco. The film's use of "fronting organizations" mirrored such representations in the tabloid press. In the beginning, Christine is very friendly to Brad, making drinks for the two of them, but when that does not work, she threatens to expose his past membership in the Communist party in Jersey City, where he had gone by the name of Frank Johnson. Brad refuses, telling her, "I graduated from you—a long time back. Same time I graduated from this," as he flips his Party card toward her. "Paste it in your scrapbook, baby—among your many souvenirs." He rejects her and the Party. Brad believes he can reveal his past to the people in his new life: "I won't be the first sucker who got into the Party—and got smart—and got out." But the Communists threaten to accuse him of the murder of a Jersey shopkeeper, and they have evidence in Brad's handwriting. Brad reluctantly returns to the Party, and they use him to promote labor agitation on the waterfront docks.

Thwarted by Brad, Christine begins a relationship with Nan's brother, Don Lowry (John Agar), against the wishes of her Party boss. The boss, Nixon, represents the cold-hearted and unemotional Communist intellectual machine. Nixon is the real bad guy of the film, who uses Christine's involvement with Don as an emotional bid to win back Brad. For Nixon, emotions are a waste of time. Christine counters that "emotion is something you're not built to understand, approve of, or appreciate. And just for the record—I don't have to work for the Party twenty-four hours a day."[59] Christine and Don actually seem quite fond of each other, but after breaking the party's rules against emotional involvement, the couple must pay with their lives. Nixon sends Christine away on assignment after it has become clear that she is in love with Don. At the airport, when she tells Don that she doesn't want to go, he asks her to marry him and leave her job. She tells him that she can never "quit her job," but does not tell him why.

Other people more perceptive than Don force the issue for him. After hearing about Don's plan to marry, a friend at work, Jim Travis, lectures Don on how he has gotten himself involved with Communists, although he is "too ignorant" of politics to realize it: "I wouldn't be lecturing you if I didn't think a lot about you and your family. There's one thing I *know*—that it's time you found out. Because they *are* a Party of few out to boss the world—every Commie has to be an active conspirator—recruit stooges—who usually don't even know they are being used. Well-meaning liberals—the underprivileged—the unemployed—and lovesick kids like you." Jim had earlier told Nan his belief that Christine was "at least a fellow-traveler—and probably a practicing Commie."

Jim's lecture prompts Don to confront Christine about her politics. She admits it's true, but tells him it should not matter because she really does love him: "I love you. I didn't at first. I used you—yes. That was my job. And I never wanted to fall in love with you. I knew it was a mistake and both of us might suffer for it. But I couldn't help myself. I love you, Don . . . and that's all that ought to matter!" But Don does not believe that any good person could ever belong to the Communist party, so Christine brings out Brad's file to show him that all kinds of people got involved in the Party.

When Nixon discovers that Christine has revealed Brad's past to Don, he threatens them both. Incensed, Don punches Nixon and heads out the door to go confront Brad about his past. Nixon tells Christine, "You were warned!" and orders his thugs to go after Don and kill him. Christine calls Nan to warn her that Don is in danger, but just as Don reaches her place he is run down by a car and killed. Nan is confused about how Christine knew what was going to happen. Melodrama ensues, with Nan asking Brad about his past: "I married you—knowing very little about you. But I trusted you. Many things have puzzled me—but I've gone on trusting you. But right now I don't." Nan confronts Christine, who tells her: "Do you know why Don was killed? Because of your husband—the great Mr. Bradley Collins! Because Don found out the great Mr. Bradley Collins is really Frank Johnson—a member of the Communist Party and working for the Party right now!"

Shortly thereafter, Christine's so-called suicide is arranged by Nixon as punishment for her betrayal. She is thrown out of a window several stories up and is impaled on an iron fence below. Even during the Cold War, misogyny plausibly trumped political hysteria, a fact which Nixon skillfully exploits as a cover-up to hide Communist activities and agents. Nixon destroys the dossier Christine had put together to expose Communist party members and explains the tidiness of his solution: "We won't bring politics into it. It is simply a suicide for love. An emotional woman—ill-balanced, as is shown by the fact that she fell insanely in love with a man younger in years, infinitely younger in experience. He is accidentally killed. She kills herself. Their case is closed."

The film ends with a showdown between Brad and Nan and the Communists. In the battle Brad dies; only Nan and Nixon survive. The Production Code mandated that all past and present sins must be addressed by the end of the film. All criminals, including former Communists, needed to be punished. In Hollywood, this meant either prison or death. The message "better dead than red" or "reds are better dead" was overtly acted out.

Gender politics play a significant role in this film. Christine's femme fatale is stereotypically gendered, and she pays with her life, but equally important here is the framing of Brad and Nan's domestic life. Brad refers constantly to man's work, emphasizing that Nan's domain is in the home. The audience is presented with the image of a stable middle class WASP family. This façade begins to crack when it is revealed that this is the story of a woman who had unwittingly married a former Communist. Brad eventually confesses everything to Nan, but his world falls apart with the unmasking of his identity as a former Communist. His marriage, his Americanness, even his masculinity, crumbles in the aftermath of his exposure. The subsequent identity crisis is so total that death is the only possible resolution.

This dramatic ending did not reflect the lived experience of those who passed. Professional ex-Communists made a good living parading their pasts at the HUAC hearings. This glaring discrepancy led reviewers to critique the relatively simplistic representation of Communist subversives by Hollywood: "If Louis Budenz and Whittaker Chambers, among others, could renounce the party, why can't a movie hero do the same for once without having to shoot it out and be killed himself in the end?"[60] Another confused reviewer noted that this film, like the similarly themed *The Red Menace*, "goes on the theory that once anybody signs up with the 'party' he is caught in its meshes forever," concluding that such blatant falsehoods ensured that this film was "hardly to be taken seriously as an expose of Communism in this country."[61] Ironically, the same events that added to the film's urgency, especially the unmasking of spies, also worked to make the film seem inadequate in its representations of the dangers of political subversion.

Woman on Pier 13 exploited anxieties about political passing by insisting that infiltrators and spies could exist within the home. The original title, *I Married a Communist*, explicitly reminded audiences that even husbands and wives could be taken in and be guilty of political "miscegenation." The film challenged the idea of the sanctity of marriage and household. Marriage was neither a safe haven nor a sacred institution immune from political subversion. As typical in anti-Communist films, personal relations might initially be presented in a sympathetic light, but ultimately even families were misled. Sympathetic, romantic, multidimensional characters and relationships were not possible. In fact, it was the opposite. Family entanglements led people into subversion.

Hollywood studios made anti-Communist films like *My Son John* and *Woman on Pier 13* to ameliorate accusations that Hollywood was left of center and a hotbed of ideological subversion. All the major studios agreed to the blacklist to avoid more direct political intervention. Dramas on-screen were mirrored by politics off-screen. Audiences understood the politicized nature of the fears in these films because of the publicity of the HUAC trials and the unmasking of political spies. Yet by portraying Communists as caricatures, alternately gangster-like or hyperintellectual, filmmakers made visible what was supposed to be an invisible threat. Filmmakers wanted to make sure that Communists, like criminals, conformed to the spirit of the Production Code and would be punished by the end of the film. Such formulaic conventions undermined their success. Hidden subversives became visible "bad guys."

However, Hollywood's anti-Communist films made up for their lack of box office success by the volumes of press coverage and analysis they generated. These films were not successful as propaganda, but they were part of a cultural dialogue about passing and identity. At the same time, even these overtly conservative films revealed postwar ideals about gender and home to be a façade and suggested there was a crisis of masculinity in the American family: themes which came to dominate filmmaking in the 1950s.

CHAPTER FIVE

THEY WALK AMONG US

Science Fiction Films and Passing Aliens

CAPGRAS SYNDROME: The patient's—a psychotic subject—delusion that a close relative or friend has been replaced by an imposter, an exact double, despite recognition of familiarity in appearance and behavior. The "imposter" is a key figure for the patient at the time of onset of symptoms; if married, always the husband or wife accordingly. The patient may also see himself as his own double.

At the movies in the late 1940s and 1950s, it was standard fare that people were not what they seemed to be. Representations of Communists passing for Americans are linked in narrative style to films about aliens passing for human. Anti-Communist films suggested the all-American next door might be a Communist, but science fiction went further by suggesting friendly neighbors might be alien invaders only pretending to be humans. It was the perfect formula to exploit the specters of passing. While science fiction films reflected cultural paranoia about Communism, they also tapped into anxieties about the nature of identity and the loss of self. The psychoanalytic demons of the mind jumped out from the screen in science fiction and horror films. The "enemy within" became the "invasion from within" as aliens took over the minds and bodies of humans.

This was the heyday of science fiction B movies in which bad things happened to good people, elaborated with fancy special effects. Popular movies included *Five* (Columbia, 1951); *Captive Women* (RKO, 1952); *The Beast from 20,000 Fathoms* (WB, 1953); *It Came from Beneath the Sea* (Columbia, 1955); *Tarantula* (Universal, 1955); *Kronos* (20th Century-Fox, 1957); *Attack of the Crab Monsters* (AA, 1957); *The Incredible Shrinking Man* (Universal, 1957); *Monster on the Campus* (Universal, 1958); *Attack of the 50-Foot Woman* (AA, 1958); *The Blob* (Paramount, 1958); *The Monster from Green Hell* (DCA, 1958); *The Fly* (20th Century-Fox, 1958); *Teenage Caveman* (AIP, 1958); and *Angry*

Red Planet (AIP, 1959). These films exploited anxieties about aliens, mutation, radiation, and atomic warfare.[1]

Science fiction was not a new genre, but the explosion of its popularity proved it resonated with audiences in postwar America, tapping into the fears and possibilities of the era. In this golden age of the genre, science fiction films spoke to postwar fears of atomic power, the possible destruction of the world, and the high cost of military or scientific arrogance, all while alluding to the existential angst of postwar identity. Horror films created awareness that "invisible" forces like atomic radiation could lead to genetic mutation or mass destruction. Films about atomic culture exploited anxieties about the future of humanity because of the fallout of radioactive waste or the dangers inherent in rivalries between military superpowers. Forces that could not be seen, like radiation, could lead to illness and death. Because the effects were not immediate, misconceptions abounded about the safety and nature of atomic energy.

Aliens came in all shapes and sizes during the 1950s. Films featuring aliens fall into two main categories: the external threat of alien invasions and the internal threat of aliens who infiltrated the earth and passed for human. External alien invasion films, epitomized by *The War of the Worlds* (1953), gave audiences a visibly defined, alien "other" that sought to destroy the earth. In external invasion films, the lines between "us and them" were clear and simple, offering a distinctly less psychological horror experience. Aliens were the bad guys; humans were the good guys. In contrast, the line between "us" and "them" was blurred in the "invasion from within" films. These films represented aliens who passed as humans, exploiting postwar fears about identity and authenticity. Aliens could be anywhere or everywhere. In these films, there was a disjuncture between hidden and performed identities and normalcy and safety.

One of the earliest alien takeover films was William Cameron Menzies's *Invaders from Mars* for 20th Century-Fox. In this 1953 film, budding young astronomer David Maclean (Jimmy Hunt) witnesses a UFO and fears that people around him are no longer who they seem to be; everyone somehow fundamentally changed. The audience knows this to be true. Hiding in a sandpit, the aliens trap people by sucking them underground, where a radio-activated control device is inserted in the back of their necks. David's father is one of the first victims of the aliens, disappearing into the sand as he investigates his son's story. He is taken over and returns home, but David senses his father has changed. Frightened, the boy warns the authorities:

"Today he acted like somebody I never saw before . . . almost as if he'd become a different person." But David quickly realizes the police are no help, as they too have been taken over. All the symbols of authority and patriarchy are possessed by the aliens.

David is put in detention, where the sympathetic Dr. Patricia Blake (Helena Carter) believes his story, protecting him from his parents, who tried to argue that David was delusional from reading too many science fiction comic books. Patricia's astronomer boyfriend, Dr. Stuart Kelston (Arthur Franz), is on hand, and he assures her that David is the "scientific type," not prone to "flights of fancy." David and Stuart then give Patricia a crash course on the history of Unidentified Flying Objects. David shows her a book on UFO sightings that includes the Lubbock Lights, an incident believed to be "UFOs flying in formation" over Texas. When asked where the aliens came and where they could be hiding, Stuart suggests the dark side of the moon: "We can only see the face of the moon. The other side has always been a dark secret." The unknown is scary and threatening, and "dark secrets" are a source of danger. Eventually the army is called in, but the soldiers and General Mayberry are possessed by the aliens. The film ends as David wakes from a dream, relieved that the terrors were not real, just as he sees a UFO outside his window. The ending blurs the line between dreams, reality, and fears.

The Lubbock Lights phenomena in 1951 generated national media attention as a possible UFO sighting, and science fiction films like *Invaders from Mars* referenced such actual events to add to their horror. There was no shortage of news reports or media materials that referenced outer space and aliens in the long 1950s. The publicity surrounding the Roswell incident in 1947 ensured that popular science fiction books like *The Flying Saucers Are Real* (1950) became bestsellers. Tabloid magazines also did their part to push conspiracy theories about aliens and government cover-ups. All these cultural currents combined to create a general familiarity about the possible existence and meanings of extraterrestrial life forms, and they made audiences more receptive to celluloid representations that fostered paranoia about alien threats.[2]

Films like *Invaders from Mars* effectively projected fears that seemingly ordinary-looking Americans were no longer who they pretended to be and that underneath their passing exteriors lurked alien and possibly sinister imposters. This framing reflected both political paranoia and threats, as well as broader postwar anxieties about the nature of authentic identity and the loss of self. Horror novelist Stephen King suggests, "When the horror movies wear their various sociopolitical hats—the B-picture as tabloid editorial—they often serve as an extraordinar[il]y accurate barometer of those things which trouble the night-thoughts of a whole society."³ Successful science fiction films, like horror films, tapped into the fears and anxieties of their era, and in the 1950s one of the most successful science fiction subgenres featured aliens passing for human.

Passing narratives like the boy's story in *Invaders from Mars* were filmic reflections of a rare psychological condition known as Capgras or "Imposter" Syndrome. This condition was originally diagnosed in the 1920s as a delusion that friends or family have been replaced by identical imposters, but it was not culturally familiar to most Americans until it became a staple in science fiction films of the 1950s. The issues and fears raised by this syndrome connected to discourses about passing. Many postwar science fiction and horror films explicitly presented aliens passing as humans, problematizing postwar concepts of identity and authenticity. In 1961, Susan Sontag perceptively argued in "The Imagination of Disaster" that these postwar science fiction films were informed not only by fears about authenticity and a loss of identity but also by the language of the couch, noting that "alien invaders practice a crime which is worse than murder. They do not simply kill the person. They obliterate him: the body is preserved but the person is entirely reconstituted as the automatized servant or agent of the alien powers . . . The person is really dead, but he doesn't know it . . . He is 'undead,' he has become an 'unperson.'" Sontag sees a repeated pattern in these films whereby individuals always fight being "taken over," but once the "deed has been done, the victim is eminently satisfied with his condition."⁴

In addition to *Invader from Mars*, the "invasion from within" scenario was featured in *It Came from Outer Space* (1953), *Invasion of the Body Snatchers* (1956), *I Married a Monster from Outer Space* (1958), and *Invisible Invaders* (1959).⁵ The ability of aliens to live among us and to escape detection by passing was the source of anxiety in these films. The alien in 1953's *Phantom from Space* was "doubly terrifying because it was invisible!" Aliens were "invisible threats," terrifying in their ability to pass undetected as normal Americans and even as spouses and neighbors.

These films were part of a shift to paranoid horror, where horror was located in the home, within the familial unit. By passing as humans, aliens "hide in plain sight." Horror no longer existed outside of American society but came from within. Capitalizing on the fears of internal threats to American society and external enemies, films with representations of passing aliens blurred the lines between external and domestic subversions. At the same time, these films played with contemporary anxieties that American soldiers had been brainwashed and indoctrinated by Communists during the Korean War.

Two films that successfully exploited anxieties about aliens passing deserve particular analysis: *Invasion of the Body Snatchers* (1956) and *I Married a Monster from Outer Space* (1958). Against these representations, the passing alien in the film *The Day the Earth Stood Still* (1951) will be considered. The trope of aliens passing as human allowed filmmakers to explore social issues and frame postwar anxieties about identity as universal. These films opened audiences to the idea of "imposter syndrome" and exploited related fears in ways that would be repeated in other science fiction films of the 1950s.

The most famous and successful of the "invasion from within" films was 1956's *Invasion of the Body Snatchers*, which presented alien invasion as an epidemic contagion. It was directed by Don Siegel and produced by Walter Wanger for Allied Artists, who described it as "science-fact."[6] Siegel and Wanger had worked together on the 1954 film *Riot in Cell Block 11*, a strong indictment of the prison system, and they took on the subject of invading aliens with the same seriousness. Based on a serial story by Jack Finney for *Collier's* magazine, *Invasion* was adapted for the screen by Daniel Mainwaring. Kevin McCarthy stars as the hero, Dr. Miles Bennell (a GP who studied psychiatry), and Dana Wynter plays his love interest, Becky Driscoll. Dr. Bennell's nurse, Sally Withers, is played by Jean Willes. Larry Gates plays another psychiatrist, Dr. "Danny" Kaufman. There is even a third psychiatrist in the film, Dr. Hall, played by Whit Bissell. Psychiatry and its explanations about identity inform the structure of the film.

While psychiatric ideas informed the film, it also invoked the paranoia of McCarthyism. Promotion materials revealed that a small American town has been taken over by something alien and evil. The aliens, giant seedpods from space, take over people in their sleep. Characters become hysterical over the fear that those closest to them are "not themselves," that they have been taken over. Uncle Ira is not Uncle Ira. These fears come true as the entire town falls prey to the alien pods and is possessed, except for a heroic few, who try to escape and warn the outside world. Ads included such tag lines as "The Nightmare That Threatens the World!," "While the earth sleeps IT happens!," and "Cell for cell . . . atom for atom . . . they capture your very soul in their creeping horror!"

Using documentary styled realism, Siegel avoided standard science fiction effects and relied more on psychological fears. The fact that the pods take over the minds and souls of people in their sleep was understood as a metaphor for American complacency on all sides of the political spectrum. The horror and suspense of the film are created not by monsters but by inverting and twisting normalcy. The town appears "normal," but normal everyday acts become sinister in their representation: "Conspiracy theories feed off the idea of the normal being deceptive."[7] The location manager looked for a small California town "surrounded by mountains" that "had to appear isolated, so that the suspenseful eeriness of plant life from another planet taking over such a small town would seem more *realistic*."[8] The mythical town was Santa Mira, California, a setting that turned the most innocuous and innocent actions into an inversion of the normal.

Originally, the script ended with Miles disheveled and hysterically screaming "You could be next!" at passing cars. However, pressure from the studio for a less depressing ending called for something more hopeful. As filmed, it is one long flashback, beginning and ending with Miles in a hospital, telling his experience to another psychiatrist, Dr. Hall. The doctors and staff believe that Miles is delusional, "as mad as a March Hare." Miles is only vindicated when they hear a news report of a freak accident on the highway involving a truck filled with strange pod-like plants. He is not paranoid. There is hope. The hospital authorities have the power to alert government agencies capable of opposing the threat and stop the invasion. Paradoxically, the representatives of authority and conformity, the FBI and hospital psychiatrists, are the only chance to stop the mindless conformity of the pods.

The movie begins in a flashback as Dr. Miles Bennell returns to his hometown. His nurse, Sally, tells him that there has been an epidemic of visitors with unusual problems, patients who think relatives are imposters. Jimmy Grimaldi (Bobby Clark) claims his mother isn't his mother. The doctor prescribes a tranquilizer and sends him home with his grandmother. Other townspeople have similar complaints, although they cannot explain what they mean; they can only say that "Uncle Ira isn't Uncle Ira." Even Miles's love interest, Becky, reveals her fears that her father isn't her father. The dialogue between Miles and Wilma Lentz (Virginia Christine) explains the situation:

WILMA: Let's have it. You talked to him . . . what do you think?
MILES: It's him . . . He's your Uncle Ira, alright.
WILMA (emphatically): He is not.
MILES: How is he different?
WILMA: That's just it, there is no difference you can actually see. He looks, sounds, acts, and remembers like Uncle Ira. (deliberately and definitively) But he isn't—there's something missing. He's been a father to me since I was a baby. Always when he talked to me there

was a special look in his eye . . . (she puts her hand to her mouth sadly). That look's gone.

MILES: What about memories? There must be certain things that only you and he would know about?

WILMA (with anguish): Oh, there are . . . I've talked to him about them. He remembers them all down to the last small detail. Just like Uncle Ira would. But Miles, there's—there's no emotion. None! (off) Just the pretense of it. The words . . . the gesture . . . the tone of the voice . . . everything else is the same but not the feeling. Memories or not, he isn't my Uncle Ira.

MILES: Now no one could possibly impersonate your Uncle Ira without you, or your Aunt Aleda, or even me seeing a million little differences.[9]

After leaving Wilma's house, Miles thinks to himself in a voice-over narration: "In the back of my mind a warning bell was ringing. Sick people who couldn't wait to see me . . . then suddenly were perfectly alright. A boy who said his mother wasn't his mother. A woman who said her uncle wasn't her uncle. But I didn't listen."

Miles treats the symptoms as paranoid delusions and tries to calm their hysteria. By the time that Miles discovers and accepts that the problem is real, it is already too late. The alien pods take over people, cell for cell and atom for atom, until they are replicas of their hosts. The pods replace the humans with all the memories and knowledge of the person they replicate, yet it is not a complete conversion. Those people who are taken over are aware of what has happened; they have become aliens who lack any of their prior emotions, from love to hate. They no longer have anxiety about identity, which is what makes them alien. Although the pods represent an alien invasion, the true horror is the loss of identity, characterized by a lack of emotion and mindless conformity: a fate, the film implies, worse than death. The film asks whether there is identity without emotion.

Miles's emotions are wrapped up in a reunion with Becky. Both have returned from Reno (with divorces) and are open to a relationship. The couple tries to date, but the strange events keep interrupting their plans. Becky and Miles discuss the "imposters" in town, but admit they are confused. They only discover the truth about the pods and how the process works after Miles's best friend Jack (King Donovan) finds the body of a man with "blank features" on his pool table and calls Miles for help. Upon examination they find the body has no fingerprints and no identity. Jack's wife Teddy (Carolyn Jones) realizes that the body was copying Jack, but wasn't "finished." Jack's "pod" opens its eyes and a cut, identical to one Jack had received earlier that evening, starts to form on his hand. Realizing Becky might be in danger, Miles goes to her house, where he finds a pod in the basement. He runs to her bedroom and carries her back to his own home.

After surviving the night, Miles seeks the aid of another psychiatrist, Dr. Danny Kaufman, who had been Miles's mentor. Kaufman surprisingly suggests the town is simply suffering from mass hysteria. Miles and the group want to accept this more rational explanation. However, when the four friends discover four pods in the greenhouse intended to replace them, they realize they are not suffering from hysteria. The couples separate to improve their chances. Miles and Becky try to escape in their car but realize that the police and gas station attendants are pods. They abandon the car and hide out in Miles's office. The next morning, pod-Jack arrives with Dr. Kaufman in tow, and they try to persuade Miles and Becky to go to sleep naturally. Dr. Kaufman eloquently extols the virtues of the pod way of life. The audience cannot be sure when people in town are still real and when they become pods. This is especially true of Bennell's mentor Dr. Kaufman, who gives the following speech:

> Less than a month ago, Santa Mira was like any other town. People with nothing but problems. Then out of the sky came a solution. Seeds drifting through space for years took root in a farmer's field. From the seeds came pods which had the power to reproduce themselves in the exact likeness of any form of life. There's no pain. Suddenly, when you're asleep, they'll absorb your minds, your memories, and you'll be born into an untroubled world.

As they hide in the office, Miles thinks about Kaufman's zombie utopia and quietly talks to Becky about the horrors of the loss of individuality and humanity. He feared this had been happening in Santa Mira even prior to the arrival of the pods: "In my practice I see how people have allowed humanity to drain away, only it happens slowly instead of all at once . . . We harden our hearts, grow callous. Only when we have to fight to stay human do we realize how precious it is."[10] The scene spells out the film's message about the loss of individuality.

Eventually Miles and Becky fight their way out of his office and onto the busy daytime street, where they try to pass as pods to escape. The line between repression and civilized conformity blurs as the pod-mobs pursue anyone who isn't exactly like them with an obsessive vengeance. The pods do not wish to kill; rather, they want to "convert" in order to expand their population. Conversion is their procreation. Here the converted people fit Sontag's template; they declare themselves happy to be pods. They have self-awareness about their hybrid human-alien identity, but believe their new identity is better. The self-knowledge of alien identity underneath the "normal" external appearance of the replaced person is passing at its best. People are right to be obsessed that others are not who they seem to be. Only when everyone not like them is taken over will the pod-imposters stop passing. Crucially, Miles and Becky are exposed as non-pods when Becky reacts with telltale emotion at the sight of a dog almost being hit by a car, but they elude the pod-mob and find shelter in a cave just outside town.

As they hide out, Becky succumbs to sleep. Miles realizes she has become a pod the moment he kisses her and there is no warmth or emotion. Her face is blank. Miles frantically runs out of their hiding place, saying in voice-over, "I'd been afraid a lot of times in my life, but I didn't know the real meaning of fear until I kissed Becky." As he thinks this, Miles runs towards the highway and into oncoming traffic, screaming: "They're here! You could be next!" The film ends as it began, with Miles hospitalized, telling his story to the staff psychiatrists.

Director Don Siegel admitted that he included psychiatrists as a means of authenticating issues about identity:

> I purposefully had the prime spokesman for the pods be a pod-psychiatrist. He speaks with authority, knowledge. He really believes that being a pod is preferable to being a frail, frightened human who cares ... The pods in my picture and in the world believe they are doing good when they convert people into pods. They get rid of pain, ill health, mental anguish. It leaves you with a dull world, but that, my dear friend, is the world in which most of us live.[11]

Dr. Danny Kaufman's role as spokesman for the pod-people is a critical indicator of the importance of the culture of the couch.

While the pods are from outer space, the fear generated is not the fear of alien invasion from an external threat; rather, it is the psychological fear about the integrity of identity and the meaning of humanity. Becky's and Miles's being exposed as human provides an interesting twist. Not only do pods pass as human, but the hero and heroine likewise try to pass as pods, a more difficult deception. Failure to suppress emotional reactions exposes their masquerade.

The film uses an epidemic of alien pods to question ideas about conformity and identity.[12] The anxieties and fears expressed about dehumanization and emotionless conformity tie into postwar cultural fears about the fluidity of racial and gender identities and confusion as to the changing status quo vis-à-vis civil rights. The fact that the town is a quintessential white-bread American town is important in locating these fears for the most privileged within American society. However, by equating rationality with dehumanization, the film suggests that usually devalued feminine qualities like emotions are the key to the survival of humanity. It is no surprise that the first character to see the pods and be replicated is Jack, a writer who is creatively inclined and more willing to challenge the rationality and logic of the world. The final message is that one has to fight to maintain an inner sense of identity. In this way, emotional signifiers made visible became the only reliable indicators of authentic human identities.

Invasion is a "highly unstable text" that can be read as an allegory about political weakness in the face of mindless conformity.[13] Contemporary critics appreciated the ironic parallels of two apparently opposite political representations. Traditional historiographical interpretations debate whether the pod-people represented Communists or American McCarthyite mobs, and an analysis of those involved in the production does not solve this debate, as they covered the spectrum of left to right politics. Wanger was a strongly left-leaning producer in the 1930s, producing such important films as *Queen Cristina* (1933) and *Stagecoach* (1939), but he became a Cold War liberal, and in 1947 he was one of the studio moguls who drafted the infamous "Waldorf statement" that initiated the blacklist. The screenwriter, Mainwaring, was more consistently leftist and deeply opposed the blacklist. Meanwhile, Richard Collins, who also worked on the script, was a HUAC informer.

Siegel himself humorously commented that he used studio executives as the role model for the pods.[14] But whatever the inspiration, dehumanization occurred through a loss of individuality, succumbing to the mentality of the mob. This film did not simply reflect political fears; it more deeply exposed anxieties about self, identity, and the meaning of human existence. It was the "quintessential paranoid film."[15] To minds predisposed to anti-Communist fears, the pods could be physical manifestations of the same anxieties and fears that J. Edgar Hoover promoted with his red-baiting discourse about the "enemy within." But the ambiguous nature of the pods, the way the alien pods can replicate and pass as anyone, meant *Invasion* could resonate with anyone's fears about passing, conformity, and hidden identities. It is this allegorical ambiguity that made science fiction films more successful than their anti-Communist filmic counterparts. Science fiction films tapped into cultural anxieties that could be interpreted in different ways by different groups.

In the 1958 film *I Married a Monster from Outer Space* (Paramount), women unknowingly married alien men who pass as humans. The domestic danger of the "enemy within" had reached the marriage bed.[16] Although the film does resort to a few requisite signifiers of the science fiction genre, with scenes of spaceships and threatening displays of firepower and ray guns, the film fosters a more general paranoia throughout the film, where the real horror is a psychological fear created by the idea that aliens can possess local men and pass as human. This alien invasion film is noteworthy for having a female lead as the protagonist, and for making gender and sexuality central issues.

Directed and produced by Gene Fowler Jr., who also directed the 1957 film *I Was a Teenage Werewolf*, the film proved popular with critics and audiences alike. The screenplay was by Louis Vittes. The cast included Gloria Talbott as Marge and Tom Tryon as her husband Bill Farrell, with John Eldredge as Chief Collins and Alan Dexter as Sam Benson. Much like in *Invasion*, the story was set in another fictional all-American town, Norrisville, California, and the location was chosen for similar reasons, playing with the "inversion of normalcy" to heighten the anxiety and horror.

The film begins at Bill's stag party on the night before his wedding to Marge. Bill is the first to leave the party and thanks his friends. On his way home, he discovers a dead body on the road. It disappears just as Bill gets out of his car, and a monster grabs him from behind. The alien turns into a vapor that surrounds Bill, who then disappears. Bill is possessed by the alien. This pattern of assault, which is repeated several times in the film, is how the aliens inhabit human form. The next day, Bill, the passing alien, is late for his wedding. The first thing Marge does when she finally sees him is give him a long kiss. Unlike in *Invasion*, where Miles knew the instant he kissed Becky she had become a pod, these aliens are more adept at passing, so Marge suspects nothing and the wedding ceremony proceeds.[17]

After they are married, Marge begins to suspect that Bill has changed. At first, only little things seem peculiar. Bill seems cold and absent-minded. He can see too clearly in the dark and he doesn't like alcohol anymore. More dramatic changes in Bill occur when Marge gives Bill a puppy for their first anniversary. The dog growls and reacts violently to Bill, although he had owned dogs "most of his life." This was a common trope in science fiction films: animals were not deceived by appearances; they recognized aliens for what they were. Bill realizes the dog is a threat, goes down to the basement and chokes the puppy, providing the first real glimpse of the dark side of the alien. Bill then lies to Marge, telling her that the collar was too tight and the dog must have choked himself. Concerned, Marge begins to write a letter to her mother: "It's been a horrible year. I'm frightened and bewildered—maybe it's me, but, oh, mama, Bill isn't the man I fell in love with—he's almost a stranger." Unsure if she is imagining things, Marge crumples up the letter and throws it away.

One evening, when Bill heads out of the house suspiciously late at night, Marge follows him, wearing only her nightgown and a raincoat. She trails him into the woods to the alien ship and discovers her husband's "secret." She sees the alien literally come out of Bill's body, leaving an empty, unresponsive shell with Bill's form as the alien enters the spaceship. Unlike other alien takeover films, where the essence of humans disappears once the replicas complete their "cell for cell" transformation, in *I Married a Monster* the real humans are kept alive in the spaceship so that they can send electrical impulses to the alien imposters to affect the masquerade. This connection between alien and human gives the passing aliens "shape, form, and even memories."

Panicking at her discovery, Marge flees the woods and runs to the local bar. She tells the patrons: "I've just seen a Monster! They look just like us!" A man responds that he sees monsters all the time, too, and he asks her how much she had to drink before she saw hers. The bartender and the patrons assume she is a lush. She attempts to alert the local authorities about the threat and goes to the police chief, who happens to be her godfather, telling him the whole story. To her relief, he says he believes her and calms her down by telling her that he is not going to call a psychiatrist, saying he "wouldn't give a nickel for Marge's cooking," but he'd bet his "whole pension on her sanity." He suggests, however, that she go back to alien-Bill to prevent his suspicions from being aroused. Marge returns home to her alien husband and comes to the dark realization that most of the town's men, including authority figures like the police and the Western Union telegraph operator, have also been taken over by the aliens.

The aliens are, however, selective in their choice of humans. They choose "suitable" bachelors, like policemen or businessmen. Others are rejected as unworthy, as in a scene where an alien-policeman comes across a young criminal but rejects him as an unsuitable candidate and kills him on the spot. Similarly, the only woman the aliens kill is labelled the "town tramp," a woman deemed "unsuitable" for procreation and therefore vaporized with their ray gun. Ironically, the alien invaders replicated conservative postwar moral values.

Marge's discovery of the truth causes her to act like a zombie herself. It is Bill's turn to tell her, "You've changed; it's as if you've gone away." With this, Marge finally confronts Bill. He explains to her that they are survivors from another planet located in the Andromeda constellation: "Our Sun became unstable so we built some spaceships, enough to get all our people away before our sun exploded. But it took time to build those ships and in that time, as our sun's rays became more intense, our women died. But we went on anyway, a race doomed to extinction." Bill admits to Marge that the men and women of his planet only came together for "breeding purposes." They now have hopes that their scientists will one day enable them to interbreed with Earth women and "revive the race." They target bachelors for the purpose of getting married and settling down to have children to repopulate the species. This process has unintended consequences, however. The passing aliens begin to "inherit" human desires in their new corporeal forms. In effect, they learn emotions. Alien-Bill tells Marge that he is learning not just "how to love," but more fundamentally "what love is." These feelings are a shock for a rational race that has no emotions.

In the context of the film, the aliens have a remarkable ability to pass. It is so complete that other alien passers have trouble "seeing" each other. A visual clue of their alien identity is revealed only when the aliens telepathically communicate with each other or when there is a flash of lightning; then for a brief moment their true faces are shown, but only to the audience. At one point, Sam and Bill talk around the issue before finally acknowledging that they are both from the alien spaceship. Sam says that he is uncomfortable "wearing this thing. The design's pretty lousy." In another scene in the town bar the aliens order drinks but do not drink them, discussing the impact of their masquerades on their sense of self.[18]

These aliens are so successful at passing that Marge and the real townsfolk concede, "You've got no way of telling whether any given man in town is a monster or not." Eventually the film does provide a reliable signifier for telling man from alien. While reproduction was the goal of the aliens, they were not capable, and this gave those who hadn't been taken over a means to identify who was who. The town doctor recognizes that the best way to sort the sterile aliens from unpossessed humans is procreation and fatherhood.[19] Since new fathers could be presumed not to have been taken over by aliens, they organize themselves as a posse with guns and dogs for an attack on the alien ship. (Apparently rallying the women in the town, who were guaranteed not to be aliens, was never an option). Sexual reproduction is the key to humanity. In the end, the aliens are attacked by the posse who shoot at the aliens as they emerge from their ship, and although guns prove ineffective, dogs manage to bring them down and kill them. The dead aliens disintegrate, allowing the young fathers to enter the ship, where they discover the kidnapped bodies of the town's men floating in air. The wires attached to them are interpreted as "some kind of broadcasting system." Simply by disconnecting the wires from the men, the aliens who have taken their form are killed.

While the ship is being attacked, alien-Bill is able to recognize the imminent danger telepathically, and together with some of the possessed policemen, he rushes to the woods to try to stop the posse from entering the spaceship. Bill watches helplessly as first each man stops in his tracks, crumples over in pain, and then loses his ability to pass as human, before finally dissolving into a jellylike substance. A closeup shot of their faces makes it clear that the aliens know their fate and can feel the process of disconnection, and yet can do nothing to stop it. The alien-Bill makes it as far as the ship, but he recognizes he has lost. He has one final conversation with Marge before he is killed. In contrast to the previous scenes that unsympathetically showed the brutal murder of two of the monster-aliens, who seemed to have no personalities or ability to communicate with the men, these scenes are sympathetically portrayed. Marge is then reunited with the human Bill, who, ironically, she never married. Their search party destroyed, the final scene shows the remaining aliens in spaceships flying away from Earth in search of another planet.

In *I Married a Monster*, the fear that the person one married might turn out to be an alien becomes prophecy. This film used passing aliens to highlight fears that people could live together intimately, even be married, and still not know each other.[20] More subversively, the film plays with standard Hollywood tropes about marriage and pressures to conform to domesticity in 1950s America. In the early scene at Bill's stag party, his friends all joke about the horrors of marriage and his last night as a free man, ordering rounds of "freedom on the rocks" and suggesting the only solution to matrimony for men is "mass suicide." One of Bill's friends even half-seriously tells him to "get in touch with me when you're getting divorced and I'll throw you a real party." In contrast to the attitudes of these human men are the alien imposter men, who want to get married, stop drinking, and most of all have children. The alien imposters are, in short, the ideal domesticated males. They wanted to be men in gray flannel suits. This framing can be viewed two ways. Having literal aliens desire and emulate this form of masculinity can be seen as a critique of this masculine ideal as unsuitable for actual men, but the film also suggests that it is these desires that make them sympathetic.

At the time, this version of "the invasion within" was interpreted as a metaphor for the threat of Communism in the 1950s. However, representations of passing aliens were not as violent or immoral as Hollywood's representations of passing Communists. Hollywood's passing aliens elicited sympathy. *I Married a Monster from Outer Space* challenges the idea that passing aliens are emotionless and devoid of feelings. The aliens learn what emotions are and even begin to feel, although ultimately they are still represented as a threat that must be destroyed. Of all the "invasion from within" films, this film locates the fear of passing within marriage. One can never be sure who is who. More importantly, the film suggests that one could have intimate relations with an alien and not be punished. This is in direct contrast to the similarly titled anti-Communist film *I Married a Communist*, where a logic of guilt-by-association meant that all who were connected to passing in some way or another enabled the Communist to pass and shared the consequences. The aliens in *I Married a Monster* demonstrate the blurring of performance and identity, privileging the humanizing effects of sex and emotion. Passing leads to a new hybrid identity that is neither alien nor human.

In stark contrast to the typical threats invoked by aliens passing as humans, the 1951 film *The Day the Earth Stood Still* featured a benign passing alien as hero. With its theme of the earth being saved by superior beings, *The Day the Earth Stood Still* is similar to several other science fiction films of the 1950s, including 1958's *The Space Children* and 1959's *The Cosmic Man*, where John Carradine's alien visitor sympathetically passes as a white human male. The explicit message of all these films was what could befall mankind if humanity did not learn how to stop wars and stop using atomic energy for weapons. The alien envoy opts to pass as human in order to learn the ways of human beings and to help humanity avoid annihilation

The Day the Earth Stood Still (20th Century-Fox) was directed by Robert Wise and produced by Julian Blaustein. Both filmmakers were pro-United Nations, and to their delight, the film won the 1952 Golden Globe Award for "Best Film Promoting International Understanding." Based on the story "Farewell to the Master" by Harry Bates and adapted for the screen by Edmond H. North, the film sought to be "as believable as possible, and put our character from the other planet right in the midst of the ordinary everyday life of people in this country." Wise added that he was "very happy to shoot in black and white to get as much of a realistic documentary feeling into it as possible, even though it was a fiction piece."[21] While the cast did not feature any big-name stars, it used real news commentators of the day like Elmer Davis, Drew Pearson, and H. V. Kaltenborn to add to the realistic effect of the story.

Michael Rennie was cast as the most important character, the alien visitor Klaatu. Rennie was a relatively unknown British actor, which the filmmakers thought was a plus. They reasoned that a popular actor like Spencer Tracy, who had also wanted the part, would not have been accepted as an alien because he had the "baggage of familiarity."[22] The role of Gort, the giant 8 foot robot, was played by Lock Martin, an actor who was over 7½ feet tall. Klaatu's earthly friend, the widow Helen Benson, was played by Patricia Neal. Helen's son Bobby was played by Billy Gray, with her unlikable boyfriend, Tom Stevens, played by Hugh Marlowe. The "world's smartest man," a mathematician named Dr. Jacob Barnhardt, who bears a "striking resemblance" to Albert Einstein, was played by blacklisted actor Sam Jaffe, another ode to the film's realism, as Jaffe was originally a mathematician before he became an actor. (Jaffe had also played a genius in *Gentleman's Agreement* as Jewish Professor Fred Lieberman.) [23]

The film opens with global news stories about a strange saucer that was too fast to be an airplane. American news commentator Elmer Davis is shown at his microphone: "We still don't know what it is or where it comes from, but there's something there. It's been tracked around the Earth by radar traveling at a rate of 4000 miles per hour. This is not another flying saucer scare. Scientists and military men are already agreed on that. Whatever it is, it's something real." News reports from around the world follow, with clips from India, France and the BBC, before American news shows a shot of the spaceship landing at a park in Washington, DC. Ironically, it lands on a symbol of America, the baseball diamond. The dramatic arrival of the ship provokes an immediate response from the military and police. Troops surround the ship, backed by tanks.

A door opens in the seamless-looking spaceship, and Klaatu emerges in a glittering silver outfit with a face mask, followed by a gigantic robot named Gort. Klaatu's first words are "we have come to visit you in peace and with goodwill" as he holds out a strange object, which turns out to merely be a gift for the president. Moments later, a "trigger-happy" soldier shoots him. The robot Gort moves in as the military backs away. His visor opens and he shoots a laser that vaporizes all of the weapons, including the tanks. Gort stops his laser attack at Klaatu's command, becoming immobile. The injured

Klaatu is taken to the military-controlled Walter Reed General Hospital, where he asks to meet all the world's leaders. Klaatu and Gort have come to Earth to demand that humans keep their fighting and weapons of mass destruction out of space, or the whole planet will be destroyed. The world leaders, however, cannot manage to arrange a meeting, much less agree on a strategy, because of the politics of the Cold War. Klaatu suggests a meeting with the United Nations to no avail. Discouraged, Klaatu decides that before making any final decision he should "become familiar with the basis for these strange unreasoning attitudes." The government representative considers his request, but replies that "under the circumstances I'm afraid that's impossible." Citing safety concerns, they seek to keep Klaatu a captive on the military base. Klaatu is forced to escape, taking the name, suitcase, and civilian clothing of a Major Carpenter.

Radio broadcasts and newspaper headlines release the news that a "monster [is] on the loose" and the "Man from Mars" has escaped. Panic in the streets ensues. Without any specific images, the public assumes that they should be on the lookout for a horrible, bug-eyed figure. Children are hurried inside their houses, and there are multiple scenes of people huddled around radios for the latest news about the alien. The news reporters try to dispel rumors that the alien is 8 feet tall or has tentacles. This atmosphere of panic is represented in great contrast to the sight of Klaatu, the "alien monster" in question, walking casually down the street wearing a nice suit and carrying an average-looking suitcase. Klaatu's guise as a passing human helps him elude authorities, who are searching for a monster with an alien form. In fact, he is "nattily attired in a business suit" with a perfect command of English and a voice that comes straight "from the BBC." Bosley Crowther described Rennie's alien as a "genteel soul," who was "charmingly suave and cosmopolitan," a humanoid "so well-mannered and peacefully inclined, that you'd hardly expect [him] to split an infinitive, let alone an atom or human head."[24]

The disjuncture between what he is and what he is expected to be allows the alien Klaatu to pass. He walks publicly without fear of discovery, conforming so completely to the visible codes of the middle class professional man that he blends into the crowd. His invisibility is aided by the film's framing techniques and his unassuming behavior. Klaatu is frequently shot from behind or in the shadows, obscuring his features. He observes more than he interacts, merely watching as the people around him go about their daily business.

In the guise of Mr. Carpenter, Klaatu quietly enters a boarding house unnoticed. He remains standing in the shadows, while the tenants watch a television broadcast, just as a real-life anchorman states that "the president has urged all citizens to be on the alert for any information about this man and to transmit such information immediately to the police, the army, or the FBI." On cue, they all turn and see Klaatu passing as Carpenter, accepting that he is just a typical man in a gray flannel suit. It is in this rooming house that Klaatu befriends a young widow, Helen, whose husband was killed in the war, and her son, Bobby. Ironically, Bobby assumes that Klaatu is an "undercover" FBI man searching for the alien, and offers his services: "Hey, Mister, can I help you look for the spaceman? I know just what he looks like—he's got a big square head with three great big eyes."

The film plays with the inability of the people to see what is right in front of them. When the landlady shows Klaatu an available room, she observes that "You're a long way from home aren't you, Mr. Carpenter?" causing Klaatu to surprisingly wonder, "How did you know," but then she adds, "Oh, I can tell a New England accent a mile away," at which he only smiles. Another scene shows tenants of the boarding house enjoying a typical breakfast, with many guests, including Klaatu, quietly reading newspapers. He is the image of respectable conformity. Against this tranquility, the only sound comes from the radio, as a news commentator intones:

> This creature, where is he? . . . Obviously the monster must be found, he must be tracked down like a wild animal, he must be destroyed, but where would such a creature hide? Would he disappear into the north woods? Would he crawl into the sewers of some great city? Everybody agrees there is great danger, the question remains, what can we do to protect ourselves? What measures can we take to neutralize this menace from another world? Destroy it? Of course, but how?

At this point, the radio is shut off, but the conversation turns to the subject of the alien. Helen argues that they shouldn't assume the "spaceman or whatever he is" means any harm or is a menace, but others ask, "Then what's he hiding for? Why doesn't he come out in the open?" to which Helen suggests that maybe he is "afraid" because "After all, he was shot the minute he landed here," and she wonders what she would do in his place. Klaatu, who had been silent, interjects, "Perhaps you'd want to know more about the people here, to orient yourself in a strange environment." The landlady interrupts, saying "There is nothing strange about Washington," putting forth her theory that the supposed spaceman is not really an alien after all, but rather a Russian and therefore a Communist agent.

In order to see Washington, Klaatu has Bobby act as his tour guide. Bobby takes him to Arlington National Cemetery, where his father is buried and then to the Lincoln Memorial, where Klaatu reads the inscription, remarking that "those are great words, that's the kind of man I want to talk to." Klaatu and Bobby also visit the spaceship site, where a curious Bobby listens to him explain the principles of nuclear-powered engines and inertia. Again, Klaatu as Carpenter is hiding in plain sight. At the site, a reporter interviews "Mr. Carpenter" and asks him if he is as "scared as the rest of us." He answers, "In a different way, perhaps; I am fearful when I see people substituting fear for reason." The disappointed reporter cuts him off as a newspaper boy runs around shouting, "Extra, Extra, Spaceman eludes police." As the crowd clamors to buy the papers, Klaatu and Bobby continue to go through Washington unnoticed.

Klaatu wants to meet the world's "best philosopher," a request that Bobby assumes means Dr. Barnhardt, the "smartest man in the world." Klaatu tracks down the professor and leaves his "calling card," writing out the solution to Barnhardt's physics equation on his blackboard. The intrigued professor requests that Mr. Carpenter be brought to him, and he is escorted by the military. The professor asks him if he has tested the theory, and Klaatu responds, "I find it works well enough to get me from one planet to another." Barnhardt promptly tells the military Captain to leave. "You have faith, Professor Barnhardt," Klaatu remarks. "It isn't faith that makes good science, Mr. Klaatu; it's curiosity," Barnhardt answers. But even Barnhardt does not see how they could get a global meeting of the intellectual elite without a show of force by the aliens. Klaatu concurs that may be the only option, and he ponders some epic violence to get the world's attention, like blowing up New York or "sinking the Rock of Gibralter." But the professor urges him to find a way to demonstrate his force without hurting people: "something dramatic, but not destructive; that's quite the problem." Their solution is to shut down all machines and electricity for half an hour, with the notable exceptions of hospitals, airplanes in flight, and the like, for safety's sake.

Both Bobby and Helen find out Mr. Carpenter's secret identity for themselves. Helen is curious about the mysterious Mr. Carpenter, and gets more suspicious when Bobby tells her that he even "helped Dr. Barnhardt with his arithmetic." When Klaatu decides he needs to return to his ship, he does not work very hard to cover his tracks. He borrows a flashlight from Bobby, who easily follows him to the park where the spaceship is located. Klaatu sends flashlight signals, activating Gort, who assaults the soldiers guarding the ship, a distraction that allows him to sneak up to and enter the spaceship. Bobby witnesses the whole thing, then runs home to tell his mother of his discovery. She dismisses his story as a "bad dream," upsetting the boy, who says, "I'd never call you a liar."

The day of Klaatu's demonstration, Carpenter shows up at Helen's work during lunch. His timing is such that the two of them are alone together in an elevator when his demonstration stops all electricity, allowing him to begin his confession in the darkness and shadows. Helen's suspicions are confirmed. Only she, not the audience, hears Klaatu's full message. However, the global impact of the event is emphasized, with shots from around the world showing bewilderment and fear. Professor Barnhardt asks his secretary Hilda whether the demonstration "frightened" her or made her feel "insecure," and he is glad she says yes.

While Helen is learning the truth of Carpenter's identity and mission, Tom is at a jeweler's, having diamonds that he found in Carpenter's room appraised, and he is told they are not from Earth. In a biblical reading, Tom would be Judas. At this point Helen believes Tom would never reveal Klaatu's secret without conferring with her first. She is wrong. The truth of Klaatu's passing identity is not safe in Tom's hands. He is a completely untrustworthy, unsympathetic character who threatens to alert the Pentagon that Mr. Carpenter is the alien. Although Helen tries to convince him that it is in the interest of the whole world not to tell, he selfishly wants the glory of Klaatu's capture.

Helen takes a cab back to the boarding house to get Carpenter, and they leave together. The military locates them and targets their cab. They do not make it back to the spaceship. Helen, who has fallen for Klaatu's charms, unsuccessfully tries to protect him. He is dramatically gunned down in the street while fleeing from the cab. Just before he dies, he whispers magic words to Helen that will prevent Gort from destroying the planet. Helen slips away to deliver the message. Gort awakens and attacks the guards, but as he turns to assault Helen, she utters, "Klaatu Barada Nikto." Instead of killing her, he takes her into the spaceship. Gort also recovers Klaatu's body, and places it inside the spaceship, where he is resurrected. In the climactic ending, the resurrected Klaatu, back in his glittering silver suit, addresses the gathered scientists and leaders gathered from around the world, giving a long final speech before he departs from Earth. He tells the diverse crowd that accepting the alien way "does not mean giving up any freedom, except the freedom to act irresponsibly," He continues:

Your ancestors knew this when they made laws to govern themselves and hired policemen to enforce them. We of the other planets have long accepted this principle, we have an organization for the mutual protection of all planets and for the complete elimination of aggression ... I came here to give you these facts, it is no concern of ours how you run your own planet, but if you threaten to extend your violence, this earth of yours will be reduced to a burned out cinder. Your choice is simple—join us and live in peace, or pursue your present course and face obliteration. We shall be waiting for your answer. The decision rests with you.

The film has often been read as a metaphor about fears and anxieties of atomic energy and Eisenhower's policy of MAD (mutually assured destruction) as a deterrence to war, but it can also be read as a critique of the American military and the government. The ambiguity of the film's message led to debates about whether the film carried a liberal or conservative message. But at its heart, *The Day the Earth Stood Still* sympathetically portrays aliens as both good and morally superior. The biblical metaphors are explicit.[25] Not only does Klaatu assume the name of Carpenter, but like Jesus, he is killed and resurrected. Before he dies, he imparts the secret of salvation, albeit to his version of Mary Magdalene. As Nora Sayre humorously pointed out, "The movie also asks how we would behave if Christ returned to Earth: the answer is that we would shoot him."[26]

Religious symbolism aside, Klaatu's representation as a passing figure is complex. First, Klaatu is not the typically threatening alien. He is intelligent and debonair, not sinister. The film suggests he merely wants knowledge about humans. This goes against more common passing narrative structures in its benign, almost humorous ruse of an intelligent alien life form that can pass undetected as a white male. Klaatu passes for his own protection, but also to protect people from themselves and their tendency to kill first and try to understand later. Passing is not threatening or tragic, merely a necessary strategy to let aliens observe Earth and its inhabitants. Here the alien is not an advance scout for an invasion, only a messenger and tourist. This is a "just visiting" level of passing. His masquerade has more in common with Gregory Peck's passing role in *Gentleman's Agreement* than it does with other examples of passing aliens in the 1950s. There is none of the wonderment or confused sense of identity experienced by the alien men in *I Married a Monster* or the threatening sense of invading doppelgangers apparent in

Invasion. Other aliens must hide their true selves or face destruction. But Klaatu does not need to pass; he chooses to. Tellingly, Klaatu's guise of white masculinity does not affect his sense of self. Klaatu is shot twice, killed, and resurrected, but he is never in crisis about who he is. This absence of anxiety about identity in *The Day the Earth Stood Still* is striking. And when his true identity is exposed, like Peck's passing journalist, his superiority revealed. Ironically, in this moment, when Klaatu stops passing, it becomes apparent that he is more of a real threat than other 1950s aliens.

Although clearly a metaphor for Cold War anxieties as well as a plug for the United Nations, the film's message is mixed. The authorities of the world need to cooperate for the common good, for all humanity, but the alternative is conformity to a galactic totalitarianism. Earth is perceived as a dangerous place because of its emotional irrationality. The peace and conformity that Klaatu demands is ironically not dissimilar to the pod-utopia of *Invasion of the Body Snatchers.* While passion, sexuality and the powers of emotions were the keys to preserving humanity in *Invasion, Invaders,* and *I Married a Monster, The Day the Earth Stood Still* suggests instead that passion and irrationality will lead to man's downfall. The happy ending is conditional on the elimination of emotion and subjugation to a higher authority. People of Earth must rise above their own "petty squabbles" or be obliterated.

Science fiction films of the 1950s dealt with anxiety and fears. They were infused with political and psychoanalytic meaning, especially in films featuring aliens passing for human. Interestingly, the intent is far more important than actuality in terms of framing passing threats. Either way, external signifiers were repeatedly shown to be inadequate to identify aliens and danger. In all of the representations of passing in this genre, the visible signifiers at first falsely indicate the humanity of the alien invaders, until visible markers re-establish the binary logic of identity by distinguishing alien from human, us versus them. But in the case of several films, *Invasion* and *I Married a Monster* in particular, this attempt to dismantle the passing narrative is not very convincing. Despite narrative resolutions that exposed and defeated the aliens, these alien takeover films opened Pandora's box by exploiting anxieties about passing and identity that could not be contained again. Aliens passing as human revealed the interconnectedness of fears about racial passing, Communism, and subversive gender or sexual identities. In fact, aliens could stand in for the undetected "other" better than any other genre of the postwar era. Science fiction films blurred the lines between psychoanalytic demons and external and domestic subversions. Audiences flocked to see science fiction films that preyed on these contemporary fears. Moreover, the fearful specter of aliens, Communists, or the "other" infiltrating American communities could not be disentangled from fears that this had already happened, that the reality of America was far different from surface illusions, and that nobody was what they seemed to be.

CHAPTER SIX

"BOTH BODY AND MEANING CAN DO A CARTWHEEL"[1]

Postwar Hollywood Masculinities and Passing Anxieties

All border towns bring out the worst in a country.[2]
—Charlton Heston in *Touch of Evil* (1958)

In the 1949 film *I Was a Male War Bride*, Cary Grant quips, "I'll have to sit here wondering what sex I am," poking fun at a postwar crisis about masculinity.[3] Passing anxieties were no longer simply about race or subversion but included gender as well. Far from being an era of stable and secure gender categories, the culture was rife with stories about an "epidemic" of gender ambiguity marked by masculine women and feminine men, and children so confused they did not know the difference.[4] *Life* magazine warned: "Spottily and sporadically, but increasingly, the sexes in this country are losing their identities . . . They are suffering from what psychiatrists call sexual ambiguity."[5] The timing of films that addressed anxieties about gender coincided with cultural fears about authenticity and identity. White masculinity in particular became a terrain fraught with anxiety.

The psychoanalytic turn in Hollywood, the dominance of Method acting, the objectification and eroticization of male bodies, and questions about the nature of identity framed evolving representations of masculinity. These images uncoupled the stable categories of gender and sexuality, opening the door to more nuanced and anxiety-ridden representations of masculinity. By analyzing the rise and fall of a new masculinity, epitomized by the "sigh guys" and "masculinity in crisis" films, it is possible to understand how the crisis developed and was represented in the culture.

Films and popular journals from the long 1950s reflected a cultural obsession with a new crisis in masculinity. *Look* magazine published a series of articles entitled "The Decline of the American Male," which later became a book in 1958.[6] This anxiety was linked to changing understanding about the nature of identity, aided and abetted by scientific studies like Kinsey's 1948 report on male sexuality, which redrew the boundaries of what constituted "normal" male sexuality, thus further aggravating fears about manhood and masculinity. In response, male roles and idols were transformed. Major films offered vivid representations of the perceived cultural emasculation of men. In the opening sequence of Billy Wilder's 1945 film *The Lost Weekend*, the leading man declares: "Sure, take a nice job, public accountant, real estate salesman—I haven't the guts—most men lead lives of quiet desperation—I can't take quiet desperation."[7] The statement foreshadowed the pervasive theme of masculine anxiety that came to dominate postwar cinema.

This crisis of masculinity appeared in westerns, melodramas, war films and science fiction. Early representations, as in films about racial passing, portrayed this crisis in a sympathetic and heroic manner. This changed in later films as ambiguity about masculinity became increasingly a symbol of a pathologically disturbed character. The strong reaction against ambiguous representations of gender matched rejections of racial ambiguity. By 1960, sympathetic representations of ambiguous masculinity disappeared. Earlier sympathetic representations include *From Here to Eternity*, *Rebel without a Cause*, *The Man in the Gray Flannel Suit*, *Tea and Sympathy*, and *The Incredible Shrinking Man*, while later pathological representations include *Vertigo*, *Psycho*, and *Suddenly, Last Summer*.

The "crisis in masculinity" films typically featured new male stars like Marlon Brando, John Kerr, Montgomery Clift, and James Dean. Brando starred in many of these films, including *The Men* (1950), *A Streetcar Named Desire* (1951), *On the Waterfront* (1954), and *The Young Lions* (1958). Montgomery Clift starred in *Red River* (1948), *A Place in the Sun* (1951) *From Here to Eternity* (1953), and *Suddenly, Last Summer* (1959). John Kerr starred in *Tea and Sympathy* (1956) and *South Pacific* (1958). Anthony Perkins starred in *Friendly Persuasion* (1956), *Fear Strikes Out* (1957), *The Lonely Man* (1957), *On the Beach* (1959), and *Psycho* (1960). Paul Newman starred in *Cat on a Hot Tin Roof* (1955) and *The Long Hot Summer* (1958). And James Dean, the quintessential image of teen male angst in *Rebel without a Cause* (1955), where he symbolically curled up in the fetal position, also starred in *East of Eden* (1955) and *Giant* (1956). Even pillars of masculinity like Gregory Peck had postwar roles that reflected this crisis of masculinity in films like *Twelve O'Clock High* (1949) and *The Man in the Gray Flannel Suit* (1956). Other established, older male stars were also subjected to less secure masculine screen personas—like Gary Cooper in *High Noon* (1952), Humphrey Bogart in *The Caine Mutiny* (1954), and James Stewart in *Vertigo* (1958).

Hollywood and the star industry changed dramatically after World War II. The rise of psychoanalytic discourse was reflected in changes to the image and status of prewar stars. As cinematic styles and topics became more gritty and realistic, the character of matinee heroes underwent corresponding changes. Writing in 1959, Robert Brustein argued that this "realistic hero" is "victimized by the confining world in which he lives . . . trapped not only in the interior of his world but in the interior of his soul. Rather than holding the world at bay with a couple of loaded pistols, he is himself held at bay by the power of his neurosis."[8] The mythic and romantic leading men of the 1920s and 1930s became the angst-ridden, flawed actors of the 1950s. In 1950, Billy Wilder's *Sunset Boulevard* featured Hollywood writer Joe Gillis (William Holden) astutely if posthumously observing that "psychopaths sell like hotcakes." The hero became the neurotic and victimized anti-hero.

Leading men who dominated the star system in the 1930s underwent dramatic image shifts. Male stars with previously stable masculine identities—like Humphrey Bogart, John Wayne, or Jimmy Stewart—had their screen images twisted, warped and pathologized. John Wayne's role in *The Searchers* (1956) was described as "a long complicated story, spread over eight or nine years. Moreover its hero, Ethan Edwards, is an unmistakable neurotic, devoured by an irrational hatred of Indians and half-breeds, shadowed by some mysterious crime."[9] Ironically, John Wayne despaired about these roles; "Ten or fifteen years ago audiences went to pictures to see men behaving like men . . . Today there are too many neurotic roles."[10] A 1955 magazine article about Burt Lancaster described the dramatic shift in masculinity:

> Here is the main difference between Lancaster and [Douglas] Fairbanks. In his tales of resources and daring, Fairbanks fulfilled himself. He belonged to an old-fashioned, more ordered world, happily pre-Freudian, in which pride in the good deed done was sufficient and the imprisoned maiden was helpless and docile, shyly accepting at last the protective gentlemanly arms of her hero. The Fairbanks outlook was practical and unquestioningly self-reliant, temptation did not exist for him, sex was never a compulsive desire but something clean and unostentatious to be expressed in the tranquil symbols of roses, pearls and moonlight. Lancaster carries with him the problems of most modern heroes. His vital and sensuous pleasure in physical sensation set him apart, but its extremes—the excess of violence, the intensified sex-warfare—betray pressures of the age of anxiety.[11]

"Neurotic" characters were so dominant that film critic Walter Lassally suggested that filmmakers deemed them necessary to appeal to modern cynical audiences: "It is the atmosphere of contemporary America—impatient and cynical, with overtones of hysteria."[12] Citing films like *East of Eden* and *Johnny Guitar*, which he described as a "post-Freudian western," Lassally argued that postwar films "bring to mind the popular radio phrase, 'You silly twisted boy,' ... manifesting itself alike in neurotic characterization and performances or a neurotic striving for effect on the part of the director."[13] The "language of the couch" had altered Hollywood's representation of gender.

Postwar images of masculinity in film were full of contradictions about masculine identity. Film provided eroticized, hypermasculine male bodies— the "age of chests"—while focusing on indicators of the internal psychological breakdown of secure masculine identities—feminized men who cried. These simultaneous representations, while contradictory, were connected. A shift occurred that blurred gender lines. Men "were becoming more like women. They were becoming 'feminized.' When they put down the gun, they put on the apron."[14]

While the screen images of older male stars like John Wayne, Jimmy Stewart, or Humphrey Bogart were twisted and pathologized, young leading stars like Marlon Brando and James Dean came pre-packaged with fractured masculinity. Their star personas off-screen reflected their characters on-screen, exuding conflicted ideas about gender and sexuality. Collectively labeled the "sigh guys" by film magazines, they were clear symbols of the ambiguous nature of postwar masculinity.[15] Together with Dean and Brando, young male stars like Rock Hudson, Montgomery Clift, Tab Hunter, Anthony Perkins, and Sal Mineo epitomized this new ideal. They were masculine yet emotional, and all were in therapy. The characters they played were emotional, passive, victimized, and even masochistic, and they were in opposition to the male authority figures usually embodied by older actors. In 1957, journalist Sidney Skolsky wrote that the "current movie heroes are boys trying to do a man's work."[16]

In their early films, these sigh guys were cast as a new kind of "hero": sensitive men, often outsiders, who take on feminine characteristics, including being objectified and victimized. Writing in 1956, filmmaker Tony Richardson noted this shift, arguing that the early 1950s saw "the emergence of a new hero—the rebel, the outsider, the protester. Whatever his surface may be, belligerent, neurotic, self-pitying, or frustrated, our hero is always deeply malcontent with the set-up as he sees it." However, he is quick to point out that of the many "disguises" of this new hero, "none has been more emulated than the version Brando and Dean have presented in American film . . . They touch the fear, the loneliness, the pallid sexual ambiguity, the vague religious yearnings of their admirers."[17]

Marlon Brando was a monumental figure in postwar Hollywood, esteemed and imitated for his acting style and his looks. He became a physical symbol of the ideals of the Method. He was explicitly acknowledged as the most important influence on other icons of new masculinity like James Dean, Montgomery Clift, and Paul Newman. Method acting was itself part of the psychoanalytic turn and the cultural search for desired authenticity at any cost.[18] Superficial performances were abandoned. "Becoming the role" was the mantra. Method actors like Brando wanted to experience their characters, not just play them. For his role a paraplegic veteran in *The Men* (1950), Brando passed as a patient at a military hospital.[19] Throughout the 1950s, Brando epitomized the versatility of the masculine image on the screen, from the bad boy biker drag in *The Wild One* (1954), to an emasculated Asian man in *The Teahouse of the August Moon* (1957), and a Southern officer in *Sayonara* (1957).

Appropriately, critics were often unwilling to separate the original posterboy of the Method from his on-screen roles. A 1954 *New York Times* article by Cecelia Ager, entitled "Brando in Search of Himself," observed: "A complicated Joe is Marlon. In all the roles he plays he is a different man. And to all who know him, likewise."[20] Brando himself suggested that his notorious public image was a "mask" he wore to protect himself, a mask that admittedly echoed his own performance as Stanley Kowalski in *Streetcar Named Desire*. The article was accompanied by a series of Brando film portraits, each showing a different identity and role, including Brando as Johnny in *The Wild Horse* (aka *The Wild One*), as Stanley Kowalski in *Streetcar Named Desire*, as Zapata in *Viva Zapata!*, as a paraplegic in *The Men*, as Mark Anthony in *Julius Caesar*, and as Napoleon in *Desiree*.

Crucially, articles like this framed Brando's many characterizations not as performances, but as a conduit for Brando to find "himself." Acting was no longer simply performance; it was therapy for the actor, and by extension, for the nation. It is ironic that the stars most associated with the "authentic" acting techniques of the Method, were themselves unable or unwilling to expose their "authentic" selves to the public, preferring instead the nonconformist masquerades of the actor.

Brando's changing representations symbolized a shift in the willingness of filmmakers to objectify the male body. His body was filmed like those of women. He filled the screen, objectified and eroticized. He flashed his chest in virtually all of his fifties roles, including *Streetcar Named Desire* and *Viva Zapata!* The image of him in his torn, wet t-shirt in *Streetcar* became an iconic representation of the period. Importantly, Brando's body made him the site of erotic gaze, both masculine and feminine. Even the censored version of the film, which edited out Stella's "excitement" at the sight of Brando, still made it explicitly clear why Stella stayed with Stanley. This focus on the male body was a radical change from filmic representations of gender and sexuality in the 1940s.

The focus on his body on screen was matched by the objectification of his star persona. Brando was featured in both gossip and entertainment magazines. Fan magazines wrote about his bad behavior, his disdain for a manicured masculinity, his unconventional love life, and his interracial affairs.[21] Headline gossip stories discussed his psychological problems or his inability to hold down a steady relationship with one woman. He was described as a "walking hormonal factory packed with animal magnetism" and as "a magnificent five-foot, nine-inch male animal with a brawler's torso and arms rippling with muscles. His sullen swagger, heavy lids and hooded eyes set in a strongly molded face, and his guttural speech mark him as the Stone Age type," then suggestively noting how "an admiring maiden sat by the hour watching Brando, his curly haired chest stripped, flex his muscles."[22]

These articles emphasized the difference between Brando's ripped t-shirt and jeans and the decade's uniform of hegemonic masculinity, the gray flannel suit. The primitive, untamed behavior and attire of stars like Brando were equated with a distilled and "authentic" form of masculinity. The ability to don or discard the rebel look highlighted the masculine body as the site of gender performance. Brando epitomized this with his bisexual appeal and his personification of masculinity through the Method ideal, combined with his contradictory insistence that the swaggering masculinity associated with him after *Streetcar* was itself another form of masquerade.

While Brando's physique was celebrated, his psychology was pathologized. One such article noted that after "six years of psychoanalysis" that "although his love life had not changed much in pattern, his party manners had . . ." It went on to suggest: "In the old days Marlon would always scratch himself wherever he happened to itch, no matter where he was at the moment or with whom. Now he manages to restrain himself."[23] A less restrained exposé was "Marlon Brando's Big Secret!" which claimed that Brando was no longer able to perform in the bedroom. The article began, "Like to know why Marlon Brando ran to the psychiatrist? What the doc told him? . . . If so, read this story—but brace yourself for SHOCKING answers!" The article suggested "the Wild One of the cinema, to put it delicately, has become the Mild One of the real-life boudoir."[24] Brando himself acknowledged that acting afforded him "the luxury of spending thousands of dollars on psychoanalysts" and that he was troubled about his "authentic" identity.[25] Brando could pass as secure masculinity on the screen, but not off.

While Brando represented a troubled but virile masculinity, Montgomery Clift was an example of a new boyish masculinity. One of the founding members of the Actors Studio, the home of the Method, Clift starred in *The Search* (1948), *Red River* (1948), *A Place in the Sun* (1951), *From Here to Eternity* (1953), *Raintree County* (1957), and *Suddenly, Last Summer* (1959).[26] He displayed such intensity in his acting that he was described in trade journals as "becoming the role."[27] Like Brando, Clift was framed in early fan magazines as a young guy in torn jeans and t-shirt who was moody and introspective. Deborah Kerr, one of his co-stars, stated in a 1953 interview that "Clift's intensity, the source of his integrity as an actor, causes him to disappear into his roles so completely that ... You have the strangest feeling he is actually experiencing the scene."[28] At the height of his career he was respected and idealized for his portrayal of this new form of masculinity: the sensitive, sexually ambiguous "sigh guy."

In 1953, Clift starred in *From Here to Eternity*. The film reinvented the war movie and provided a representational blueprint of the new masculinity. Clift plays antihero Private Robert E. Lee Prewitt, a new type of American hero, defined by alienation and sensitive masculinity rather than macho confidence and brute strength. But he is not alone: all the sympathetic male characters in this film exhibit degrees of an independence-at-all-costs mentality that borders on masochism. And they all pay for it. These characters are threatened and beaten in attempts to make them submit to the system. Frank Sinatra's portrayal of Private Angelo Maggio was especially masochistic: a man determined to challenge the warden of the stockade, who dies rather than give Sergeant James R. ("Fatso") Judson (Ernest Borgnine) the satisfaction of breaking him. Prewitt also dies trying to return to his unit as Pearl Harbor is attacked (and he is symbolically killed by "friendly fire").[29] Viewed against the sensitivity and alienated masculinity of Prewitt and Maggio, Fatso is a vision of uncontrolled sadism, a type of masculinity nourished by institutions like the American military. This role was similar to Hume Cronyn's fascist warden in the prison film *Brute Force* (1947). Hollywood suggested that men who thrived on the abuse of institutional power were themselves inescapably psychotic. Representations of tough guys as psychopaths played in opposition to the more sensitive and nurturing masculinity exhibited by the new heroes of the 1950s.

Like Clift, fellow "sigh-guys" James Dean and Sal Mineo were representative of the new sensitive masculinity and ambiguous sexuality in *Rebel without a Cause* (Warner Bros., 1955). James Dean starred in only three Hollywood films (two of them released after his death). Nonetheless, his star persona and the discourse surrounding his life and death are inescapably linked to representations of youth and masculinity in the fifties. Sam Astrachan wrote about Dean and Brando for the *New Republic*, calling them "The New Lost Generation." Referring to the iconic status of Dean, Astrachan commented: "In each of the Dean roles, the distinguishing elements are the absence of his knowing who he is, and what is right and wrong. Dean is always mixed-up and it is this that has made him so susceptible to teen-age adulation . . . In James Dean, his movie roles, his life and death, there is a general lack of identity."[30]

Elia Kazan, who directed James Dean in *East of Eden*, was less than kind in his evaluation of Dean's acting abilities and character: "He was never more than a limited actor, and he was a highly neurotic young man—obviously sick, and he got more so . . . most of all I had the impression of someone who was a cripple inside."[31] Another interview noted how Dean "feels that his continuing attempt to find out just where he belongs is the source of his strength as an actor."[32] The adjective most used to describe Dean was "lost." He was in constant anguish and confusion over his identity, as *Variety* pointed out: "His ability to get inside the skin of youthful pain, torment, and bewilderment is not often encountered."[33] Dean's star image was framed as an amalgamation of fellow actors Marlon Brando and Montgomery Clift, both of whom he copied and worshipped. Whether a sign of Dean's confusion over his identity or of his sense of humor, Dean signed letters "Love, Jim (Brando Clift) Dean."[34]

Rebel without a Cause, directed by Nicholas Ray, was released shortly after Dean's death in 1955. Based on case studies, the film highlighted the anxieties of the postwar American teenager. Ray consulted psychologists, juvenile police officers, and social workers to add to the films authentic portrayal of teenage angst and juvenile delinquency. Ray also hired Dr. Douglas M. Kelley, "the internationally known professor of criminology (U of C at Berkeley)," who was also the "chief psychiatrist at the Nuremberg Trials," to advise him on the psychiatric motivations of the characters in the film, thereby providing authenticity.[35]

But Ray was not the only person influenced by the language of the couch. Screenwriter Stewart Stern admitted that he was "hot" with therapy while writing the script.[36] He also mined his high school experiences and time spent in the military to help portray in the script the difficult decisions of trying to fit in and whether or not to befriend someone who wasn't "in." The army gave him insight about the masquerade of tough masculinity. This informed *Rebel*—"especially this whole question of the masks we feel we need to wear in front of others—and what *exactly* defines a 'man.' I wanted to say something about that in the script, and I thought that the Jim Stark-Plato relationship was striving for that."[37] Masquerades of masculinity and the need to define manliness are echoed throughout the film.

Reflecting psychoanalytic ideas, the film blames parents for the anxieties of the teenagers. A poster for the film asserted, "Maybe the police should have picked up the parents instead . . ." Other tag lines for the film included "Jim Stark—a kid in the year 1955—what makes him tick . . . like a bomb?" and "J.D. James Dean! Juvenile Delinquent! Just Dynamite!"[38] A reviewer noted Nicholas Ray's dramatizing of his own "Freudian contentions," especially in regard to the parental figures.[39] The parents in the film are all inadequate, yet the alienation and confused identities of their teenage children speak to greater issues than bad parental role models. Most of Dean's confused outbursts were unfocused: "If I had one day when I didn't have to be all confused and ashamed of everything—or I felt I belonged someplace." The film injected an obsessive focus about the anxiety of juvenile identity into family melodrama, making it a cornerstone of the therapeutic fifties.

Rebel centers on three troubled teenagers, all of whom come from dysfunctional homes. Plato (Sal Mineo) has parents who are wealthy but absent. Judy (Natalie Wood) has a father who is uncomfortable with her emerging sexuality and treats her with cold hostility. Jim (James Dean) has parents (Jim Backus and Ann Doran) who fail to perform appropriate parental and gender roles. His dad wears an apron and does not stand up to his domineering wife. In a press release, Jim Backus described his part: "I play a weak-kneed father, a man who is under the complete domination of his wife." The release described Dean's character as "a high school boy filled with confusion about his role in life. Because of his 'nowhere' father in the film, Dean does not know how to be a man. Because of his mother, he anticipates destruction in all women."[40] In an iconic scene, Jim screams, "You're tearing me apart!" to his parents. It was the scream of a generation, resonating with teenagers in the angst-ridden fifties.

Jim, Judy, and Plato all negotiate coming of age. In the absence of adult guidance and acceptance, the trio creates its own ideal family.[41] The triangulated subtext of Jim, Judy, and Plato, although readable as sexual in the final film, was carefully denied by the film producers.[42] Plato's adoration of Jim is telling when viewers see a picture of Alan Ladd hanging in Plato's locker. According to comments made by Warner Bros. executive Steve Trilling, the script originally had Jim kissing Plato in a "paternalistic" way, but instead in the final print Jim just stroked Plato's head.[43] The screen version made Plato's adoration of Jim clear but left ambiguity about Jim's adolescent sexuality intact. Ambiguous masculinity implicated sexuality as likewise unfixed.

Rebel stakes out the middle ground of desired masculinity. Judy's boyfriend Buzz Gunderson (Corey Allen), the leader of the gang of kids at the school, is contrasted with Plato, the sensitive outcast, but neither of them is allowed to survive; only Jim survives. Crucially, Jim Stark is located between the masculine extreme of the tough and aggressive Buzz (who dies in the chicken run) and the worship of Plato (who dies in a confrontation with the police). Like Dean himself, Jim is represented as being in touch with his feelings and in pain because of that. Judy reinforces the desirability of this ambiguous middle ground when she tells Jim that women want a man who is really strong, by which she says she meant being willing and able to stand by those, like Plato, on the outside of the norm, but also able to be gentle and sweet. In the end Jim's softer and fractured masculinity is the only one that survives and has a future.

Rebel without a Cause revealed the contradictions and complexities behind Hollywood's representation of gender. Stern admitted he "couldn't wait to blame the parents," condemning the gender ambiguity of Jim's parents as dangerously bad. Yet the product of that ambiguity was James Dean's alter ego Jim Stark, the most imitated and worshipped icon of teenage masculinity in the 1950s. To add to the conflation or confusion of the star with the role, there was the knowledge that Dean insisted the character's first name be the same as his.[44] Sal Mineo likewise admitted that Plato's crush on Jim was replicated by his crush on Dean.[45]

The heroic portrayal of Jim Stark's ambiguous, softer masculinity complicates the film's critique of the crisis generated by inadequate gender role models, which was echoed further by James Dean's own iconic persona. Dean was celebrated for his rebellious "teenager" image on the screen, but part of Dean's status reflected how perfectly his confused sexuality and ambiguous masculinity fit with postwar anxieties of identity: "None could claim, like James Dean in the fifties, to be speaking for and in the idiom of its own generation."[46] Dean's early tragic death solidified his status permanently as the sexually ambiguous young male icon of the 1950s.[47]

Following the release of *Rebel*, *Life* magazine turned to psychiatric experts to analyze the "rampant" postwar gender crisis: "One of the worst aspects of the general situation [of sexual ambiguity] . . . is that it tends to repeat itself in magnified form with each new generation. The masculinized mother and feminized father produce girls who are even more masculine, boys who are even more feminine."[48] However, if *Rebel* condemned Jim's father as being too effeminate, other films were critical of fathers who were too domineering and tough.

An overabundance of masculine qualities was seen as triggering neurotic behavior in children, as was the case in *Fear Strikes Out* (Paramount, 1957). Directed by Robert Mulligan, it was based on the "true" story of baseball player Jimmy Piersall (Anthony Perkins). Piersall battled mental illness to become a major league ballplayer. The cause of his nervous breakdown was his domineering father who was obsessed with perfection for his son. The film ends happily: psychological treatment allows Jimmy to overcome the fears instilled in him by his father and to play ball again for a professional team; he even gets the girl. In both *Fear Strikes Out* and *Rebel without a Cause*, the gendered ambiguity of the characters played by Dean and Perkins was sympathetically portrayed. Jim Stark and Jimmy Piersall were the heroes of these films, not fearful examples of disturbed masculinity. The cause of their identity crisis lay with their parents.

Stars like Montgomery Clift and James Dean became popular because their personas resonated with cultural anxieties about the inherent instability of gender identities. They were anxiety-ridden icons of an insecure age: "Dean was the dead-end kid of the therapeutic fifties, the ideal hero, the perfect patient. As with Perkins, trying to be tough drove him crazy. If the teenager in *Werewolf* was born to be bad, Dean was born to the couch, a sick boy, not an evil one."[49] Anxiety-ridden young stars with their trips to the psychiatrist's office, their neuroses, and their wild, uncontrolled behavior and unconventional sexual liaisons, were perfectly suited to a cultural climate marked by crisis. New young male stars who were dubbed the "bad boys" of Hollywood appeared in the papers as much for the dramas of their personal lives and their brushes with the law as for their characterizations in films. Their escapades fed their "star personas" off the screen, while on the screen they redefined representations of masculinity and complicated gender.

The objectified, troubled male stars like Dean and Brando placed fractured masculinities on display. Deep-seated anxieties about authentic identities operated in juxtaposition to visible images of masculine chests that essentialized male bodies. Male bodies asserted a stable masculinity that their identities lacked. The physicality of both male and female bodies became paramount: "the fifties are marked by the emergence of sexual extremes–the ultrafeminine Monroes and Mansfields with large breasts and tiny waists, and the super-masculine Lancasters and Mitchums with their large shoulders and narrow hips."[50]

This was the "age of the chest," a site of exaggerated gender and eroticism for both men and women.[51] The physiques of leading men were objectified, eroticized, and celebrated. Male stars wore ripped t-shirts revealing shaved masculine chests, while women sported full-figured torpedo bras. William Holden went shirtless in *Picnic*. Burt Lancaster's physique was a crucial part of his role in *The Rose Tattoo*. Yul Brynner and Charlton Heston exposed muscular bodies in *The Ten Commandments*. Fan magazines, with headlines like "Hollywood's Muscle Men and Pin-Up Pretties," hinted that young stars like Rock Hudson, Burt Lancaster, and Kirk Douglas were cast as much for their muscular torsos as for their acting talent.[52] Kirk Douglas admitted he had to show off his torso to get the part in *Champion*. He behaved, he said, just like the "starlets do. I took off my jacket and shirt, bared my chest and flexed my muscles."[53] A 1954 *Life* magazine article suggested it was hard to tell whether Rock Hudson's fan appeal "lies primarily with his 'basic honesty' or with his bare chest."[54] The cheesecake of the 1940s became the beefcake of the 1950s.

Anxieties evoked by invisible social categories in the 1950s led to a process of physical overcompensation. The more invisible the category of identity (gender, sexuality, religion, or race), the more intense the cultural desire to mark the body.[55] Gender identity was proscribed by clothes and body types that unconvincingly tried to make irrefutable the connection between sex and gender. Stabilizing gender roles through clothing suggested gender anxiety, not security. Fashion trends emphasized and caricatured gender, with cinched waist, flared skirts, and torpedo bras for women, and gray suits or rebellious t-shirts, and leather jackets for men.[56] Ironically, the use of fashion to mark gender highlighted how gender and sexuality were manufactured.

These manufactured trends in clothing were mirrored in corporate culture. The gray flannel suit became another form of drag. While it was a symbol of hegemonic corporate masculinity, it was also the ultimate masquerade of masculinity. The reliance of highly gendered physical codes and fashion made it easy for people to pass, especially in drag, increasing the cultural disconnect between identity and external representation. The conformist suit of the corporate world disrupted the norms it set out to regulate. Clothes making the man became a truism. Image-based conformity increased the possibility of transgression. Anyone could don the suit and perform white middle-class masculinity.

Darryl Zanuck's *The Man in the Gray Flannel Suit* (20th Century-Fox, 1956) symbolized the emptiness and problematic masculinity of the faceless postwar businessman.[57] Nunnally Johnson adapted the Sloan Wilson novel and directed the film. It starred Gregory Peck as Tom Rath, with Jennifer Jones as his wife, Betsy. A box office success, it was the quintessential corporate-culture film. In the film, everyman Rath returns home from war and becomes a Madison Avenue executive. Wilson's confused postwar "hero" narrates:

> I really don't know what I was looking for when I got back from the war, but it seemed as though all I could see was a lot of bright young men in gray flannel suits rushing around New York in a frantic parade to nowhere. They seemed to me to be pursuing neither ideals nor happiness—they were pursuing a routine. For a while I thought I was on the side lines watching the parade, and it was quite a shock to glance down and see that I too was wearing a gray flannel suit.[58]

The overarching theme of the film is trying to balance getting ahead with the competing demands of family life. The film suggests that the pressure to conform crippled rather than defined a man's identity. Rath negotiates an increasingly fractured identity as a veteran, businessman, husband, and a father.

In reviews of the film, movie magazines presented the "Man in the Gray Flannel Suit" as the hegemonic symbol of masculinity in the 1950s, noting how this image of masculinity was ironically defined by its lack of individuality.[59] The suit, *Life* magazine suggested, was such a good disguise that Gregory Peck passed unnoticed as a commuter while researching his role for the film: "So well camouflaged was Peck by his protective gray coloration that few of the people he was studying guessed they were brushing elbows with a celebrity."[60] *The Man in the Gray Flannel Suit* was the perfect symbol of the costs of maintaining the performance of masculinity, and it echoed anxieties about the pressures and lack of authenticity in men's lives.

Similarly, in 1956 Nicholas Ray directed *Bigger than Life*; a film explicitly tying the postwar crisis about masculinity to a conformist culture awash in psychoanalytic jargon and miracle drugs. James Mason produced and starred in the film as Ed Avery, a schoolteacher attired in gray suits, whose masculine guise is crumbling. Unbeknownst to his wife, he has to moonlight as a taxi driver to support his middle class fantasy. Avery is a man crippled by severe pain and diagnosed as terminal, but a doctor offers him an experimental treatment of the hormone cortisone. This miracle drug saves his life but turns him into an increasingly erratic and violent symbol of fractured masculinity as the excess hormone makes him insane. The central male character devolves, becoming addicted and out of control. Ed goes from a sympathetic, average schoolteacher, an anxiety-ridden but nice guy, to a brutish, hormonal masculine caricature. Mason performed crippled masculinity very well in *Island in the Sun, A Star Is Born*, and *Bigger than Life*.

While dramatic films like *The Man in the Gray Flannel Suit* and *Bigger than Life* made visible the anxiety and performance of masculinity, science fiction films like *The Incredible Shrinking Man* (1957) and *Attack of the 50 Foot Woman* (1958) went further, arguing that masculinity itself was in jeopardy.[61] Directed by Jack Arnold and written by Richard Alan Simmons and Richard Matheson, *The Incredible Shrinking Man* starred Grant Williams as Scott Carey, and Randy Stuart as Louise Carey, featuring the tag lines "Hour by hour he gets smaller-and-smaller!" / "Moment by moment the terror mounts!" Carey is exposed to a strange mist that causes him to become smaller and smaller. No longer metaphoric, the world becomes a physically terrifying place for a little man. In contrast, Nancy Archer (Allison Hayes) grew in *Attack of the 50 Foot Woman* (1958): "See a female Colossus ... her mountainous torso, skyscraper limbs, giant desires!" Shrinking men and giant women captured the fear that categories of sex and gender were out of control.

The meaning of gender and sexuality was changing as films tried to push the boundaries of representation. Attempts at depicting deviant sexualities were hampered by film regulations aimed at denying explicit representations or even explicit references to any sexuality. Due in part to the restrictions of the Production Code, sexuality was often represented by gender performance. Inferences about sexuality were projected, not made explicit. The silence about sexuality in films granted interpretive freedom to spectators who were accustomed to reading what was prohibited by the Code. Both screenwriters and audiences were adept at interpreting the codes and sexual meanings in film narratives.

Rebel without a Cause subtly touched upon issues of sexuality in connection with a crisis about masculinity, but that was not its main theme. It was left to other Hollywood films to go beyond subtext and explicitly represent sexualities deemed deviant by the Production Code. Groundbreaking and destabilizing gender representations, varying from sensitive men and aggressively masculine women to depictions of homosexuality, were represented in postwar films. Writers like Tennessee Williams, who explored the links between gender, sexuality, and psychology in his literary works, provided source material for Hollywood films. Many of Williams's "Freudian fables of repression" were adapted to the screen in the 1950s, including *A Streetcar Named Desire* (1951), *Cat on a Hot Tin Roof* (1958), and *Suddenly, Last Summer* (1959).[62] Williams's nuanced use of psychology allowed taboo topics of sexuality to be addressed in Hollywood films, including female promiscuity, homosexuality, and incest. These films made explicit the fears about the boundaries of gender and sexuality.

It is ironic that an industry built on the performance of idealized gender and heterosexual roles helped to subvert the imagined stable boundaries of gender and sexuality. Conflicts of interest emerged between filmmakers, who wanted to push boundaries, and the PCA and studio executives, who wanted to censor materials. Any films featuring taboo topics were sure to be discussed in the media, making it questionable whether omissions or censoring really worked. Movies are not produced and consumed in a vacuum. Movie productions led to a resurgence of interest in the plays or books they were based on, ensuring recognition of what changes were made and why. And if anyone in the audience failed to understand, there were plenty of film critics who acted to remind them.

Explicit discussions in movie magazines and the popular press insured that even when topics were not directly acknowledged, audiences knew what was being discussed. Films like *Rope* (1948), *Young Man with a Horn* (1950), *Cat on a Hot Tin Roof* (1955), *Suddenly, Last Summer* (1959), and *Tea and Sympathy* (1956) addressed issues of homosexuality.[63] These films show the failure of censors to erase representations of deviant sexualities. Although these films did erase direct references to sexuality to pass the Production Code, the behaviors and psychologies were named in film reviews, assuring that audiences understood the implied behaviors. Critics, reviewers and audiences filled in the blanks left by filmmakers.[64]

As a case in point, magazine reviews of *Cat on a Hot Tin Roof* (1958) made explicit the homosexual relationship between Brick (Paul Newman) and his buddy that the studio and PCA had tried hard to eliminate. This film, directed by Richard Brooks, was adapted from a Tennessee Williams play for MGM. In a Production Code memo regarding *Cat on a Hot Tin Roof*, the attempt to erase deviant sexualities is clear: "This outline would stress the father-son relationship as the central theme. It would omit any inference of homosexuality. The son's problem would be that he had idealized the older football player, and looked up to him as a father—and this has always rankled with the father."[65] This was done to the satisfaction of the PCA, but somehow did not affect how audiences read the film when it was released. A *Reporter* review plainly referred to the "inference of homosexuality" that the PCA had excised: "The great menace to all these plotters [to get Big Daddy's favor] is the younger son, Brick, a retarded juvenile, an alcoholic, and an apparent homosexual. Despite all this he is Big Daddy's favorite and, perversely, he cares nothing for the old man's money but takes a masochistic delight in heading for skid row."[66] Another reviewer stated: "Brick Pollit, her husband, lackadaisically played throughout the film by Paul Newman, drinks and avoids his wife because he suffers a guilt complex concerning his feeling that he 'let down' a former school chum in the latter's hour of emotional need. Even without specifics, the homosexual nature of the attraction between the two boys is not left in doubt for those familiar with the Williams play."[67] If Maggie (Elizabeth Taylor) was framed as "the troubled, childless, unsatisfied wife of the drunken scion of a rich Southern planter," the film left no question as to why she was unsatisfied.

Themes of fractured masculinity, confused sexuality, and performance were echoed in other Hollywood films. Alfred Hitchcock reveled in the art of playing with the boundaries of identity. In many respects he was "the perfect director for the anxiety-ridden long 1950s."[68] His lifelong interest in Freudian psychology informed both how he selected stories and how they were treated in film. From *Rope* (Warner Bros., 1948) to *Psycho* (Paramount, 1960), his films showed an explicit fascination with voyeurism, making the audience complicit, and he subverted notions of normalcy, finding horror in the small town and the family. Hitchcock used Hollywood stars from the previous era, twisting and distorting their images on-screen and making audiences uncomfortably complicit, creating suspense in the process.

Rope is an excellent example because of its explicit content and its interpretation of postwar culture. At its center, this film portrayed a controversial story about a murder with both homosexual and Jewish overtones that bore similarities to the famous Loeb-Leopold case.[69] Such overtones were explicitly denied by Jack Warner in a letter to Mr. Barney Balaban from Paramount Pictures in New York. Balaban had written Warner to warn of the controversies which would be raised by the film. Because he believed the film's story was based on the "real" murder case involving "Jewish boys," Balaban worried that it "could not help but have an adverse influence on the standing of our Jewish people in the nation." Jack Warner responded to Balaban to calm his fears, stating in a letter dated March 5th, 1948: "I have talked to Alfred Hitchcock, the Producer and Director of this picture and he emphatically told me that it has nothing to do with the Loeb-Leopold case. Furthermore, the action takes place in New York and no Jewish characters are portrayed in the picture." He continued: "Very confidentially, Barney, had you or someone else called my attention to the resemblance between the case and this picture before the picture was made, Warner Bros. would not have made any deal to release the picture."[70] Despite the denials of those involved, when it was released in 1948 most reviewers mentioned the Loeb-Leopold case within the first paragraph, although some sarcastically noted that "any resemblance to persons or events is purely coincidental."[71] Another writer quipped that the meal on the chest was definitely "non-Kosher."[72] The lack of explicitly Jewish characters and the "imagined" plot did not prevent many people from connecting the film to the well-known case. Nor was the film any more effective at erasing the homosexual overtones.

Arthur Laurents wrote the screenplay for *Rope*, which starred Farley Granger (Phillip) and John Dall (Brandon) as two rich young men who commit murder as an intellectual exercise. Interestingly, the characters paralleled hidden Communists: overly educated intellectuals who are vaguely Jewish and exhibit an effeminate masculinity with homosexual connotations. James Stewart starred as their former teacher, Rupert Cadell, who inspired them with his philosophic theories. Frank Capra argued that "when you're dealing in the world of ideas and you want your character to be on a higher intellectual plane . . . you turn to persons like Jimmy Stewart because he has the look of the intellectual about him."[73] Stewart was the embodiment of "all-American" righteous intellectuals who triumphed in films like *Mr. Smith Goes to Washington*. In *Rope*, Stewart was once again an intellectual. But here the integrity and charm of his character became a portrayal of disturbed masculinity.

The heterosexuality of Stewart's character and his adoring students was also questionable. In spite of PCA intents, advertisements for *Rope* suggested a sexual relationship between men: "Nothing ever held you like Alfred Hitchcock's 'Rope,'" but one poster had the smaller lines "In one man's hands . . . Rope is a deadly weapon . . . In one man's arms . . . LOVE is a shameful thing!" Another poster read: "Nothing ever held you like its SUSPENSE! Nothing ever held you like its FALSE LOVE!" The poster even had a quote by J. Edgar Hoover, exclaiming: "Never saw anything like its terrific suspense! It leaves you breathless!"[74] The film was accepted by some censors and banned by others.[75] The erasure of homosexuality was a questionable success, because reviewers commented on its elimination from the script. The film was the perfect example of how audiences interpreted films beyond the dictates of the code.

Although films like *Rope* raised questions about the meaning of masculinity and sexuality, no film tried harder to disconnect sexuality from signifiers of masculinity than *Tea and Sympathy* (MGM, 1956), directed by Vincente Minnelli. Based on Robert Anderson's Broadway play, the film asks, "What is manliness?"[76] Anderson tried to argue that the film "doesn't actually deal with homosexuality, but only with the impact the false charge has on the boy."[77] Nonetheless, the *Time* review indicated that although Hollywood had bought the rights to this play based on its popularity, it then sat on it for quite some time because of its subject matter.[78] When the film was finally made, any suggestions of homosexuality as the problem confronting young Tom were carefully censored, and certainly the movie did tone down the explicit references to homosexuality that were evident in the Broadway play, but the PCA and the studio denied the inference about sexuality to no avail. All the mainstream reviews and discussions of this film reinserted the question about sexuality as if it had been explicitly addressed in the film.

Tea and Sympathy focuses on a young man at a prep school, Tom Lee (John Kerr), who is accused of being a "sissy" and then has an affair with the headmaster's wife, Laura Reynolds (Deborah Kerr) to make him a man. Leif Erickson played the headmaster, Bill Reynolds, whose wife Laura provides the "tea and sympathy" to the boys at the school. All three leads originated the roles on Broadway. Pandro Berman, the film's producer, noted how the boy "is regarded by fellow students and the housemaster as an 'off-horse' because he doesn't flex his muscles . . . To them he is soft physically and becomes suspect. They conveniently pigeonhole their standards for manliness and anyone who doesn't conform is an odd ball."[79] Tom is a shy, quiet, and gentle young man who is interested in classical music and plays tennis, not football. He sews buttons on his own shirts, often likes to be solitary, and reads. He is even given the part of "Lady Teazle" in the school production of *The School for Scandal*. In short, Tom "does not conform to the clichés of adolescent masculine behavior . . . [and] from that evil gossip begins to grow."[80] These characteristics and activities earn him the nickname "Sister Boy" at the boarding school. As "Sister Boy," Tom is framed as a "sissy" and taunted by class-mates, who suspect him of being a homosexual. He begins to doubt his own masculine and therefore sexual identity. Confused, he says he wants to learn how to behave like a man.

John's roommate tries to defend Tom, teaching him how to walk "more manly" and explaining the "male facts of life." But these lessons do not resolve Tom's identity crisis. He even considers suicide after an attempt to seduce a woman dubbed the "campus chippy" (Norma Crane) ends in failure and ridicule. The film ends with his heterosexual manhood restored only after having sex with Laura. The headmaster's wife commits adultery, sacrificing her marriage in an effort to "save" Tom and "restore his soul by giving him her body."[81] Or, as another reviewer put it, Kerr's actions "furnish him with incontestable proof that his fears are groundless."[82] The film suggests that he will in fact finally be able to "walk like a man."

The adaptation of the play from Broadway to film involved a number of changes.[83] PCA dictates decried a high cost for adultery and a postscript was added, implying that the affair ruined Laura's life. In addition, there were specific changes designed to erase any suggestion that the headmaster and Tom might be homosexuals. For instance, in the film version, the sight of Tom "sitting on a beach with several faculty wives, sewing a button on a shirt" was the trigger for his nickname "Sister Boy" the *Time* magazine review noted that this was toned down from the original play, where Tom "was accused of lying naked on a beach with a schoolmaster who was generally suspected of homosexuality" and that only after this story went "the rounds" through the school did the other fellows start "calling him 'Sister Boy.'"[84] In the film version, gender performance was conflated with sexuality, an act that framed masculinity as something that could be taught and performed. Failure to perform appropriate masculinity was equated with homosexuality.

A key message was that masculinity had to be performed and monitored. It was not innate. Walking like a man made you a man. The flip side was that men who did not follow these normative performances risked censure and ridicule. Tom's anxieties and fears were about his sexual identity, and so was his cure. No matter how much Laura tried to stabilize Tom's sexuality, the film showed that heteronormative masculinity was a matter of masquerade and performance.

In the original play, the hypermasculinity of the brawny and athletic Headmaster Bill Reynolds (Leif Erickson) was coded as overcompensation for repressed homosexual desires: "Left out—at great cost to the dramatic motivation—is the schoolmaster's fear of his own latent homosexuality. We don't understand what motivates his hounding of the boy . . ."[85] *Variety* also commented on the change: "The housemaster part, played with muscle-flexing exhibitionism by Leif Erickson, has lost some of its meaning . . . In the original his efforts at being 'manly' and his hatred for Kerr carried the suggestion that, indeed, he was trying to escape some kind of effeminate quirk in his own makeup. This suggestion is diluted in the film."[86] Similarly, one reader commented, "Playgoers could not escape the latent homosexuality of Tom's housemaster, Bill Reynolds, and to a lesser degree of Tom's schoolmates. But this facet of the drama is lost to the moviegoer."[87] In both the play and the film, Laura challenged her husband, arguing that his idea of masculinity was too narrow and that perhaps his hostility toward Tom was reflective of something he "fears in himself."

Tom and the headmaster represent opposing views of masculinity. Tom was a "Sister Boy," while the headmaster is a "hearty extrovert whose biceps are bigger than his hatband."[88] Tom has many feminine characteristics. He is portrayed as passive, reflective, emotional, and vulnerable. The *Hollywood Reporter* noted: "John Kerr does a good job, guiding his character on the hairline between sensitivity and effeminacy."[89] In keeping with the spirit of the times, Tom's version of masculinity was the decidedly more sympathetic representation.

If the question of the film was "What is manliness?" the answer kept step with new conceptions of masculinity. The 1950s context of the sigh guys and gender ambiguity ensured that Tom Lee was the hero. Thomas Wood wrote, "This is the era of the off-horse, and the world has found its champion in the form of a fictitious, prep school boy named Tom Lee."[90] If Tom Lee was a poster-boy for the new man, then Laura was the film's most vocal champion of that form of masculinity. Echoing Judy's voiced ideal of masculinity in *Rebel*, Laura articulates the film's plea for the new masculinity: "Manliness is not all swagger and swearing and mountain climbing . . . Manliness is also tenderness and gentleness and consideration."

The celebration of a new masculinity represented by male icons like John Kerr, James Dean, Montgomery Clift, and Tony Perkins did not last. There was a backlash against the confusion and anxiety that such fluidity promoted. By the end of the 1950s, gender ambiguity became psychotic rather than sympathetic. Sexual fluidity and ambiguously feminized men "had to be repudiated."[91] In 1958, Jimmy Stewart's portrayal of masculinity in Alfred Hitchcock's *Vertigo* signaled a representational shift away from the heroic "feminized" masculinity towards a more unsympathetic framing of disturbed masculinity. Stewart starred as the disturbed policeman/detective John "Scottie" Ferguson, with Kim Novak in the dual role of Madeleine Elster/Judy Barton, and Barbara Bel Geddes as Scottie's longtime companion, Marjorie "Midge" Woods.[92]

Hitchcock took Jimmy Stewart's "nice guy" image and distorted it, making him a disturbingly obsessive character with debilitating psychiatric issues. Stewart's gentler masculinity, in which he projected an emotional openness and a sexual immaturity, becomes suggestively indicative of neurosis. In *Vertigo* Scottie Ferguson becomes a symbol of an impotent disturbed masculinity. The film opens with him running across rooftops in San Francisco. He suffers from acrophobia, and an untimely attack of vertigo means he cannot save a fellow officer. Because of this, he quits the police force and suffers a mental breakdown. He is hired by an old college classmate, Gavin Elster (Tom Helmore), to shadow his wife Madeleine because he fears she may be suicidal. The plot hinges on Ferguson's belief that Madeleine is obsessed with her great-grandmother Carlotta Valdez, who committed suicide at Madeleine's age of twenty-six. Madeleine is a typical icy Hitchcock blonde who seems no more real than the portrait of Carlotta that she habitually sits in front of at the Palace of the Legion of Honor. Yet this woman quickly becomes the focus of Ferguson's obsessive interest. In his role as detective, Scottie wanders around San Francisco, shadowing Madeleine and displaying an eerie capacity for voyeurism, a favorite obsession in Hitchcock films.

Throughout the film, Ferguson is framed by women: Midge, Madeleine, Judy, and Judy performing Madeleine. In many respects, Midge is the only stable character in the film, but she is on the periphery of the psychological dramas as both Ferguson's and Madeleine's identities slowly unravel. The very matter-of-fact Midge recognizes his growing fascination with Madeleine but does not try to remold herself. Her attempt at self-makeover is limited to painting a portrait of Carlotta with her own face, an attempt at humor that does not go over well with him. This suggests Midge is in love with him, even though she broke off their engagement.

Later in the film, Ferguson is unable to stop Madeleine's suicide at the San Juan Bautista tower because of his vertigo. Following her death, he has another breakdown and is placed in a mental hospital for his "morbid depression." As one reviewer put it, Stewart "goes off his rocker (Stewart acting insane is like Novak acting like being in love)."[93] At the hospital the almost catatonic Ferguson is unmoved by Midge's visits. When he is finally released from the mental hospital over a year later he develops a "morbid obsession" with Madeleine, seeing her likeness everywhere. Finally, he sees a brunette woman, Judy Barton, who has a "remarkably similar" face and questions her. A flashback sequence shows Judy's memory of the events. It is the only time that the film shifts from Stewart's perspective and revealing that Judy was hired by Gavin to act as Madeleine to conceal the murder of his wife.

There is a staggering multiplicity to the levels of masquerade: Kim Novak performing Judy, who had only been pretending to be Madeleine, who was in turn pretending to be possessed by Carlotta.[94]

When Ferguson realizes that Judy is Madeleine, he sadistically manipulates and transforms her into his Pygmalion fantasy of her earlier incarnation. He takes her to a fancy salon to buy an identical gray suit and the exact color and kind of shoes Madeleine wore. Finally he focuses on her hair, making her dye it the same color blonde. She is reluctant, but says "If I change the color of my hair, will you love me?" Ferguson tells her, "I need you to be Madeleine for a while, then we'll both be free." He takes Judy back to the Mission, the scene of the crime and confronts her about Gavin: "He made you over, just like I made you over—only better. Not only the clothes and the hair, but the looks and the manner and the words. Did he train you? Did he tell you exactly what to do? What to say?" In his anger, Ferguson reasserts his masculinity, curing his vertigo and dragging her up the tower. The appearance of a nun startles them, and Judy accidentally falls to her death. Judy's transformation back into Madeleine is complete. Throughout the film, the line between the real and fantasy is blurred.

In *Vertigo* the instability and anxiety about gender was reinforced by its insistence that feminine identity was inauthentic. Kim Novak's multiple feminine performances—symbolized physically by the shift from blonde to brunette and back again—shows the degree to which feminine gender performances are constructed. Films in general presented brunettes as more authentic than blondes. Novak was a reluctant star who was herself nothing more than a product of the studio's and the director's construction. James Harvey writes that "Even at the peak of her stardom most of Novak's publicity seemed to be about what a miracle had been worked *on* her, by Harry Cohn and his studio. *Time* magazine did a 1956 cover story about her, offering her the ambiguous accolade of being (as they claimed) the first 'truly manufac-tured' star."[95] Postwar fan magazines became increasingly explicit that femi-nine ideals embodied by stars like Novak were manufactured constructions, a shift reinforced by unmasking narratives in films like *Vertigo*.

The filmic transformation of Judy back into Madeleine suggests a misogy-nistic manipulation of the feminine image that lies at the heart of gender constructions. The film illustrates the dark side of Pygmalion fantasies, where the actress/woman lacks agency in her own construction. The artifice of Kim Novak's performance as Judy/Madeleine was in keeping with other hypercon-structed feminine performances of the fifties, except it went further in forcing an uncomfortable recognition that both Novak and her dual role were shaped by masculine authority: by Ferguson on the screen, and by Hitchcock off the screen. But at least on the screen, Ferguson's desire to manipulate and mold Judy into his ideal feminine construction is represented as disturbed. In the end, Stewart's "nice guy" persona unravels. Ferguson becomes unsympathetic through his cruelty to Judy, culminating in her death. By then, he is not just a broken man, but a murderous psychopath.

It is instructive to compare *Vertigo* with *Rebel without a Cause*. Both Scottie Ferguson (Stewart) and Jim Stark (Dean) are reluctant catalysts in the deaths of men who are their peers. In *Vertigo*, the officer dies because of Stewart's vertigo; in *Rebel*, Buzz dies in a contest of masculinity. Both films end with tragic death scenes. In *Vertigo*, Judy (who loves Ferguson) dies; in *Rebel*, Plato (who loves Jim) dies. Yet for all their parallels, what these films say about masculinity is decidedly different. *Rebel* ends tragically yet optimistically with the hope that Jim may be able to claim an in-between space of masculinity, tough and manly yet honest to his emotional center. Dean's portrayal became an iconic symbol for "his generation." So effective was the universal appeal of this theme that audiences overidentified with Dean. In contrast, Hitchcock made the character of Ferguson so disturbed that identification was difficult. Even if audiences sympathized with his manipulations or his obsessive love for a created feminine ideal over a real woman, it would be hard to identify with the character. The viewer's sympathy shifted away from Ferguson to Judy. By the film's end, he is a broken, neurotic man with little future who no longer speaks for anyone.

While early films like *From Here to Eternity* or *The Man in the Gray Flannel Suit* showed a crippled masculinity, they also revealed a shift in ideals about masculinity. Frank Sinatra and Montgomery Clift in *From Here to Eternity* displayed an almost masochistic willingness to fight, and indeed to die, for the right cause. They represented a new kind of anti-hero that was clearly differentiated from prewar and wartime representations of masculinity. The new masculinity was softer but more complex and more nuanced.

In these postwar films, the stability between masculinities and femininities blurred as Hollywood leading men became victimized, objectified, and emotionally unstable. James Dean and Montgomery Clift epitomized the gentler, confused masculinity in their iconic roles in such films as *Rebel without a Cause* and *From Here to Eternity*. These sympathetic representations of unstable and confused masculinity were short-lived. By the late fifties, men who did not know how to be men were at best pathetic and at worst psychotic. Films like *Vertigo* and *Psycho* suggested disturbed men who were personal failures. "Momism" had come a long way in a decade. While James

Dean's strong mother in *Rebel* made him confused and angst-ridden, Tony Perkin's mother in Hitchcock's *Psycho* (1960) made him a psychotic killer.[96]

The repudiation of ambiguous gender representations on the screen signaled postwar anxieties about identity that had consequences off the screen, especially for the male stars that had so epitomized those ideals. Because of his image-changing role in *Psycho* (1960), Tony Perkins went from being a rising star, able to get boyish leading man roles in films like *The Actress* (1953), *Friendly Persuasion* (1956), and *On the Beach* (1959), to being typecast as a caricatured symbol of psychotic gender identity. This sigh guy became indicative of disturbed masculinity. None of the other "sigh guys" fared much better.

There was an equally drastic devolution in the star persona of Montgomery Clift, who went from being a sensitive and charismatic "sigh guy" in the early postwar years to a feminized neurotic by the end of the 1950s.[97] He was the same actor with the same tendencies and characteristics, but shifting discourses meant that his antisocial behavior and sexual ambiguity became signs of a disturbed pathology. A car accident in 1957 only heightened his alienation, compounded by the fact that all the fan magazines and the scandal tabloids began to freely allude to his breakdowns, neuroses, bisexuality, and alcohol and drug addictions. One tabloid used the dramatic headline "Memo to: MONTY CLIFT, Subject: YOUR DEATH." The tabloid editors pleaded with the star: "Read the pattern of your life—and run, do not walk to the nearest analyst. You can reverse your path to self-destruction—but time is running short."[98]

New male icons like Clift and Brando were more explicitly objectified than earlier leading men, but they were also pathologized. Even the dead icon James Dean was not immune. One tabloid pointedly asked: "Was Jimmy Dean a Psycho?" The article negatively described the star as "withdrawn, friendless, suspicious, uncooperative, [and] rude," noting that "He betrayed a near psychopathic personality, with alternative fits of despondency and wild jubilation."[99] It concluded: "No doubt about it, Dean wasn't improving at the time his Porsche crumpled him in that last embrace. His popularity would soon skyrocket, but as a man he was beginning to fold."[100] The author hoped that teenagers would find a healthier Hollywood star to worship and emulate.

The postwar crop of male icons did not carry over well into the 1960s. By the end of the fifties these new masculine icons, represented by James Dean, Montgomery Clift, and Anthony Perkins, had either died or become representative of a twisted and disturbed masculinity that was no longer viewed sympathetically. Clift and Perkins never emerged from the psychological roles which had defined their earlier movie roles. If Brando had become a powerful symbol of objectified masculinity in the 1950s, by the end of the fifties, Clift and Perkins became symbols of pathologized masculinity.

By 1960 the "sigh guys" were passé, a lost masculine ideal; the new heroic masculinity was once again tough and stoic, as in the chest-baring epics of *Ben-Hur* (1959) and *Spartacus* (1960). However, a return to unambiguous gender representations allowed filmmakers the license to treat gender performance in a more playful way. Arguably no film better represents the sea change in representations of gender identities than Billy Wilder's *Some Like It Hot* (MGM, 1959). On the surface, this film was the most explicit instance of passing in films of the fifties, and yet it was the least connected to the crisis of identity that defined Hollywood's representations of gender and sexuality. Films like *From Here to Eternity, Rebel without a Cause, Tea and Sympathy*, and *Vertigo* were saturated with anxiety, both in the narratives and in how the film's stars were framed. In contrast, *Some Like It Hot* reveled in gender masquerade and passing in suggestively transgressive ways, devoid of such underlying anxieties on or off the screen. The difference in gendered representations and how its stars were represented marked more than just a genre difference between musical comedies and dramas; it marked a shift away from the postwar crisis about identity.

Some Like It Hot employed cross-dressing and gendered masquerades throughout the film. The story begins in 1929 with Joe (Tony Curtis) and Jerry (Jack Lemmon) working as musicians in Chicago speakeasies. They accidentally witness the St. Valentine's Day massacre, and to avoid being recognized and killed by the gangsters involved, they must hide out. To escape, they disguise themselves as women, Josephine and Daphne, respectively. To quote *Variety*, the story "revolves around the age-old theme of men masquerading as women."[101] Reviewers described them as "a couple of Charley's aunts."[102] In their new feminine guises Joe/Josephine and Jerry/Daphne join an all-girl band. Top-billed Marilyn Monroe plays Sugar Cane, one of the band's members, and she quickly becomes the main object of both Lemmon's and Curtis's affections.

The romantic antics in the film are predictably complicated. Joe/Josephine tries to romance Sugar, and in doing so enacts yet another identity, that of an impotent and wealthy playboy. Meanwhile Jerry, as Daphne, is "chased by a millionaire playboy determined to marry a blonde."[103] The rich playboy in question is Osgood Fielding III (Joe E. Brown), and he works hard to court Daphne/Jerry. In a scene where they tango together to the tune of "La

Cumparsita," Osgood has to tell him, "You're leading again." Jerry apologizes, and they continue to dance. Osgood is entranced by Daphne and is willing to negotiate the assumed gender roles. At the end of the film, Osgood even asks Daphne to marry him as they sail off into the sunset. When Daphne/Jerry reveals that he is a man, Osgood responds with the film's classic line, "Nobody's perfect." Comedy allows the film to suggest that stable categories of sexuality and gender are just not that important.

A crucial scene sets up the conflicted identity dynamics of gender passing. As the "all-girl" band heads to Florida on a train, Jerry watches the girls in their nightclothes. Joe advises him: "Steady, boy. Just keep telling yourself you're a girl." Jerry repeats over and over to the rhythm of the train: "I'm a girl. I'm a girl. I'm a girl..." Taking this mantra to heart, Lemmon as Daphne quickly embraces the femininity of the part, more so than Curtis. The press emphasized Lemmon's innate masculinity and his difficulty in correctly donning the wigs and flapper skirts to play the part. The *Los Angeles Mirror News*, with the headline "The Secrets of Acting Like a Lady," stated:

> It's hard enough for most youngsters to act like ladies ... but for Jack Lemmon it is understandably even harder. Lemmon isn't exactly a female impersonator. But a series of plot turns do result in his disguising himself as a girl ... Lemmon confesses his masquerade won't really fool anybody in the audience. His native masculinity assures that. But the disguise must be good enough to deceive the other characters in the movie. 'It's like a suspense story where the audience knows the killer, but the guys up on the screen don't,' he laughs ...[104]

Lemmon confessed that shaving his legs was not that difficult (and was necessary for authenticity); the "hardest" part of the masquerade was learning how to walk in high heels.

In the end, casting Lemmon and Curtis as cross-dressers was like Hollywood's practice of casting a white person in the role of blacks passing for whites. It was Hollywood studios hedging their bets. They wanted to suggest Lemmon's successful gender performance of femininity while maintaining that there is an innate masculinity to the actor and the character he plays. This emphasis on the stable masculinity and heterosexuality of the two male stars was a common theme in the media. One ad proclaimed: "She's Young ... She's Engaged ... She Uses After-Shave Lotion! She's Tony Curtis in *Some Like It Hot*." Reviewers noticed that Tony Curtis made a prettier woman than Lemmon, but they inevitably also noted that Curtis was married to the

beautifully feminine Janet Leigh.[105] Dick Williams wrote, "Female impersonation in movies is risky but there is never a descent to the limp-wrist, swish
kind of humor. Tony and Jack make convincing, good-looking females, but
there is no doubt left that they are really hearty males with a strong predi-
lection for dames."[106] Williams reassured readers that transvestism was not
homosexuality. But stability was easier to assert than maintain. The film
showed that gender could easily subvert as well as maintain the binaries of
masculine and feminine or heterosexuality and homosexuality.

Some Like It Hot enacted multiple gender masquerades. Curtis performed
masculine and feminine identities with equal zest. He was Tony Curtis performing as Joe and Josephine and Junior as Cary Grant. He perfectly paro-
died Cary Grant's distinctive screen persona, revealing even this ideal of
masculinity to be a mask: "Curtis is given opportunity to be manly and a
sort of super-wolf when, during a double masquerade, he assumes a Cary
Grant voice and a set of psychiatric jargon by which he induces Marilyn
Monroe to plead for the privilege of seducing him."[107] Curtis's masculine
performance of Grant's screen persona was deliberate. There were handwrit-
ten notes on the working script telling Curtis to perform "Cary Grant once
more."[108] The rumors that Curtis worshipped Grant and that he used Grant's
voice and mannerisms to woo his wife Janet Leigh only added to the levels
of masquerade.

In the end, the film suggested that the flapper dresses and the masculine
playboy costumes were comparable masquerades for an actor to assume. The
masks were all equivalent. By extension, the film suggested that star personas
of the actors playing the roles of pretty-boy masculinity, blonde bombshell, or
everyman were as carefully constructed and performed as the characters. The
star persona "Tony Curtis," the Hollywood moniker of Bernie Schwartz, was a
performance, as were Marilyn Monroe's and Jack Lemmon's constructed star
personas. Wilder used Curtis and Monroe to call attention to performance.

Despite the film's willingness to focus on gender as performance, it did
not represent "masculinity in crisis." The characters were not victimized or
objectified, nor tormented about their identity. Instead, gender boundaries
were transgressed in the spirit of fun. It was presumably funny to watch
men undergo the rigors of learning to dress and act like women. The guise
of female impersonation by actors focused on the comedic possibilities, and
the degree of illusion achieved was limited. In Hollywood comedies, men
reluctantly cross-dressed. They were victims of circumstance and were not
meant to be convincing. The gender masquerade was never presented as
a personal choice or part of their identity. Furthermore, such passing was

only convincing within the film's narrative; neither Curtis nor Lemmon were made up to be passable women. The *Motion Picture Herald* noted, "Why the spectacle of two healthy, hearty males in female disguise should prove still to be so funny is for psychiatrists to explain."[109] The spectacle of men in drag was not only funny for the audience to watch, but fun for the actors to perform.

From the late 1940s to the end of the 1950s, Hollywood's representation of masculinity shifted dramatically. Parallels between films depicting racial passing and masculinity in crisis clearly emerge. Early representations of masculinity in crisis were sympathetically portrayed; their ambiguous behavior and identities framed as offering new possibilities in a rigid and unjust world. Like racial indeterminacy, gender ambiguity and sexual fluidity were represented as positive traits in masculine star personas, both on and off the screen. This was epitomized in the sympathetic characters played by Montgomery Clift in *From Here to Eternity*, John Kerr in *Tea and Sympathy*, and James Dean in *Rebel without a Cause*. Against this ideal, tough guys were the psychopaths representing disturbed masculinity. However, the idealization of sensitive masculinity and sexual ambiguity as embodied by the "sigh guys" was temporary. Portrayals of ambiguous masculinity were repudiated by the end of the fifties. Objectified masculinity remained, but without the off-screen psychoanalytic connotations of stars like Brando and Clift. Ambiguity about gender became a sign of a pathological personal failure. Individuals who crossed boundaries became psychotic. By the decade's end, Dean's Rebel became Perkins's Psycho.

In its own way, Hollywood came to terms with the "crisis of identity" that defined the postwar period. Jerry (Jack Lemmon) and Joe (Tony Curtis) may have feared for their lives in running from the mob, but they were never worried about their gendered identities: "Lemmon and Curtis, high-heeled, padded, and bewigged are bust-deep in splendid slapstick all the way . . . As for Miss Monroe, she is, as usual, an extremely effective female impersonator, herself."[110] In some ways, Monroe enacted the greatest gender masquerade of all.

Michael Rennie as Klaatu the passing alien in *The Day the Earth Stood Still* (Twentieth Century-Fox, 1951), directed by Robert Wise. Digital frame enlargement.

Klaatu camouflaged in the gray flannel suit at the Lincoln Memorial, with young Bobby (Billy Gray) as his guide, in *The Day the Earth Stood Still*. Digital frame enlargement.

Dean Stockwell surprised by his reflection as *The Boy with Green Hair* (RKO, 1948), directed by Joseph Losey. Digital frame enlargement.

FBI agent Stedman (in the ubiquitous gray flannel suit) pressures Lucille (Helen Hayes) to inform on her son, with the Jefferson Memorial as backdrop: *My Son John* (Paramount, 1952), directed by Leo McCarey. Digital frame enlargement.

Communist reflections in *My Son John*. The dramatic car chase scene: Robert Walker (as John) flees in a taxi with his former Communist comrades in pursuit. Digital frame enlargement.

The "sigh guys": Montgomery Clift and Frank Sinatra present a new kind of hero in *From Here to Eternity* (Columbia Pictures, 1953), directed by Fred Zinnemann. Digital frame enlargement.

Private Peter Moss (James Edwards) and Finch (Lloyd Bridges) as reunited buddies in *Home of the Brave* (Stanley Kramer Productions, 1949), directed by Mark Robson. Digital frame enlargement.

Representing the postwar ideal of the "melting pot" platoon in *Home of the Brave*. Digital frame enlargement.

Moss breaks down as Finch dies in his arms in *Home of the Brave*. Digital frame enlargement.

Objectified masculinity: Marlon Brando bares his chest in *Viva Zapata!* (Twentieth Century-Fox, 1952), directed by Elia Kazan. Digital frame enlargement.

Burt Lancaster bares his chest: *From Here to Eternity*. Digital frame enlargement.

Ambiguous masculinity as heroic: Tony Perkins as baseball player Jimmy Piersall in *Fears Strikes Out* (Paramount, 1957), directed by Robert Mulligan. Digital frame enlargement.

The cry of a generation: James Dean's teenage angst in *Rebel without a Cause* (Warner Bros., 1955), directed by Nicholas Ray. Digital frame enlargement.

The parents are to blame: Dean's father (Jim Backus) wears an apron in *Rebel*. Digital frame enlargement.

Fractured masculinity on display: James Mason in *Bigger than Life* (Twentieth Century-Fox, 1956), directed by Nicholas Ray. Digital frame enlargement.

Tough guys are psycho: Sgt. "Fatso" Judson (Ernest Borgnine) in *From Here to Eternity*. Digital frame enlargement.

Contrasting femininity: Lauren Bacall's masculinized femininity against Doris Day's demure feminin- ity in *Young Man with a Horn* (Warner Bros., 1950), directed by Michael Curtiz. Digital frame enlargement.

Paranoid masculinity: a hysterical Kevin McCarthy in *Invasion of the Body Snatchers* (Allied Artists and Walter Wanger Productions, 1956), directed by Don Siegel. Digital frame enlargement.

Judy Holliday as accused wife Doris Attinger on the stand: *Adam's Rib* (MGM, 1949), directed by George Cukor. Digital frame enlargement.

Judy Holliday imagined as a man: *Adam's Rib*. Digital frame enlargement.

"Joan in Jeans" as victorious female masculinity: Joan Crawford takes charge in the western *Johnny Guitar* (Republic Pictures, 1954), directed by Nicholas Ray. Digital frame enlargement.

Mercedes McCambridge's disturbed femininity shoots it out with Joan Crawford (and loses) in the finale of *Johnny Guitar*. Digital frame enlargement.

The upstart, ingénue, and seasoned actress: Anne Baxter, Bette Davis, and Marilyn Monroe, with George Sanders in *All about Eve* (Twentieth Century-Fox, 1950), directed by Joseph Mankiewicz. Digital frame enlargement.

The finale in *All about Eve*:
endless reflections of an
aspiring actress. Digital
frame enlargement.

Framing the intimate
boundaries of Southern
female identity: Jeanne
Crain, Ethel Waters, and
Ethel Barrymore in *Pinky*
(Twentieth Century-Fox,
1949), directed by Elia
Kazan. Digital frame
enlargement.

Joanne Woodward as Eve Black in *The Three Faces of Eve* (1957), directed by Nunnally Johnson. Digital
frame enlargement.

Judy Holliday as the platinum blonde phenomenon Billie Dawn in *Born Yesterday* (Columbia Pictures, 1950), directed by George Cukor. Digital frame enlargement.

Holliday reveals hidden desires of the blonde in *Born Yesterday*. Digital frame enlargement.

Iconic blonde bombshell: Marilyn Monroe as Lorelei performing her signature number, "Diamonds Are a Girl's Best Friend," in *Gentlemen Prefer Blondes* (Twentieth Century-Fox, 1953), directed by Howard Hawks. Lorelei's blondeness is enhanced by the dark mesh veils on all the other women. Digital frame enlargement.

Jane Russell as Dorothy, the only woman in the frame surrounded by men, after "Ain't There Anyone Here for Love?" in *Gentlemen Prefer Blondes*. Digital frame enlargement.

Jane Russell as Dorothy performing Monroe as Lorelei for the French courts in *Gentlemen Prefer Blondes*. Digital frame enlargement.

Jennifer Jones and Jorja Curtright as Han Suyin and Suzanne discuss passing and identity over tea in a Hong Kong café in *Love Is a Many Splendored Thing* (Twentieth Century-Fox, 1955), directed by Henry King. Digital frame enlargement.

Marlon Brando falls for the androgynous charms of Miiko Taka in *Sayonara* (William Goetz Productions, 1957), directed by Joshua Logan. Digital frame enlargement.

Ricardo Montalban at ease with gender (and racial) masquerade in *Sayonara*. Mirrored reflections speak to the elasticity of identity. Digital frame enlargement.

Imitative (mirrored) identities: Susan Kohner as Sarah Jane, the passing daughter, and Juanita Moore as Annie, the concerned mother, in *Imitation of Life* (Universal-International, 1959), directed by Douglas Sirk. Digital frame enlargement.

Distraught Sarah Jane stops passing and acknowledges her mother in death, the finale of *Imitation of Life*. Digital frame enlargement.

An impossible romance: Harry Belafonte and Joan Fontaine in *Island in the Sun* (Twentieth Century-Fox, 1957), directed by Robert Rossen. Digital frame enlargement.

Transgressive yet permissible: Dorothy Dandridge and John Justin find romance and a happy ending in *Island in the Sun*. Digital frame enlargement.

The dark side of the Pygmalion fantasy: Jimmy Stewart as Ferguson and Kim Novak as Judy confront their images at the dress shop where he forces her transformation back to Madeleine, in *Vertigo* (Paramount, 1958), directed by Alfred Hitchcock. Again, mirrors in the scene heighten the ambiguity between projected appearances and imagined real identities, with Hitchcock's patently uneasy reflections on gender and power adding to the tension. Digital frame enlargement.

Kim Novak is blonde once more in *Vertigo*. Digital frame enlargement.

Art imitates life: Lana Turner takes the witness stand in *Peyton Place* (Twentieth Century-Fox, 1957), directed by Mark Robson. Digital frame enlargement.

Performing gender and celebrity: Tony Curtis impersonates Cary Grant to seduce Marilyn Monroe as Sugar Kane in *Some Like It Hot* (MGM, 1959), directed by Billy Wilder. Digital frame enlargement.

Happy endings: Joe E. Brown and Jack Lemmon dance the tango in *Some Like It Hot*. Digital frame enlargement.

CHAPTER SEVEN

HOLLYWOOD'S POSTWAR FEMININE MASQUERADES

Masculine Women, Blonde Goddesses, and Passing for Normal

Everybody hides behind plain brown wrappers.[1]
—Diane Varsi in *Peyton Place* (1957)

While a common theme in the 1950s was "what makes a man a man," Hollywood also questioned what made a woman. Films like *Johnny Guitar*, *Calamity Jane*, *Sayonara*, and *Touch of Evil* featured masculine women who played with categories of masculinity. At the same time films like *Gentlemen Prefer Blondes* and *All about Eve* suggested that women were performing femininity. Other films, like *Peyton Place*, raised the issue of "passing for normal." Even Hollywood films that epitomized gender as a stable binary construct suggested the artificiality of gender roles. Actresses performing actresses and the ideal of the blonde sex symbol were an important part of Hollywood's postwar representations of femininity. Such idealized, overly constructed gender representations highlighted rather than negated the ambiguity of gender. Gender was understood as performance.

The perceived lack of rigid and stable boundaries between postwar masculinity and femininity created anxieties that men were becoming feminized and women masculinized and that gendered categories were collapsing, all of which Hollywood both magnified and reflected. However, representations of actresses cross-dressing in masculine attire were only one strand of film images that highlighted the mutability and passing possibilities of gender. Femininity itself was suggestively constructed as a passing performance. Films showed women how to be women and how to give socially acceptable gendered performances to fit into society. This included how to achieve the physically desired look of blonde femininity and how to pass like everyone else. Narratives suggested everything was a passing performance. Films offered blueprints of how to perform femininity and respectability successfully and how to disguise inappropriate details like illegitimate children, premarital sex, or extramarital affairs.

Hollywood's images of feminine masculinity contributed to perceptions that gender categories were breaking down, but they were framed differently than the cross-dressing antics of Jack Lemmon or the ambiguous masculinity of postwar "sigh guys." These transgressive acts, unlike those performed by their male counterparts, did not symbolize confusion or a psychological crisis. Explicit crises about gender were absent from the narratives of these films. Representations of ambiguous women, unlike narratives of masculinity, resisted focusing on anxiety. Cross-dressing men were assumed to be passing within the context of the film, whereas women who performed masculinity or passed as men were always understood to be female, even when instances of "mistaken identity" occurred.

Hollywood had a long movie tradition of women dressing as men, including Marlene Dietrich in *Morocco* (1930), Greta Garbo in *Queen Cristina* (1933), Katharine Hepburn in *Sylvia Scarlett* (1935), or Veronica Lake in *Sullivan's Travels* (1941). However, by the 1950s, the context of these representations changed with the shifts in understandings about gender and identity. The artificial construction of gender and sexuality became progressively more visible. Androgynous cross-dressing women appeared in films like *The Member of the Wedding* (1953), *Calamity Jane* (1953), *Johnny Guitar* (1954), *Sayonara* (1957), *Touch of Evil* (1958), and *South Pacific* (1958). Masculine or "butch" women, like their effeminate male counterparts, suggested nonnormative sexuality, but these signifiers were never consistent or stable. Even culturally loaded signifiers, such as instances of cross-dressing and drag, could be fluid in their meanings.

One such film with evolving gender representations was Fred Zinnemann's *The Member of the Wedding* (Columbia, 1952). Similar to *Tea and Sympathy*, this film looks at adolescent gender issues in its focus on a girl who acted and dressed more like a boy. Based on Carson McCullers's play, the film starred Julie Harris as young tomboy Frankie Addams. While it pushed boundaries of gender and sexual identity, it kept the issue within the safer context of a coming-of-age story.[2] Frankie's "tomboy" is a rite of passage that gives way to an "adult" acceptance of femininity.

Many unlikely postwar films, including *South Pacific* (1958), *Sayonara* (1957), and *Touch of Evil* (1958), used cross-dressing and drag performances suggestively. *South Pacific* highlighted gender antics in the Thanksgiving Follies camp show scene where nurse "Nellie" (Mitzi Gaynor) dons a male sailor's uniform to comedic effect. She comes out onto the stage singing: "My doll is as dainty as a sparrow / Her figure is something to applaud / Where she's narrow she's narrow as an arrow/ And she's broad where a broad should be broad! A 101 lbs of fun, that's my little honey-bun . . . I'm her booby, she's my trap." Then her "honey-bun" comes on stage: Luther Billis (Ray Walston) dressed in comic drag in a skirt, a coconut bra, and a grass hairdo. This cross-dressing scene is unusual in that both male and female drag performances were used for comedic effect, but they existed within the context of military traditions of transvestism and camp to "entertain" the troops.[3]

Similarly, Joshua Logan's *Sayonara* (Warner Bros., 1957), hyped for its "daring interracial romance," was more transgressive in its play with representations about the fluidity of gender, even if its gender masquerades were explored within the safer context of a foreign and exotic culture, the world of Japanese theatre. Mexican-born Ricardo Montalban is particularly notable for his gender and racial blurring performance as Japanese Kabuki actor Nakamura, who performs both male and female characters in his stage roles. In a promotional interview for the film, Montalban stated that he was "fascinated by what he saw backstage at the Kabuki theatres," and that "Female impersonators are able to portray femininity to a greater extent than a woman. They have observed movements that women are not even aware of. An idealization of womanhood is projected through their performance. This Japanese art is in no way comparable to what we in America call female impersonators."[4]

Sayonara featured not only female impersonators, like Nakamura in the Kabuki theatre, but radical male impersonators, who performed in the revered fictional all-female Matsubayashi theatre (likely based on Japan's famous Takarazuka Theatre). Members of this female theatre troupe were secluded from the public and not allowed to socialize outside. Utilizing a standard Hollywood trope about forbidden love, Major Gruver (Marlon Brando), a US airman stationed in Kobe, falls in love with a member of this troupe, Hana Ogi (Miiko Taka). When Gruver first spots Hana, she is dressed in male attire, and her strikingly masculine look piques his curiosity. Throughout their courtship, she appears in various manifestations of both racial and gender drag, including a western tuxedo with top hat and tails. The constant fluidity of her racial and gender representations extends the transgressive nature of their relationship.[5] However, in the end Hana must give up not only her career but also the fluidity of her gendered performances, once she becomes Gruver's military wife. This progressive ending, with its interracial marriage, is muted by Hana's transformation into a traditionally subservient woman.[6] But even this conservative reassertion of gender norms and national hierarchies does not erase the gender play that came before.

In contrast to the sympathetic gender fluidity in *Sayonara*, gender ambiguity was pathologized in *Touch of Evil* (Universal, 1958). Written and directed by Orson Welles, *Touch of Evil* starred Charlton Heston as Mexican detective Ramon Miguel ("Mike") Vargas, Janet Leigh as his wife Susan Vargas, and Welles himself as Captain Hank Quinlan, a corrupt cop. It also starred Joseph Calleia as Sergeant Pete Menzies, with cameos by Dennis Weaver, Marlene Dietrich, and Mercedes McCambridge. While McCambridge was "unbilled," contemporaneous reviewers mentioned her remarkable cameo, giving her credit for an amazing performance.[7] As part of a gang that attacks, drugs, kidnaps, and apparently rapes Susan Vargas, McCambridge's portrayal of a pathologically masculine woman echoed the film's larger theme of the inherent and dangerous ambiguity of border spaces.

This film was set in the fictional American-Mexican border town of Los Robles, a space where normative laws and boundaries are destabilized. Borders are most clearly defined by understanding those who can cross versus those who cannot. The space mimics passing subjects who likewise cross borders of identity, allowing us to see where the edges and boundaries are, always in opposition to categories that remained fixed: "Borders are set up to define the places that are safe and unsafe, to distinguish us from them."[8] The denizens of Los Robles were treated with contempt by authorities as the bastard children of unrecognized interracial and international boundaries. The film's narrative makes clear that borders were spaces inadequately guarded by laws, and the space was inherently corrupt. As Mike Vargas says, "Border towns bring out the worst in a country."

Touch of Evil explicitly outlined the dangers of porous spaces that existed between the defined categories of nation, state, culture, race, gender, and sexuality. Thus, border towns were spaces where racial, gender, and national identities blurred, and laws ceased to be meaningfully operative. In this context, McCambridge's representation of butch femininity, although brief, acted as a reminder that gender boundaries between masculine and feminine were permeable, rendering binary categories meaningless. Judith Halberstam places McCambridge's cameo as one of the most "iconic predatory butches" in American film.[9]

While Mercedes McCambridge's performance of the butch biker was praised, the character was pathologized. This duality echoed broader cultural attitudes about masculine women on and off the screen in postwar America.

In *Life* magazine, psychiatrists claimed that sexual ambiguity was rampant and dangerous, and American postwar culture needed fixed gender ideals. In 1956, *Life* posited that men "should admire [women] not for the cut of their trousers, figuratively or literally, but for their miraculous, God-given, sensationally unique ability to wear skirts, with all the implications of that fact," although it went on to admit how "masculine garb, popularized in the 1940s by Marlene Dietrich, typified women's equality."[10] Thus, the desire to promote definite feminine ideals was complicated by the ongoing cultural tendency to equate masculine women with power and equality, especially when embodied by powerful female star personas.[11]

Lauren Bacall, as psychoanalyst Amy North in *Young Man with a Horn* (Warner Bros., 1950), represents both the strengths and pathologies that masculine women suggested in postwar film. Bacall's demeanor and performance as North was quite similar to her prior "tough girl" roles in films like *The Big Sleep* (1946) and *Key Largo* (1948), but here the attitude bordered on pathological. Directed by Michael Curtiz, *Young Man with a Horn* told the story of jazz musician Rick Martin (Kirk Douglas) who marries Amy North (Bacall). The film was based on real life trumpeter Bix Beiderbecke. Amy describes herself as an "intellectual mountain-goat," and when Rick meets her she is studying psychiatry to be a doctor. This explicitly puts psychoanalysis front and center in the storyline, as when she tells Rick his horn is his "alter ego," which, she explains, "simply means your other self." Amy has no interest in listening to jazz, just analyzing it. However, the film's representation of psychoanalytic ideas goes far deeper than Amy's pseudo-psychoanalytic ramblings. Martin's trumpet is framed as a "fetish," and his obsession with the perfect note is more the cause of his nervous breakdown than his suspicions that Amy is not normal.

A love triangle adds to the film's psychoanalytic mix. In contrast to Bacall's strong and professional Amy North, Doris Day is Jo Jordan, the properly feminine "good" girl singer who competes for Martin's affections. Amy tells Rick, "Jo's interesting, isn't she? So simple and uncomplicated. Must be wonderful to wake up and know just what door you're going through. She is so terribly normal." Later, unaware that he has just married her, Jo warns Rick about Amy: "I know her much better than you. She's a strange girl . . . But inside, way inside, she is all mixed up. She's wrong for you." In the end, Amy does not stand by her man; only dutiful Jo shows up at the rehab sanitarium to support Martin. Jordan (Day) and North (Bacall) are contrasted as extremes of femininity. While North is shown throughout in feminine clothes, her clinical interest in sexuality and emotion, because of her desired profession, is itself framed as psychologically disturbing and indicative of a deviant sexuality. In opposition to Jordan's supportive femininity, North's butchness became suggestive. *Young Man with A Horn* was unusual in its portrayal of North's sexuality based on Bacall's projection of masculine attitudes and not masculine looks.

Similarly, *Adam's Rib*, a Katharine Hepburn vehicle from 1949, played with culturally enforced distinctions between masculine and feminine and made ideas about gender identity and equity the focus. This MGM film was a big hit with Hepburn being praised as its star. Beautifully written by husband and wife team Ruth Gordon and Garson Kanin and directed by George Cukor, the film was billed as a battle of the sexes that focused on the legal and marital battles of two lawyers, District Attorney Adam Bonner (Spencer Tracy) and his wife Amanda (Hepburn). The married lawyers end up on opposing sides of a court case where a young woman named Doris Attinger (Judy Holliday) is accused of shooting her philandering husband. Adam is the prosecutor, and Amanda acts for her defense, seeing the case as a feminist issue because women are held to different standards than men. Amanda argues that a man trying to defend his marriage against the encroachment of a "wolf" would not be found guilty, and neither should a woman. Then she asks the jury to imagine the sex of all characters as opposite, so that the defendant Doris is a man, and the husband and the wolf are women, which they do. The convincing gender reversal wins Amanda the court case, but it is Adam's gender masquerade that saves their marriage when he performs sensitive masculinity, proving that men too can be passingly feminine to get what they want from a relationship. And *Adam's Rib* was not alone in its focus on the postwar re-negotiation of gender ideologies. Films like *I Was a Male War Bride* (1949), starring Cary Grant and Ann Sheridan, and *The Lieutenant Wore Skirts* (1956) starring Tom Ewell and Sheree North, also addressed these issues to great effect.

However, while actresses like Lauren Bacall and Katharine Hepburn were celebrated for such strong performances, they were pathologized for the same attributes. Not every actress was allowed to cross gender boundaries with impunity. There was a sharp contrast between discourse about representations of masculine masquerade on the screen and actresses who dressed the part off the screen. This was reinforced by exposés claiming to "unmask" the real person behind Hollywood stars. Assigning meaning to ambiguous gender characteristics by inferring sexuality was a staple of postwar fan and scandal magazines, which used language that reflected the psychoanalytic turn in popular culture.

A *Private Lives* article on Katharine Hepburn ("Katie Hepburn's Sex Hex!") assaulted her looks and questioned whether she had a "masculine complex."[12] It also included a photo of Hepburn with a baseball bat and the slogan "Batter up, Dr. Kinsey!" A 1953 *Confidential* article on the androgynous actress implied she had a "masculine complex," using such phrases as "Hollywood's Torrid Tomboy," "tomboy tendencies," and "panties phobia" to explain why she always wore pants: "She's as muscular as they come, a throwback to her childhood days when, with her two brothers, she worked out on athletic paraphernalia and developed biceps through wrestling and boxing matches. In fact, she used to shave her head so she could butt better and keep opponents from getting their hands in her hair."[13] Articles on other actresses suggested that preference for male attire was a sign of a non-normative sexuality. An article on actress Lizabeth Scott indicated she always wore "men's" PJs, and suggested she might be a "baritone babe."[14] The sheer quantity of tabloid gossip about the sex lives and behaviors of the stars implied that deviant sexualities were rampant in Hollywood, including rumors of Brando's many wild orgies or of Sinatra's reaction to his wife Ava Gardner's relationship with Lana Turner.[15]

After the war, magazines used the language of the couch to pathologize movie stars, even while idolizing them. Female actresses became either oversexed, like Marilyn Monroe, or sexually deviant, like Lizabeth Scott, or both:

> Some [actresses] continue to play their screen parts off-screen. The great lover on film tries to become one in real life. The celluloid siren jumps from one bedroom to another to prove that she's really as sexy as the world thinks . . . it becomes a chase after sensation and novelty. It may account for the fact that so many stars have heterosexual affairs one day and homosexual ones the next. It's a change . . . people who become actors are often those who are not sure of their own identities . . . "They just don't know who they are or what they want to be, so they become actors and try one role after another."[16]

Like fears about the hidden identities of others, the projected sexuality of stars was feared to be one more mask.[17] The potential invisibility of "sexual deviants" and their ability to pass were a threat to the fabric of American society. *Coronet* warned, "While the appearance of most of these unfortunates may betray them to watchful persons, other sex aberrants look, act, and dress like anyone else. It is they who are the real threat. For, until an overt action is committed, their victims sense no danger."[18] The lack of visible indicators complicated representations of gender and sexuality both on and off the screen, and contradictory messages abounded. If women wearing men's PJ's was a signifier of their sexuality, then how were audiences supposed to read Miiko Taka's masculine drag in *Sayonara*? Or how would they read the gender ambiguity expressed in Hollywood's female-centric westerns, like Doris Day in *Calamity Jane* or Joan Crawford's "Joan in Jeans" performance in *Johnny Guitar*?[19]

Although usually a masculine genre that excluded women except as prostitutes or token love interests, westerns for the first time in the 1950s featured strong female leads. Female characters assumed attitudes and attires usually reserved men, donning the cowboy uniform of jeans, guns, hats, and frontier independence. Female-centric westerns included Doris Day in *Calamity Jane* (1953), Joan Crawford in *Johnny Guitar* (1954), Barbara Stanwyck in both *Cattle Queen of Montana* (1954) and *Forty Guns* (1957), Jane Russell as Calamity Jane in *The Paleface* (1948) and as Belle Starr in *Montana Belle* (1952), and Yvonne De Carlo (as yet another representation of Calamity Jane) in *Calamity Jane and Sam Bass* (1949).[20] Anne Baxter also played a "pistol-packing tomboy" as the lone female in William A. Wellman's *Yellow Sky* (1948).[21]

Doris Day in *Calamity Jane* and Joan Crawford in *Johnny Guitar* represent different takes on straddling the masculine-feminine performance, one comic, the other dramatic. While *Calamity Jane* is a musical comedy with a Technicolor feel that captures the lighter side of the decade, *Johnny Guitar* is darker and is also the most original western of the 1950s. Both films were popular at the box office and are cited by film theory as texts open to queer appropriation.[22] The cross-dressing masquerades played with gender boundaries, but never questioned the passing implications of the characters.

Calamity Jane was created by Warner Bros. as a star vehicle for the "ineffably androgynous" Doris Day.[23] Set in Deadwood, Dakota Territory, the film was premiered in this South Dakota town in 1953 and based on the life of Calamity Jane. Day plays her as a frontier tomboy who claims femininity to win the love of Wild Bill Hickok (Howard Keel). The studio pushed it as a love story. As the 1953 *New York Journal-American* put it: "'Calamity Jane': GAY TECHNICOLOR WESTERNER: Doris Day Gives Legend a New Slant ... Here Calamity's a warbling tomboy and Wild Bill's a singing gambler, and, what's more, the two fall in love and get married."[24] Framed as a tomboy's coming-of-age story, her sexual maturity is predicated on the adoption of feminine dress and behavior. What is different from Elizabeth Taylor in *National Velvet* or Julie Harris in *The Member of the Wedding* is that Calamity is an adult woman, not an adolescent.

Research by the studio discovered that Calamity "dressed by preference in male attire, frequently a suit of fringed buckskin, and few persons ever saw her in women's apparel."[25] She appears in the film dressed in a masculine frontier outfit, appropriating both male and Native American cultural signifiers, including leather buckskins, a coonskin cap, and a shotgun. Her job is suitably masculine, guarding a stagecoach. Posters for the film, however, feminized the cowboy outfit, showing Calamity/Day with fringed leather shorts, guns and holster, a fringed vest, a long-sleeved white shirt which shows her stomach, cute leather-fringed gloves, and cowboy boots.[26] Day was both the girl next door and "Calamity," the gender-bending western hero. In such publicity shots, the historically masculine Calamity looks more like a Dallas Cowboy cheerleader than a frontier cowboy.

Most of the action takes place in the Golden Garter saloon in Deadwood, where Calamity's tomboy-like drag is accepted by the locals. And she is not alone in crossing gender lines. At the saloon, there is a misunderstanding about gender expectations because of the androgynous name of the booked performer, Frances Fryer (Dick Wesson), who is then forced by the manager to pass as an actress because the audience wants to see a woman on stage. The performance fails. To stop the patrons from rioting, Calamity boasts that she will bring a real actress to Deadwood, the beautiful Adelaid Adams (Gale Robbins). Calamity Jane heads east to Chicago to track down Adams. Because of her masculine attire, she is mistaken for a man, first by a prostitute and then by Katie (Adams's maid). While Calamity is unable to bring back the real Adelaid Adams, she brings back Adelaid's maid, Katie Brown (Allyn Ann McLerie), who herself passed as the famed actress. Other characters are also passing, including the cross-dressing actor who tries to pass himself off as a feminine "Frances Fryer." The cross-dressing allows for confusion and mistaken identities, undermining the stability of signifiers about gender and sexual identity.

While living with Katie, Calamity learns how to be a woman from her feminine roommate. She becomes a lady to secure the heterosexual love of Hickok. The transformation from tomboy to lady parallels the comedic education of men learning to perform feminine drag. Calamity is taught how to walk, how to apply makeup, and how to appear feminine. There is a step-by-step process as she learns the skills to pass in the part. She learns how to perform femininity. As Hickok says, with a little work, Calamity could be "a passable pretty gal." Katie also transforms Calamity's cabin into a site of feminine domesticity to the tune of "A Woman's Touch." The song plays with the irony and comedy of gender when cross-dressing is involved, and

Day's award-winning song "Secret Love" has been celebrated as an anthem of queer desire.[27] Like *Some Like It Hot*, *Calamity Jane* plays with gender, cross-dressing and sexuality, but the ending could also be viewed as a return to appropriate gender roles and heteronormativity.

In *Johnny Guitar* (1954), Joan Crawford offered a more destabilizing and convincing portrait of masculine femininity. Written by Philip Yordan and directed by Nicholas Ray for Republic Pictures, the film was a traditional western with a male lead. When Ray asked Crawford to star he had to promise her the leading role. Yordan talked to Crawford about the original script:

> She says: "It's nonsense. I have no part. I just stand around and walk around with boots on and have a few stupid scenes." I said, "Well, what's your idea?" She says, "There's Sterling Hayden in the picture and he's not much and some other actor and he's not much and Ward Bond, one of the actors who John Ford is always using in those pictures with [John] Wayne, and he's not much. So I want to play the man. I want to shoot it out in the end with Mercedes McCambridge, and instead of me playing with myself in a corner, let Sterling play with himself in a corner and I'll do the shoot-out." I said, "Ah, uh, um . . . if I do that, will you do the picture?" She says, "Yeah." I said, "Okay."[28]

Crawford agreed to star, and nothing was changed except the gender of the lead. With Ray as director and Crawford in the lead, the movie became the best example of gender ambiguity and role reversal in the western genre of the 1950s. It is also loaded with psychoanalytic language, coded subtext of homosexuality, feminist statements, and political allegory filled with anti-HUAC subtext.[29]

Johnny Guitar is the story of conflict between bankers, ranchers, and the encroaching railroad for control of the west. At the center is Vienna (Joan Crawford), who represents a western vision of the self-made woman, rising from working in saloons to owning one: a successful entrepreneur, if not entirely respectable. The economic fight is mirrored by the conflict between Vienna and Emma Small (Mercedes McCambridge).[30] Vienna is in love with Johnny Logan, aka Johnny Guitar (Sterling Hayden), while Emma is infatuated with the Dancin' Kid (Scott Brady), although one reviewer argued there were "doubts" about "her vague and underplayed attachment to Scott Brady, leader of a trio of dubious citizens."[31] When respected townfolk form a lynching posse to destroy Vienna's and the Kid's gang, the film suggests that Emma's personal obsession and vendetta against Vienna is driving the conflict. The film ends in a dramatic shootout between Emma and Vienna.

The *Cue* review summed it up as follows:

Conceived in the mystic, folksy, sentimental Frankie and Johnnie tradition, this is basically an off-beat tale of the deathless love of a gunman turned guitar player (Sterling Hayden) for a femme fatale who runs a desert town saloon (Miss Crawford). This lady, torn between love and hate for her man Johnny Guitar, is simultaneously being stalked in a murderous female feud by a psychopathic hussy (Mercedes McCambridge) who is jealous of the saloon gal's fatal fascination for another killer man known as the Dancin' Kid (Scott Brady).[32]

Contemporary reviews responded to the tough, masculine image:[33] "Joan Crawford plays essentially the role Van Helfin played in SHANE . . ."[34] *Los Angeles Times' This Week Magazine* wrote: "Miss Crawford wears jeans, totes a gun, narrowly escapes drowning and forest fire, and is threatened with lynching. This is the first time in fiction dealing with the chivalrous Wild West that a female has ever worn a noose around her neck."[35] Molly Haskell wrote that Crawford, as "the outrageous gun-toting Vienna . . . alternates between masculine and feminine elements of her personality with a bravura that is grand and funny without ever being ludicrous or demeaning."[36]

In *Pix* magazine, Joan is flanked by her film posse in a black western outfit: "Wearing the tightest jeans since Marlon Brando in *The Wild One*, Joan Crawford faces hostile townsfolk with her henchmen."[37] Another picture was captioned: "the ladies take over. Men stand by while Joan and rival Mercedes McCambridge shoot it out." Reviewers recognized that in the film women played roles traditionally reserved for men but they were silent about what this meant.

In the film Crawford's masculine dress is not addressed as a plot device. Unlike Day's Calamity Jane, Crawford's Vienna never has to reclaim her femininity. She is comfortable in the masculine cowboy outfit of black jeans and shirt and in the white dress she wears when the posse comes to burn down her saloon. She performs both feminine and masculine masquerades with equal strength. Vienna's devoted saloon keeper Sam pays her the compliment that "I have never met a woman who was more man!"

Emma, on the other hand, who always appears as the decorous lady and symbol of feminine respectability, becomes increasingly twisted as the film develops. The lasting impression, noted by reviewers, was the underlying psychopathic turn of Emma's character. *Variety* derided Emma as a "bitter, frustrated leader of a nearby community who has egged the ranchers and others into taking her side by using their fear of the settlers and fences that will come with the rails."[38] Other reviewers used stronger language, describing her not only as a "psychopathic hussy" but also as a "perfect balladic image of the jilted gal with a psychopathic hate" and the "neurotic 'respectable' woman who leads her fellow citizens in the war against Crawford."[39]

Emma's obsession with Vienna also garnished speculation by film critics. *Cue* and *Variety* expressed doubts about Emma's affections for Kid, implying other unspoken feelings were behind her character's motivation. Emma's "psychopathology" was understood as a coded euphemism for lesbian desire.[40] However, the film's ultimate transgressive potential is not with the subtext but with the ending. The final showdown between Vienna/Crawford and Emma/McCambridge remains a landmark image in cinema history: two women fighting it out according to the rules of the old west.

Films like *Sayonara*, *Calamity Jane*, and *Johnny Guitar* showed gender masquerade, highlighting women performing masculinity. Stars Miiko Taka, Doris Day, and Joan Crawford adeptly performed androgynous characters, helping to destabilize normative categories of gender. Crawford's Vienna was the most ambiguous, because her behavior and clothes were not used as a narrative device, and she was never forced to reclaim femininity. This was in marked contrast to Day's Calamity Jane, which replicated the comedic steps necessary for men to become women as passable female impersonators. However, in the narrative of the film, Calamity's authentic gender identity is never questioned. Neither Calamity nor Vienna experience a crisis about their androgynous gender masquerades. At no time did the films suggest that the failure to perform appropriate feminine ideals was indicative of a pathological identity or that such masculine attributes would lead to a nervous breakdown.

Representations of masculine woman existed in sharp contrast with the psychological discomfort suggested by representations of effeminate men. Men unsure about their masculinity experienced crisis because their gender and sexual identities were in jeopardy. Masculinity was more prized, more central. Accordingly, the cost of failing to learn gendered performance was higher for men than for women. But this was also partly because of the pretense that being a man was natural and lacked conscious effort. Unlike masculinity, femininity was never assumed to be something innate. It was always understood to be a construction.

Playing the woman was hard work. In *All about Eve*, Margo Channing (Bette Davis) tells her friend, "It's one career all females have in common whether we like it or not—being a woman. Sooner or later we've got to work at it, no matter how many other careers we've had or wanted." The idea that women perform femininity was not new; what was new was the relationship between acting, performance, and identity. Audiences were encouraged to peak behind the curtain and see how representations of femininity were masks that could be taken on or off. The 1950s films *Sunset Boulevard* (1950), *All about Eve* (1950), *Singing in the Rain* (1951), *The Bad and the Beautiful* (1952), *A Star Is Born* (1954), *The Big Knife* (1955), and *The Goddess* (1958) all showed the ugliness behind performance and the cracks in the façade of star personas.

The year 1950 saw the release of *All about Eve*, based on Mary Orr's story, "The Wisdom of Eve."[41] The critically acclaimed film was a box office hit nominated for fourteen Oscars in 1950 and taking home six. Produced by Darryl F. Zanuck for Twentieth Century-Fox, it was directed by Joseph L. Mankiewicz, who also wrote the screenplay. The movie starred Bette Davis as Margo Channing and Gary Merrill as her boyfriend, Bill Simpson.[42] Character actress Thelma Ritter played Margo's companion, Birdie Coonan. Celeste Holm played Karen Richards, Margo's best friend and wife of the playwright Lloyd Richards (Hugh Marlowe); therefore, she was "of the Theatre only by marriage." The young actress Eve Harrington was played by Anne Baxter. Rounding out the cast was Marilyn Monroe as Miss Caswell, a "graduate of the Copacabana School of Dramatic Art," and George Sanders as the theatre critic Addison DeWitt, described as possessing an "un-distilled Satanic quality."[43]

The film opens with Eve receiving the Sarah Siddons Award for Distinguished Achievement in Theatre. A flashback shows her rise to fame after her arrival in New York the year before. Karen Richards found Eve backstage and invited her to meet Margo Channing. Eve confesses she had watched every performance of Margo Channing in "Aged in Wood" in New York and was a self-avowed fan. Eve had first seen Margo perform in San Francisco and claimed it had changed her life. Eve relates her life story for them:

I guess it started back home—Wisconsin—I was an only child. I used to make-believe a lot when I was a kid. I acted out all sorts of things ... Somehow acting and make-believe began to fill up my life more and more. It got so I couldn't tell the real from the unreal, except that the unreal seemed more real to me.

Her dad was a farmer, so they were poor:

> I had to help out. So I quit school and went to Milwaukee. Became a
> secretary. In a brewery. When you're a secretary in a brewery it's pretty
> hard to believe you're anything else. Everything is beer. It wasn't much
> fun, but it helped at home, and there was a little theatre group there
> like a drop of rain in the desert . . . That's where I met Eddie . . . Then
> the war came and we got married. Eddie was in the Air Force. They
> sent him to the South Pacific . . .

Eve explains how she decided to stay in San Francisco after getting the news
that Eddie had been killed. Eve's version of her identity, including passing as
a war widow, is constructed to ensure a connection to Margo. Birdie responds
to her tale with a wisecrack: "What a story, everything but the bloodhounds
snapping at her rear end."

The film's plot then follows Eve's rise in the acting world. Eve moves in
with Margo, becomes her understudy, seduces Karen's husband Lloyd after
trying to seduce Bill, and finds her match in Addison DeWitt, with whom
she strikes a "devil's bargain" to make it to the top of the theatre world. The
film ends with Eve's own adoring fan, Phoebe (Barbara Bates), president of
her high school's "Eve Harrington Fan Club," pretending to be Eve in front of
the three-way mirror in Eve's bedroom, holding Eve's Sarah Siddons Award.
The three-way mirror creates hundreds of reflections of the artificial Eve
bouncing off each other.

All about Eve critiqued the artificiality of the world of acting and performance. Eve betrayed everyone by passing as something other than what she
was. Throughout the film Eve is shown performing both on and offstage. The
skillful manipulation of those around her is framed as a vice, not a virtue. As
the ideal of an innocent, idealistic, and demure young woman, Eve matched
the film's opening narration: "Eve. Eve, the Golden Girl. The cover girl, the
girl next door, the girl on the moon . . ." Eve became the embodiment of what
people wanted to see in her. But Eve was a manufactured lie, an extension of
her acting and desire for make-believe. According to Mankiewicz, "Gertrude
Slescynski (the name and person Eve was born with but had discarded) had
rendered herself literally nonexistent. Not one facet of Gertrude's previous
life did she consider worthy of inclusion in the Eve Harrington she fabricated
for the wooing of Margo and the others."[44] She was an unsympathetic fiction,
a false identity with a fictive past created to become Margo's confidante and
her protégé. Eve was "relentlessly on the make" and filled with an "insatiable

need and greed," who "is confronted in the end—as all Eves must be and are—by an acute awareness that she has been servicing a bottomless pit. A void. Her ego? That Self without which nobody is anybody? The Eves—male and/or female—have none."[45]

Birdie was the only one who questioned Eve's motives.[46] When Margo describes Eve as "loyal and efficient," Birdie quips, "Like an agent with only one client." Margo asks: "She only thinks of me, doesn't she?" To which Birdie responds: "Well, let's say she thinks only *about* you ... like she's studying you, like you was a play or a book or a set of blueprints—how you walk, talk, eat, think, sleep." Margo defends Eve, but begins to question Eve's motives and actions. Margo's suspicions are compounded by the anxieties of aging as an actress and as a woman. In the end, Eve takes over Margo's position as a top Broadway star. Eve reaches the top of the theatre world as the star in a play written by Lloyd and directed by Bill.

Eve's downfall only comes with her unmasking by DeWitt. When Eve tells him that Lloyd will leave Karen and marry her, DeWitt lets her know how much he knows about her "real" identity:

> To begin with, your name is not Eve Harrington; it's Gertrude Slescyn-ski. It's true your parents were poor, they still are. They would like to know how you are and where. They haven't heard from you in three years ... It's also true that you worked at a brewery, but life in the brewery was not as dull as you pictured it. In fact, it got less and less dull until your boss's wife had your boss followed by detectives ... the $500 you got to get out of town brought you straight to New York, didn't it? ... There was no Eddie, no pilot. That was not only a lie it was an insult to dead heroes and the women who loved them.

"Eve Harrington" was a fiction that Gertrude Slescynski enacted to become an actress and a celebrated Broadway star.

Eve's narrative fictions, her passing strategies, erased her working-class background and allowed entry into Margo's world. Passing as social strategy was conflated with her ability to perform as an actress. Ingénues must appear naïve and young but be ruthless and conniving in order to survive in the world of the theatre. After Margo is told that Eve took her place at a reading, she asks DeWitt about her performance. He responds:

> I've lived in the theatre as a trappist monk lives in his faith. I have no other world. No other life. And once in a great while I experience that

moment of revelation which all true believers wait and pray—you were one ... Hays another ... Eve Harrington will be among them ... It wasn't a reading; it was a performance. Brilliant. Vivid. Something made of music and fire. In time she'll be what you are.

A reviewer commented on the relationship between Eve and Baxter: "Anne Baxter's ambitious actress is an amazingly accurate characterization. For all the ruthlessness in the part Miss Baxter makes you understand that this is the only way her success could be achieved. She's a terrible woman, but you sympathize with her just the same."[47] Bette Davis commented: "Anne was really playing a double role: one thing on the surface, another underneath. I called it the 'sweet bitch.' Her part was more difficult than mine."[48] Tellingly, most reviews hyped Anne Baxter as the authentic ingénue that Eve only pretended to be.

Eve's fictive pasts and shifting identities, her passing as an innocent ingénue, were part of her skill as an actress. And within the film, all those who should know—directors, critics and playwrights—think that Eve is a great actress. Moreover, in the end Eve's professional rewards for performing duplicitous masquerades were high since she conquered the theatre world, which was, as Margo put it, "All the world's religions rolled into one and we're the gods and goddesses." Actresses had to be adept at passing to be successful. Stars were idealized precisely because they could be anything or anyone, barring ruptures between their images and their identities. Actresses playing actresses invited contradictions.

Because performance confused the lines between acting and identity, it left others confused about issues of authenticity. The fundamental lack of authenticity inherent in all acting was equated with disturbed psychology. At Margo's party, DeWitt argued: "By and large we are concentrated gatherings of neurotics, egomaniacs, emotional misfits and precocious children." He continued:

Every now and then some elder statesman of the theatre or cinema assures the public that actresses and actors are just plain folks, ignoring the fact that their greatest attraction to the public is their complete lack of resemblance to normal human beings. We all have abnormality in common. We're a breed apart from the rest of humanity, we theatre folk. We are the original displaced personalities.

Critics agreed: "This film leaves one with the impression that anyone earning his living in the theatre is at best a wild-eyed, anti-social neurotic, and at worst a soulless psychopathic creature devoid of any human feeling, and who manipulates and destroys whoever crosses his path, for his own aggrandizement."[49] *Time* magazine commented that "the story of Eve's success proves her less a Cinderella than a Lady Macbeth."[50]

Tellingly, the only authentic characters in the film are Karen and Birdie, those who do not act for a living. They did not need to perform or pass. In contrast, actresses had to separate internal "selves" from "public" personas. Away from the theatre with Karen, Margo questions who she is:

> MARGO: "So many people know me. I wish I did. I wish someone would tell me about me."
>
> KAREN: "You're Margo, just Margo."
>
> MARGO: "What is that? Besides something spelled out in light-bulbs, I mean. Besides something called a temperament, which consists mostly of swooping about on a broomstick and screaming at the top of my voice. Infants behave the way I do, you know, they carry on and misbehave, they'd get drunk if they knew how, when they can't have what they want, when they feel unwanted or insecure, or unloved . . . More than anything in this world, I love Bill, and I want Bill, and I want him to want me, but me, not Margo Channing, and if I can't tell them apart how can he?"
>
> KAREN: "Well, why should he and why should you?"
>
> MARGO: "Bill's in love with Margo Channing—he's fought with her, worked with her, and loved her. But ten years from now Margo Channing will have ceased to exist, and what's left will be what?"

Margo is unsure about who she is and worries about the age difference between herself and Bill (who is eight years younger).

Time magazine described Margo as "volatile, egocentric, and uninhibited, a great stage personality whose bitter anxiety over encroaching middle age blights both her career and her love affair with a younger director."[51] At the same time, the film addresses the diminished career opportunities for an aging female actress. Mankiewicz argued:

> In the role of Margo Channing I wanted to dramatize the trauma and terror with which many actresses approach both aging and the transition from married actress to just married woman . . . Forty years of age. Four-O. Give or take a year, the single most critical milestone in the life of an actress . . . who for the first time is having to decide whether

to play the mother of a late teenager ... It is a bitterly sad point of no return for an actress ... The personality aliases left for her to assume would now become inevitable character roles and—if she was unlucky enough to go on and on—caricatures ... Women's lib has quite a point to make here: about a society which can evolve and foster a set of standards by which, at roughly forty, the female actress is required to foreswear the public projection of romantic and sexual allure—while the male actor carries on blithely.[52]

Margo worried that her advancing age would limit her ability to get good roles. Conflating the performance on-screen with the actress off-screen, audiences would understand that Bette Davis faced the same problems.

If *All about Eve* suggested that the line between authentic identities and acting performances was ambiguous, it also suggested sexual fluidity. Great acting, like passing, created anxiety because the projection of one false identity implicated others, with sexual identity revealed to be as much a performance as gender. Representing an inverse take on the casting couch, the ingénue Eve seduces whoever might help her career. The film suggests a homoerotic undercurrent to Eve's and Margo's relationship, who are framed briefly as an idyllic couple. Margo's love interest, Bill, left for California the same evening they all met Eve. In a voice-over, Margo remembers: "That same night, we sent for Eve's things. She moved into the little guest room on the top floor ... The next three weeks were out of a fairy tale, and I was Cinderella in the last act. Eve became my sister, lawyer, mother, friend, psychiatrist, and confidante ... The honeymoon was on." By seducing Margo, Eve was able to supplant faithful defender Birdie on the domestic front in the relentless pursuit of her ambitions.

A profession based on passing and performance had a price. Unlike the crisis of masculinity films, where bad gender role models or rampant gender ambiguity in the culture was blamed for gender confusion, women had no one to blame but themselves. The film suggested that ambitious actresses like Margo had to sacrifice normative gender identities for their careers, a theme reflected in other 1950s films about actresses. Lana Turner's role as the great theatre actress Lora Meredith in *Imitation of Life* was a more sympathetic echo of Eve. Lora's self-described backstory about her start in the theatre paralleled Eve's fictional tale, complete with a husband who died, and it intimated how the local theatre was "like a drop of rain on the desert" that kept them going until they reached New York and were able to realize their dream of being actresses. In these films, actresses were caught between imagined off-screen authentic identities and their public passing performances. Bordering on cautionary tales, characters like Eve and Lora were celebrated as great actresses, yet pathologized as unnatural women.

All about Eve presented a range of women's roles and depicted the fine line between what constituted necessary passing performances for an actress both on and off the stage, to achieve professional status and what crossed the line as an unacceptable lack of authenticity. The line between acting and passing became blurred. The character of Eve revealed the framework for gendered passing performances based on social norms and strictures. The movie also pushed the envelope about sexuality, even though the original plan for Eve to be a lesbian became suggestive rather than explicit.[53] *All about Eve* is an excellent model of the inauthentic and unsympathetic woman whose character makes up one passing fiction after another in order to achieve her ambitions and who is duly punished. Most importantly, this film suggested the subterfuges necessary to succeed both as an actress in the theatrical profession and as a woman in American society, as well as the costs of such subterfuge.

Like the 1950s, this film is all about identity. Margo wonders who she is behind her masks. Other characters wonder who Eve really is and whether actresses can ever stop performing. Actresses in *All about Eve* echoed postwar concerns about the nature of identity and the distrust of passing fictions while celebrating great actors and actresses. In so doing, this film revealed the cracks in postwar constructions of femininity and authenticity. For their portrayals, both Anne Baxter and Bette Davis were nominated for Best Actress at the 1950 Academy Awards. Tellingly, however, these two brunettes lost out to brash blonde newcomer Judy Holliday for her comic performance as Billie Dawn in *Born Yesterday*.[54]

In 1951, the *New York Times* noted how blondes dominated the box office on the stage and screen:

As the thespian spring approaches, the voice of the dumb blonde is heard throughout the land. The psychosomatic Adelaide of "Guys and Dolls," the diamond-driven Lorelei of Little Rock, and Dagmar, the platinum ph.d. of Channel 4, are all having their peroxide innings at the box office as the paying customers seek blonde shelter from bomb talk. And now, inexorably, the durable Billie Dawn, the Brooklyn Galatea of "Born Yesterday"—"the dumbest broad of them all" according to one awed critic—has been nominated for an Academy Award, an upstart challenger to such long-standing brunette intellects as Miss Gloria Swanson and Miss Bette Davis.[55]

Judy Holliday was one of many blonde archetypes that abounded in this period, from the girl next door to sex symbols to wise-cracking dames. Different filmmakers utilized different types of blondes. Hitchcock preferred the "drawing room ice queen" blondes of Grace Kelly, Eva Marie Saint, Doris Day, and Janet Leigh, rather than those like Marilyn Monroe or Jayne Mansfield who, he commented, had "sex written on their face."[56] Actresses like Monroe and Holliday utilized variations on the "dumb blonde" performance to make their mark in Hollywood films. As the *New York Times* noted, blondes in the 1950s were all the rage.

While the manufactured blonde starlet was not new, its association with femininity, whiteness, and class changed. Blondeness became the ideal of the perfect woman. Blondeness was equated with whiteness, and blondes in films signified the height of feminine performance: "Erasing one's difference, assimilating, was a sign of Americanness. And assimilation meant passing for white. Beauty standards were white. So were the models of the family and gender."[57] The blonde craze developed in response to challenges to white supremacy and WASP ideals from the emerging civil rights movement.[58]

The blonde woman was a symbol of the manufactured white female and the privileges of white femininity. Blondeness in all its facets was inextricably linked with whiteness, class, and feminine performance. As much as any other factor, this "blonde function" contributed to visible constructions of identity.[59] Like the ubiquitous "man in the gray flannel suit," blondeness invited a duplicity that facilitated blurring the line between gender performance and authentic identity. In Hollywood there was little faith in the idea of a "natural" blonde. "Platinum blondes" in postwar films became the most recognizably constructed signs of racial and gender identity in the 1950s.

Films like Hitchcock's *Vertigo* made audiences confront the artificiality of the spectacle, acknowledging how femininity was performance. The misogyny behind the power to mold women was disturbingly illuminated. As both a blonde and a brunette, the artifice of Kim Novak's roles as Judy/Madeleine was molded by masculine authorities, on-screen by Ferguson (Stewart) and off-screen by Hitchcock. In the 1950s, Hollywood made it explicit that gender was socially constructed.

Blondeness as a manufactured commodity could be packaged and bought. It was sold in a bottle as a lifestyle choice. While it created a white feminine ideal, it also meant anyone could buy platinum hair and pass as a blonde. Understanding blondeness as a bottled commodity subverted notions of authentic white identity. Blondeness afforded women another mask for racial and ethnic passing that existed outside class distinctions as the desired representation of a sexualized feminine beauty. Blondeness was therefore intimately connected to the performance of whiteness. Blonde beauty was hyped as attainable precisely because it was artificial.

An extreme but fun example of the blonde function is the low-budget horror film *She Devil* (1957), directed by Kurt Neumann. A young woman named Kyra Zelas (Mari Blanchard) is given an experimental serum developed by Dr. Dan Scott (Jack Kelly) to treat her terminal tuberculosis. He designed the serum to allow animals to adapt to any threat in their environment. Kyra is not only cured, but becomes indestructible. Tellingly, her adaptive superpowers quickly transform her from mousy brunette into blonde femme fatale, an alter ego she uses to manipulate men who all fall in love with her and to "hide in plain sight." At will, she can shift between her brunette and blonde identity, allowing her to commit crimes and then escape detection. Passing only as a glamourous blonde in public and keeping her brunette self a secret, she literally gets away with murder.

Kyra instinctively lies that her new blonde appearance is a just a bottled makeover, but Dr. Scott's housemate and colleague Dr. Richard Bach (Albert Dekker) becomes suspicious and steals a sample of her hair. The microscope confirms his fear that Kyra's hair is not chemically treated or dyed, but natural. Both men worry about the implications of her "natural [blonde] pigmentation" and decide she is too dangerous to live. Together the two male doctors who created her destroy her. The film ends with Kyra losing her goddess-like glow and reverting to her dark-haired self before dying from the tuberculosis. Although lacking in subtlety, this horror film exposes a common 1950s construct: blondeness as both desired ideal and dangerously duplicitous.

An indelible take on the bottled blonde archetype was created by Judy Holliday in George Cukor's *Born Yesterday* (Columbia, 1950), an image more evocative of working-class feminine ideals. Based on the Broadway play by Garson Kanin, the film suggested women that needed to be taught how to act like a "lady," a construction that was anything but natural. The dynamic trio of Holliday, Kanin, and Cukor ensured that a depth of social commentary made it into the comedy; the film was filled with references to 1940s left-wing ideals, echoing themes from the 1948 Progressive party platform.[60] Holliday (who was neither blonde nor dumb) played the character of a former Brooklyn showgirl, tough-talking platinum blonde Billie Dawn, for which she won Best Actress. William Holden played a journalist who was hired by her corrupt boyfriend, Harry Brock (Broderick Crawford). Holden was supposed to tutor her in how to overcome her "crass" and typically "dumb (but really not so dumb) blonde" behavior, to teach her social sophistication so that she could pass as a respectable middle-class American woman suitable for him to marry. Instead, Holliday and Holden teach each other about American history, democracy, and the virtue of wearing glasses. The dumb blonde "broad" becomes enlightened and intellectually curious, and the journalist has his faith restored.

A more interesting lesson here is how Holliday (nee Tuvim) applied the power of the feminine performance from her screen role to her real life. Because of her left-wing sensibilities, feminism, and Popular Front politics, Holliday was targeted as a "Red" by HUAC in 1951, but she had created such a convincing and formidable blonde persona in her *Born Yesterday* role that she was able to use it on Congress.[61] In her testimony before the Committee, Holliday played the part as the dumb but not so dumb blonde celluloid heroine Billie Dawn, and this time, the performance earned her more than awards. It stopped her from being blacklisted or having to name names. Judy Holliday proved that the blonde function could be used by actresses to their own advantage.

Of all the blonde archetypes of the 1950s, Marilyn Monroe was the most iconic symbol of the blonde function.[62] Her public performance was contrasted and read against her original brunette roots. Norma Jeane performed Marilyn, who performed the dumb sex goddess of the screen. Like Brando, it was hard to separate the actor from the performance. Appropriately, Monroe was also a devotee of Freud and the psychoanalytic shift. In 1953, Monroe was quoted in the *New York Times* about her religious differences with her friend Jane Russell, who was at the time also her costar in the upcoming film *Gentlemen Prefer Blondes*: "'Jane,' says Miss Monroe, 'who is deeply religious, tried to convert me to her religion and I tried to introduce her to Freud. Neither of us won.'"[63]

Monroe may have begun her screen career playing bit parts like Miss Casswell in *All about Eve*, but she came to symbolize fifties blonde performance in films like *Monkey Business* (1952), *Niagara* (1953), *How to Marry a Millionaire* (1953), and *Some Like It Hot* (1959). So successful was she that in Billy Wilder's *The Seven Year Itch* (1955), Monroe simply played The Girl. When Richard (Tom Ewell) buzzes her into the apartment building, Monroe as The Girl embodies "the 1950s Hollywood ideal of white femininity: white skin, platinum hair, white dress, white earrings, white sandals—not to mention the white bread and potato chips in her grocery bag."[64] Molly Haskell notes, "The times being what they were, if she hadn't existed, we would have had to invent her." [65]

Monroe's most iconic blonde performance was as Lorelei Lee in Howard Hawks's 1953 musical *Gentlemen Prefer Blondes.*[66] While Jane Russell received top billing, it made a star of Monroe.[67] Based on Anita Loos's 1920s novel, the story was updated for the 1950s. The hyperfeminine constructions of Dorothy (Russell) and Lorelei (Monroe) highlighted the performative aspects of gender and sexuality. The film opens with Lorelei and Dorothy singing "Two Little Girls from Little Rock." The women make no pretense about their desire to find suitable men for marriage. For Dorothy, this means a good-looking man, and for Lorelei, someone who is rich. Allusions to unhappy love affairs justify their calculating nature. In the film, Dorothy and Lorelei use their femininity not only to marry but also to improve their social status.

In an important courtroom scene, the usually brunette Dorothy passes as her blonde friend to keep Lorelei out of jail. Dorothy performs Lorelei's signature number, "Diamonds Are a Girl's Best Friend," in Lorelei's blonde drag, copying the look and the attitude. Russell as Dorothy's performance of Lorelei was no less constructed than Monroe's own construction of Lorelei. The blonde bombshell was a mask that could be performed by other women. The only person to see through the impersonation is Dorothy's beau, Malone (Elliot Reid), who threatens to expose Dorothy to the court. Dorothy as Lorelei silences him, however, explaining that Dorothy really loved him but she would not be happy if he did anything to hurt Lorelei.

While the film exposes the artificiality of femininity, it also plays with ideas of sexuality. In the narrative, Dorothy and Lorelei are committed as much to each other as to the men they finally marry. The men in the film quite literally disappear into the background. When Dorothy sings her famous number "Ain't There Anyone Here For Love?" the men's Olympic team members become physical props for the song.[68] The sexual innuendo is reinforced when she grabs two tennis rackets, asking, "Doubles anyone? Court's free!" In the final scene, Dorothy and Lorelei walk down the aisle together as the camera focuses on them, not their adoring husbands. The grooms become "bystanders" to Dorothy and Lorelei's "performance of victorious femininity."[69]

The unabashed celebration of the blonde as artificial in *Gentlemen Prefer Blondes* reflected wider cultural discourses about gender performance. It was a strange truism that a post-war culture obsessed with authenticity was also obsessed with the blonde image. This film destabilized gender and sexuality by placing the emphasis on the careful performances necessary for a sex goddess out to catch a millionaire. Taken together, Hollywood films suggested that all representations of iconic postwar femininity, especially blonde femininity, were passing performances. One reviewer quipped: "As for Miss Monroe, she is, as usual, an extremely effective female impersonator, herself."[70] Monroe candidly admitted she knew how to perform "Marilyn."

Actresses like Judy Holliday and Marilyn Monroe epitomized the successfully constructed blonde persona, but blondeness as desired ideal was a gender performance that invited racial transgressions. The 1955 film *Love Is a Many Splendored Thing* offers a good example. Hyped for its complex representations of interracial loves and racial indeterminacy, this film also showcased how blondeness implicated passing identities. Directed by Henry King and adapted from the semi-autobiographical novel by Han Suyin, the film is set in 1949 Hong Kong. The British colony offers a perfect setting to explore boundaries between race, gender, and competing cultural ideologies. Jennifer Jones was cast in the lead as the widowed Eurasian doctor Han Suyin (which raised controversies of its own).[71] Dr. Suyin's husband was a Nationalist General shot by the communists, which posits her as a politically good Chinese in the Cold War ethos of the 1950s. William Holden is the male romantic lead, Mark Elliot, the white American correspondent with a wife whom he doesn't love but cannot divorce.

More important here is the supporting role of Dr. Suyin's friend Suzanne (Jorja Curtright), who is also Eurasian but dramatically dyes her hair blonde and passes for English. The film's portrayal of two differing Eurasian women—Han and Suzanne—subverts ideas of a singular (and appropriate) racial identity by framing the issue as one of competing cultural forces rather than essentialist categories. In a scene at a café where the two women are having lunch they discuss the pros and cons of passing in Hong Kong. Suzanne tells her: "I pass for English now; I hope you won't give me away." Han responds: "Oh, Suzanne, you should be proud to be Eurasian and proud of your Chinese heritage." But Suzanne challenges this framework: "Nonsense. You can't be two things at once, and I advise you pass for English."

Suzanne's choice to pass is motivated by her desire to be a suitably British-looking mistress to her white married lover, hospital director Humphrey Palmer-Jones (Torin Thatcher). In this way, Suzanne personified the interconnectedness of race and sexuality, demonstrating racial flexibility but also a more rigid conception of gender performance. Her racial passing was inseparable from her carefully constructed gendered and sexually available performance as a "blonde" white woman. Suzanne's assumption of whiteness owes more to Marilyn Monroe's or Judy Holliday's blonde performance than it does to cultural depictions of mulattoes in crisis found in films like

Imitation of Life, a performance based as much on gendered strategies for survival as on ideas of race.

In films like *Born Yesterday* and *Love Is a Many Splendored Thing*, women learned class and racially based feminine behavior in order to pass in different societal circles. Representations of gender, sexuality, race, and class intertwined in Hollywood's framing of love, respectability, and security. This gender performance formula was replicated in other 1950s narratives, including *Gigi* and *A Star Is Born*, and of course most famously in *My Fair Lady*, the 1956 Broadway musical adaptation of *Pygmalion*.[72] While the "Pygmalion syndrome" and gender masquerades have a textual antiquity, as do cross-dressing and role reversals, postwar questions about authenticity and the nature of identity complicated how these narratives were viewed. The psychoanalytic turn directly informed how postwar images of women were coded in class and racialized terms as well as what constituted normalcy.

The psychoanalytic intersections of race, class, and gender identity all came together in the 1957 film *The Three Faces of Eve*, directed by Nunnally Johnson. Joanne Woodward starred in this "true story" of a Georgia housewife with multiple personalities, based on the book by Drs. Corbett Thigpen and Harvey M. Cleckley, the therapists who treated the real Eve. Alistair Cooke introduces the film, authenticating its verisimilitude. Not surprisingly, a male psychiatrist is the authority in the film, and he not only diagnoses Eve, but defines what her normal feminine identity should be. The film reflects postwar tropes about race and gender. The racialized characteristics evoked by Eve's differing personalities are explicit, down to their names. Her first personality is "Eve White," designated a lower-class "white trash" Southern woman who is abused by her husband. The second personality is "Eve Black," revealed to be a wild woman whose behavior is associated with a sexualized blackness (including a proclivity for jazz music), vividly described by Bosley Crowther as "a loose, lurid creature with a brash go-to-hell attitude."[73] Woodward's performance of blackness as this personality echoes other racially indeterminate characters in fifties films, like Sarah Jane in *Imitation of Life* or Jocelyn in *Island in the Sun*. Moreover, Eve Black is fully aware of Eve White and everything she does, and she can even pass herself off as the other personality when she chooses. Significantly, however, Eve White blacks out when the other personalities come to the fore. It is not surprising that the black personality can pass, whereas the white identity is not even aware. With the aid of psychiatrists, a third personality finally emerges, a healthy one that is neither wild nor white trash, and tellingly, is also less Southern. Eve becomes the desired middle-class white woman and is cured.

Eve's on-screen transformation into desired ideals by helpful professionals was mirrored off-screen. Georgia-born Joanne Woodward won the Academy Award for this performance, with critics praising her Southern authenticity. The irony was not lost on her; as she claimed in interviews, "It was the easiest role I ever did."[74] Appropriately, Woodward was a devotee of psychoanalysis and the Method. In earlier roles Woodward admitted she had carefully worked with vocal coaches to erase all traces of her Southern accent and background in order to conform to the more generic (if vaguely Midwestern) white middle-class ideal that Hollywood favored and propagated.[75] Woodward had worked hard to appear natural and authentic, but once again the American starlet was revealed to be a carefully constructed performance at odds with her real story.

The acknowledged artificiality of femininity and gender fed broader cultural fears that identities were no longer fixed and stable. Films and audiences wondered if everyone was passing in one way or another. While the idea of normalcy was celebrated in prescriptive literature, it became increasingly difficult to find it in films. American towns became bastions of secrets and pathological anxiety. *Rebel without a Cause* featured a town full of teenage angst, masculine anxiety, and neurotics. In *Bad Day at Black Rock*, the town was filled with dark secrets, a decayed and ignorant place that was part of America's past, not its future. But no film captured the hypocrisy of small town America better than Mark Robson's 1957 adaptation of Grace Metalious's novel *Peyton Place*.[76] Although chided by critics, the book broke all sales records after its release in 1956.[77] Metalious, dubbed "Pandora in Blue Jeans" by the press, was loved in the big cities but vilified in her hometown for exposing their secrets.[78] *Life* magazine wrote of the controversy:

> Grace Metalious, author of one of the most popular novels in the country, is easily the most unpopular novelist—and resident—in Gilmanton, New Hampshire. Her novel, *Peyton Place*, is a brawling story of violence and sex in a New England town which citizens of Gilmanton consider a scandalous portrayal of their town. "She's written a dirty story about us," complains a bitter citizen.[79]

The film adaptation of Peyton Place was critically and financially successful, garnering nominations for nine Academy Awards, including Best Picture. Filmed in Camden, Maine, it starred Lana Turner as Constance MacKenzie, with Diane Varsi as her daughter Allison. Turner was unquestionably the biggest star of this ensemble drama, though the central character is the daughter.

Told from Allison's perspective, the narrative is a remembrance of her life in the New England town she grew up in during the 1940s, as part of the high school graduating class of 1941. The supporting cast included Russ Tamblyn as Norman Page and Hope Lange as Selena Cross, Allison's two best friends. Lee Philips played Michael Rossi as the new principal of the high school and Constance's romantic interest. Lloyd Nolan starred as Dr. Matthew Swain, who knew the town's secrets, the sins hidden behind the whitewashed exteriors and picket fences. While the film was less graphic than the novel, it still included rape, incest, adultery, illegitimacy, murder, and nudity. An apt tagline stated, "Small town America will never be the same again."

The film begins as Allison learns a lesson in the gender politics of a small town. Miss Thornton (Mildred Dunnock), the beloved teacher, is skipped over for a promotion for principal. Instead, the town hires a man from the outside, Mr. Rossi. Allison expresses her disappointment and disillusionment, but Miss Thornton tells her: "A person doesn't always get what she deserves. Remember it. If there is anything in life you want go and get it. Don't wait for anybody to give it to you."

Life in Peyton Place was not the stuff of fairy tales. Allison declares in a voiceover that "everybody hides behind plain brown wrappers." Allison's mother Constance was stifling to live with as "the only perfect person" in the town. This was only appearance, however; Constance passed as a widow, creating a fiction of a deceased husband to explain her pregnancy after she returned alone to her hometown.[80] Class and geography intersect. Constance was able to pass off her youthful indiscretion and project unquestioned respectability, aided by the geography of her affair, which was safely situated in the big city.

Allison's best friend Norman had a domineering mother who became jealous if he spent time with anyone else, making him feel "maladjusted." Echoing the narrative of Tea and Sympathy, Norman feared he was becoming a "sissy," his worries magnified because he hated being at home and spending all his time in the library. Another student named Rodney (Barry Coe) hated his family, especially his overly domineering and cheating father whom he viewed as a hypocrite. Rodney's father disapproved of his relationship with Betty (Terry Moore) because he viewed her as the "town tramp." His father told him: "I can understand you wanting to see the girl, but not in public." Rodney responded: "Okay, nobody's fighting you. I'll be as big a Harrington as you. I'll marry a cold fish from Boston, have one child, and cheat for the rest of my life." To ensure his obedience, Rodney's father buys him a new convertible.

However, the most dramatic situation is that of Selena, Allison's other best friend. While her home was framed as rustic and pastoral, with sheep roaming the grounds, inside, her drunken stepfather Lucas (Arthur Kennedy) beat her because she was provocative. Her mother Nellie (Betty Field) was too ineffectual and frightened to help.[81] The escalating violence of Selena's home life pushed the boundaries on representations of incest and sexual violence. Just before her graduation, Selena is assaulted and raped by her stepfather. The scene then dramatically cuts to the next day's graduation ceremony and Allison's valedictorian speech: "The world outside waits for you; it is a world full of love and rich in opportunity; there may be dangers [as the camera cuts to a shot of Selena's solemn face in her graduation gown], but if you hold firm to your purpose and your ideals, you'll storm the ramparts of success; tomorrow you grow up and your true happiness begins." The students applaud but the camera focuses on Selena's sad face. The film juxtaposes hope for the future against the dark secrets that are coming to light.

The film emphasized the sharp distinction between public and private spaces and public and private selves. It inverted ideas of safety; private spaces supplanted public spaces as places of fear and terror. *Peyton Place* framed the home as a place to escape, not a safe haven. Moreover, while the townspeople all had secrets, they were gendered in nature, and the stakes were higher for women than for men. Women were the gatekeepers of appearance. The film repeatedly showed the direct connection between a women's status, her public persona, and her appearance. The issue of pregnancy for unmarried women was serious.[82]

However, the passing fictions of feminine respectability were not accessible to all women. Constance's performance as a widow was not a social strategy Selena could use when she discovered she was pregnant. Instead, Selena asked Dr. Swain for an abortion. He refused because it was illegal, but changed his mind when he realized what had happened. A child of incest trumped ethical or moral concerns about abortion. Swain confronted Lucas and had him sign a confession and leave town. Selena's mother knew the truth but could not face it and in despair she committed suicide, symbolically, in Allison's closet. Later, Lucas returned from the Navy and Selena killed him. The murder set the stage for the final dramatic courtroom scene following Selena's arrest.

In court, Dr. Swain drew back the curtains of false appearances. All of the town's secrets were revealed as Peyton Place was put on trial. The doctor admitted that he had "assisted" Selena "in a miscarriage," and then continued indicting the whole town: "We are all prisoners of each other's gossip, killed by each other's whispers, and it's time it stopped . . . Selena's been living in a prison of her own long enough, one we helped build."[83] With this testimony, Selena is acquitted, and as the storm of a trial settles, the chastised townsfolk wait outside to congratulate her. Reconciled, they find a "season of love." With their secrets revealed the town and Selena find happiness.

Peyton Place was a massive hit for the 20th Century-Fox Studio, aided mainly by the popularity of its source, but the off-screen scandal of its star Lana Turner while the film was in theatres did not hurt, either.[84] The media played with the slippage between the trial in the film and Turner's own murder trial. In 1958, Life magazine juxtaposed pictures of Turner on the stand with stills from her movies, including The Postman Always Rings Twice and Peyton Place: "Lana had been nominated for an Academy Award ... but this was a dramatic, personal triumph far beyond anything she had achieved as an actress."[85] The publicity was good for film, helping to keep box office attendance healthy. And while critics jested over whether Turner gave the better performance on or off the screen, she did receive an Oscar nomination for her role in the film. The film also received eight other nominations, including Best Picture, Best Director for Robson, and Best Supporting Actress nominations for both Diana Varsi and Hope Lange.

Despite the sentimental conclusion, Peyton Place suggested that the idealized, harmonious small town and the American values it epitomized were an illusion. Although the idea that ordinary people had dark secrets was not new, Peyton Place created a benchmark for unmasking Americans and was a crucial reflection of postwar anxieties about authenticity and passing. Metalious's narrative was so effective that the term "Peyton Place" entered the cultural vocabulary as shorthand for the hypocrisy and falseness of picture-perfect towns. No one was what he or she appeared to be; everyone passed to appear normal to others. Trading on the language of the couch, the film suggested that such passing created pathology. Both the novel and the film adaptation reached unprecedented numbers of people with this message, giving voice to concerns about authenticity and the linkages between public and private personas. Peyton Place reflected fears that the search for authenticity so intrinsic to postwar culture had led to the inverse, a culture defined by the anxiety that identities and lives lacked authentic meaning. Passing specters became internalized. Normalcy, even in the heartland, was an illusion at best. Americans were shown as leading imitative rather than authentic lives. Echoing other films of the era, Peyton Place highlighted the masks worn to project normal gender and sexual identities in American culture, suggesting that all Americans were passing in some form or another.

CONCLUSION

If the "fundamental problem" of the 1950s was that of "personal identity," it was a problem that America's "dream factory" reflected.[1] Following the Second World War, Hollywood embraced the psychoanalytic turn and dreams of authenticity, while channeling fears that like the atom the inner world of identity and Self was irreparably split. Passing became the central metaphor for anxiety about authenticity and identity. Representations of passing related to discourse about authenticity and identity extended far beyond issues of race or racial indeterminacy. The possibility that aliens could pass as humans, Communists could pass as Americans, men could pass as women, women could pass as men, and homosexuals could pass as heterosexuals fueled a decade of anxiety and fear. *Ebony*'s suggestion that five to ten million blacks were passing unbeknownst to white America mirrored J. Edgar Hoover's multitudes of hidden Communist subversives, the "enemy within," who were dispersed throughout the country in universities, government positions, and most insidiously, in Hollywood. On and off the screen, Hollywood was a flashpoint for expressing and targeting these fears.

Over time, the specter of passing shifted from being an externalized fear about how others were perceived to an internalized fear that individual identities and the external markers of identity might be inauthentic. Blondeness and the gray flannel suit were just masks. The epistemological questions raised by Langston Hughes's short story about passing mirrored broader cultural anxieties about the instability and fragility of categories of race, class, gender, and sexuality—all of which Hughes himself epitomized. On March 26, 1953, just a year after he published his successful 1952 short story collection *Laughing to Keep from Crying*, Hughes was investigated by HUAC for Communist beliefs in a televised hearing.[2] Hughes recanted his earlier beliefs, refused to name names, and was still exonerated. Hughes's own experiences showed an American culture that was just as defined by anxiety about hidden political and sexual identities as about racial identities. The question of who was passing for whom took on greater significance.

Like Hughes and his story, Hollywood's myriad representations of passing in films between 1947 and 1960 illuminate the contradictory discourses about identity that coexisted in postwar American culture. Films revealed a disjuncture between narrative ideas that championed authenticity as desirable and the inherent implication of the film medium that any projection of identity was merely a performance. Likewise, Hollywood's openness to sexual fluidity and gender ambiguity, embodied by new star personas and ideals, operated in and around conservative discourse about the imperatives of stable and authentic (or normal) identities, and vice versa. In this reading, overtly discussed fears about Communists or blacks passing undetected in WASP middle-America, which Hollywood reflected, did not help restabilize American identity into clearly defined categories; in fact, it only served to complicate a deeper crisis about the nature of gender, race, and sexuality and ultimately added to anxieties that everyone was passing for something else. In *All about Eve*, Addison DeWitt claims that it is their collective "ab-normality" that makes theatre people so unique and different from "normal" Americans, but other films from the 1950s expose the anxiety that no one is really normal when judged according to standards set by impossible cultural ideals. Authentic identities were elusive and imagined. In postwar America, everyone was passing.

AFTERWORD AND ACKNOWLEDGMENTS

This book is primarily a cultural and social history of the United States in the postwar era, but any history about identity, anxiety, passing, and films must acknowledge a rich, theoretical base that transcends discipline. By combining diverse and divergent threads of scholarship from multiple disciplines, a richer and more nuanced view of postwar American culture emerges. Analyzing passing and Hollywood films was both a fun exploration and a means to open up new historical perspectives on mid-century America and American cinema. Indebted to the insights of both film theorists and historians, this book joins others who seek to historically contextualize theoretical discourses about race, gender, and sexuality and to create important counternarratives about the long 1950s.

While films serve as the primary evidentiary source, other documents were utilized from a variety of archives and source materials. The most extensive collection of film files exists in the Margaret Herrick Library of the Academy of Motion Picture Arts and Sciences (AMPAS) in Beverley Hills, which houses Academy Film Archives and the Production Code Administration (PCA) Archives. The Harry Ransom Humanities Research Center at the University of Texas at Austin holds important collections, including the David O. Selznick Papers. The Bowling Green University Popular Culture Archives has an almost complete collection of extremely popular postwar tabloid magazines like *Confidential*, *Suppressed*, *Whisper*, and *Private Lives*, important source materials for the type of scandals that sold best, and more importantly, for how such scandals were framed by the gossip press. The Special Collections at the Cinema-Television Library and the Warner Bros. Archive (WB), both at the University of Southern California, offer extensive collections on their films. The Film and Television Archive (ARSC) at the University of California at Los Angeles allows scholars to view old television series, such as episodes of the 1950s *Confidential File* series, including "Daytime Whites." The Library of Congress has an abundance of useful materials, especially copies of unreleased films about the Hollywood blacklist. The released FBI Hollywood surveillance files available on microfilm at the University of California at Berkeley is another helpful resource.

Collectively, these archival materials provided cultural and political contexts for understanding American society during the long 1950s. Other documents include published materials from the McCarthy era and the

Hollywood Ten, as well as accounts and memoirs written by individuals in Hollywood. The final but invaluable sources are the many important popular magazines and newspapers like the *New York Times*, *Sight and Sound*, *Hollywood Reporter*, *Los Angeles Times*, *Variety*, *Life*, *Newsweek*, and *Ebony*. All these magazines spanned the entire era, from 1947 to 1960.

Writing a book is a long-drawn-out and usually solitary process, but it would not have been possible without the help of many people over the years. First, I want to thank the amazing team at University Press of Mississippi who worked hard to bring this book to publication. I am indebted to the kindness and efforts of Leila Salisbury, Valerie Jones, Anne Stascavage, John Langston, and designer Pete Halverson, as well as the readers for their generous comments. On a more personal level, I would like to thank all the colleagues, friends, and family members who have been invaluable in seeing this project through to the finish line; they surely know who they are, but a few in particular must be mentioned. Robin and Jeet deserve a shout-out for giving both my writing and me incredible support. Thanks also to Sam, JJ, Michele, Catherine, Leslie, and Sharon for their help of various forms over the years, as well as to my sister Becky and my brother Den. Special thanks go to RJ, who has been a great friend and an excellent reader/editor through so many drafts and incarnations of this manuscript. Thanks is also due to Molly Ladd-Taylor. Most of all I would like to thank my parents Jane and David.

NOTES

INTRODUCTION

1. William Shakespeare, *Othello*, Act 1, Scene 1, Line 68.

2. Langston Hughes, "Who's Passing for Who?," in *Langston Hughes Short Stories*, ed. Akiba Sullivan Harper (New York: Hill and Wang, 1996), 170–74. Originally published in Hughes's short story collection *Laughing to Keep from Crying* (1952).

3. Hughes, "Who's Passing for Who?," 173.

4. Important studies on racial passing include Werner Sollors, *Neither Black nor White yet Both: Thematic Explorations of Interracial Literature* (New York: Oxford University Press, 1997); Gayle Wald, *Crossing the Line: Racial Passing in Twentieth-Century U.S. Literature and Culture* (Durham, NC: Duke University Press, 2000); Maria Carla Sanchez and Linda Schlossberg, ed., *Passing: Identity and Interpretation in Sexuality, Race, and Religion* (New York: New York University Press, 2001); and Pamela L. Caughie, *Passing and Pedagogy: The Dynamics of Responsibility* (Urbana and Chicago: University of Illinois Press, 1999).

5. The "long 1950s" has been used by historians to refer to the decade and a half following the Second World War, with variation as to the exact start and end dates depending on the scholar's focus. In this work, I use the phrase as a short-hand to refer to the period from 1947 to 1960.

6. Henry Louis Gates Jr., *Thirteen Ways of Looking at a Black Man* (New York: Random House, 1997), 207.

7. Elaine K. Ginsberg, ed., *Passing and the Fictions of Identity* (Durham and London: Duke University Press, 1996), 8.

8. Sollors, *Neither Black nor White*, 247–48.

9. Ian F. Haney Lopez, *White by Law: The Legal Construction of Race* (New York: New York University Press, 1996); Werner Sollors, *Interracialism: Black-White Intermarriage in American History, Literature, and Law* (Oxford, New York: Oxford University Press, 2000); Peggy Pascoe, *What Comes Naturally: Miscegenation Law and the Making of Race in America* (Oxford: Oxford University Press, 2009).

10. "Whiteness" studies share analytic focus with passing. See Richard Dyer, *White* (London and New York: Routledge, 1997); bell hooks, "Representations of Whiteness," in bell hooks *Black Looks: Race and Representation* (Toronto: Between the Lines, 1992); David R. Roediger, ed., *Black on White: Black Writers on What It Means to Be White* (New York: Schocken Books, 1999); Gwendolyn Audrey Foster, *Performing Whiteness: Postmodern Re/Constructions in the Cinema* (New York: State University of New York Press, 2003); and Daniel Bernardi, ed., *Classic Hollywood, Classic Whiteness* (Minneapolis: University of Minnesota Press, 2001).

11. Lisa M. Anderson, *Mammies No More: The Changing Image of Black Women on Stage and Screen* (Lanham: Rowman & Littlefield, 1997); and Wald, *Crossing the Line.*

12. Reba Lee, *I Passed for White* (New York: Longman, 1955) and Fay Liddle Coolidge, *Black Is White* (New York: Vantage, 1958). An incomplete list of post-passing magazine articles includes Fred Demery, "I Lived Two Lives for 30 Years," *Ebony* (December 1958): 156–62; "Why I Never Want to Pass," *Ebony* (June 1959): 49–52, 54; "Have Negroes Stopped Passing?," *Jet* (September 13, 1956): 10–12; "I'm Through with Passing," *Ebony* (March 6, 1951): 22–27; Janice Kingslow, "I Refuse to Pass," *Negro Digest* (May 1950): 30; and "Why 'Passing' Is Passing Out," *Jet* (July 17, 1952): 12–13. For a discussion of the phenomenon of post-passing stories, see Wald, *Crossing the Line,* 116–51.

13. Other important novels focusing on racial passing include William and Ellen Craft, *Running a Thousand Miles to Freedom* (1860), Mark Twain, *Puddn'head Wilson* (1894), Frank Waldo, *Our America* (1919), Walter White, *Flight* (1926), Jessie Faucet, *Plum Bun* (1929), and George Schuyler, *Black No More* (1931). Passing was most thoroughly explored as a literary theme in the 1920s and 1930s, especially by writers of the Harlem Renaissance. However, later works included Lillian Smith, *Strange Fruit* (1944) and Gwendolyn Brooks, *A Street in Bronzeville* (1945). See Sollors, *Neither Black nor White.* See also M. Giulia Fabi, *Passing and the Rise of the African American Novel* (Urbana and Chicago: University of Illinois Press, 2001).

14. It should be noted that Hughes was consistent in how he framed issues of racial passing in his writings. His 1934 satire of *Imitation of Life,* called "Limitations of Life," also humorously exposed the contradictions and issues of racial indeterminacy and racial passing. What was dramatically different is the cultural context in which these texts were read.

15. Kephart, "The 'Passing' Question," *Phylon* 10 (1948): 336.

16. Wald, *Crossing the Line,* 23.

CHAPTER 1

1. Quote under heading "Atomic Age," in *Time,* August 20, 1945, 29.

2. Quote appears in the "U.S. at War" section under the heading "The Bomb" in *Time,* August 20, 1945, 19.

3. Ellen Herman, *The Romance of American Psychology* (Berkeley: University of California Press, 1996): 133–34.

4. Ellen Schrecker, *Many Are the Crimes: McCarthyism in America* (Boston: Little, Brown and Company, 1998): 203.

5. Alan Nadel, *Containment Culture* (Durham, NC: Duke University Press, 1995); Steven J. Whitfield, *The Culture of the Cold War,* 2nd ed. (Baltimore: John Hopkins University Press, 1991); Paul Boyer, *By the Bomb's Early Light: American Thought and Culture at the Dawn of the Atomic Age* (New York: Pantheon, 1985).

6. Irving Howe, "This Age of Conformity," *Partisan Review* 21 (January–February 1954): 1.

7. The phrase "age of anxiety" was first used in this context by historian Arthur Schlesinger Jr., who borrowed his wording from poet W. H. Auden. Arthur M. Schlesinger, *The Vital Center* (Boston: Houghton Mifflin, 1949).

8. Jerome F. Shapiro, *Atomic Bomb Cinema: The Apocalyptic Imagination in Film* (New York: Routledge, 2002).

9. Joel Foreman, ed., *The Other Fifties: Interrogating Midcentury American Icons* (Urbana and Chicago: University of Illinois Press, 1997); Stephanie Coontz, *The Way We Never Were: American Families and the Nostalgia Trap* (New York: Basic Books, 1999); Joanne Meyerwitz, ed., *Not June Cleaver: Women and Gender in Postwar America, 1945–1960* (Philadelphia: Temple University Press, 1994); Wini Breines, *Young, White, and Miserable: Growing Up Female in the Fifties* (Boston: Beacon Press, 1992).

10. Susan Hegeman, *Patterns for America: Modernism and the Concept of Culture* (Princeton, New Jersey: Princeton University Press, 1999): 103.

11. Margaret Mead, *And Keep Your Powder Dry: An Anthropologist Looks at America* (New York: William Morrow, 1942). Prewar bestsellers in cultural anthropology that were influential included Margaret Mead's *Coming of Age in Samoa: A Psychological Study of Primitive Youth for Western Civilization* (1928; repr., New York: William Morrow, 1973), and Ruth Benedict's *Patterns of Culture* (1934; repr., New York: Houghton Mifflin, 1989).

12. For an early analysis of these studies, see Milton Singer, "A Survey of Culture and Personality Theory and Research," in *Studying Personality Cross Culturally*, ed. Bert Kaplan (New York: Harper and Row, 1961), 9–90, especially 43–57.

13. Herman, *Romance of American Psychology*, 33.

14. Lois W. Banner, *Intertwined Lives: Margaret Mead, Ruth Benedict, and Their Circle* (New York: Knopf, 2003).

15. Northrop Frye, *Anatomy of Criticism: Four Essays* (Oxford: Oxford University Press, 2000).

16. Erikson was a key part of the postwar shift in how culture and identity were understood. Warren Susman writes, "From the end of the 1940s to almost the end of the 1950s the problem was fundamentally redefined as that of personal identity. Who could object to seeing this as the age of Erik Erikson?" Warren I. Susman, *Culture as History: The Transformation of American Society in the Twentieth Century* (New York: Pantheon Books, 1984): 284.

17. Lionel Trilling, *Sincerity and Authenticity: The Charles Eliot Norton Lectures, 1969–1970* (Cambridge, Massachusetts: Harvard University Press, 1971).

18. Susman, *Culture as History*, 284.

19. Herman, *Romance of American Psychology*, 292.

20. Carl Degler, *In Search of Human Nature: The Decline and Revival of Darwinism in American Social Thought* (Oxford: Oxford University Press, 1991): viii.

21. Gunnar Myrdal, *An American Dilemma: The Negro Problem and Modern Democracy*, 20th anniversary ed. (New York: Harper & Row, 1962).

22. The 1944 documentary *The Negro Soldier* was a filmic response to the Double V campaign. It was made both as propaganda to promote enlistment by African American men and as a progressive call to end discrimination and racial segregation. The film,

written by Carlton Moss and produced by Frank Capra, was viewed as a "turning point" in representations of blacks and became required viewing in the army. See Thomas Cripps and David Culbert, "The Negro Soldier (1944): Film Propaganda in Black and White," *American Quarterly*, 31, no. 5 (Winter 1979): 616–40.

23. Herman, *Romance of American Psychology*, 181–84.

24. Walter A. Jackson, *Gunnar Myrdal and American's Conscience: Social Engineering and Racial Liberalism, 1938–1987* (Chapel Hill: University of North Carolina Press, 1990).

25. Myrdal, *American Dilemma*; Abram Kardiner and Lionel Ovesey, *The Mark of Oppression: Explorations in the Personality of the American Negro* (Cleveland: World Publishing Company, 1951); Gordon W. Allport, *The Nature of Prejudice*, 1979.

26. Harry Truman, *To Secure These Rights: The Report of the President's Committee on Civil Rights* (Washington, DC: Government Printing Office, 1947).

27. Elaine Tyler May, *Homeward Bound: American Families in the Cold War Era* (New York: Basic Books, 1988). Nadel, *Containment Culture*.

28. Steven Cohan, *Masked Men: Masculinity and the Movies in the Fifties* (Blooming-ton and Indianapolis: Indiana University Press, 1997), and Anna Creadick, "Incredible/ Shrinking Men: Masculinity and Atomic Anxiety in American Postwar Science Fiction Film" in *Fear Itself: Enemies Real and Imagined in American Culture*, ed. Nancy Lusignan Schultz, (West Lafayette, Indiana: Purdue University Press, 1999), 285–300.

29. Herman, *Romance of American Psychology*.

30. Eva S. Moskowitz, *In Therapy We Trust: America's Obsession with Self-Fulfillment* (Baltimore and London: John Hopkins University Press, 2001), 169.

31. Ads blamed the pressures of modern life, claiming the monotony and pressure of daily life created "anxiety-ridden housewives" and "stressed out" businessmen in need of something to help them "cope." Drugs like Seconal and Miltown were solutions. See Janet Walker, "Couching Resistance: Women, Film, and Postwar Psychoanalytic Psychiatry," in *Psychoanalysis & Cinema*, ed. E. Ann Kaplan (New York: Routledge, 1990), 143–62. See also William Chafe, *The Unfinished Journey: America since World War II*, 2nd ed. (Oxford: Oxford University Press, 1986): 126.

32. Joanne Meyerwitz, *How Sex Changed: A History of Transsexuality in the United States* (Cambridge: Harvard University Press, 2002).

33. John D'Emilio, *Sexual Politics, Sexual Communities: The Making of a Homosexual Minority in the United States, 1940–1970* (Chicago: University of Chicago Press, 1983); Liz Kennedy, *Boots of Leather, Slippers of Gold* (New York: Routledge, 1993); Allan Berube, *Coming Out under Fire: The History of Gay Men and Women in World War II* (New York: Plume, 1991).

34. David Riesman, *The Lonely Crowd: A Study of the Changing American Character* (New Haven: Yale University Press, 1950).

35. Singer, "A Survey of Culture and Personality Theory and Research," 9–90.

36. Helen Leland Witmer and Ruth Kotinsky, eds., *Personality in the Making: The Fact-Finding Report of the Midcentury White House Conference on Children and Youth* (New York: Harper, 1952); Beatrice B. Whiting, ed., *Six Cultures: Studies of Child Rearing* (New York: John Wiley and Sons, 1963).

37. Herman, *Romance of American Psychology*, 187.

38. Phillip Wylie, *Generation of Vipers* (New York: Rinehart, 1942).

39. Edward A. Strecker, *Their Mothers' Sons: The Psychiatrist Examines an American Problem* (New York: J. B. Lippincott Co., 1947) and Ferdinand Lundberg and Marynia F. Farnham, MD, *Modern Woman: The Lost Sex* (New York: Harper and Brothers, 1947).

40. Erik Erikson was an influential dissenting voice against "momism," noting how there were so many experts "decrying the mothers of this country as 'Moms' and as a 'generation of vipers'" that it had become "a manifest literary sport." "Who is this 'Mom'?" he asks, and "How did she lose her good, simple name? How could she become an excuse for all that is rotten in the state of the nation and a subject of literary temper and tantrums?" Erikson, *Childhood and Society*, 2nd ed. (New York: W. W. Norton, 1950): 288–89.

41. For an analysis of Wertham's life and work, see Bart Beaty, *Fredric Wertham and the Critique of Mass Culture: A Re-Examination of the Critic Whose Congressional Testimony Sparked the Comics Code* (Jackson: University Press of Mississippi, 2005).

42. A. L. Kroeber and Clyde Kluckholm, *Culture: A Critical Review of Concepts and Definitions* (New York: Vintage, 1952).

43. The results of Whiting's studies were later published. Beatrice B. Whiting, ed., *Six Cultures: Studies of Child Rearing* (New York: John Wiley and Sons, 1963).

44. Elie A. Cohen, *Human Behavior in the Concentration Camp* (New York: Grossett and Dunlap, 1953).

45. Alfred C. Kinsey, *Sexual Behavior in the Human Male* (Philadelphia: Saunders, 1948) and *Sexual Behavior in the Human Female* (Philadelphia: Saunders, 1953).

46. Jonathan Gathorne-Hardy, *Sex, The Measure of All Things: A Life of Alfred C. Kinsey* (London: Chatto & Windus, 1998) and James H. Jones, *Alfred C. Kinsey: A Public/Private Life* (New York: W.W. Norton, 1997).

47. Jennifer Terry, *An American Obsession: Science, Medicine, and Homosexuality in Modern Society* (Chicago: University of Chicago Press, 1999): 303.

48. Margaret Mead, *Sex and Temperament in Three Primitive Societies* (New York: Mentor Books, 1950).

49. Herman, *Romance of American Psychology*.

50. Original emphasis, Erikson, *Childhood and Society*, 24.

51. Erikson, *Childhood and Society*, 406–7.

52. Erikson, *Childhood and Society*, 407.

53. J. Edgar Hoover quoted at a HUAC hearing in 1947 in the documentary *Hollywood on Trial* (1976). A James Gutman/ David Helpern Jr. Production. Narrated by John Huston.

54. For contextualization on racial aspects of the investigations and the blacklist, see also Penny M. Von Eschen, *Race against Empire: Black Americans and Anticolonialism, 1937–1957* (Ithaca, NY: Cornell University Press, 1996).

55. Richard M. Fried, *Nightmare in Red: The McCarthy Era in Perspective* (New York: Oxford University Press, 1990); and David Caute, *The Great Fear: The Anti-Communist Purge under Truman and Eisenhower* (New York: Simon and Schuster, 1978).

56. Chafe, *The Unfinished Journey*, 105.

57. Literary critic Robert Corber connects fears about sexuality and passing queers to Cold War anxieties: "One of the consequences of the definition of homosexuality and lesbianism as threats to national security was that in the 1950s sexual orientation became as crucial a determinate of social identity as race and gender." Robert Corber, *In the Name of National Security: Hitchcock, Homophobia, and the Political Construction of Gender in Postwar America* (Durham: Duke University Press, 1993): 9.

58. Terry, *American Obsession*, 343.

59. John D'Emilio, "The Homosexual Menace: The Politics of Sexuality in Cold War America," in *Passion and Power: Sexuality in History*, eds. Kathy Peiss and Christina Simmons (Philadelphia: Temple University Press, 1989), 226–40.

60. Amy Knight, *How the Cold War Began: The Gouzenko Affair and the Hunt for Soviet Spies* (Toronto: McClelland & Stewart, 2005); David K. Johnson, *The Lavender Scare: The Cold War Persecution of Gays and Lesbians in the Federal Government* (Chicago: University of Chicago Press, 2004).

61. Whitfield, *Culture of the Cold War*, 45.

62. See Kenneth Frank, "America on Guard: Homosexuals, Inc.," *Confidential* 2, no. 2 (May 1954): 18–19; Brooks Martin, "Lavender Skeletons," *Confidential* 1, no. 3 (July 1953): 34–35; Elliot Weems, "Why They Call Broadway The 'Gay' White Way," *Tip-Off: The Magazine of Inside Exclusives* (April 1956): 40–41, 72–73; Bruce Cory, "The Lowdown on That 'Disorderly Conduct' Charge Against Tab Hunter," *Confidential* (September 1955): 18–19, 60; Kenneth McLain, "The Untold Story of Marlene Dietrich," *Confidential* (July 1955): 22–25, 56, 58; Jack Schantz, "How Taxpayers Support Our Ambassadors of Gay Will," *Whisper* 10, no. 3 (March 1956): 18–19, 59.

63. May, *Homeward Bound*, 95.

64. FBI *Confidential Files. Communist Activity in the Entertainment Industry. FBI Surveillance Files on Hollywood 1942–1958*, ed. Daniel J. Leab (Bethesda, MD: University Publications of America, 1991), 14 Microfilm Reels.

65. Bosley Crowther, "Will Film-Making Be Complicated by the 'Un-American' Probers?" *New York Times*, November 2, 1947, unpaginated.

66. Eric Bentley, *Thirty Years of Treason: Excerpts from Hearings before the House Committee on Un-American Activities, 1938–1968* (New York: Viking Press, 1971); John Cogley, *Report on BLACKLISTING - Movies* (The Fund for the Republic, 1956); Gary Carr, *The Left Side of Paradise: The Screenwriting of John Howard Lawson* (Ann Arbor, Michigan: UMI Research Press, 1984); and Walter Goodman, *The Committee: The Extraordinary Career of the House Committee on Un-American Activities* (New York: Farrar, Straus & Giroux, 1968).

67. A lot has been published both by and about the Hollywood Ten. See Bernard F. Dick, *Radical Innocence: A Critical Study of the Hollywood Ten* (Lexington: University of Kentucky Press, 1989); Elia Kazan, *A Life* (New York: Knopf, 1988); Arthur Miller, *Timebends: A Life* (New York: Grove Press, 1987); Lester Cole, *Hollywood Red: The Autobiography of Lester Cole* (Palo Alto, Ca: Ramparts Press, 1981); Herbert Biberman, "*Salt of the Earth: The Story of a Film*"; Dalton Trumbo, *The Time of the Toad: A Study of the Inquisition in America* (New York: Harper and Row, 1972; a collection of Dalton Trumbo's letters was

published in Helen Manfull, ed., *Additional Dialogue, 1942–1962* (New York: M. Evans, 1970); Edward Dmytryk wrote several books, including his autobiography, *It's a Hell of a Life, But Not a Bad Living* (New York: Times Books, 1978) and *Odd Man Out: A Memoir of the Hollywood Ten* (Carbondale: Southern Illinois University Press, 1995).

68. The "Hollywood Ten" short documentary was made under the auspices of The Film Division of the Southern California Chapter, National Council of Arts, Sciences, and Professions. This documentary was included on the 1999 DVD release of *Salt of the Earth*.

69. Quoted in the "Hollywood Ten" short documentary (included on the 1999 DVD release of *Salt of the Earth*).

70. Victor S. Navasky, *Naming Names* (New York: Viking Press, 1980), and Larry Ceplair and Steven Englund, *The Inquisition in Hollywood: Politics in the Film Community, 1930–1960* (Berkeley: University of California Press, 1983).

71. Ronald Reagan, quoted in a 1970s interview, in the documentary *Hollywood on Trial* (1976): "There never was a blacklist—it was forced by the American people who would refuse to see films with un-American people in them . . . It was a confused time, but I don't think that there's any blame that can be assessed against anyone." His statement goes against evidence to the contrary; see *Red Channels: The Report on Communist Influence in Radio and Television* (New York: American Business Consultants, 1950) and John Cogley, *Report on Blacklisting II: Radio-Television* (New York: Fund for the Republic, 1956).

72. For a detailed history of the production and response to this film, see: James J. Lorence, *The Suppression of "Salt of the Earth": How Hollywood, Big Labor, and Politicians Blacklisted a Movie in Cold War America* (Albuquerque: University of New Mexico Press, 1999).

73. Paul Buhle and Dave Wagner, *Hide in Plain Sight: The Hollywood Blacklistees in Film and Television, 1950–2002* (New York: Palgrave Macmillan, 2003).

74. Gladwin Hill, "Stars Fly to Fight Inquiry into Films: Broadcast by Players and Others, including 4 Senators, Assails House Committee," *New York Times* (October 27, 1947), A. The story details the radio broadcast aptly titled "Hollywood Fights Back" (aired on ABC radio) that began with keynote speaker Myrna Loy declaring that "We question the right of Congress to ask any man what he thinks on political issues" and ended with Judy Garland urging people to write Congress to protest the Committee's inquiry.

75. Paul Buhle and Dave Wagner, *Radical Hollywood: The Untold Story behind America's Favorite Movies* (New York: The New Press, 2002): 382.

76. There were too many headlines and articles about stars that confessed to being "duped" or publicly had to recant earlier beliefs to fully list here. Examples include the story about Edward G. Robinson, "Actor Admits Reds Used Him as 'Sucker'" *New York Times* (May 1, 1952), in which he was cleared of being a Communist, but guilty of being "duped" by Communist Front Organizations. Or Peter Kihss, "Robert Rossen Admits He Gave Reds $40,000," *New York Times*, May 8, 1953, in which Rossen not only "publicly repented" his refusal to name names in 1951, but emphasized he had "voluntarily returned" to HUAC to set that right because "he had decided that no person should put his single individual morality above national security." See also "Red Dupes Artists, Senate Group

Says: Judy Holliday, 3 Others Cited to Show Communists Trick Entertainers with 'Causes,'" *New York Times*, September 25, 1952; "Lucille Ball Tells of 1936 Red Links: But House Group Says There Is No Evidence Actress Ever Joined the Party," *New York Times*, September 13, 1953. These articles were reprinted in Gene Brown, ed., *The New York Times Encyclopedia of Film 1952–1957* (New York: TIMES BOOKS, 1984).

77. Michael Rogin, *Ronald Reagan, the Movie, and Other Episodes in Political Demonology*: 239.

78. A. H. Weiler, "Movie Maker Hires Blacklisted Writer," *New York Times*, January 20, 1960; and Murray Schumach, "Trumbo Will Get Credit for Script: Spartacus' Authorship to Be Attributed to Blacklisted Writer by U-I Studio," *New York Times*, August 8, 1960.

79. *The Miracle* (*Il Miracolo*), based on a story by Federico Fellini, was a 1948 Roberto Rossellini short film, which generated controversy and accusations of "sacrilegious" and communist-inspired atheism. Rossellini's film was bundled with two other short films and released in the US in 1950 under the title *Ways of Love* (original titled *L'amore*). See Alan F. Westin, "The Miracle Case: The Supreme Court and the Movies," in *The Movies in Our Midst: Documents in the Cultural History of Film in America*, ed. Gerald Mast (Chicago: University of Chicago Press, 1982), 604–9.

80. Whitfield, *Culture of the Cold War*, acknowledgments page.

81. Hortense Powdermaker, *Hollywood: The Dream Factory* (New York: Little, Brown and Company, 1950).

82. Powdermaker, *Hollywood*, 12.

83. Powdermaker, *Hollywood*, 307–9.

84. "Cinema Reviews," *Time*, October 16, 1950, 74.

85. Powdermaker, *Hollywood*, 254.

86. Martha Wolfenstein and Nathan Leites, *Movies: A Psychological Study* (New York: Hafner Publishing Company, 1950).

87. Wolfenstein and Leites, *Movies*, 291.

88. Norman N. Holland, "Psychiatry in Pselluloid," *The Atlantic Monthly* 203:2 (February 1959): 105–7.

89. Tony Richardson, "The Method and Why: An Account of the Actors' Studio." *Sight & Sound: The Film Quarterly*, 26, no. 3 (Winter 1956–57): 133.

90. Lee Strasberg, *A Dream of Passion: The Development of the Method* (Boston: Little, Brown, 1987).

91. Thomas H. Pauly, *An American Odyssey: Elia Kazan and American Culture* (Philadelphia: Temple University Press, 1983).

92. Richardson, "The Method and Why," 134.

93. Louis Giannetti and Scott Eyman, *Flashback: A Brief History of Film* 3rd ed. (Englewood Cliffs, New Jersey: Prentice Hall, 1996), 270.

94. The Oxford English Dictionary uses the following definition: "subtext. †1. [sub- 3 a] Text appearing below other text on the page. *Obs*. 2. [SUB- 5 c] An underlying theme in a piece of writing (esp. in novel or play). Also *transf.* 1950 E.R. HAPGOOD tr. C. *Stanislavski's Building Character* viii. 113 'What do we mean by subtext? What is it that lies beneath the actual words of a part? ... It is the manifest, the inwardly felt expression of a human being

in a part, which flows uninterruptedly beneath the words of a text, giving them life and a basis for existing." *Oxford English Dictionary*, 2nd ed., s.v. "subtext." Quote appears in the "U.S. at War" section under the heading "The Bomb" in *Time*, August 20, 1945, 19.

96. Erikson, *Childhood and Society*, 406.

CHAPTER 2

1. Langston Hughes, "Fooling Our White Folks," *Negro Digest* 8.6 (April 1950): 38–41. Reprinted in *The Collected Works of Langston Hughes*, ed. Christopher C. De Santis, vol. 9, *Essays on Art, Race, Politics, and World Affairs*, 314.

2. Thomas Cripps, *Hollywood's High Noon: Moviemaking and Society before Television)*, 195.

3. Cripps, *Hollywood's High Noon*, 195.

4. Cripps, *Hollywood's High Noon*, 141.

5. Wald, *Crossing the Line*, 89.

6. Bosley Crowther, *New York Times*, March 16, 1952, unpaginated.

7. Peter Roffman and Jim Purdy, *The Hollywood Social Problem Film: Madness, Despair, and Politics from the Depression to the Fifties* (Bloomington: Indiana University Press, 1981): viii.

8. *Variety* frequently provided commentaries on such trends in filmmaking. "'Message' Pix Have Quality: Negro Themes B.O., Red Cycle Sags," *Variety* ,October 19, 1949, 1, 63.

9. Frank Sinatra (As told to Allan Morrison), "The Way I Look at Race: Singer protests use of racial epithets, calls bigotry a 'disease,'" *Ebony* (July 1958): 35–44.

10. "Rated Must-See Film: Paves the Way for Three Others," *Hollywood Reporter*, July 25, 1947, 6.

11. Dore Schary, "Letter from a Movie-Maker: *Crossfire* as a Weapon against Anti-Semitism," *Commentary* (1947): 344–47. Contained in the *Crossfire* file, MHL-AMPAS.

12. Film critic Rose Pelswick quoted in "*Crossfire* Draws Salvo of Praise from N.Y. Reviewers: Bold Handling of Hot Theme Lauded," *Hollywood Reporter*, July 25, 1947, 2.

13. Judith E. Smith, *Visions of Belonging: Family Stories, Popular Culture, and Postwar Democracy, 1940–1960* (New York: Columbia University Press, 2004): 150.

14. Buhle and Wagner, *Radical Hollywood*, 389.

15. Edward Dmytryk comments taken from the Program Notes of a retrospective of his films in 1977 (the "RKO years"). Program notes by Mitch Tuchman, in *Crossfire* file, MHL-AMPAS.

16. James Agee, "Films," *The Nation*, August 2, 1947, unpaginated clipping in *Crossfire* file, MHL-AMPAS.

17. Film noir and message films were linked, both in terms of the filmmakers who made them and the stylistic techniques they employed. Thomas Cripps suggests: "Perhaps the message movie and the film noir were two sides of the same political coin . . . Both genres emerged in response to the disillusion brought about by war." Cripps, *Hollywood's High Noon*, 215. See also James Naremore, *More Than Night: Film Noir in Its Contexts* (Berkeley: University of California Press, 1998, 2008).

18. "Movie of the Week: Crossfire," *Life*, June 30, 1947, 71.

19. Schary, "Letter from a Movie-Maker": 344–47. Elliot Cohen, "Reply," *Commentary* (1947): 347–48. Letters in *Crossfire* file, MHL-AMPAS.

20. Schary, "Letter from a Movie-Maker": 344–47.

21. Cohen, "Reply": 347–48.

22. Virginia Wright, Drama Editor, "Crossfire," *Daily News*, March 9, 1948, 23, 26.

23. Wright, "Crossfire": 23, 26.

24. Wright, "Crossfire": 23.

25. Wright, "Crossfire": 23, 26.

26. Ceplair and Englund, *The Inquisition in Hollywood*, and Dmytryk, *Odd Man Out*.

27. Jesse Zunser, film critic from *Cue*, as quoted in "Rated Must-See Film; Paves Way for Three Others," *Hollywood Reporter*, July 25, 1947, 2.

28. "Racial Intolerance Feature in Full Swing," *Los Angeles Times*, March 6, 1947. Unpaginated clipping from the *Crossfire* file, MHL-AMPAS.

29. Zunser, "Rated Must-See Film," 2.

30. The next collaboration between Carl Foreman and Stanley Kramer would be another military-themed social problem film, *The Men* (1950); tackling the topic of disabled veterans, starring Marlon Brando. Shortly thereafter, Foreman was targeted by HUAC and blacklisted. He moved to England. Kramer continued working in Hollywood.

31. For a look at the production of this film see: Thomas Brady, "Crusade in Hollywood," *New York Times*, March 6, 1949.

32. "'Brave' Secret," *Variety*, March 23, 1949, 20.

33. Michael Rogin, *Blackface, White Noise: Jewish Immigrants in the Hollywood Melting Pot* (Berkeley: University of California Press, 1996), 228. Buhle and Wagner were more dismissive of the theme change in *Home of the Brave*: "That a victimized Jew could become black as easily as a victimized gay soldier could become Jewish in *Crossfire* was unsurprising in Hollywood, where it was just part of the transfer of victimhood." Buhle and Wagner, *Radical Hollywood*, 393. For a different perspective and detailed account of the debates surrounding this change in *Home of the Brave*, see also Smith, *Visions*, 134–39.

34. "Home of the Brave: First film about anti-Negro bias made in secret by Hollywood ex-GIs," *Ebony* (June 1949): 60.

35. Bosley Crowther, "Movie Review: Home of the Brave," *New York Times*, May 13, 1949.

36. Caption on the poster for the film in *Ebony* (July 1949).

37. Thomas Doherty, *Projections of War: Hollywood, American Culture, and World War II* (New York: Columbia University Press, 1993).

38. Thomas Cripps, *Making Movies Black: The Hollywood Message Movie from World War II to the Civil Rights Era* (New York: Oxford University Press, 1992); 220.

39. "Home of the Brave," 59.

40. Judith Smith notes *Home of the Brave* playwright Arthur Laurents "later described the relationship of the soldier buddies as homosexual," but in the film this remained subtext. Smith, *Visions*, 135.

41. The poem *The Coward* is attributed in the on-screen film credits to Eve Merriam.

42. Most reviews read the ending as progressive, but it too is a mixed message when analyzed. Scholars like Thomas Cripps have rightly noted that the visual pairing of Mingo and Moss at the end of the film "inadvertently" equates disability with race, "inviting a reading that one complete black soldier equaled one damaged white one." Cripps, *Making Movies Black*, 225.

43. See Berube, *Coming Out under Fire*.

44. Ruth Feldstein, *Motherhood in Black and White: Race and Sex in American Liberalism, 1930–1965* (Ithaca NY: Cornell University Press, 2000), 40.

45. "Review: *Home of the Brave*," *Time*, May 9, 1949, 100.

46. One of the strongest critics of the film was Manny Farber in his review: Manny Farber, "Review," *Nation*, May 21, 1949, 590–91.

47. Quoted in "Film Has Telling Lines on Bigotry," *Ebony* (June 1949), 62. Print media like *Ebony* were no less prone to mixed messages, as in this case where on the same page as this review for *Home of the Brave*, an ad for a skin product promised "double strength skin whitener." As in women's magazines, advertisers were not above exploiting racist and sexist ideologies to sell products.

48. Donald Bogle, *Toms, Coons, Mulattoes, Mammies, & Bucks: An Interpretative History of Blacks in American Films* (New York: Viking Press, 1973), 146.

49. Dore Schary, *Heyday* (Boston: Little & Brown, 1979), 157.

50. Thomas F. Brady, "Hollywood Tackles the Facts of Life: Several Films Being Made about Racial Issues," *New York Times*, March 16, 1947.

51. Wartime and postwar white progressives wanted to use racial passing to suggest the permeability of boundaries previously seen as uncrossable and to encourage white audiences to "see through" supposed racial differences in a common humanity. Here's where challenging the Nazi "racialization" of Jews and Jewishness and the obsession with Jewish blood (itself modeled on US white supremacists) seemed like a good starting place, and influenced the narrative strategy in films like *Crossfire* and *Gentleman's Agreement*.

52. "*Gentlemen's Agreement*: New Daring Movie Exposes 'Nice People' Who Spread Racial Hatred," *Ebony* (January 1948), 17.

53. Laura Z. Hobson, *Laura Z.: A Life* (New York: Arbor House, 1983): 345–65.

54. Quoted in George F. Custen, *Twentieth Century's Fox: Darryl F. Zanuck and the Culture of Hollywood* (New York: Basic Books, 1997, 294.

55. Quote from 1947 promotional trailer for the film.

56. Movie-tone News promo for *Gentlemen's Agreement*, 1947.

57. Original emphasis. Quoted in Brady, "Hollywood Tackles the Facts of Life."

58. Quoted in Neal Gabler, *An Empire of Their Own: How the Jews Invented Hollywood* (New York: Anchor Books, 1989), 349.

59. Gabler, *Empire of Their Own*, 299–300, 349–50.

60. Smith, *Visions*, 161–62.

61. Rogin, *Blackface, White Noise*.

62. Hobson, quoted in Smith, *Visions*, 157.

63. Laura Z. Hobson, *Laura Z.: A Life* (New York: Arbor House, 1983).

64. Gabler, *Empire of Their Own*, 348.

65. Lou Hollis, "The Name Ain't the Same in Movieland!," *Hush-Hush* 1, no. 3 (September 1955): 39.

66. Hollis, "Name Ain't the Same," 38–39, 61; "Name Game: What are the Real Names of the Stars?," *The Lowdown* 1, no. 4 (August 1955): 38–39; "Name Game: What are the Real Names of the Stars?," *The Lowdown* 1, no. 7 (February 1956): 42–43.

67. Gabler, *Empire of Their Own*, 301.

68. Rankin's speech quoted in Gordon Kahn, *Hollywood on Trial* (New York: Boni & Gaer, 1948): 176–77.

69. Victor S. Navasky, *Naming Names* and Gabler, *Empire of Their Own*. Paul Buhle and Dave Wagner, *Blacklisted: The Film Lover's Guide to the Hollywood Blacklist* (New York: Palgrave Macmillan, 2003).

70. Penelope Houston, "Mr. Deeds and Willie Stark," *Sight and Sound* 19, no. 7 (November 1950), 279.

71. Quoted in George Custen, *Twentieth Century's Fox: Darryl F. Zanuck and the Culture of Hollywood*.

72. The conflicted production of *The Boy with Green Hair* prefigured growing political conflicts within Hollywood. Liberal Dore Schary was one of the producers of this film for RKO, but the studio became more conservative when anti-Communist Howard Hughes took over. The director of this film, Joseph Losey, was later blacklisted in 1951, and moved to Europe.

73. "*The Boy with Green Hair*: Unusual Film Fantasy Blasting Color Prejudice Finally Released after Studio Battle," *Ebony* (December 1948), 60.

74. Bogle, *Toms, Coons, Mulattoes, Mammies and Bucks*, 144.

75. Cripps, *Making Movies Black*: 219–20.

76. Roi Ottley, "5 Million U.S. White Negroes," *Ebony* (March 1948): 20–21.

77. "PASSING," *Ebony* (May 1949), 27, 29.

78. Documentary: *Confidential File*. "Daytime Whites." Producer: Ben Pivar. Directors: Ben Pivar and Irvin Reishner. Writers: Paul V. Coates ("reporter") and James Peck (c. 1955). "Summary: Filmed sequence dramatizing the problems addressed in the program: the story of a young secretary in New York City who is black and is passing for white." UCLA, Film and Television Archive (ARSC).

79. Ottley, "5 Million U.S. White Negroes": 20–21.

80. "White by Day … Negro by Night," *Ebony* (April 1952). This article discussed "occupational" whites and featured a "photographic" quiz entitled "Which is Negro? Which is White?" This format was very similar to another quiz layout in the earlier "White Negroes" edition of *Ebony* in 1948.

81. "PASSING," *Ebony* (May 1949), 30.

82. "PASSING," 30.

83. Allison Graham, *Framing the South: Hollywood, Television, and Race during the Civil Rights Struggle* (Baltimore and London: John Hopkins University Press, 2001), 39.

84. Rogin, *Blackface, White Noise*, 209–50.

85. Ottley, "America's Five Million White Negroes," 28.

86. Margaret Lillard, "Reunion celebrates friendship and revolutionary film," *Globe and Mail*, July 28, 1989, C8.

87. De Rochemont produced "The March of Time" newsreels and some WWII war documentaries like *We Are the Marines* (1942). He also helped to define stylized film noirs in spy thrillers like *Boomerang!* (1947) and *House on 92nd Street* (1945). His penchant for producing "real life" stories led to his designation as the "father of the docudrama."

88. This incident was fictional, and the black press heavily critiqued its inclusion because it implied a false equivalency to prejudice. See Smith, *Visions*, 180–81.

89. "Review of *Lost Boundaries*," *Variety*, June 29, 1949, 14, 20. This review describes but does not analyze the implications of this framing of Harlem, an omission that contrasts with how the scene was almost universally critiqued in the black press.

90. Gayle Wald argues that Howard's crisis about race provoked an equal crisis about security and masculinity, but that the "boundaries of class" were upheld even when racial boundaries were "lost." Wald, *Crossing the Line*, 82–115.

91. The shortcomings and contradictions of the film have been well-documented by film historians. See Cripps, *Making Movies Black*, 226–32.

92. *Lost Boundaries* poster ad, *Ebony* (July 1949), 3.

93. Richard Winnington, "Critics Forum: Negro Films," *Sight and Sound* 18 (January 1950), 28.

94. "*Lost Boundaries*," *Ebony* (July 1949), 53.

95. "*Lost Boundaries*," 53.

96. "Review of *Lost Boundaries*," *Variety*, June 29, 1949, 14, 20.

97. "Review of *Lost Boundaries*," 14, 20.

98. "TV in South Also Bans 'Boundaries'; Won't Play Patsy," *Variety*, August 24, 1949, 1, 63. "MPAA May Join with De Rochemont to Fight Southern 'Boundaries' Ban," *Variety*, August 31, 1949, 4.

99. The director was originally John Ford, but after many problems on set, he was replaced. Most egregious was Ford's appalling treatment of Ethel Waters, generally belittling her as "Aunt Jemima." Waters recalled he was "so cruel" she "almost had a stroke." See Cripps, *Making Movies Black*, 236. See also Donald Bogle, *Heat Wave: The Life and Career of Ethel Waters* (New York: HarperCollins, 2011).

100. "Review of *Pinky*," *Variety*, October 5, 1949, 8.

101. "Review of *Pinky*," *Variety*, 8.

102. Lisa M. Anderson, *Mammies No More: The Changing Image of Black Women on Stage and Screen*.

103. Wald, *Crossing the Line*, 100.

104. Wald, *Crossing the Line*, 100.

105. Anderson, *Mammies No More*, 60.

106. Francis Harman in a letter, "Some Comments and Suggestions re PINKY," sent March 8, 1949 (to Philip Dunne and/or Darryl Zanuck), in *Pinky* PCA file.

107. Response to Francis Harman from Darryl F. Zanuck in a letter dated March 30, 1949, in *Pinky* PCA file.

108. *Time*, October 10, 1949, 68; "Review of *Pinky*," *Variety*, October 5, 1949, 8.

109. *Time*, October 10, 1949, 68. Similarly, Bosley Crowther gave the film a mixed review: "By giving a winning personality to the much-abused girl Jeanne Crain successfully channels resentment against these bitter experiences to you ... [But] this scan of a social problem has certain faults and omissions which may be resented and condemned ... The 'old mammy' sentiment is extolled. And a passion for paternalism is very obvious at the picture's core." Bosley Crowther, "Review of 'Pinky,' Zanuck's Film Study of Anti-Negro Bias in Deep South, Shown at Rivoli," *New York Times*, September 30, 1949.

110. Cripps, *Making Movies Black*, 215–49.

111. "Review of *Pinky*," *Variety*, 8.

112. "*Pinky*: Story on girl who passes will be most debated film of the year," *Ebony* (September 1949), 23.

113. "Zanuck Made Movie Despite Criticism of Racial Theme," *Ebony* (September 1949), 25.

114. "Zanuck Made Movie Despite Criticism of Racial Theme," 25.

115. Quoted in Doug McClelland, *Forties Film Talk: Oral Histories of Hollywood, with 120 Lobby Posters* (Jefferson, North Carolina: McFarland & Company, 1992), 270.

116. Ward, *Crossing the Color Line*, 116–51.

117. Richard Winnington, "Critics Forum: Negro Films," *Sight and Sound* (January 1950), 28.

118. "Zanuck Made Movie Despite Criticism of Racial Theme," 25.

119. "'Message' Pix Must Have Quality; Negro Themes B.O., Red Cycle Sags," *Variety*, October 19, 1949, 1, 63.

120. Susan Courtney, *Hollywood Fantasies of Miscegenation: Spectacular Narratives of Gender and Race, 1903–1967* (Princeton and Oxford: Princeton University Press, 2005), 171.

121. Wald, *Crossing the Line*, 93–94.

122. Ralph Ellison, "Review of *Pinky*" in *Shadow and Act* (New York: Random House, 1953): 273–81.

123. Excerpts of letter, "Philip Dunne to Darryl F. Zanuck, February 2, 1949, Philip Dunne Collection, Doheny Library, USC." Quoted in Custen, *Twentieth Century's Fox*, 300–301.

124. Darryl F. Zanuck to Charles Einfeld, February 10, 1949, Philip Dunne Collection, Doheny Library, USC. Reprinted in Custen, *Twentieth Century's Fox*.

125. Philip Dunne's promotional piece "An Approach to Racism" discusses the production of *Pinky* and his intents as co-author of the script. Undated article in *Pinky* file, MHL-AMPAS.

126. Wendy Doniger, *The Woman Who Pretended to Be Who She Was: Myths of Self-Imitation* (Oxford: Oxford University Press, 2005): 183–84.

CHAPTER 3

1. Glen O. Gabbard and Krin Gabbard, *Psychiatry and the Cinema*, 2nd ed. (New York: American Psychiatric Press, 1999).

2. "Hollywood Headshrinkers Squeal on the Stars!" *Hush-Hush: What You Don't Know about the People You Know* 2, no. 5 (January 1956): 50.

3. "Hollywood Headshrinkers Squeal on the Stars!": 17–19, 50, 51.

4. "Hollywood Headshrinkers Squeal on the Stars!": 50–51.

5. Esme Corrado, "The Truth about Psychiatry and Hollywood Love," *Uncensored* 5, no. 3 (August 1956): 22–23, 64.

6. Corrado, "Truth about Psychiatry and Hollywood Love," 23.

7. Victoria Thorn, "Are Most Movie Stars Mentally Ill?: yes! says a psychiatrist, and the facts are even worse than people think!" *Confidential* 8, no. 8 (October 1960): 20–23, 60, 62.

8. Thorn, "Movie Stars Mentally Ill?": 20–23, 60, 62.

9. "Broadway 'Oriental': Juanita Hall Scores Her Second Stage Hit in Eastern Role." *Ebony* (March 1959): 128.

10. "I'm Through with Passing," *Ebony* (March 1951): 22–24.

11. Frank Sinatra (as told to Allan Morrison), "The Way I Look at Race: Singer protests use of racial epithets, calls bigotry a 'disease,'" *Ebony* (July 1958), 43.

12. Journalist Thomas Pryor contrasts Sidney Poitier to previous black "entertainers" like Lena Horne, Eartha Kitt, Paul Robeson, and Ethel Waters, among others, and suggests how significant the progress of his particular rise to stardom was, arguing that "Poitier does not dance or sing. He is the first of his race to reach the top of the Hollywood ladder solely on the basis of acting ability." Thomas M. Pryor, "A 'Defiant One' Becomes a Star," *New York Times*, January 25, 1959. See also Lerone Bennett Jr., "Hollywood's First Negro Movie Star: Sidney Poitier breaks film barrier to become screen idol," *Ebony* (May 1959): 100–103, 106–8.

13. Dandridge made the cover of *Life* magazine with this role. "Dorothy Dandridge: Hollywood's Fiery Carmen Jones," *Life*, November 1, 1954.

14. Quote originally from Louie Robinson's "Why Dandridge Can't Kiss Her White Film Lover: Torrid New Story Stars Interracial Love Code Debate," *Jet*, December 13, 1956, 56–61. Quoted in Marguerite H. Rippy, "COMMODITY, TRAGEDY, DESIRE: Female Sexuality and Blackness in the Iconography of Dorothy Dandridge," in *Classic Hollywood, Classic Whiteness*, ed. Daniel Bernardi, 192.

15. Rippy, "COMMODITY, TRAGEDY, DESIRE," 194.

16. See Petey Williams, "What Price Hollywood Morals: Some May Fly in the Face of Convention," *Suppressed* 1:6 (November 1954): 45–52; Jacques Du Bec, "Eartha Kitt and Her Santa Baby: Arthur Loew Jr.," *Confidential* 2, no. 6 (January 1955): 18–19, 51–52; Jacqueline Tracy, "How Pearl Bailey Hooked a White Husband!," *Whisper* 9, no. 2 (August 1955): 16–17, 60; Sherman Griswold, "Marshall Field's Daughter—Rebel with a Cause: She defied the racial taboos of her social set to prove that love is a multi-colored thing . . .," *Confidential* 4, no. 1 (March 1956): 32–33, 58, 60; D. Loring Taylor, "They Were a Real 'Gone' Threesome . . . Orson Welles, his Chocolate Bon Bon, and the Whoopsy Waiter!," *Confidential* 5, no. 1 (March 1957): 16–17, 48, 50; Matt Williams, "S-H-H! Have You Heard the Latest about Sammy Davis Jr.?," *Confidential* 4, no. 1 (March 1956): 12–15, 51–52; Hy Steirman, "Kim Novak and Sammy Davis, Jr.: Who Broke Up Their Romance?," *Confidential* 6, no. 5 (December 1958): 14–15, 50, 52.

17. Lary May, *The Big Tomorrow: Hollywood and Politics of the American Way* (Chicago and London: University of Chicago Press, 2000), 211.

18. "Racy or Racist?: What Is It the 'Expose' Magazines Think They're Exposing in All Those Articles?" in the short-lived magazine *Celebrities Answer (to the Scandal Magazines)* 1, no. 1 (July 1957): 37–39.

19. "Racy or Racist?": 39.

20. Dai Vaughan, "Sapphire," Peter G. Baker, ed., *Films and Filming* 5, no. 9 (June 1959), 25.

21. Cripps, *Making Movies Black*, 263.

22. On Zanuck's ambitions about this production, see George F. Custen, *Twentieth Century's Fox: Darryl F. Zanuck and the Culture of Hollywood* (New York: Basic Books, 1997).

23. Excerpts of letter (dated May 13, 1955) from Geoffrey Shurlock (at PCA) to Harry Cohn (at Columbia Pictures), in *Island in the Sun* PCA file.

24. From a letter (dated July 19, 1956) from Truman K. Gibson, Jr. to Colonel Frank McCarthy (at 20th Century-Fox), in *Island in the Sun* PCA file.

25. Fred Hift, *Variety*, June 19, 1957, un-paginated clipping in *Island in the Sun* file, MHL-AMPAS.

26. The film was in the year's top ten according to the *Variety* box office reports (June 1957).

27. For a look at the draw and star power of Belafonte at the time of this film's release, see Judith E. Smith, *Becoming Belafonte: Black Artist, Public Radical* (Austin: University of Texas Press, 2014).

28. From a letter dated July 19, 1956 to Colonel Frank McCarthy at 20th Century-Fox, in *Island in the Sun* PCA file.

29. "Hollywood's Summer Films Tackle Some Sweaty Topics with Varying Success," *Life*, July 22, 1957, unpaginated clipping in *Island in the Sun* PCA file.

30. "Appendix: The Motion Picture Production Code" in Leonard J. Leff and Jerold L. Simmons, *The Dame in the Kimono: Hollywood Censorship and the Production Code from the 1920s to the 1960s* (London: Weidenfeld and Nicolson, 1990), 285.

31. Geoffrey Shurlock officially took over as director of the Production Code Administration from Joseph Breen in 1954, and promptly made amendments to ease restrictions on taboo subjects like miscegenation and profanity. Immediate press response to changes in the Code include, "Revised Pix Code OKs Miscegenation, Drinking, Smuggling If 'In Good Taste,'" *Variety*, September 15, 1954, 3, 16; and "Dope, Kidnapping and Other Tabu Plots OK under Revised Film Code," *Variety*, December 12, 1956, 1–20. See also Leff and Simmons, *The Dame in the Kimono*, 216; and Thomas Doherty, *Hollywood's Censor: Joseph I. Breen and the Production Code Administration* (New York: Columbia University Press, 2007).

32. "RE: ISLAND IN THE SUN (20th Century-Fox)" memo by Geoffrey M. Shurlock in his capacity as head of the Production Code Administration, dated June 18, 1956, in *Island in the Sun* PCA file.

33. Cripps, *Making Movies Black*, 265. See also Bosley Crowther, "Color or Class: Are Issues Evaded in 'Island in the Sun'?" *New York Times*, June 23, 1957, and Albert Johnson, "Black Brown and Beige," *Film Quarterly* 13, no.1 (Autumn 1959): 39–41.

34. "RE: ISLAND IN THE SUN (20th Century-Fox)".

35. Courtney, *Hollywood Fantasies of Miscegenation*: 216–17.

36. Excerpts of letter (dated May 13, 1955) from Geoffrey Shurlock (at PCA) to Harry Cohn (at Columbia Pictures), in *Island in the Sun* PCA file.

37. This compromise was much discussed. See "To Kiss or Not to Kiss Is Question Which Upset Cast," *Ebony* (July 1957), 34. See also Bosley Crowther, "Color or Class: Are Issues Evaded in 'Island in the Sun'?," *New York Times*, June 23, 1957. However, even the compromises were too much for some, see "Belafonte Gets Dixie Threats for Movie Role," *Jet*, January 3, 1957.

38. Belafonte talked about his marriage to Julie Robinson, his second wife, and the public attention it received, in part because he was such a big star but also, he believed, simply because being an interracial couple in 1950s America was considered newsworthy (and the added showbiz gossip that Julie was a former girlfriend of Marlon Brando also fueled interest). See Harry Belafonte, "Why I Married Julie," *Ebony* (July 1957), 90–95.

39. Many credit Fannie Hurst's relationship with Zora Neale Hurston (who acted as secretary, "chauffeur," and "companion") as offering a template for the interracial pairing of the two women in the novel and as an influence more generally on her interest in representing issues of gender, racial identity, and passing. See Mary Ann Doane, *Femme Fatales: Feminism, Film Theory, Psychoanalysis* (New York: Routledge, 1991): 233–35. See also Abe C. Ravitz, *Imitations of Life: Fannie Hurst's Gaslight Sonatas* (Carbondale: Southern Illinois University Press, 1997).

40. Bosley Crowther, "Detergent Drama: 'Imitation of Life' in Familiar Soapy Vein," *New York Times*, April 19, 1959. L.E.R., "'Imitation of Life' Film Tear-Evoking Production," *Hollywood Citizen-News*, March 21, 1959. Unpaginated clippings from *Imitation of Life* file, MHL-AMPAS.

41. Hal Erikson, *New York Times*, (1959). Unpaginated clipping in *Imitation of Life* file, MHL-AMPAS.

42. Caughie, *Passing and Pedagogy*, 195.

43. Jack Moffitt, "Hunter and Sirk Remake Better Than '34 Original," *Hollywood Reporter*, February 3, 1959.

44. Quoted in "Sirk on Sirk: Jon Halliday Interview," reprinted in *Imitation of Life: Douglas Sirk, Director*, ed. Lucy Fischer, 229.

45. "Film Review: Imitation of Life," *Variety*, February 3, 1959, unpaginated clipping in *Imitation of Life* file, MHL-AMPAS.

46. Feldstein, *Motherhood in Black and White*, 123.

47. Richard Dyer, "Four Films of Lana Turner," in *Imitation of Life*, 186–206.

48. Jack Moffitt, "Hunter and Sirk Remake Better Than '34 Original," *Hollywood Reporter*, February 3, 1959, 3. Clipping in *Imitation of Life* file, MHL-AMPAS.

49. "Film Review: Imitation of Life," *Variety*.

50. "*Imitation of Life* Well Titled," *Los Angeles Times*, March 20, 1959. Unpaginated clipping in *Imitation of Life* file, MHL-AMPAS.

51. Kohner's casting was a variation/conflation of what Michael Rogin called "civil rights blackface." Rogin, *Blackface, White Noise*, 302.

52. Bosley Crowther, "Detergent Drama: *Imitation of Life* in Familiar Soapy Vein," *New York Times*, April 19, 1959.

53. Synopsis contained in the *Imitation of Life* folder, MHL-AMPAS.

54. On the "radical female homosociality" of this film, where the two mothers form an interracial couple that can be read as miscegenation, see Patricia White's *Uninvited: Classical Hollywood Cinema and Lesbian Representability* (Bloomington: Indiana University Press, 1999): 109–11.

55. From the film synopsis contained in the *Imitation of Life* folder, MHL-AMPAS.

56. Rainer Werner Fassbinder, "Imitation of Life," in *Imitation of Life, Douglas Sirk, Director*, 244.

57. BBC2 documentary *Behind the Mirror: A Profile of Douglas Sirk* (1979). This documentary interview with Sirk was produced and hosted by Mark Shivas.

58. 1950s audiences would have understood that the scene referenced/replicated the actual "doll tests" done in 1940 and 1941 by psychologist Kenneth Clark, whose study was cited in *Brown v. Board of Education* as evidence that segregation hurt the social development of black children.

59. Quoted from the BBC2 documentary *Behind the Mirror*.

60. As Valerie Smith notes, this framing conflates the "daughters' rejection of their own subordinate status with their rejection of their mothers, readers or viewers are manipulated into criticizing rather than endorsing these non-compliant light-skinned women." Smith, *Not Just Race, Not Just Gender: Black Feminist Readings* (New York: Routledge, 1998), 39.

61. "*Imitation of Life*: Juanita Moore Stars in New Version of Film," *Ebony* (April 1959): 70.

62. "Imitation of Life: Production Notes," in *Imitation of Life: Douglas Sirk, Director*, 185.

63. Original emphasis. Moffitt, "Hunter and Sirk Remake Better Than '34 Original," 3.

64. BBC2 documentary *Behind the Mirror*.

65. "Sirk on Sirk: Jon Halliday Interview," in *Imitation of Life: Douglas Sirk, Director*, 228.

66. "Sirk on Sirk: Jon Halliday Interview," 228.

67. Michael Stern, "Imitation of Life," in *Imitation of Life, Douglas Sirk, Director*, 285.

68. Both Mary Ann Doane and Ruth Feldstein have noted how the film creates a parallel between Sarah Jane and Lora and between passing and acting. See Feldstein, *Motherhood in Black and White*, 124. See also Doane, *Femmes Fatales*, 236.

69. Poster ad for *Imitation of Life* in *Ebony* (April 1959), 105.

70. Quotes from the BBC2 documentary *Behind the Mirror*.

71. Moffitt, "Hunter and Sirk Remake Better Than '34 Original," 6.

72. Moffitt, "Hunter and Sirk Remake Better Than '34 Original," 3.

73. "L.A. Negro Paper Refuses *Imitation* Ads; U-I Hits Back," *Hollywood Reporter*, February 2, 1959, unpaginated clipping in *Imitation of Life* file, MHL-AMPAS.

74. "L.A. Negro Paper Refuses *Imitation* Ads."

75. Ottley, "5 Million U.S. White Negroes."

CHAPTER 4

1. Gracie Allen, "Hollywood Nursery Rhymes," *Variety*, January 5, 1949, 56.

2. Penelope Houston, "Mr. Deeds and Willie Stark," *Sight & Sound* 19, no. 7 (November 1950): 276–85.

3. Chafe, *Unfinished Journey*, 99.

4. Richard M. Fried, *Nightmare in Red: The McCarthy Era in Perspective* and David Caute, *The Great Fear: The Anti-Communist Purge under Truman and Eisenhower*.

5. Quoted in Chafe, *Unfinished Journey*, 99.

6. Quoted in Navasky, *Naming Names*, 24.

7. Douglas publicly deplored the growing culture of fear in the *New York Times*: "The Communist threat inside the country has been magnified and exalted far beyond its realities. Irresponsible talk by irresponsible people has fanned the flames of fear. Accusations have been loosely made. Character assassinations have become common . . . Fear has driven more and more men and women in all walks of life either to silence or to the folds of the orthodox. Fear has mounted—fear of losing one's job, fear of being investigated, fear of being pilloried. This fear has stereotyped our thinking, narrowed the range of free public discussion, and driven many thoughtful people to despair." William O. Douglas, "The Black Silence of Fear," *New York Times Magazine*, January 13, 1952, 7, 37–38. See also William Douglas, *The Court Years, 1939–1975: The Autobiography of William O. Douglas* (New York: Random House, 1980).

8. Schrecker, *Many Are the Crimes*, 190–200.

9. William O. Douglas, "The Black Silence of Fear."

10. Robert Griffith, *The Politics of Fear: Joseph R. McCarthy and the Senate* (Lexington: University Press of Kentucky, 1970); and Caute, *The Great Fear.*

11. Navasky, *Naming Names.*

12. Caute, *The Great Fear;* Fried, *Nightmare in Red;* and Whitfield, *The Culture of the Cold War.*

13. Whitfield, *Culture of the Cold War*, 27. Allen Weinstein, *Perjury: The Hiss-Chambers Case* (New York: Knopf, 1978).

14. Whittaker Chambers, *Witness* (Chicago: Henry Regnery, 1952).

15. Jurors were interviewed for the documentary *The Trials of Alger Hiss* (1979), directed by John Lowenthal.

16. John P. Roche, *The Quest for the Dream: The Development of Civil Rights and Human Relations in Modern America* (New York: Macmillan, 1963).

17. "'The Black Silence of Fear' that Supreme Court Justice William O. Douglas deplores in Document 22 seemingly blanketed the nation, and meaningful political dissent all but withered away." Schrecker, *Age of McCarthyism*, 93.

18. Martin Bauml Duberman, *Paul Robeson* (New York: Knopf, 1988).

19. Corber, *In the Name of National Security*, 10.

20. John Lukacs, *Historical Consciousness*, rev. ed., (New York: Schocken Books, 1985), 379.

21. Lukacs, *Historical Consciousness*, 343.

22. Lela Rogers issued this public statement in the late 1940s in response to the controversy of HUAC's investigation of Hollywood. Quoted in the documentary *Hollywood on Trial* (1976).

23. Whitfield, *Culture of the Cold War*, 103.

24. Einstein's statement, written on May 16, 1953, quoted in Thomas Doherty, *Cold War, Cool Medium: Television, McCarthyism, and American Culture* (New York, Columbia University Press, 2003), 87.

25. Matthew Cvetic, *I Was a Communist for the FBI* (originally published as a serial for the *Saturday Evening Post*); Herbert Philbrick, *I Led Three Lives: Citizen, "Communist," Counterspy* (Washington, DC: Capital Hill Press, 1953, 1972); Angela Calomaris, *Red Masquerade: Undercover for the FBI* (Philadelphia: Lippincott, 1950); Hede Massing, *This Deception* (New York: Duell, Sloan and Pearce, 1951); and Herbert L. Packer, *Ex-Communist Witness* (Stanford: Stanford University Press, 1962).

26. Doherty, *Cold War, Cool Medium*, 140.

27. Tag line featured on a promotional poster for the film, in *I Was a Communist for the FBI* file, MHL-AMPAS.

28. Michael Barson, *"Better Dead Than Red!": A Nostalgic Look at the Golden Years of Russiaphobia, Red-baiting, and Other Commie Madness* (New York: Hyperion, 1992).

29. Caloamazonmaris, *Red Masquerade*, 265.

30. Philbrick *I Led Three Lives*, 235.

31. Philbrick, *I Led Three Lives*, appendix.

32. Philbrick, *I Led Three Lives*, 184–85.

33. Doherty, *Cold War, Cool Medium*, 148.

34. Dialogue quoted in Karel Reisz's review of the film. As a left-wing director, Reisz was part of the blacklisted film community working in Europe in the 1950s, influencing his critique. See Karel Reisz, "Hollywood's Anti-Red *Boomerang*: Apple Pie, Love and Endurance versus The Commies," *Sight & Sound: The Film Quarterly* 22, no. 3 (January–March, 1953), 132–37, 148.

35. Nora Sayre, "Cold War Cinema II," *The Nation*, March 3, 1979, 245.

36. Original emphasis. Whitfield, *Culture of the Cold War*, 141.

37. "Film Reviews: *Conspirator*," *Variety*, August 3, 1949, 16.

38. "Message Pix Must Have Quality; Negro Themes B.O., Red Cycle Sags," *Variety*, October 19, 1949, 1, 63.

39. For instance, *My Son John* ranked in the top-ten list of 1952 films by the NBR, and, as noted, *I Was a Communist for the FBI* was misguidedly nominated for "Best Documentary" at the Academy Awards in 1951. See Alan G. Fetrow, *Feature Films, 1950–1959: A United States Filmography* (Jefferson: North Caroline: McFarland & Company, 1999), 288.

40. Alex Barris, "On the Screen: My Son John," *The Globe and Mail* (May 26, 1952): 14.

41. Schrecker, *Many Are the Crimes*, 142.

42. Robert Warshow, *The Immediate Experience: Movies, Comics, Theatre, and Other Aspects of Popular Culture*, enlarged ed. (Cambridge, Massachusetts: Harvard University Press, 2001), 134–35. Previously published as "Review of *My Son John*" for the *American Mercury* (June 1952). Warshow was a cultural analyst who wrote a series of essays on

American popular culture from 1947 until his early death at the age of thirty-seven in 1955.

43. Warshow, *Immediate Experience*, 136, 140–41.

44. Reisz, "Hollywood's Anti-Red *Boomerang*," 148.

45. Rogin, *Ronald Reagan: The Movie*, 250.

46. Warshow, *Immediate Experience*, 134–35.

47. Vito Russo, *The Celluloid Closet: Homosexuality in the Movies* (New York: Harper, 1987), 94–95, 99.

48. The death of Walker forced the filmmakers to be creative to finish *My Son John*, a circumstance noted in film reviews. See Bosley Crowther, "Review of *My Son John*," *New York Times*, April 9, 1952, unpaginated.

49. Warshow, *Immediate Experience*, 133.

50. Rogin, *Ronald Reagan: The Movie*, 247.

51. Warshow, *Immediate Experience*, 140.

52. Stevenson would later go on to a career of directing fluffy family fare, working mainly for Disney films. His films included: *Old Yeller* (1957), *The Absent-Minded Professor* (1961), *That Darn Cat!* (1965), *The Love Bug* (1968), and *Bedknobs and Broomsticks* (1971). His most famous film was *Mary Poppins* (1964).

53. Whitfield, *Culture of the Cold War*, 141.

54. TMP's "One Man's Battle with Communism," *New York Times*, June 16, 1950, clipping in *Woman on Pier 13* PCA file.

55. TMP's "One Man's Battle with Communism."

56. Gene Arneel, "Review," *Motion Picture Daily* (September 21, 1949), unpaginated clipping in *Woman on Pier 13* PCA file.

57. Daniel Mainwaring, quoted in Patrick McGilligan, ed., *Backstory 2: Interviews with Screenwriters of the 1940s and 1950s*, 197.

58. PCA concerns listed in *Woman on Pier 13*, PCA file.

59. Sic from script. Robert Stevenson, *The Woman on Pier 13*, RKO Classic Screenplays (New York: Frederick Ungar Publishing, 1976).

60. TMP, Film Review, "One Man's Battle with Communism."

61. Edwin Schallert, "*I Married a Communist* Follows Thriller Format," *Los Angeles Times*, October 10, 1949, clipping in *Woman on Pier 13* PCA file.

CHAPTER 5

1. See Kevin Heffernan, *Ghouls, Gimmicks, and Gold: Horror Films and the American Movie Business, 1953–1968* (Durham: Duke University Press, 2004), and Cyndy Hendershot, *I Was a Cold War Monster: Horror Films, Eroticism, and the Cold War Imagination* (Bowling Green: Bowling Green University Popular Press, 2001).

2. "AP Wires Burn with 'Captured Disc' Story," *Daily Illini*, July 9, 1947; "'Disc' Near Bomb Test Site Is Just a Weather Balloon," *New York Times*, July 9, 1947; "Army, Navy Move on 'Flying Disc' Rumors," *El Paso Herald-Post*, July 9, 1947.

3. From Stephen King's "Danse Macabre," excerpted in *Invasion of the Body Snatchers: Don Siegel, director*, ed. Al La Valley (New Brunswick: Rutgers University Press, 1989), 198.

4. Susan Sontag, "The Imagination of Disaster," in *Against Interpretation and Other Essays* (New York: Farrar, Straus & Giroux, 1961): 221–22.

5. *Invisible Invaders* (1959), directed by Edward L. Cahn, featured invisible men from the moon who come to Earth and inhabit bodies of dead people. The film powerfully suggests there are greater things to fear than death, like becoming "less than human."

6. Quote from Wanger in an unpaginated publicity file clipping contained in the *Invasion of the Body Snatchers* file, MHL-AMPAS.

7. Stuart Samuels, "The Age of Conspiracy and Conformity: *Invasion of the Body Snatchers* (1956)" in *American History/ American Film: Interpreting the Hollywood Image*, ed. John E. Connor and Martin A. Jackson (New York: Frederick Ungar Publishing, 1979, 1980), 209.

8. My emphasis. Quote from the film's publicity release, contained in the *Invasion of the Body Snatchers* file, MHL-AMPAS.

9. Entire script reprinted in *Invasion of the Body Snatchers: Don Siegel, Director*, ed. Al La Valley.

10. Miles's speech echoed the filmmaker's own fears of what was happening to society in Eisenhower's America. Comments made in program notes, *Invasion of the Body Snatchers* file, MHL-AMPAS.

11. Don Siegel quoted in the program notes of *Cinema Texas*, 13, no. 2 (October 5, 1977), in *Invasion of the Body Snatchers* file, MHL-AMPAS.

12. Al La Valley, *Invasion of the Body Snatchers*, and Mark Jancovich, *Rational Fears: American Horror in the 1950s* (Manchester and New York: Manchester University Press, 1996).

13. La Valley, "Introduction," in *Invasion of the Body* Snatchers, ed. Al La Valley, 4.

14. Siegel quoted in an unpaginated interview contained within the *Invasion of the Body-Snatchers* file, MHL-AMPAS.

15. Leslie Y. Rabkin, *The Celluloid Couch: An Annotated International Filmography of the Mental Health Professional in the Movies and Television, from the Beginning to 1990* (Lanham, Md.: The Scarecrow Press, 1998), 148.

16. Adrian Turner connects Cold War fears and domestic anxieties in his analysis of the film: "Here the allegorical red is not under the bed but literally in it ..." Adrian Turner, *Hollywood 1950s* (New York: Gallery Books, 1986): 49.

17. Per Schelde argues that the marriage in this film between an actual alien and a human woman is an extreme representation of the idea that men and women are different species; a commonly expressed anxiety in the gender obsessed 1950s. Per Schelde, *Androids, Humanoids, and Other Science Fiction Monsters: Science and Soul in Science Fiction Films* (New York: New York University Press, 1993): 103.

18. Michael Lee argues the coded representations of male aliens here with their "double life" can be read as a metaphor for homosexuality. See Michael Lee, "Ideology and Style in the Double Feature *I Married a Monster from Outer Space* and *Curse of the Demon*" in *Horror at the Drive-In: Essays in Popular Americana*, ed. Gary D. Rhodes, (Jefferson,

North Carolina: McFarland & Company, 2003), 71. See also Harry Benshoff, *Monsters in the Closet: Homosexuality and the Horror Film* (Manchester: Manchester University Press, 1997).

19. In the 1998 remake of this film (with its slightly shorter title of *I Married a Monster*) a slight twist used alcohol as a signifier about which men were still human; human males became "visible" because they still drank alcohol (most of the bars in town had shut down because of the alien influx).

20. Mark Jancovich analyzes the film in relation to cultural anxieties about marriage and conformity. See Jancovich, *Rational Fears*, 78.

21. Quoted in "Making the Earth Stand Still" Documentary (1995), included on 2004 Studio Classics DVD release.

22. Robert Wise's observations on casting choices, quoted in "Making the Earth Stand Still."

23. Sam Jaffe, who had received an Oscar nomination for his role in *Asphalt Jungle* (1950), was named in the second round of Hollywood HUAC hearings in 1951 and was blacklisted for several years, returning to the screen with a part in *The Barbarian and the Geisha* in 1958. Paul Buhle and Dave Wagner, eds. *Blacklisted: The Film Lover's Guide to the Hollywood Blacklist* (New York: Palgrave Macmillan, 2003). See also Peter Biskind, *Seeing Is Believing: How Hollywood Taught Us to Stop Worrying and Love the Fifties* (New York: Henry Holt, 1983), 153.

24. Bosley Crowther, "Emissary from Planet Visits Mayfair Theatre in '*Day the Earth Stood Still*,'" *New York Times*, September 19, 1951. Un-paginated file clipping from *The Day the Earth Stood Still* file, MHL-AMPAS.

25. Peter Biskind and others argue that this film equates Klaatu "with Christ himself," and that it acted as a critique "of the witch-hunt and the cold war [that] skated close to the edge of permissible dissent." Biskind, *Seeing*, 152–58.

26. Nora Sayre, *Running Time: Films of the Cold War* (New York: Dial Press, 1982), 196.

CHAPTER 6

1. Mikhail Bakhtin, *Rabelais and His World*, Helene Iswolsky, trans., (Bloomington: Indiana University Press, 1984), 415.

2. Heston as "Mike" Vargas speaking to his wife Susan in Orson Welles's *Touch of Evil* (1958).

3. Howard Hawks directed *I Was a Male War Bride* (Twentieth Century-Fox, 1949), known for his role reversal comedies that played with conventional gender ideas.

4. Herman, *Romance of American Psychology*, 279.

5. Robert Coughlan, "Changing Roles in Modern Marriage" *Life*, December 24, 1956, 109. See also Keith Sward, "Boy and Girl Meet Neurosis," *The Screen Writer* (September 1948): 8–26.

6. Both series and book were edited by *Look* editors under the same title, *The Decline of the American Male* (New York: Random House, 1958).

7. *Lost Weekend* was based on the novel by Charles Jackson (originally published in 1944).

8. Robert Brustein, "The New Hollywood: Myth and Anti-Myth" (1959), in *The Movies in Our Midst: Documents in the Cultural History of Film in America*, ed. Gerald Mast (Chicago: University of Chicago Press, 1982), 689. Originally appeared in *Film Quarterly* in 1959.

9. Lindsay Anderson, "Film Review: *The Searchers*," *Sight and Sound* 26, no. 2 (Autumn 1956): 94–95.

10. Reprinted in Cohan, *Masked Men*, 202.

11. James Morgan, "Hecht-Lancaster Productions," *Sight & Sound* 25, no. 1 (Summer 1955): 38–42, 55.

12. Walter Lassally, "The Cynical Audience," *Sight and Sound* 26, no. 1 (Summer 1956): 12–13.

13. Lassally, "Cynical Audience," 12–15.

14. Biskind, *Seeing*, 257.

15. Sidney Skolsky, "The New Look in Hollywood Men," *Photoplay* (July 1957): 41–43, 111–12; "Sigh Guy Monty Clift," *Movie Glamour Guys* (1949): 4–5. See also Cohan, *Masked Men*.

16. Skolsky, "New Look in Hollywood Men."

17. Tony Richardson, "The Method and Why: An Account of the Actors' Studio," *Sight & Sound: The Film Quarterly* 26, no. 3 (Winter 1956–57), 133–36.

18. Lionel Trilling, *Sincerity and Authenticity: The Charles Eliot Lectures, 1969–1970* (Cambridge: Harvard University Press, 1971): 134–43.

19. Brando recalled: "I played a young army lieutenant, Ken Wilocek, whose spine had been smashed by a sniper's bullet in the closing days of the war. I had no idea what it was like to be confined in a wheelchair . . . so I asked to be admitted to the Birmingham Veterans Hospital in southern California as a paralyzed veteran with a background similar to Ken Wilocek's . . . For three weeks I tried to do everything the patients did and learn what their lives were like." Quoted in Marlon Brando, *Songs My Mother Taught Me*. With Robert Lindsey. (New York: Random House, 1994): 147.

20. Cecelia Ager, "Brando in Search of Himself," *New York Times Magazine*, July 25, 1954), 24, 33.

21. Harper Babst, "Marlon Brando's Weird Love Life: Hollywood He-Man Dates Like Mad, Gets Engaged, Then Runs for Cover. Basically Afraid of Women, He's Been Known to Tell a Girl: 'I'd Like to Make Love to You but It Gives Me a Headache,' *On the QT* 2, no. 4 (March, 1957): 19–21, 54–55. Kenneth G. McLain, "Why Marlon Brando Isn't Even Half Safe: Here's what his best friends won't tell him," *Confidential* 2, no. 3 (July 1954): 34–35, 52–55. Another gossip story was about Brando's "interracial affair" with "tan tootsie" Jerri Gray. See Horton Streete, "What the Gossip Columns Missed: It Was Scandalous Way to Behave . . . even for Marlon Brando," *Confidential* 4, no. 5 (November, 1956): 31–33, 48.

22. Babst, "Brando's Weird Love Life," 54; and McLain, "Brando Isn't Even Half Safe," 35.

23. Babst, "Brando's Weird Love Life," 54.

24. Raymond Dumaret, "A Close Friend Lets the Cat Out of the Bag and Reveals: Marlon Brando's Big Secret!" *Whisper* 9, no. 2 (August 1955): 19–21, 50–51.

25. Brando, *Songs My Mother Taught Me*, 243.

26. Patricia Bosworth, *Montgomery Clift: A Biography* (New York: Bantam, 1979).

27. "Sigh Guy Monty Clift": 4–5.

28. Kerr is quoted in Maxine Arnold, "Nobody Asked Him," *Photoplay* (Dec. 1953): 52–53, 87–90.

29. By the end of *From Here to Eternity* two of the three male "heroes" were dead, making it easy to argue the film reflected a postwar crisis about masculinity, but Sam Girgus goes further and argues the film "projects the collapse of masculinity." See Girgus, *Hollywood Renaissance*, 151.

30. Sam Astrachan, "The New Lost Generation," *New Republic* (February 4, 1957), 17.

31. Kazan quoted in Donald Spoto, *Rebel: The Life and Legend of James Dean* (New York: HarperCollins, 1996), 165.

32. "Moody New Star," *Life*, March 7, 1955.

33. "Movie Reviews," *Variety*, Oct. 19, 1955.

34. Spoto, *Rebel*, 160.

35. "Rebel without a Cause," Press Release, in "Rebel without a Cause" file 705, WB Archives, USC.

36. William Baer, "An Interview with Stewart Stern," *Michigan Quarterly Review* 38, no. 4 (Fall 1999): 580–604.

37. Baer, "An Interview with Stewart Stern," 585.

38. Promotional posters in the "Rebel without a Cause" file 705, WB Archives, USC.

39. Derek Prouse, "Review: *Rebel without a Cause*," *Sight and Sound* 25, no. 3 (Winter 1955–56): 161, 164.

40. *Rebel without a Cause* Press Release, *Rebel* file 705.

41. Michael DeAngelis, *Gay Fandom and Crossover Stars: James Dean, Mel Gibson, and Keanu Reeves* (Durham & London: Duke University Press, 2001), 54.

42. In 1974 *Rolling Stone* magazine did a feature story on *Rebel without a Cause* with James Dean on the cover, stating: "With the emergence of the anti-hero—usually an androgynous adolescent—the Fifties explored the topic of bisexuality. By allowing Plato to play a homosexual counterpoint in *Rebel*, the basic question—How can you become a man?—became more complex." *Rolling Stone*, June 20, 1974, 58.

43. Trilling's comments written on unpaginated looseleaf paper contained in the *Rebel without a Cause* file, WB Archives, USC.

44. Spoto, *Rebel*, 217.

45. Derek Marlowe, "Soliloquy on James Dean's Forty-fifth Birthday," *New York Magazine*, Nov. 8, 1976.

46. Peter John Dyer, "Youth and the Cinema: The teenage rave," *Sight and Sound: The International Film Quarterly* 29, no. 1 (Winter 1959–60), 27.

47. In 1959, journalist Peter Dyer noted the undiminished influence of the James Dean phenomenon: "There is barely a teenage film made over the past three years which does not reflect, in some degree, the Dean legend; just as there is barely a film industry

outside of Hollywood which does not have its own James Dean star. With his death, screen teenagers everywhere closed their ranks . . . To try to understand the extremism of Hollywood's teenage cult . . . one has only to look back briefly to the emotional climate following Dean's death. 'The career of James Dean has not ended. It has just begun; and remember, God Himself is directing the production.' This was the conclusion of the Rev. Xen Harcey's eulogy at the actor's funeral. Two years later, 8,000 letters a month were still addressed to Dean's home, some asking for souvenirs, such as a piece of his smashed car, others writing to him as if he were still alive. Dedicated Deans (430,000 members), Dean's Teens (393,000) and James Dean's Memorial Club (330,000) were just three of the 360 fan clubs which sprang up all over the States . . ." Dyer, "Youth and the Cinema," 29.

48. Robert Coughlan, "Changing Roles in Modern Marriage," *Life*, December 24, 1956, 112.

49. Biskind, *Seeing*, 261.

50. Rebecca Bell-Metereau, *Hollywood Androgyny*, New York: Columbia University Press, 1993, 94.

51. A writer for *Playboy* used this term, perceptively noting that the 1950s were the "age of the chest" for both the male and female bodies. See Richard Armour, "Age of the Chest," *Playboy* (July 1958): 57, 65. See also Cohan, *Masked Men*: 184–89.

52. Many magazines explicitly discussed the physiques of the male stars with headlines like "Hollywood's Muscle Men and Pin-Up Pretties," *Movieland* (October, 1954): 48–55.

53. Kirk Douglas, *The Ragman's Son: An Autobiography* (New York: Simon, 1989), 129.

54. "A Hollywood Album of Male Appeal," *Life* (May 31, 1954), 96. Quoted in Cohan, *Masked Men*, 164–65.

55. On the need to mark "illegible" bodies, see Linda Schlossberg, "Introduction: Rites of Passing," in *Passing: Identity and Interpretation in Sexuality, Race, and Religion*, eds. Maria Carla Sanchez and Linda Schlossberg (New York: New York University Press, 2001), 2.

56. Valerie Steele, *Fifty Years of Fashion: New Look to Now* (New Haven, CT: Yale University Press, 1997): 1–48.

57. Magazines like *Life* emphasized the anxiety of the masculine role. See "Man in a Gray Flannel Trap" *Life*, April 9, 1956, 111–14, clipping in *The Man in the Gray Flannel Suit* PCA file.

58. Sloan Wilson, *The Man in the Gray Flannel Suit* (New York: Simon and Schuster, 1955), 272.

59. Jack Moffat, "Review of *The Man in the Gray Flannel Suit*," *Hollywood Reporter*, March 30, 1956, unpaginated clipping in *The Man in the Gray Flannel Suit* PCA file.

60. "Suiting Up as a Suburbanite Movies," *Life*, November 7, 1955, 135.

61. *Attack of the 50 Foot Woman* (1958), directed by Nathan Juran and written by Mark Hanna.

62. Allison Graham, "'The Loveliest and Purest of God's Creatures': *The Three Faces of Eve* and the Crisis of Southern Womanhood," in *Classic Hollywood, Classic Whiteness*, ed. Daniel Bernardi, 97. See also James Gilbert, *Men in the Middle: Searching for Masculinity in the 1950s* (Chicago & London: The University of Chicago Press, 2005), 13.

63. Russo, *Celluloid Closet*.

64. Chon Noriega, "'Something's Missing Here!': Homosexuality and Film Reviews During the Production Code Era, 1934–1962," *Cinema Journal* 30 (1990): 20–41.

65. Production Code Administration memo, dated June 23rd, 1955, in the *Cat on a Hot Tin Roof* PCA file.

66. Unpaginated clipping from the *Reporter*, August 13, 1958, in the *Cat on a Hot Tin Roof* PCA file.

67. "Film Review," *Films in Review* 9, no. 8 (October 1958), 454.

68. M. Keith Booker, *The Post-Utopian Imagination: American Culture in the Long 1950s* (Westport, Connecticut: Greenwood, 2002), 147.

69. This story was remade in the late fifties as *Compulsion* (1959), with the same subject matter as *Rope*—yet another variation of the 1920s Leopold and Loeb murder case—but much more explicitly treated. This film was based on the book (and stage play) by Meyer Levin, and starred Dean Stockwell and Bradford Dillman as the boys.

70. Letter dated March 5, 1948 from Jack Warner to Mr. Barney Balaban [Paramount Pictures Inc. NY]. Letter contained in *Rope* file, WB Archives, USC.

71. Unpaginated review clipping contained in the *Rope* file, WB Archives, USC.

72. Unpaginated review clipping contained in the *Rope* file, WB Archives, USC.

73. Joseph McBride, *Frank Capra: The Catastrophe of Success* (New York: Simon and Schuster, 1992), 385.

74. All the tag lines are on posters contained in the promotional material from the *Rope* file, WB Archives, USC.

75. A page in file 2701 of the Warner Bros. Archives had a list of censorship "rulings." Kansas, Alberta, and New York passed "Rope" with "No eliminations." British Columbia and Chicago gave it an "Adult." And Atlanta, Memphis, and Seattle all "Banned" it. Contained in *Rope* file, WB Archives, USC.

76. Quoted in Thomas M. Pryor "Hollywood Clicks: M-G-M Solves Its 'Tea and Sympathy' Script Problem—Of Alec Guinness," *New York Times*, September 25, 1955. Unpaginated review clipping in *Tea and Sympathy* file, MHL-AMPAS.

77. "'Tea, Sympathy' May Duck the Code," *Variety* (December 16, 1953). Review clipping in *Tea and Sympathy* file, MHL-AMPAS.

78. "For almost a year the Hollywood censors and the studio bosses hassled over the weighty problems the film posed. Is the U.S. moviegoer old enough to be told that there is such a thing as homosexuality? Is it decent to suggest that there are worse things than adultery? The answer to both questions was a resounding no, and the studio applied the fig leaf to the offending parts . . . but the sex is still fully in evidence. Indeed, the censor seems in most instances to have used the fig leaf as his own eye patch." *Time*, October 8, 1956, unpaginated clipping in *Tea and Sympathy* file, MHL-AMPAS.

79. Quoted in Thomas M. Pryor "Hollywood Clicks: M-G-M Solves Its *Tea and Sympathy* Script Problem—Of Alec Guinness," *New York Times*, September 25, 1955, clipping in *Tea and Sympathy* file, MHL-AMPAS.

80. Barbara L. Goldsmith, "Fall Films and a New Star," *Woman's Home Companion* (October 1956), clipping in *Tea and Sympathy* file, MHL-AMPAS.

81. *Time*, October 8, 1956, clipping in *Tea and Sympathy* file, MHL-AMPAS.

82. "Low Key and Offbeat," *Newsweek*, October 1, 1956, clipping in *Tea and Sympathy* file, MHL-AMPAS.

83. "Review of *Tea and Sympathy*," *Saturday Review*, September 22, 1956, in *Tea and Sympathy* file, MHL-AMPAS.

84. *Time*, October 8, 1956, clipping in *Tea and Sympathy* file, MHL-AMPAS.

85. "Review of *Tea and Sympathy*," *Saturday Review*, September 22, 1956. Edwin Schallert, "'Tea and Sympathy' Likely to Provoke Mixed Reaction," *Los Angeles Times*, October 4, 1956. Unpaginated review clippings from *Tea and Sympathy* file, MHL-AMPAS.

86. "*Tea and Sympathy*," *Variety*, September 26, 1956, 3, 15, in *Tea and Sympathy* file, MHL-AMPAS.

87. Letter to the *Times* from Rev. C. E. Egan Jr. (from Easton, Conn.). "Opinions from Readers: *Tea and Sympathy* Elicits Diverse Reactions to Theme and Content," *New York Times*, October 14, 1956, unpaginated clipping in *Tea and Sympathy* file, MHL-AMPAS.

88. *Time*, October 8, 1956, clipping in *Tea and Sympathy* file, MHL, AMPAS.

89. "*Tea and Sympathy* Is a Fine Deeply Moving Film," *Hollywood Reporter*, September 25, 1956, 3, 11, clipping in *Tea and Sympathy* file, MHL-AMPAS.

90. Thomas Wood, "*Tea and Sympathy* Comes to the Movies," *New York Herald Tribune*, Sunday, July 1, 1956, unpaginated clipping in *Tea and Sympathy* file, MHL-AMPAS.

91. Biskind, *Seeing*, 340–41.

92. Upon release, *Vertigo* was panned with reviews critiquing both the film and the stars. One review said that it "pursues its theme of false identity with such a plodding persistence," that "the audience has long since had kittens" and also noted "the spectacle of Kim Novak playing a dual identity role with equal ineptitude . . ." "SR Goes to the Movies: The Sweet Smell of Excess," *Saturday Review*, June 7, 1958. Another review heavily critiqued the film's "implausible" plot and "bad" acting. "Film Review," *Films in Review* 9, no. 6 (June–July 1958), 334.

93. "Film Review," *Films in Review* 9, no. 6 (June–July 1958), 334.

94. Paula Marantz Cohen, "Hitchcock's Revised American Vision: The Wrong Man and Vertigo" in *Hitchcock's America*, eds. Jonathan Freedman and Richard Millington. (New York: Oxford University Press, 1999): 155–72.

95. James Harvey, *Movie Love in the Fifties* (New York: Alfred A. Knopf, 2001), 78.

96. Dyer's review summarizes Perkin's disturbed character in *Psycho*: "A shy young matricide who lugs his dear departed out of her grave, preserves her for ten years alongside the rest of his specimens in a swamp-bordering motel, speaking to and for her, dressing in her clothes, murdering any girl whose attraction for him might make the possessive old thing jealous, until the only way he can survive a rapidly growing burden of understandable embarrassment is by seeking total refuge in his mother's identity . . ." Peter John Dyer, "Film Review: Psycho and The Apartment," *Sight and Sound* 29, no. 4 (Autumn 1960): 195–96.

97. Cohan, *Masked Men*, 225–26.

98. *Confidential* 6, no. 4 (October 1958), 10.

99. "Was Jimmy Dean a Psycho?," *On the QT* 2, no. 4 (March 1957): 38–39, 58–59.

100. "Was Jimmy Dean a Psycho?," 59.

101. *Variety*, February 25 1959, in *Some Like It Hot* file, MHL-AMPAS.

102. "Some Like It *Hot* Not as Hot as Expected," *Los Angeles Times*, September 4, 1959, in *Some Like It Hot* file, MHL-AMPAS

103. "Review of *Some Like It Hot*," *Motion Picture Herald*, January 31, 1959, in *Some Like It Hot* file, MHL-AMPAS.

104. "Secrets of Acting Like a Lady," *Los Angeles Mirror-News*, March 28, 1959, unpaginated clipping 1 in *Some Like It Hot* file, MHL-AMPAS.

105. Ed Sikov, *Laughing Hysterically: American Screen Comedy of the 1950s* (New York: Columbia University Press, 1994): 133–34.

106. Dick Williams, *Mirror-News*, February 27, 1959, un-paginated clipping in *Some Like It Hot* file, MHL-AMPAS.

107. "Billy Wilder Pic Distills Laughs from Dry Era," Hollywood Reporter, February 25, 1959, unpaginated clipping in *Some Like It Hot* file, MHL-AMPAS.

108. Notes made on page 133 of the script, reprinted in *Billy Wilder's Some Like It Hot, The Funniest Film Ever Made: The Complete Book*, ed. Alison Castle (Koln: Taschen, 2001), 22.

109. Vincent Canby, "Review," *Motion Picture Herald*, March 7, 1959, unpaginated clipping in *Some Like It Hot* file, MHL-AMPAS.

110. "Movie Review," *Newsweek*, April 6, 1959, unpaginated clipping in *Some Like It Hot* file, MHL-AMPAS.

CHAPTER 7

1. Quote by Allison MacKenzie (played by Diane Varsi) from the film version of *Peyton Place*.

2. Bell-Metereau, *Hollywood Androgyny*, 98–99.

3. Susan Sontag, "Notes on 'Camp,'" in *Against Interpretation and Other Essays* (New York: Farrar, Straus & Giroux, 1961): 275–92.

4. Ray Falk, "Sayonara' Now Spells Change," *New York Times*, March 10, 1957.

5. Gina Marchetti, "Contradiction and Viewing Pleasure: The Articulation of Racial, Class, and Gender Differences in Sayonara," in *Multiple Voices in Feminist Film Criticism*, eds. Diane Carson, Linda Dittmar, and Janice R. Welsh (Minneapolis: University of Minnesota Press, 1994): 248–49.

6. Graham, *Framing the South*, 67–80.

7. Like other reviews, the *Los Angeles Examiner* reporter noted the "unbilled" cameo appearances by Dietrich, Zsa Zsa Gabor, and especially by Mercedes McCambride, who was distinguished by "a crew-cut, leather jacket, and an unsavory spot of dialogue." Kay Proctor, "'Touch of Evil' Sure Is a Mess," *Los Angeles Examiner*, April 24, 1958, Section 3, 6.

8. Gloria Anzaldua, *Borderlands/ La Frontera: The New Mestiza* (San Francisco: Aunt Lute Books, 1987), 3.

9. Judith Halberstam, *Female Masculinity* (Durham and London: Duke University Press, 1998): 196–97.

10. Robert Coughlan, "Changing Roles in Modern Marriage," *Life*, December 24, 1956, 113, 118.

11. Richard Dyer, *Stars* (London: BFI, 1979, 1998), 58.

12. "Katie Hepburn's Sex Hex!" *Private Lives* 1, no. 9 (January 1956): 6–9, 54.

13. The article went on to note that as a kid "Katie liked to be called 'Jimmy' [and] often beat up bullies," a background which helped her "inject realism" into her fights in *Warrior's Husband*. Eugene Harte, "Katharine Hepburn: Hollywood's Torrid Tomboy—She once ripped off her panties and gave them to a stagehand. Another time she bathed in the nude. Here's the story-behind-the-story of a gal whose love life has been a subject of vicious speculation for years," *Confidential* 1, no. 4 (August 1953): 36, 37, 47, 50, 51.

14. Matt Williams, "Just a Routine Check, Ma'am ... and Out Popped Lizabeth Scott in the Call Girls' Call Book," *Confidential* 3, no. 4 (September 1955): 32–33, 50. See also Walt Truman, "Hollywood's No. 1 Madame," *Whisper* 9, no. 2 (August 1955): 41–43, 52.

15. Gossip about Frank Sinatra, Ava Gardner, and Lana Turner include the "dual" *Private Lives* articles, "What Shocked Frankie? What Happened When Frankie Found Two Drunk Beauties in His House?" and "Lana and Ava: Hollywood's Warmest Friendship!" *Private Lives and Private Affairs, Two Magazines in One!* 1, no. 5 (March, 1955): 6–11.

16. Victoria Thorn, "Are Most Movie Stars Mentally Ill?: yes! says a psychiatrist, and the facts are even worse than people think!" *Confidential* 8, no. 8 (October 1960): 20–23, 60, 62.

17. There are many studies of Hollywood stars and sexuality, including William J. Mann, *Behind the Screen: How Gays and Lesbians Shaped Hollywood 1910–1969* (New York: Viking, 2001) and Diana McLellan, *The Girls: Sappho Goes to Hollywood* (New York: LA Weekly Book for St. Martin's Press, 2000). For an analysis of scandal magazines and gay affairs, see also Adrienne L. Mclean and David A. Cook, eds., *Headline Hollywood: A Century of Film Scandal.* (New Brunswick, New Jersey: Rutgers University Press, 2001); and David Ehrenstein, *Open Secret: Gay Hollywood, 1928–1998* (New York: William Morrow and Company, 1998). Ehrenstein goes into depth on *Confidential's* exposés of gay leading men (like Tab Hunter, Rock Hudson, and Liberace), and looks at other controversial topics, including Ingrid Bergman's pregnancy out of wedlock (for which she was denounced on the floor of Congress).

18. Ralph H. Major Jr., "New Moral Menace to Our Youth," *CORONET* (September 1950): 101–8.

19. "Joan in Jeans: Screen's first lady doffs her mink to show they're mighty tough in the West," *Pix*, October 2, 1954), 42; and "Joan in Jeans," The *Los Angeles Times' This Week Magazine*, April 11, 1954. Clippings in *Johnny Guitar* file, MHL-AMPAS.

20. Allan Dwan directed *Montana Belle* (1952) and *Cattle Queen of Montana* (1954), Samuel Fuller directed *Forty Guns* (1957), George Sherman directed *Calamity Jane and Sam Bass* (1949), and Norman McLeod directed the comedy-western *The Paleface* (1948) with Jane Russell as Calamity Jane opposite Bob Hope.

21. Bosley Crowther, "Review of *Yellow Sky*," *New York Times*, February 2, 1949.

22. See Russo, *Celluloid Closet*; Robert J. Corber, *Cold War Femme*, White, and *Uninvited*; Ellis Hanson, ed., *Out Takes: Essays on Queer Theory and Film* (1999); *Queer Looks:*

Perspectives on Lesbian and Gay Film and Video, eds. Martha Gever, John Greyson, and Pratibha Parmar (New York: Routledge, 1993).

23. Eric Savoy, "'That Ain't All She Ain't,'" *Out Takes: Essays on Queer Theory and Film*, edited by Ellis Hanson, 161. See also Corber, *Cold War Femme*, Chapter 6, "Doris Day's Queer Normativity": 154–83.

24. *New York Journal-American*, Thursday, November 5, 1953, 20, in *Calamity Jane* file, WB Archives, USC.

25. Letter to the studio research department from Nell Perrigoue of the Deadwood Chamber of Commerce (Deadwood, South Dakota), dated March 1940, from *A South Dakota Guide* of the American Guide Series. From USC File 1010 (which also contained various memos and letters to and from the research dept., as well as a copy of *LIFE AND ADVENTURES OF CALAMITY JANE, By HERSELF*), in *Calamity Jane* file, WB Archives, USC.

26. Poster contained in *Calamity Jane* File 648 A: clippings and posters, WB Archives, USC.

27. Eric Savoy calls this scene "little closet on the prairie," as it parodies 1950s ideals of a feminine domestic bliss and butch-femme roles. Their actions accompanying the song features Jane chopping wood and other masculine tasks while Katie cooks and cleans. Savoy, "'That Ain't All She Ain't,'" 173.

28. Philip Yordan quoted in *Backstory 2: Interviews with Screenwriters of the 1940s and 1950s*, ed. Patrick McGilligan, 353.

29. See: J. Hoberman, "Johnny Guitar," *Village Voice*, January 13–19, 1982, and Myron Meisel, "Johnny Guitar," *Filmex*, March 5, 1980, clippings in *Johnny Guitar* file, MHL-AMPAS.

30. A review notes how Mercedes McCambridge "comes off excellently as the main threat to the heroine's life, proving as she did in her Academy Award winning assignment in 'All the Kings Men,' that a super-forceful ----- is just what she needs. As the leader of the townspeople against suspected outlaws she is relentlessly determined to see Miss Crawford hanged or shot, if not also drawn and quartered. And you never doubt she means business." Edwin Schallert, "Joan Crawford Hits Tough Stride," *Los Angeles Times*, May 6, 1954, unpaginated clipping in *Johnny Guitar* file, MHL-AMPAS.

31. Schallert, "Joan Crawford Hits Tough Stride."

32. "Joan Crawford Hits Them with Wide Open Spaces," *Cue*, June 5, 1954, unpaginated clipping in *Johnny Guitar* file, MHL-AMPAS.

33. "Joan in Jeans," *Los Angeles Times' This Week Magazine*, April 11, 1954; "Review of *Johnny Guitar*," *Variety*, May 5, 1954; Milton Luban, "Inept Yarn Matched by Megging, Acting," *Hollywood Reporter*, May 5, 1954; Schallert, "Joan Crawford Hits Them with Wide Open Spaces"; "Joan Crawford Hits Tough Stride," *Los Angeles Times*, May 6, 1954; Kay Proctor, "'Johnny Guitar' Arizona Saga," *Los Angeles Examiner*, May 6, 1954; Bosley Crowther, "Review," *New York Times*, May 28, 1954. Clippings in *Johnny Guitar* file, MHL-AMPAS.

34. Bosley Crowther, *New York Times*, May 28, 1954, 19.

35. "Joan in Jeans," *Los Angeles Times*.

36. Molly Haskell, *From Reverence to Rape: The Treatment of Women in the Movies* (Baltimore: Penguin Books, 1973, 1974), 176.

37. "Joan in Jeans: Screen's first lady doffs mink to show they're mighty tough in the west," *Pix*, October 2, 1954, 43, clipping in *Johnny Guitar* file, MHL-AMPAS.

38. "*Johnny Guitar* Review," *Variety*, May 5, 1954, unpaginated clipping in *Johnny Guitar* file, MHL-AMPAS.

39. "Joan Crawford Hits Them with Wide Open Spaces," *Cue*, June 5, 1954, and Proctor, "'Johnny Guitar' Arizona Saga." Reviews in *Johnny Guitar* file, MHL-AMPAS.

40. For an analysis of the coding of lesbian desire in films, see White, *Uninvited*; Corber, *Cold War Femme*; and Russo, *Celluloid Closet*.

41. Many books have been written about this film, including a retrospective account by Mankiewicz. See Joseph Mankiewicz and Gary Carey, *More about All about Eve* (New York: Random House, 1972) and Sam Staggs, *All about All About Eve* (New York: St. Martin's, 2000). See also Russo, *Celluloid Closet*; Haskell, *Reverence to Rape*; Judith Roof, *All about Thelma and Eve: Sidekicks and Third Wheels* (Urbana: University of Chicago Press, 2002); and Kenneth Turan, "A Sparkling 'Eve': Joseph L. Mankiewicz's 1950 hit 'All about Eve,' re-released in a newly restored print, still crackles," *Los Angeles Times*, November 3, 2000, F2, F13.

42. "Cinema Reviews," *Time*, October 16, 1950, 75, in *All about Eve* file, MHL-AMPAS.

43. Letter to the editor, "Dissenting Opinion," *New York Times*, November 5, 1950.

44. Joseph L. Mankiewicz, "All about the Women in 'All about Eve,'" *New York*, October 16, 1972, 37–42, in *All about Eve* file, MHL-AMPAS.

45. Mankiewicz, "All about the Women in 'All about Eve,'" 37–42, in *All about Eve* file, MHL-AMPAS.

46. For an important analysis of Thelma Ritter's character and the function of the sidekicks in general, see Roof, *All about Thelma and Eve*.

47. "Darryl Zanuck, Mankiewicz, Davis, Baxter Score Hits," *Hollywood Reporter*, September 13, 1950.

48. Davis quoted in Staggs, *All about All about Eve*, 102.

49. "Dissenting Opinion: Letter to the Screen Editor," *New York Times*, November 5, 1950.

50. "Cinema Reviews," *Time*, October 16, 1950, 75, in *All about Eve* file, MHL-AMPAS.

51. "Cinema Reviews," *Time*, 75.

52. Mankiewicz, "All about the Women in 'All about Eve'": 37–42, in *All about Eve* file, MHL-AMPAS.

53. See Russo, *Celluloid Closet*, 94.

54. Conventional wisdom is that Baxter and Davis effectively cancelled each other out at the Academy Awards, leaving an opening for Holliday to win. Brunette Gloria Swanson, nominated for her role in *Sunset Boulevard*, also lost out. See Staggs, *All about All about Eve*.

55. Helen Markel Herrmann, "Hey-Hey-Day of a 'Dumb' Blonde: Judy Holliday's whinny and wiggle make her the nation's favorite nitwit—but she isn't," *New York Times*, March 4, 1951, 16, 44. For a similar take on the genius of Holliday, see also Winthrop Sargeant, "Judy

Holliday: 'Born Yesterday's' Not So Dumb Blonde Prefers Slacks to Minks, Likes Proust, Hates Hollywood, Hopes to Someday Play Ophelia," *Life*, April 2, 1951, 107–8, 111–18.

56. Susan Jhirad, "Hitchcock's Women," *Cineaste* 13, no. 4 (1984): 30–33.

57. Wini Breines, "Postwar White Girls' Dark Others," in *The Other Fifties: Interrogating Midcentury American Icons*, ed. Joel Foreman, 69.

58. Cohan, *Masked Men*, 13.

59. On the social function of the "blonde" in terms of framing ideals of femininity and whiteness, see Richard Dyer, *White* (London and New York: Routledge, 1997). See also Sabrina Barton, "Crisscross: Paranoia and Projection in *Strangers on a Train*," *Camera Obscura* 25–26 (1991): 74–100.

60. Holliday, Cukor, and Kanin worked together on several films, notably *Adam's Rib*, that Cukor directed, Kanin co-wrote with wife Ruth Gordon, and Holliday performed the "scene stealing" role of Doris Attinger alongside Katharine Hepburn. Like Holliday, Kanin and Gordon were deemed "Reds" by HUAC in 1951. See Judith Smith, "Judy Holliday's Urban Working-Girl Characters in 1950s Hollywood Film," in *A Jewish Feminine Mystique?: Jewish Women in Postwar America*, eds. Hasia R. Diner et al (New Jersey: Rutgers University Press, 2010): 160–76.

61. Thomas J. Foley, "Oscar Winners Judy Holliday and Jose Ferrar Linked to Red Groups: House Probers Name Stars, 47 Others," *New York Times*, April 5, 1951, 1, 4. Regarding Holliday's performing "Billie Dawn" before HUAC, see Gary Carey, *Judy Holliday: An Intimate Life Story* (New York: Seaview Books, 1982).

62. Dyer, *White*. Monroe was featured in too many articles and on too many magazine covers to fully list, but included *Life*, *Time*, and of course the inaugural cover of *Playboy*. See "Marilyn Monroe: The Talk of Hollywood," *Life*, April 7, 1952, 101–4; "Marilyn Monroe," *Time*, August 11, 1952, 74–82; "What Makes Marilyn," *Playboy*, no. 1, 1953: 17–19.

63. Barbara Berch Jamison, "Body and Soul: A Portrait of Marilyn Monroe Showing Why Gentlemen Prefer That Blonde," *New York Times*, July 18, 1953.

64. Barton, "Face Value," 139.

65. Molly Haskell, "We Would Have Had to Invent Her," in, *All the Available Light: A Marilyn Monroe Reader*, ed. Yona Zeldis McDonough (New York: Simon and Schuster, 2002), 115.

66. "Marilyn Takes Over as Lorelei." *Life*, May 25, 1953, 79–81.

67. Jane Russell received top billing for the film as Monroe was not yet a star. Jonathan Rosenbaum notes that Russell "was paid $200,000 for her part (and got top billing), while Monroe, on her Fox salary and not yet a star, got only $500 a week." Jonathan Rosenbaum, *Placing Movies: The Practice of Film Criticism* (Berkeley: University of California Press, 1995), 99.

68. McCarthy, *Howard Hawks*, 508. Vito Russo's *Celluloid Closet* interprets the scene with a similar reading.

69. Barton, "Face Value," 129.

70. "Review of *Some Like It Hot*," *Newsweek*, April 6, 1959, clipping in *Some Like It Hot* file, MHL-AMPAS.

71. See Gina Marchetti, "White Knights in Hong Kong: *Love Is a Many Splendored Thing* and *The World of Suzie Wong*," in *Romance and the 'Yellow Peril': Race, Sex, and Discursive Strategies in Hollywood Fiction* (1993): 109–24.

72. *Gigi* (USA, 1958), directed by Vincente Minnelli, won the Oscar for Best Picture. Music was written by Frederick Loewe, with lyrics and screenplay written by Alan Lerner. The film, starring Louis Jordan and Leslie Caron, based on Colette's writings, explicitly dealt with the grooming of a young girl to be a courtesan/ mistress for wealthy men. *My Fair Lady*, a very successful musical adaptation of George Bernard Shaw's *Pygmalion*, likewise concerned the gender education of a young woman designed to "pass her off" as a "lady."

73. Bosley Crowther, "Review: *The Three Faces of Eve*," *New York Times*, September 27, 1957.

74. Allison Graham, *Framing the South*, 50. Previously published as "Joanne Woodward: The Fugitive Kind," *Look*, December 23, 1959, 123.

75. See Graham, *Framing the South*, 42–53.

76. Emily Toth, *Inside Peyton Place: The Life of Grace Metalious* (1981; repr. Jackson: University Press of Mississippi, 2000).

77. Jane Hendler, *Best-Sellers and Their Film Adaptations in Postwar America: From Here to Eternity, Sayonara, Giant, Auntie Mame, Peyton Place* (New York: Peter Lang Publishing, 2001).

78. Her hometown of Gilmanton, New Hampshire, apparently never did forgive her for the novel; see Joelle Farrell, "'Pandora in Blue Jeans' Lives On: Film about 'Peyton Place' author opens old town wounds," *Concord Monitor*, March 26, 2006.

79. *Life*, November 12, 1956, 104.

80. Regina G. Kunzel, "White Neurosis, Black Pathology: Constructing Out-of-Wedlock Pregnancy in the Wartime and Postwar United States," in *Not June Cleaver: Women and Gender in Postwar America 1945–1960*, ed. Joanne Meyerowitz (Philadelphia: Temple University Press, 1994), 307.

81. Sayre, *Running Time*, 102.

82. See Rickie Solinger, *Wake Up Little Susie: Single Pregnancy and Race before Roe v. Wade* (New York: Routledge, 1992).

83. The Production Code made it clear that films could not say nor advocate abortion, so having a doctor admit to "assisting a miscarriage" flaunted the Code.

84. Richard Dyer argues: "More than one newspaper described her testimony as 'the greatest performance of her life.' Whether or not this was fair of the press, the confusion was compounded by the purely coincidental release of *Peyton Place* around the time of the trial. In it, Turner's big scene has her breaking down in sobs on the witness stand, just as she did at the Stompanato trial." Richard Dyer, "Four Films of Lana Turner," in *Imitation of Life, Douglas Sirk, Director*, ed. Lucy Fischer (New Brunswick, NJ: Rutgers University Press, 1991), 203.

85. "Lana's Plea for Daughter Is Real-Life Drama Triumph," *Life*, April 21, 1958, 21.

CONCLUSION

1. Susman, *Culture as History*, 284.
2. *The Collected Works of Langston Hughes*, ed. Christopher C. De Santis, vol. 9, *Essays on Art, Race, Politics, and World Affairs*, xv.

BIBLIOGRAPHY

ARCHIVAL SOURCES

"Biography Files." Margaret Herrick Library, Academy of Motion Picture Arts and Sciences, Los Angeles, California.

"David O. Selznick Files." Harry Ransom Humanities Research Center, University of Texas at Austin.

FBI Confidential Files. Communist Activity in the Entertainment Industry. FBI Surveillance Files on Hollywood, 1942–1958. Edited by Daniel J. Leab. Bethesda, MD: University Publications of America, 1991. 14 Microfilm Reels.

"General Subject Files." Margaret Herrick Library, Academy of Motion Picture Arts and Sciences, Los Angeles, California.

Motion Picture and Television Reading Room, Library of Congress, Washington, DC.

Motion Picture Sound and Video Branch, NNSM, Department of Defense Archives, College Park, Maryland.

Popular Culture Research Collections, Popular Culture Library, Bowling Green State University.

"Production Code Administration Files (PCA Files)." Margaret Herrick Library, Academy of Motion Picture Arts and Sciences, Los Angeles, California.

The UCLA Film and Television Archives, University of California at Los Angeles.

Warner Bros. Archives, School of Cinema-Television, University of Southern California.

PRIMARY DOCUMENTS

Agee, James. *Agee on Film: Criticism and Comment on the Movies*. New York: Modern Library, 2000. First published in 1958 by McDowell, Obelensky.

Ager, Cecelia. "Brando in Search of Himself." *New York Times Magazine* (July 25, 1954), 24, 33.

Allport, Gordon W. *The Nature of Prejudice*. Don Mills, Ont.: Addison-Wesley Pub. Co., 1954. Reprinted as the unabridged 25th anniversary ed., with introduction by Kenneth Clark and foreword by Thomas Pettigrew in 1979. Page references are to the 1979 edition.

Armour, Richard. "Age of the Chest." *Playboy*, January 1956, 57, 64.

Astrachan, Sam. "The New Lost Generation," *New Republic*, February 4, 1957, 17.

Baer, William. "An Interview with Stewart Stern." *Michigan Quarterly Review* 38, no. 4 (Fall 1999): 580–604.

Behlmer, Rudy, ed. *Memo from Darryl F. Zanuck: The Golden Years at Twentieth Century-Fox*. Foreword by Philip Dunne. New York: Grove, 1993.

Belafonte, Harry. "Why I Married Julie," *Ebony*, July 1957, 90–95.

"Belafonte Gets Dixie Threats for Movie Role," *Jet*, Jan 3, 1957.

Bell, Daniel. ed., *The New American Right*. New York: Criterion, 1955.

Biberman, Herbert. "*Salt of the Earth*": *The Story of a Film*. Boston: Beacon, 1965.

Brando, Marlon with Robert Lindsey. *Songs My Mother Taught Me*. New York: Random House, 1994.

Brown, Gene, ed. *The New York Times Encyclopedia of Film*. New York: Times Books, 1984.

Calomaris, Angela. *Red Masquerade*. Philadelphia: Lippincott, 1950.

Chambers, Whittaker. *Witness*. New York: Random House, 1952.

Cogley, John. *Report on Blacklisting II: Radio-Television*. New York: Fund for the Republic, 1956.

Cole, Lester. *Hollywood Red: the Autobiography of Lester Cole*. Palo Alto, Calif.: Ramparts, 1981.

Coughlan, Robert. "Changing Roles in Modern Marriage." *Life*, December 24, 1956, 108–18.

Crowther, Bosley. "Color or Class: Are Issues Evaded in *Island in the Sun*?," *New York Times*, June 23, 1957.

———. "Detergent Drama: *Imitation of Life* in Familiar Soapy Vein," *New York Times*, April 19, 1959.

———. "Review: *The Three Faces of Eve* (1957)," *New York Times*, September 27, 1957.

———. "Review: *Yellow Sky*," *New York Times*, February 2, 1949.

———. "Will Film-Making Be Complicated by the 'Un-American' Probers?," *New York Times*, November 2, 1947.

Cvetic, Matthew. *I Was a Communist for the FBI*. (First serialized in *Saturday Evening Post* under the title "I Posed as a Communist for the FBI" in 223, no. 4, July 22, 1950.

The Decline of the American Male. Edited by *Look* editors. New York: Random House, 1958.

"Dope, Kidnapping, and Other Tabu Plots OK Under Revised Film Code." *Variety*, December 12, 1956, 1–20.

Dmytryk, Edward. *It's a Hell of a Life, But Not a Bad Living*. New York: Times Books, 1978.

———. *Odd Man Out: A Memoir of the Hollywood Ten*. Carbondale: Southern Illinois University Press, 1995.

Douglas, Kirk. *The Ragman's Son: An Autobiography*. New York: Simon, 1989.

Douglas, William O. "The Black Silence of Fear." *New York Times Magazine*, January 13, 1952, 5, 7, 37–38.

Dyer, Peter John. "Film Review: *Psycho* and *The Apartment*." *Sight and Sound* 29, no. 4 (Autumn 1960): 195–96.

———. "Youth and the Cinema: The Teenage Rave." *Sight & Sound: The International Film Quarterly* 29, no. 1 (Winter 1959/60): 26–30, 51.

Ellison, Ralph. *Invisible Man*. 1952. 30th anniversary ed. New York: Random House, 1982.

———. *Shadow and Act*. 1953. Vintage reissue ed. New York: Random House, 1995.

Erikson, Erik. *Childhood and Society*. 1950. 2nd ed. New York: W. W. Norton & Company, 1963.

Fast, Howard. *Being Red: A Memoir*. New York: Dell, 1990.

Geisel, Theodor Seuss. *The Sneetches and Other Stories*. 1961; repr. New York: Random House, 1989.

Goldman, Eric F. *The Crucial Decade and After: America, 1945–1960*. New York: Vintage Books, 1956, 1960.

Harte, Eugene. "Katharine Hepburn: Hollywood's Torrid Tomboy—She once ripped off her panties and gave them to a stagehand. Another time she bathed in the nude. Here's the story-behind-the-story of a gal whose love life has been a subject of vicious speculation for years." *Confidential* 1, no. 4 (August 1953), 36, 37, 47, 50, 51.

Hellman, Lillian. *Scoundrel Time*. Boston: Little, Brown, 1976.

Herrmann, Helen Markel. "Hey-Hey-Day of a 'Dumb' Blonde: Judy Holliday's whinny and wiggle make her the nation's favorite nitwit—but she isn't." *The New York Times Encyclopedia of Film, 1947–1951*. New York: Times Books, 1984.

Hollis, Lou. "The Name Ain't the Same in Movieland!" *Hush-Hush* 1, no. 3 (September 1955): 38–39, 61.

Houston, Penelope. "Mr. Deeds and Willie Stark." *Sight & Sound: The International Film Quarterly* 19, no. 7 (November 1950): 276–79, 285.

Hughes, Langston. "Who's Passing for Who?," in *Langston Hughes Short Stories*, edited by Akiba Sullivan Harper, 170–74. Introduction by Arnold Rampersad. New York: Hill and Wang, 1996.

———. *Essays on Art, Race, Politics, and World Affairs*. Edited by Christopher C. De Santis. Vol. 9 of *The Collected Works of Langston Hughes*. Columbia and London: University of Missouri Press, 2003.

Hurst, Fannie. *Imitation of Life*. New York: Harper & Row, 1933.

"Joan in Jeans." *Los Angeles Times' This Week Magazine*, April 11, 1954.

"Joan in Jeans: Screen's first lady doffs her mink to show they're mighty tough in the West." *Pix*, October 2, 1954, 42.

Jowitt, Earl. *The Strange Case of Alger Hiss*. Garden City, New York: Doubleday & Company, 1953.

Kahn, Gordon. *Hollywood on Trial: The Story of the 10 Who Were Indicted*. New York: Boni & Gaer, 1948.

Kardiner, Abram, and Lionel Ovesey. *The Mark of Oppression: Explorations in the Personality of the American Negro*. Cleveland: World Publishing Company, 1951.

"Katie Hepburn's Sex Hex!" *Private Lives* 1, no. 9 (January 1956): 6–9, 54.

Kazan, Elia. *A Life*. New York: Knopf, 1988.

Kinsey, Alfred C. *Sexual Behavior in the Human Male*. Philadelphia: Saunders, 1948.

———. *Sexual Behavior in the Human Female*. Philadelphia: Saunders, 1953.

Kroeber, A. L., and Clyde Kluckholm. *Culture: A Critical Review of Concepts and Definitions*. New York: Vintage, 1952.

Lassally, Walter. "The Cynical Audience." *Sight & Sound: The International Film Quarterly* 26, no. 1 (Summer 1956): 12–15.

Lundberg, Ferdinand, and Marynia F. Farnham, MD, *Modern Woman: The Lost Sex*. New York: Harper and Brothers, 1947.

Major, Jr., Ralph H. "New Moral Menace to Our Youth." *Coronet*, September 1950, 101–8.

Mankiewicz, Joseph L. "All about the Women in 'All about Eve.'" *New York*, October 16, 1972, 37–42.

"Marilyn Monroe: The Talk of Hollywood." *Life*, April 7, 1952, 101–4.

"Marilyn Monroe." *Time*, August 11, 1952, 74–82.

"Marilyn Takes Over as Lorelei." *Life*, May 25, 1953, 79–81.

McClelland, Doug. *Forties Film Talk: Oral Histories of Hollywood, with 120 Lobby Posters*. Jefferson, North Carolina: McFarland, 1992.

Mead, Margaret. *And Keep Your Powder Dry: An Anthropologist Looks at America*. New York: William Morrow, 1942.

Miller, Arthur. *Timebends: A Life*. New York: Grove, 1987.

———. "Why I Wrote *The Crucible*: An Artist's Answer to Politics." *New Yorker*, October 21, 1996, 158–64.

Myrdal, Gunnar. *An American Dilemma: The Negro Problem and Modern Democracy*. 20th anniversary ed. New York: Harper & Row, 1962.

"Name Game: What Are the Real Names of the Stars?" *The Lowdown* 1, no. 4 (August 1955): 38–39.

Packer, Herbert L. *Ex-Communist Witness*. Stanford: Stanford University Press, 1962.

Powdermaker, Hortense. *Hollywood: The Dream Factory*. New York: Little, Brown and Company, 1950.

Red Channels: The Report on Communist Influence in Radio and Television. New York: American Business Consultants, 1950.

"Revised Pix Code OKs Miscegenation, Drinking, Smuggling If 'In Good Taste.'" *Variety*, September 15, 1954, 3, 16.

Richardson, Tony. "The Method and Why: An Account of the Actors' Studio." *Sight & Sound: The Film Quarterly* 26, no. 3 (Winter 1956–57): 133–36.

Riesman, David. *The Lonely Crowd: A Study of the Changing American Character*. New Haven: Yale University Press, 1950.

Sapir, Edward. "Why Cultural Anthropology Needs the Psychiatrist." *Psychiatry* 1 (February 1938), 10.

Schallert, Edwin. "Joan Crawford Hits Tough Stride." *Los Angeles Times*, May 6, 1954.

"Sigh Guy Monty Clift." *Movie Glamour Guys* (1949): 4–5.

Singer, Milton. "A Survey of Culture and Personality Theory and Research." In *Studying Personality Cross-Culturally*, edited by Bert Kaplan. New York: Harper & Row, 1961.

Skolsky, Sidney. "The New Look in Hollywood Men." *Photoplay* (July 1957): 41–43, 111–12.

Sontag, Susan. *Against Interpretation and Other Essays*. New York: Farrar, Straus & Giroux, 1961.

Sward, Keith. "Boy and Girl Meet Neurosis." *The Screen Writer*, September 1948, 8–26.

Thorn, Victoria. "Are Most Movie Stars Mentally Ill?: yes! says a psychiatrist, and the facts are even worse than people think!" *Confidential* 8, no. 8, October 1960, 20–23, 60, 62.

"To Kiss or Not to Kiss Is Question Which Upset Cast," *Ebony*, July 1957, 34.

Trilling, Lionel. *Sincerity and Authenticity: The Charles Eliot Norton Lectures, 1969–1970*. Cambridge, Massachusetts: Harvard University Press, 1972.

———. *The Liberal Imagination: Essays on Literature and Society*. New York: Viking, 1950.

Truman, Harry. *To Secure These Rights: The Report of the President's Committee on Civil Rights*. Washington, DC: Government Printing Office, 1947.

Truman, Walt. "Hollywood's No. 1 Madame." *Whisper* 9, no. 2 (August 1955): 41–43, 52.

Trumbo, Dalton. *The Time of the Toad: A Study of the Inquisition in America*. 1949; repr. New York: Harper and Row, 1972.

———. *Additional Dialogue: Letters of Dalton Trumbo, 1942–1962*. Ed. Helen Manfull. New York: M. Evans, 1970.

Twain, Mark. *The Tragedy of Pudd'nhead Wilson*. 1894. Reprint, New York: Penguin Books, 1980.

"What Shocked Frankie? What Happened When Frankie Found Two Drunk Beauties in His House?" and "Lana and Ava: Hollywood's Warmest Friendship!" *Private Lives and Private Affairs, Two Magazines in One!* 1, no. 5, March 1955, 6–11.

Whyte, William H. Jr. *The Organization Man*. New York: Simon, 1956.

Whiting, Beatrice B., ed., *Six Cultures: Studies of Child Rearing*. New York: John Wiley and Sons, 1963.

Williams, Matt. "Just a Routine Check, Ma'am . . . and Out Popped Lizabeth Scott in the Call Girls' Call Book." *Confidential* 3, no. 4, September 1955), 32–33, 50.

Wilson, Sloan. *The Man in the Gray Flannel Suit*. New York: Simon and Schuster, 1955.

Witmer, Helen Leland, and Ruth Kotinsky, ed., *Personality in the Making; The Fact-Finding Report of the Midcentury White House Conference on Children and Youth*. New York: Harper, 1952.

Wylie, Phillip. *Generation of Vipers*. New York: Rinehart, 1942.

Wolfenstein, Martha, and Nathan Leites. *Movies: A Psychological Study*. New York: Hafner Publishing, 1950.

SECONDARY SOURCES

Anderson, Lisa M. *Mammies No More: The Changing Image of Black Women on Stage and Screen*. Lanham: Rowman & Littlefield, 1997.

Ball, Terence. "The Politics of Social Science in Postwar America." In *Recasting America: Culture and Politics in the Age of Cold War*, edited by Lary May, 76–92. Chicago: University of Chicago Press, 1989.

Banner, Lois W. *Intertwined Lives: Margaret Mead, Ruth Benedict, and Their Circle*. New York: Knopf, 2003.

Barrios, Richard. *Screened Out: Playing Gay in Hollywood from Edison to Stonewall*. New York: Routledge, 2003.

Barson, Michael. *"Better Dead than Red!": A Nostalgic Look at the Golden Years of Russiaphobia, Red-baiting, and Other Commie Madness*. New York: Hyperion, 1992.

Barton, Sabrina. "Crisscross: Paranoia and Projection in *Strangers on a Train*." *Camera Obscura* 25–26 (1991): 74–100.

———. "Face Value." In *All the Available Light: A Marilyn Monroe Reader*, edited by Yona Zeldis McDonough, 120–41. New York: Simon and Schuster, 2002.

Beaty, Bart. *Fredric Wertham and the Critique of Mass Culture: A Re-Examination of the Critic Whose Congressional Testimony Sparked the Comics Code*. Jackson: University Press of Mississippi, 2005.

Bell-Metereau, Rebecca. *Hollywood Androgyny.* 2nd ed. New York: Columbia University Press, 1993.

Benshoff, Harry. *Monsters in the Closet: Homosexuality and the Horror Film.* Manchester: Manchester University Press, 1997.

Bernardi, Daniel, ed. *Classic Hollywood, Classic Whiteness.* Minneapolis: University of Minnesota Press, 2001.

Berube, Allan. *Coming Out under Fire: The History of Gay Men and Women in World War Two.* 1990. Reprint, New York: Plume, 1991.

Biskind, Peter. "Rebel without a Cause: Nicholas Ray in the Fifties." *Film Quarterly* (Fall 1974): 32–38.

———. *Seeing Is Believing: How Hollywood Taught Us to Stop Worrying and Love the Fifties.* 1983. Reprint, New York: Henry Holt, 2000.

Black, Gregory D. *Hollywood Censored: Morality Codes, Catholics, and the Movie.* Cambridge: Cambridge University Press, 1994.

Bogle, Donald. *Heat Wave: The Life and Career of Ethel Waters.* New York: HarperCollins, 2011.

———. *Toms, Coons, Mulattoes, Mammies and Bucks: An Interpretative History of Blacks in American Film.* New York: Viking, 1973.

Booker, M. Keith. *The Post-Utopian Imagination: American Culture in the Long 1950s.* Westport, Connecticut: Greenwood, 2002.

Bosworth, Patricia. *Montgomery Clift: A Biography.* New York: Bantam, 1979.

Boyer, Paul. *By the Bomb's Early Light: American Thought and Culture at the Dawn of the Atomic Age.* New York: Pantheon, 1985.

Breines, Wini. *Young, White, and Miserable: Growing Up Female in the Fifties.* Boston: Beacon, 1992.

Brown, Peter Harry. *Kim Novak: The Reluctant Goddess.* New York: St. Martin's, 1986.

Bruzzi, Stella. *Undressing Cinema: Clothing and Identity in the Movies.* London and New York: Routledge, 1997.

Butler, Judith. *Gender Trouble: Feminism and the Subversion of Identity.* London: Routledge, 1990.

———. "Lana's 'Imitation': Melodramatic Repetition and the Gender Performative." *Genders* 9 (1990): 1–18.

———. *Bodies That Matter: On the Discursive Limits of "Sex."* New York: Routledge, 1993.

Buhle, Paul, and Dave Wagner, eds. *Blacklisted: The Film Lover's Guide to the Hollywood Blacklist.* New York: Palgrave Macmillan, 2003.

Buhle, Paul, and Dave Wagner. *Hide in Plain Sight: The Hollywood Blacklistees in Film and Television, 1950–2002.* New York: Palgrave Macmillan, 2003.

———. *Radical Hollywood: The Untold Story behind America's Favorite Movies.* New York: The New Press, 2002.

Byars, Jackie. *All That Hollywood Allows: Re-Reading Gender in 1950s Melodrama.* Chapel Hill and London: University of North Carolina Press, 1991.

Carr, Gary. *The Left Side of Paradise: The Screenwriting of John Howard Lawson.* Ann Arbor, Michigan: UMI Research, 1984.

Carson, Diane, and Linda Dittmat, eds. *Multiple Voices in Feminist Film Criticism*. Minneapolis: University of Minnesota Press, 1994.

Castle, Alison. ed., *Billy Wilder's "Some Like It Hot," The Funniest Film Ever Made: The Complete Book*. Koln: Taschen, 2001.

Caughie, Pamela L. *Passing and Pedagogy: The Dynamics of Responsibility*. Urbana and Chicago: University of Illinois Press, 1999.

Caute, David. *The Great Fear: The Anti-Communist Purge under Truman and Eisenhower*. New York: Simon and Schuster, 1978.

Ceplair, Larry, and Steven Englund. *The Inquisition in Hollywood: Politics in the Film Community, 1930–1960*. Garden City, NY: Anchor/Doubleday, 1980.

Chafe, William. *The Unfinished Journey: America since World War II*. 1986. 2nd ed. Oxford: Oxford University Press, 1991.

Cohan, Steven. *Masked Men: Masculinity and the Movies in the Fifties*. Bloomington and Indianapolis: Indiana University Press, 1997.

Cohen, Paula Marantz. "Hitchcock's Revised American Vision: The Wrong Man and Vertigo." In Jonathan Freedman and Richard Millington, eds., *Hitchcock's America*. New York: Oxford University Press, 1999: 155–72.

Coontz, Stephanie. *The Way We Never Were: American Families and the Nostalgia Trap*. New York: Basic Books, 1999.

Corber, Robert J. *Cold War Femme: Lesbianism, National Identity, and Hollywood Cinema*. Durham and London: Duke University Press, 2011.

———. *In the Name of National Security: Hitchcock, Homophobia, and the Political Construction of Gender in Postwar America*. Durham, NC: Duke University Press, 1993.

Courtney, Susan. *Hollywood Fantasies of Miscegenation: Spectacular Narratives of Gender and Race, 1903–1967*. Princeton and Oxford: Princeton University Press, 2005.

Creadick, Anna. "Incredible/Shrinking Men: Masculinity and Atomic Anxiety in American Postwar Science Fiction Film." In *Fear Itself: Enemies Real and Imagined in American Culture*, edited by Nancy Lusignan Schultz. West Lafayette, Indiana: Purdue University Press, 1999.

Cripps, Thomas. *Making Movies Black: The Hollywood Message Movie from World War II to the Civil Rights Era*. New York: Oxford University Press, 1992.

———. *Slow Fade to Black: The Negro in American Film, 1900–1942*. Oxford: Oxford University Press, 1993.

Cripps, Thomas, and David Culbert. "The Negro Soldier (1944): Film Propaganda in Black and White." *American Quarterly* 31, no. 5 (Winter 1979): 616–40.

Custen, George F. *Twentieth Century's Fox: Darryl F. Zanuck and the Culture of Hollywood*. New York: Basic Books, 1997.

Dick, Bernard F. *Radical Innocence: A Critical Study of the Hollywood Ten*. Lexington: University of Kentucky Press, 1989.

DeAngelis, Michael. *Gay Fandom and Crossover Stars: James Dean, Mel Gibson, and Keanu Reeves*. Durham & London: Duke University Press, 2001.

Degler, Carl. *In Search of Human Nature: The Decline and Revival of Darwinism in American Social Thought*. Oxford: Oxford University Press, 1991.

D'Emilio, John. "The Homosexual Menace: The Politics of Sexuality in Cold War America." In *Passion and Power: Sexuality in History*, edited by Kathy Peiss and Christina Simmons. Philadelphia: Temple University Press, 1989. 225–40.

———. *Sexual Politics, Sexual Communities: The Making of a Homosexual Minority in the United States, 1940–1970.* Chicago: University of Chicago Press, 1983.

Doane, Mary Ann. *Femmes Fatales: Feminism, Film Theory, Psychoanalysis.* New York and London: Routledge, 1991.

Doherty, Thomas. *Cold War, Cool Medium: Television, McCarthyism, and American Culture.* New York: Columbia University Press, 2003.

———. *Hollywood's Censor: Joseph I. Breen and the Production Code Administration.* New York: Columbia University Press, 2007.

———. *Projections of War: Hollywood, American Culture, and World War II.* New York: Columbia University Press, 1993.

Doniger, Wendy. *The Woman Who Pretended to Be Who She Was: Myths of Self-Imitation.* Oxford: Oxford University Press, 2005.

Doty, Alexander. *Flaming Classics: Queering the Film Canon.* New York: Routledge, 2000.

Draper, Ellen. "'Controversy has probably destroyed forever the context': The *Miracle* and Movie Censorship in America in the Fifties." *The Velvet Light Trap* 25 (Spring 1990): 69–79.

Duberman, Martin Bauml. *Paul Robeson.* New York: Knopf, 1988.

Dyer, Richard. *White.* London and New York: Routledge, 1997.

———. *Stars.* 1979. New ed. London: BFI, 1998.

———. *Now You See It: Studies on Lesbian and Gay Film.* London: Routledge, 1990.

———. *The Matter of Images: Essays on Representation.* London: Routledge, 1993.

Ehrenreich, Barbara. *The Hearts of Men: American Dreams and the Flight from Commitment.* New York: Doubleday, 1983.

Fabi, M. Giulia. *Passing and the Rise of the African American Novel.* Urbana and Chicago: University of Illinois Press, 2001.

Feldstein, Ruth. *Motherhood in Black and White: Race and Sex in American Liberalism, 1930–1965.* Ithaca, NY: Cornell University Press, 2000.

Fischer, Lucy, ed. *Imitation of Life: Douglas Sirk, Director.* New Brunswick, NJ: Rutgers University Press, 1991.

Foreman, Joel, ed. *The Other Fifties: Interrogating Midcentury American Icons.* Urbana and Chicago: University of Illinois Press, 1997.

Foster, Gwendolyn. *Performing Whiteness: Postmodern Re/Constructions in the Cinema.* New York: State University of New York Press, 2003.

Foucault, Michel. *Discipline and Punishment: The Birth of the Prison.* New York: Vintage Books, 1995.

Freedman, Jonathan, and Richard Millington, eds. *Hitchcock's America.* New York: Oxford University Press, 1999.

Fried, Richard. *Nightmare in Red: The McCarthy Era in Perspective.* New York: Oxford University Press, 1990.

Friedrich, Otto. *City of Nets: A Portrait of Hollywood in the 1940s*. New York: Harper & Row, 1986.

Gabbard, Glen O., and Krin Gabbard. *Psychiatry and the Cinema*. 2nd ed. American Psychiatric, 1999.

Gabler, Neal. *An Empire of Their Own: How the Jews Invented Hollywood*. New York: Anchor Books, 1989.

Garber, Marjorie. *Vested Interests: Cross-Dressing and Cultural Anxiety*. New York and London: Routledge, 1992.

Gates, Henry Louis Jr. *Thirteen Ways of Looking at a Black Man*. New York: Random House, 1997.

Gathorne-Hardy, Jonathan. *Sex, the Measure of All Things: A Life of Alfred C. Kinsey*. London: Chatto & Windus, 1998.

Gever, Martha, John Greyson, and Pratibha Parmar, eds., *Queer Looks: Perspectives on Lesbian and Gay Film and Video*. New York: Routledge, 1993.

Giannetti, Louis, and Scott Eyman. *Flashback: A Brief History of Film*. 3rd ed. Englewood Cliffs, New Jersey: Prentice Hall, 1996.

Gilbert, James. *Men in the Middle: Searching for Masculinity in the 1950s*. Chicago & London: The University of Chicago Press, 2005.

Ginsberg, Elaine K., ed. *Passing and the Fictions of Identity*. Durham and London: Duke University Press, 1996.

Girgus, Sam B. *Hollywood Renaissance: The Cinema of Democracy in the Era of Ford, Capra, and Kazan*. Cambridge: Cambridge University Press, 1998.

Goodman, Walter. *The Committee: The Extraordinary Career of the House Committee on Un-American Activities*. New York: Farrar, Straus & Giroux, 1968.

Graham, Allison. *Framing the South: Hollywood, Television, and Race during the Civil Rights Struggle*. Baltimore and London: John Hopkins University Press, 2001.

Griffith, Robert. *The Politics of Fear: Joseph R. McCarthy and the Senate*. Lexington: University Press of Kentucky, 1970 & 1987.

Halberstam, Judith. *Female Masculinity*. Durham and London: Duke University Press, 1998.

Hanson, Ellis. ed. *Out Takes: Essays on Queer Theory and Film*. Durham, NC: Duke University Press, 1999.

Harvey, James. *Movie Love in the Fifties*. New York: Knopf, 2001.

Haskell, Molly. *From Reverence to Rape: The Treatment of Women in the Movies*. Baltimore: Penguin Books, 1974.

———. "We Would Have Had to Invent Her." In *All the Available Light: A Marilyn Monroe Reader*, edited by Yona Zeldis McDonough, 113–19. New York: Simon and Schuster, 2002.

Heffernan, Kevin. *Ghouls, Gimmicks, and Gold: Horror Films and the American Movie Business, 1953–1968*. Durham: Duke University Press, 2004.

Hegeman, Susan. *Patterns for America: Modernism and the Concept of Culture*. Princeton, New Jersey: Princeton University Press, 1999.

Hendershot, Cyndy. *I Was a Cold War Monster: Horror Films, Eroticism, and the Cold War Imagination*. Bowling Green: Bowling Green University Popular Press, 2001.

Hendler, Jane. *Best-Sellers and Their Film Adaptations in Postwar America: "From Here to Eternity," "Sayonara," "Giant," "Auntie Mame," "Peyton Place."* New York: Peter Lang Publishing, 2001.

Henriksen, Margot A. *Dr. Strangelove's America: Society and Culture in the Atomic Age.* Berkeley: University of California Press, 1997.

Herman, Ellen. *The Romance of American Psychology: Political Culture in the Age of Experts.* Berkeley: University of California Press, 1995.

hooks, bell. "Representations of Whiteness." In bell hooks, *Black Looks: Race and Representation,* 165–78. Toronto: Between the Lines, 1992.

Huggins, Nathan Irvin. "Passing Is Passé." In *Revelations: American History, American Myths,* edited by Brenda Smith Huggins, 245–46. New York: Oxford University Press, 1995.

Jackson, Walter A. *Gunnar Myrdal and American's Conscience: Social Engineering and Racial Liberalism, 1938–1987.* Chapel Hill: University of North Carolina Press, 1990.

Jancovich, Mark. *Rational Fears: American Horror in the 1950s.* Manchester and New York: Manchester University Press, 1996.

Johnson, David K. *The Lavender Scare: The Cold War Persecution of Gays and Lesbians in the Federal Government.* Chicago: University of Chicago Press, 2004.

Jones, James H. *Alfred C. Kinsey: A Public/Private Life.* New York: W.W. Norton, 1997.

Kaplan, E. Ann, ed. *Psychoanalysis & Cinema.* New York: Routledge, 1990.

Kashner, Sam, and Jennifer MacNair. *The Bad and the Beautiful: Hollywood in the Fifties.* New York: W. W. Norton, 2002.

Kennedy, Liz. *Boots of Leather, Slippers of Gold.* New York: Routledge, 1993.

Klapp, Orrin E. *Heroes, Villains, and Fools: The Changing American Character.* Englewood Cliffs, NJ: Prentice Hall, 1962.

Klinger, Barbara. *Melodrama and Meaning: History, Culture and the Films of Douglas Sirk.* Bloomington: Indiana University Press, 1994.

Knight, Amy. *How the Cold War Began: The Gouzenko Affair and the Hunt for Soviet Spies.* Toronto: McClelland & Stewart, 2005.

Kroeger, Brooke. *Passing: When People Can't Be Who They Are.* New York: Public Affairs, 2003.

Lawrence, Amy. "American Shame: *Rope,* James Stewart, and the Postwar Crisis in American Masculinity." In *Hitchcock's America,* edited by Jonathan Freedman and Richard Millington., 55–76. Oxford: Oxford University Press, 1999.

Lee, Michael. "Ideology and Style in the Double Feature *I Married a Monster from Outer Space* and *Curse of the Demon.*" In *Horror at the Drive-In: Essays in Popular Americana,* edited by Gary D. Rhodes, 67–78. Jefferson, North Carolina: McFarland, 2003.

Lippe, Richard. "Montgomery Clift: A Critical Disturbance" *CineAction!* 17 (1989): 36–42.

Lipsitz, George. *The Possessive Investment in Whiteness: How White People Profit from Identity Politics.* Philadelphia: Temple University Press, 1998.

Lopez, Ian F. Haney. *White by Law: The Legal Construction of Race.* Critical America Series. New York: New York University Press, 1996.

Lorence, James J. *The Suppression of "Salt of the Earth": How Hollywood, Big Labor, and Politicians Blacklisted a Movie in Cold War America.* Albuquerque: The University of New Mexico Press, 1999.

Lubin, Alex. *Romance and Rights: The Politics of Interracial Intimacy, 1945–1954.* Jackson: University Press of Mississippi, 2005.

Lukacs, John. *Historical Consciousness.* Rev. ed. New York: Schocken Books, 1985.

Lucanio, Patrick. *Them or Us: Archetypal Interpretations of Fifties Alien Invasion Films.* Bloomington & Indianapolis: Indiana University Press, 1987.

Lunbeck, Elizabeth. *The Psychiatric Persuasion.* Princeton, New Jersey: Princeton University Press, 1994.

MacDougall, Robert. "Red, Brown and Yellow Perils: Images of the American Enemy in the 1940s and 1950s." *Journal of Popular Culture: Comparative Studies in the World's Civilization* 32, no. 4 (Spring 1999), 59–75.

Mann, William J. *Behind the Screen: How Gays and Lesbians Shaped Hollywood 1910–1969.* New York: Viking, 2001.

Marchetti, Gina. *Romance and the 'Yellow Peril': Race, Sex and Discursive Strategies in Hollywood Fiction.* Berkeley: University of California Press, 1993.

Mast, Gerald, ed. *The Movies in Our Midst: Documents in the Cultural History of Film in America.* Chicago: University of Chicago Press, 1982.

May, Elaine Tyler. *Homeward Bound: American Families in the Cold War Era.* New York: Basic Books, 1988.

May, Lary. *The Big Tomorrow: Hollywood and the Politics of the American Way.* Chicago: University of Chicago Press, 2000.

———, ed. *Recasting America: Culture and Politics in the Age of Cold War.* Chicago: University of Chicago Press, 1989.

McCann, Graham. *Rebel Males: Clift, Brando and Dean.* London: Hamish Hamilton, 1991.

McCarthy, Todd. *Howard Hawks: The Grey Fox of Hollywood.* New York: Grove, 1997.

McDonough, Yona Zeldis, ed. *All the Available Light: A Marilyn Monroe Reader.* New York: Simon and Schuster, 2002.

McGilligan, Patrick, ed. *Backstory 2: Interviews with Screenwriters of the 1940s and 1950s.* Berkeley: University of California Press, 1991.

McGilligan, Patrick, and Paul Buhle. *Tender Comrades: A Backstory of the Hollywood Blacklist.* New York: St. Martin's, 1997.

Meyerwitz, Joanne, ed. *Not June Cleaver: Women and Gender in Postwar America 1945–1960.* Philadelphia: Temple University Press, 1994.

———. *How Sex Changed: A History of Transsexuality in the United States.* Cambridge: Harvard University Press, 2002.

Modleski, Tania. "The Incredible Shrinking He(r)man: Male Regression, the Male Body, and Film." *Differences* 2, no. 2 (1990): 55–75.

Moskowitz, Eva S. *In Therapy We Trust: America's Obsession with Self-Fulfillment.* Baltimore and London: John Hopkins University Press, 2001.

Nadel, Alan. *Containment Culture: American Narratives, Postmodernism, and the Atomic Age.* Durham and London: Duke University Press, 1995.

Naremore, James. *More Than Night: Film Noir in Its Contexts*. Berkeley: University of California Press, 2008.

Navasky, Victor S. *Naming Names*. New York: Viking, 1980.

Noriega, Chon. "'Something's Missing Here!': Homosexuality and Film Reviews During the Production Code Era, 1934–1962." *Cinema Journal* 30 (1990): 20–41.

Oshinsky, David. *A Conspiracy So Immense: The World of Joseph McCarthy*. New York: Free Press, 1983.

Pascoe, Peggy. *What Comes Naturally: Miscegenation Law and the Making of Race in America*. Oxford: Oxford University Press, 2009.

Pauly, Thomas H. *An American Odyssey: Elia Kazan and American Culture*. Philadelphia: Temple University Press, 1983.

Polan, Dana. *Power and Paranoia: History, Narrative, and the American Cinema, 1940–1950*. New York: Columbia University Press, 1986.

Powell, A. D. *"Passing" for Who You Really Are: Essays in Support of Multiracial Whiteness*. Palm Coast: Backintyme, 2005.

Rabkin, Leslie Y. *The Celluloid Couch: An Annotated International Filmography of the Mental Health Professional in the Movies and Television, from the Beginning to 1990*. Lanham, Md.: Scarecrow Press, 1998.

Rasmussen, Birgit Brander, Irene J. Nexica, Eric Klinenberg, and Matt Wray, eds. *The Making and Unmaking of Whiteness*. Durham and London: Duke University Press, 2001.

Ravitz, Abe C. *Imitations of Life: Fannie Hurst's Gaslight Sonatas*. Carbondale: Southern Illinois University Press, 1997.

Ray, Susan, ed. *I Was Interrupted: Nicholas Ray on Making Movies*. Berkeley: University of California Press, 1993.

Rippy, Marguerite H. "Commodity, Tragedy, Desire: Female Sexuality and Blackness in the Iconography of Dorothy Dandridge." In *Classic Hollywood, Classic Whiteness*, edited by Daniel Bernardi, 178–209. Minneapolis: University of Minnesota Press, 2001.

Roche, John Pearson. *The Quest for the Dream: The Development of Civil Rights and Human Relations in Modern America*. New York: Macmillan, 1963.

Roediger, David R., ed. *Black on White: Black Writers on What It Means to Be White*. New York: Schocken Books, 1999.

———. *The Wages of Whiteness: Race and the Making of the American Working Class*. 1991. Rev ed. London: Verso, 1999.

Roffman, Peter, and Jim Purdy. *The Hollywood Social Problem Film: Madness, Despair, and Politics from the Depression to the Fifties*. Bloomington: Indiana University Press, 1981.

Rogin, Michael. *Blackface, White Noise: Jewish Immigrants in the Hollywood Melting Pot*. Berkeley: University of California Press, 1996.

———. *Ronald Reagan, the Movie: and Other Episodes in Political Demonology*. Berkeley: University of California Press, 1987.

Roof, Judith. *All about Thelma and Eve: Sidekicks and Third Wheels*. Urbana and Chicago: University of Illinois Press, 2002.

Rosenbaum, Jonathan. *Placing Movies: The Practice of Film Criticism*. Berkeley: University of California Press, 1995.

Rosenstone, Robert. *Visions of the Past: The Challenge of Film to Our Idea of History.* Cambridge: Harvard University Press, 1995.

Ross, Steven J., ed. *Movies and American Society.* Oxford: Blackwell, 2002.

Rossinow, Doug. *The Politics of Authenticity: Liberalism, Christianity, and the New Left in America.* New York: Columbia University Press, 1998.

Russo, Vito. *The Celluloid Closet: Homosexuality in the Movies.* Rev. ed. New York: Harper & Row, 1987.

Samuels, Stuart. "The Age of Conspiracy and Conformity: *Invasion of the Body Snatchers* (1956)." In *American History/American Film: Interpreting the Hollywood Image,* edited by John E. Connor and Martin A. Jackson, 203–18. Foreword by Arthur M. Schlesinger, Jr. New York: Frederick Ungar Publishing Co., 1979.

Sanchez, Maria Carla, and Linda Schlossberg, eds. *Passing: Identity and Interpretation in Sexuality, Race, and Religion.* New York: New York University Press, 2001.

Sarris, Andrew. *You Ain't Heard Nothing Yet: The American Talking Film History and Memory, 1927–1949.* New York: Oxford University Press, 1998.

Savoy, Eric. "'That Ain't All She Ain't: Doris Day and Queer Performativity." In *Out Takes: Essays on Queer Theory and Film,* edited by Ellis Hanson, 151–82. Durham, NC: Duke University Press, 1999.

Sayre, Nora. *Running Time: Films of the Cold War.* New York: Dial, 1982.

———. *Previous Convictions: A Journey through the 1950s.* New Brunswick, NJ: Rutgers University Press, 1995.

Schanke, Robert A., and Kim Marra, eds. *Passing Performances: Queer Readings of Leading Players in American Theater History.* Ann Arbor: University of Michigan Press, 1998.

Schatz, Thomas. *Boom and Bust: American Cinema in the 1940s.* Berkeley: University of California Press, 1999.

Schelde, Per. *Androids, Humanoids, and Other Science Fiction Monsters: Science and Soul in Science Fiction Films.* New York: New York University Press, 1993.

Schrecker, Ellen W. *No Ivory Tower: McCarthyism and the Universities.* New York: Oxford University Press, 1986.

———. *Many are the Crimes: McCarthyism in America.* Boston: Little, Brown, 1998.

Sedgwick, Eve Kosofsky. *Epistemology of the Closet.* Berkeley and Los Angeles: University of California Press, 1990.

Shapiro, Jerome F. *Atomic Bomb Cinema: The Apocalyptic Imagination in Film.* New York: Routledge, 2002.

Sherwin, Martin J. *A World Destroyed: Hiroshima and the Origins of the Arms Race.* New York: Knopf, 1975.

Showalter, Elaine. *Sexual Anarchy: Gender and Culture at the Fin de Siecle.* New York: Penguin Books, 1990.

Sikov, Edward, ed. *Laughing Hysterically: American Screen Comedy of the 1950s.* New York: Columbia University Press, 1994.

Smith, Judith E. *Becoming Belafonte: Black Artist, Public Radical.* Austin: University of Texas Press, 2014.

———. *Visions of Belonging: Family Stories, Popular Culture, and Postwar Democracy, 1940–1960.* New York: Columbia University Press, 2004.

———. "Judy Holliday's Urban Working-Girl Characters in 1950s Hollywood Film." In *A Jewish Feminine Mystique?: Jewish Women in Postwar America,* edited by Hasia R. Diner et al, 160–76. New Brunswick, NJ: Rutgers University Press, 2010.

Smith, Valerie. *Not Just Race, Not Just Gender: Black Feminist Reading.* New York and London: Routledge, 1998.

Solinger, Rickie. *Wake Up Little Susie: Single Pregnancy and Race Before Roe v. Wade.* New York: Routledge, 1992.

Sollors, Werner. *Neither Black nor White yet Both: Thematic Explorations of Interracial Literature.* New York: Oxford University Press, 1997.

———. *Interracialism: Black-White Intermarriage in American History, Literature, and Law.* Oxford, New York: Oxford University Press, 2000.

Somerville, Siobhan B. *Queering the Color Line: Race and the Invention of Homosexuality in American Culture.* Durham, NC: Duke University Press, 2000.

Spoto, Donald. *Rebel: The Life and Legend of James Dean.* New York: HarperCollins, 1996.

Staggs, Sam. *All about "All about Eve": The Complete Behind-the-Scenes Story of the Bitchiest Film Ever Made.* New York: St. Martin's, 2000.

Steele, Valerie. *Fifty Years of Fashion: New Look to Now.* New Haven, CT: Yale University Press, 1997.

Strasberg, Lee. *A Dream of Passion: The Development of the Method.* Boston: Little, Brown, 1987.

Strecker, Edward A. *Their Mothers' Sons: The Psychiatrist Examines an American Problem.* New York: J. B. Lippincott Co., 1947.

Susman, Warren I. *Culture as History: The Transformation of American Society in the Twentieth Century.* New York: Pantheon Books, 1984.

Terry, Jennifer. *An American Obsession: Science, Medicine, and Homosexuality in Modern Society.* Chicago: University of Chicago Press, 1999.

Toth, Emily. *Inside Peyton Place: The Life of Grace Metalious.* 1981. Reprint, Jackson: University Press of Mississippi, 2000.

Vera, Hernan, and Andrew M. Gordon. *Screen Saviors: Hollywood Fictions of Whiteness.* Lanham: Rowman & Littlefield, 2003.

Wald, Gayle. *Crossing the Line: Racial Passing in Twentieth-Century U.S. Literature and Culture.* Edited by Donald E. Pease. Durham: Duke University Press, 2000.

Warren, Bill. *Keep Watching the Skies! American Science Fiction Movies of the Fifties.* London: McFarland, 1982.

Whatling, Clare. *Screen Dreams: Fantasising Lesbians in Film.* Manchester: Manchester University Press, 1997.

White, Patricia. *Uninvited: Classical Hollywood Cinema and Lesbian Representability.* Bloomington: Indiana University Press, 1999.

Whitfield, Stephen J. *The Culture of the Cold War.* 1991. 2nd ed. Baltimore: Johns Hopkins University Press, 1996.

Williams, Linda. *Playing the Race Card: Melodramas of Black and White from Uncle Tom to O. J. Simpson.* Princeton, NJ: Princeton University Press, 2001.

Wilton, Tamsin, ed. *Immortal Invisible: Lesbians and the Moving Image.* London: Routledge, 1995.

Wood, Michael. *America in the Movies Or, "Santa Maria, It Had Slipped My Mind."* 1975. Reprint, New York: Columbia University Press Morningside ed., 1989.

Wood, Robin. *Hitchcock's Films Revisited.* Rev. ed. New York: Columbia University Press, 2002.

SELECT FILMOGRAPHY

FEATURE FILMS

Adam's Rib
> Rel. 1949, B&W, 101 min., MGM
> Prod: Lawrence Weingarten; Dir: George Cukor; Screenplay: Ruth Gordon and Garson Kanin.

All about Eve
> Rel. 1950, B&W, 138 min., Twentieth Century-Fox
> Prod: Darryl F. Zanuck; Dir: Joseph L. Mankiewicz; Screenplay: Joseph L. Mankiewicz; Cine: Milton Krasner; Ed: Barbara McLean. Nominated for 14 Oscars, with 6 wins.

Attack of the 50-Ft Woman
> Rel. 1958, B&W, 65 min., Allied Artists/ Woolner Brothers
> Prod: Bernard Woolner; Dir: Nathan Hertz Juran; Screenplay: Mark Hanna.

Bad Day at Black Rock
> Rel. 1955, color, 81 min., MGM
> Prod: Herman Hoffman and Dore Schary; Dir: John Sturges; Screenplay: Millard Kaufman, adapted by Don McGuire, based on a story by Howard Breslin.

Bigger than Life
> Rel. 1956, color, 95 min., Twentieth Century-Fox
> Prod: James Mason; Dir: Nicholas Ray; Screenplay: Cyril Hume and Richard Maibaum, uncredited writing by Clifford Odets, Nicholas Ray and James Mason.

Born Yesterday
> Rel. 1950, B&W, 102 min., Columbia Pictures Inc.
> Prod: S. Sylvan Simon; Dir: George Cukor; Screenplay: Garson Kanin and Albert Mannheimer, based on the stage play by Garson Kanin. Rated in the top 5 moneymakers of 1950 by *Hollywood Reporter*.

The Boy with Green Hair
> Rel. 1948, color, 82 min., RKO Pictures
> Prod: Dore Schary; Dir: Joseph Losey.

Calamity Jane
> Rel. 1953, color, 101 min., Warner Bros. Pictures, Inc.
> Prod: William Jacobs; Dir: David Butler; Screenplay: James O'Hanlon; Music: Ray Heindorf. "Secret Love" won Oscar for Best Song.

Cat on a Hot Tin Roof
> Rel. 1958, color, 108 min., Metro-Goldwyn-Mayer (MGM)
> Prod: Lawrence Weingarten; Dir: Richard Brooks; Screenplay: Richard Brooks and James Poe, based on the play by Tennessee Williams.

Crossfire
>   Rel. 1947, B&W, 85 min., RKO Pictures, Inc.
>   Prod: Adrian Scott; Dir: Edward Dmytryk; Exec. Prod: Dore Schary; Screenplay: John Paxton, based on Richard Brook's novel *The Brick Foxhole*.

The Day the Earth Stood Still
>   Rel. 1951, B&W, 92 min., Twentieth Century-Fox
>   Prod: Julian Blaustein; Dir: Robert Wise; Screenplay: Edmund H. North, based on story by Harry Bates; Cine: Leo Tover.

Fear Strikes Out
>   Rel. 1957, B&W, 101 min., Paramount Pictures Corp.
>   Prod: Alan Pakula; Dir: Robert Mulligan; Screenplay based on the book *Fear Strikes Out: The Jim Piersall Story* by James A. Piersall (Boston, 1955).

From Here to Eternity
>   Rel. 1953, B&W, 118 min., Columbia Pictures Corp.
>   Prod: Buddy Adler; Exec. Prod: Harry Cohn; Dir: Fred Zinnemann; Screenplay: Daniel Taradash, based on a novel by James Jones; Cine: Burnett Guffrey; Ed: William A. Lyon. Filmed in Hawaii at the Schofield Barracks. Listed # 2 on *Variety*'s Top Twenty Moneymaker list for 1953.

Gentleman's Agreement
>   Rel. 1947, B&W, 118 min., Twentieth Century-Fox
>   Prod: Darryl F. Zanuck; Dir: Elia Kazan; Screenplay: Moss Hart, based on Laura Z. Hobson's novel. Oscar for Best Picture. Ranked in top ten of *Variety*'s box office money-makers list for 1947.

Gentlemen Prefer Blondes
>   Rel. 1953, color, 97 min., Twentieth Century-Fox
>   Prod: Sol C. Siegel; Dir: Howard Hawks; Screenplay Charles Lederer, based on the 1927 play by Anita Loos.

Giant
>   Rel. 1956, color, 198 min., Warner Bros. Pictures, Inc.
>   Prod: George Stevens and Henry Ginsberg; Dir: George Stevens; Screenplay: Fred Guiol and Ivan Moffat, based on the novel by Edna Ferber; Cine: William C. Mellor and Edwin DuPar; Ed: William Hornbeck, Philip W. Anderson, and Fred Bohanen. Filmed in Texas. Listed # 3 on both *Hollywood Reporter*'s and *Variety*'s Top Twenty Moneymaker list for 1957.

Home of the Brave
>   Rel. 1949, B&W, 88 min., United Artists
>   Prod: Stanley Kramer; Dir: Mark Robson; Screenplay: Carl Foreman, based on the 1945 play by Arthur Laurents; Cine: Robert De Grasse. Carl Foreman was nominated by the Writers Guild of America, 1950, for the Robert Meltzer Award (Screenplay Dealing Most Ably with Problems of the American Scene).

I Married a Monster from Outer Space
>   Rel. 1958, B&W, 78 min., Paramount Pictures
>   Prod: Gene Fowler Jr.; Dir: Gene Fowler Jr.; Screenplay: Louis Vittes; Cine: Haskell B. Boggs.

I Want to Live!

Rel. 1958, B&W, 120 min., Figaro.

Prod: Walter Wanger; Dir: Robert Wise; Screenplay by Nelson Gidding and Don Mankiewicz, based on letters by Barbara Graham.

I Was a Communist for the FBI

Rel. 1951, B&W, 83 min., Warner Bros. Pictures, Inc.

Prod: Bryan Foy; Dir: Gordon Douglas; Screenplay: Crane Wilbur, based on *I Posed as a Communist for the FBI* by Matt Cvetic as told to Pete Martin. Nominated for "Best Documentary" at the 1951 Academy Awards.

Imitation of Life

Rel. 1959, color, 124 min. Universal-International

Prod: Ross Hunter; Dir: Douglas Sirk; Screenplay: Eleanore Griffin and Allan Scott, based on the novel by Fannie Hurst; Cine: Russell Merry; Ed: Milton Carruth. Listed # 4 on *Variety*'s Top Twenty Moneymaker list for 1959.

The Incredible Shrinking Man

Rel. 1957, B&W, 81 min., Universal International Pictures

Prod: Albert Zugsmith; Dir: Jack Arnold; Screenplay: Richard Matheson, based on the novel of the same name by Richard Matheson.

Invaders from Mars

Rel. 1953, B&W, 78 min., Edward L. Alperson Productions

Prod: Edward L. Alperson; Dir: William Cameron Menzies; Screenplay: Richard Blake.

Invasion of the Body Snatchers

Rel. 1956, B&W, 80 min., Allied Artists and Walter Wanger Productions

Prod: Dir: Don Siegel; Screenplay Daniel Mainwaring, based on Jack Finney's *Collier's* magazine serial.

Island in the Sun

Rel. 1957, color, 119 min., Twentieth Century-Fox

Prod: Darryl F. Zanuck; Dir: Robert Rossen; Screenplay Alfred Hayes, based on Alec Waugh's novel. One of top-grossing films of 1957.

Johnny Guitar

Rel. 1954, color, 116 min., Republic Pictures

Prod: Herbert J. Yates; Dir: Nicholas Ray; Screenplay: Philip Yordan. Theme song by Peggy Lee.

Lost Boundaries

Rel. 1949, B&W, 99 min., Louis De Rochemont Associates

Prod: Louis De Rochemont; Dir: Alfred L. Werker; Screenplay: Virginia Shaler and Eugene Ling, with screen adaptation by Charles palmer, based on William L. White's *Document of a New England Family.*

Love Is a Many Splendored Thing

Rel.1955, color, 102 min., Twentieth Century-Fox

Prod: Buddy Aadler; Dir: Henry King; Screenplay: John Patrick, based on the novel *A Many Splendored Thing* by Han Suyin.

The Man in the Gray Flannel Suit
 Rel. 1956, color, 152 min., Twentieth Century-Fox
 Prod: Darryl F. Zanuck; Dir: Nunnally Johnson; Screenplay: Nunnally Johnson, based
 on the novel by Sloan Wilson.

The Member of the Wedding
 Rel. 1952, B&W, 93 min., Stanley Kramer Productions
 Prod: Stanley Kramer, Edna Anhalt and Edward Anhalt; Dir: Fred Zinneman; Screen-
 play: Edna Anhalt, based on the novel by Carson McCullers.

My Son John
 Rel. 1952, B&W, 122 min., Paramount
 Prod: Leo McCarey; Dir: Leo McCarey; Screenplay: Myles Connolly, adapted by John
 Lee Mahin and Leo McCarey; Cine: Harry Stradling.

Peyton Place
 Rel. 1957, color, 162 min., Twentieth Century-Fox
 Prod: Jerry Wald; Dir: Mark Robson; Screenplay: John Michael Hayes, based on the
 novel by Grace Metalious; Cine: William C. Mellor; Ed: David Bretherton. Listed # 2
 on both *Hollywood Reporter*'s and *Variety*'s top box office moneymakers list for 1958.

Pinky
 Rel. 1949, B&W, 102 min., Twentieth Century-Fox
 Prod: Darryl F. Zanuck; Dir: Elia Kazan (John Ford, uncredited); Screenplay: Philip
 Dunne and Dudley Nichols, based on the novel *Quality* by Cid Ricketts Sumner; Cine:
 Joseph MacDonald. All three actresses nominated for Oscars. Listed #2 on *Variety*'s
 list of top box office moneymakers in 1949.

Rebel without a Cause
 Rel. 1955, color, 111 min., Warner Bros. Pictures, Inc.
 Prod: David Weisbart; Dir: Nicholas Ray; Screenplay: Stewart Stern, from an adapta-
 tion by Irving Shulman of a story by Nicholas Ray inspired from the story "The Blind
 Run," title from a book by Robert M. Lindner (1944); Cine: Ernest Haller; Ed: William
 Ziegler; Production Design: William Wallace; Music: Leonard Rosenman. Tied for #11
 on *Variety*'s Top Twenty Moneymaker list for 1956.

Rope
 Rel. 1948, B&W, 80 min., Warner Bros. (later Distributed by Universal Pictures)
 Prod: Alfred Hitchcock; Dir: Alfred Hitchcock; Screenplay: Arthur Laurents, based
 on the play by Patrick Hamilton, and the adaptation by Hume Cronyn; Cine: William
 V. Skall; Ed: William H. Ziegler.

Salt of the Earth
 Rel. 1954, B&W, 94 min., Independent Production Company with Intl Union of Mine,
 Mill & Smelter Workers
 Prod: Paul Jarrico and Jules Schwerin; Dir: Herbert J. Biberman; Screenplay: Michael
 Wilson; Music: Sol Kaplan. Blacklisted film.

Sayonara
 Rel. 1957, color, 147 min., William Goetz Productions
 Prod: William Goetz; Dir: Joshua Logan; Screenplay: Paul Osborn, based on novel by
 James A. Michener.

She Devil
> Rel. 1957, B&W, 77 min., Twentieth Century-Fox Film Corporation
> Prod: Kurt Neumann; Dir: Kurt Neumann; Screenplay: Carroll Young and Kurt Neumann, based on story by Stanley G. Weinbaum.

A Streetcar Named Desire
> Rel. 1951, B&W, 125 min., Warner Bros. Pictures, Inc.
> Prod: Charles K. Feldman; Dir: Elia Kazan; Screenplay: Tennessee Williams, based on Oscar Saul's adaptation of the play by Tennessee Williams; Cine: Harry Stradling; Ed: David Weisbart; Art Dir: Richard Day; Set Decoration: George James Hopkins; Music: Alex North. Listed # 5 on *Variety's* Top Twenty Moneymaker list for 1951.

Some Like It Hot
> Rel. 1959, B&W, 122 min., Metro-Goldwyn-Mayer (MGM)
> Prod: Dir: Billy Wilder; Screenplay by Billy Wilder and I.A.L. Diamond. Nominated for 7 Oscars. Named #1 comedy of the 20th century by the American Film Institute.

South Pacific
> Rel. 1958, color, 151 min., 171 min., Twentieth Century-Fox
> Prod: Buddy Adler; Dir: Joshua Logan; Cine: Leon Shamroy; Screenplay: Paul Osborn, adapted from the musical by Richard Rodgers and Oscar Hammerstein II and Joshua Logan, based on *Tales of the South Pacific* by James A. Michener.

Tea and Sympathy
> Rel. 1956, color, 122 min., Metro-Goldwyn-Mayer (MGM)
> Prod: Pandro S. Berman; Dir: Vincente Minnelli; Screenplay Robert Anderson, based on his play.

The Three Faces of Eve
> Rel. 1957, B&W, 91 min., Twentieth Century-Fox
> Prod: Nunnally Johnson; Dir: Nunnally Johnson; Screenplay: Nunnally Johnson, based on the book by Corbett H. Thigpen, MD.

Touch of Evil
> Rel. 1958, B&W, 93 min., 108 min., Universal
> Prod: Albert Zugsmith; Dir: Orson Welles; Screenplay: Orson Welles, adapted from an earlier script by Paul Monash, based on the 1956 novel *Badge of Evil* by Whit Masterson.

Vertigo
> Rel. 1958, color, 128 min., Paramount
> Prod: Alfred Hitchcock; Dir: Alfred Hitchcock; Screenplay: Samuel Taylor and Alec Coppel, based on the 1954 French novel *D'entre les Morts* by Pierre Boileau and Thomas Narcejac.

The Woman on Pier 13 (aka I Married a Communist)
> Rel. 1949, B&W, 73 min., RKO Pictures
> Prod: Jack J. Gross; Dir: Robert Stevenson; Screenplay: Robert Hardy Andrews and George W. George.

Young Man with a Horn
> Rel. 1950, B&W, 112 min., Warner Bros. Pictures, Inc.
> Prod: Jerry Wald; Dir: Michael Curtiz; Screenplay: Carl Foreman and Edmund H. North, based on Dorothy Baker's 1938 novel inspired by the life of jazz musician Bix Beiderbecke.

DOCUMENTARY FILMS/TELEVISION

Army-McCarthy Hearings, 5-4-54 to 6-17-54
  Library of Congress Cinema and Television Reading Room.
Behind the Mirror: A Profile of Douglas Sirk
  Rel. 1979, BBC. Produced and hosted by Mark Shivas. An hour of the documentary featured on the Criterion Collection DVD edition of *All That Heaven Allows* (1955), released in 2001.
The Celluloid Closet
  Rel. 1996, HBO and Sony Pictures Classics. Produced and Directed: Rob Epstein and Jeffrey Friedman; Cine: Nancy Schreiber; Screenplay: Rob Epstein, Jeffrey Friedman and Sharon Wood, based on the book by Vito Russo. Narration written by Armistead Maupin. Narrated by Lily Tomlin.
Confidential File: Reporter Anthology, episode "Daytime Whites"
  Rel. 1955, KTTV Los Angeles. Prod: Ben Pivar; Dir: Ben Pivar and Irvin Reishner; Writers: Paul V. Coates and James Peck; Host/ Narrator: Paul Coates; Episode Summary: "Filmed sequence dramatizing the problems addressed in the program: the story of a young secretary in New York City who is black and is passing for white." Classic TV Archive, Film and Television Archive (ARSC) at UCLA.
Hitchcock, Selznick and the End of Hollywood
  Rel. 1998, 86 min., PBS American Masters Series. Produced and directed by Michael Epstein; Cine: Michael G. Chin; Ed: Bob Eisenhardt.
Hollywood on Trial
  Rel. 1976, 105 min., Cinema Associates and Lumiere. Prod: James C. Gutman, Frank Galvin and Juergen Hellwig. Dir: David Helpern Jr.; Cine: Barry Abrams; Screenplay: Arnie Reisman. Narrated by John Huston. Nominated for the Oscar for Best Documentary in 1977.
The Hollywood Ten
  Rel. 1950, B&W, 15 min., Film Division of the Southern California Chapter, National Council of the Arts, Sciences and Professions. Dir: John Berry. Featured on the Criterion Collection of *Salt of the Earth* (1954) DVD, released in 1999.
Legacy of the Hollywood Blacklist
  Unreleased. 1987, 60 min. Dir: Judy Chaikin. Incomplete version available in the Library of Congress Cinema and Television Reading Room.
The Post-War Era: Film Noir and the Hollywood Ten
  Undated. Time-Life Television. 20 min. Library of Congress Cinema and Television Reading Room.
Testimony of Bishop G. Bromley Oxnam before HUAC, July 21, 1953
  30 min., 1953. Library of Congress Cinema and Television Reading Room.
The Trials of Alger Hiss
  1979, 110 min., 164 min, History on Film. Produced and Directed by John Lowenthal; Ed: Marion Kraft. Library of Congress Cinema and Television Reading Room.

INDEX

CPSIA information can be obtained at www.ICGtesting.com
Printed in the USA
BVOW02*1912130316

440044BV00003B/4/P